WILHELM II
AND
THE GERMANS

WILHELM II AND THE GERMANS

A Study in Leadership

THOMAS A. KOHUT

New York   Oxford
OXFORD UNIVERSITY PRESS
1991

Oxford University Press

Oxford New York Toronto
Delhi Bombay Calcutta Madras Karachi
Petaling Jaya Singapore Hong Kong Tokyo
Nairobi Dar es Salaam Cape Town
Melbourne Aukland

and associated companies in
Berlin Ibadan

Published by Oxford University Press, Inc.
200 Madison Avenue, New York, New York 10016

Oxford is a registered trademark of Oxford University Press

Library of Congress Cataloging-in-Publication Data
Kohut, Thomas August
Wilhelm II and the Germans: a study in leadership /
Thomas A. Kohut.
p. cm.
Includes bibliographical references and index.
ISBN 0-19-506172-1
1. Wilhelm II. German Emperor, 1859–1941—Psychology. 2. Germany—
Kings and rulers—Psychology. 3. Germany—Politics and
government—1871–1933. 4. Leadership. I. Title: Wilhelm 2 and
the Germans. II. Title: Wilhelm Two and the Germans.
DD229.K54 1991
943.08′4′092—dc20   90-42490 CIP
[B]

9 8 7 6 5 4 3 2 1

Printed in the United States of America
on acid-free paper

For Susan

Acknowledgments

Studying Kaiser Wilhelm II for fifteen years has been a trying experience. Although never boring, Wilhelm II was not a particularly pleasant person who surrounded himself with other not particularly pleasant people. And he was the leader of a nation in which aggressive nationalism, imperialism, racism, social antagonism, and sexism were prevalent. Nevertheless, my purpose in writing this book is not to condemn Wilhelm II or the Germans but rather to understand him and through him and popular reactions to him to understand something of them.

Whatever unpleasantness I experienced in studying the Kaiser has been more than offset by my pleasure at the generous advice and support I received from colleagues and friends over the course of this project. Perhaps my first debt of gratitude is owed my first professor of history, Robert E. Neil of Oberlin College. It was because of him that I became a historian. Professor Neil's observation in a lecture course that it was appropriate for the Kaiser to have lent his name to the period of German history between 1890 and 1914 sparked my interest both in the personification inherent in the notion of "Wilhelmian Germany" and in Wilhelm II's function as the personal symbol of the nation, the function to which he devoted so much of his time and energy and which historians have tended to ignore or dismiss.

I also wish to acknowledge Nathaniel London, a psychoanalyst, with whom I launched my first systematic effort to understand the Kaiser. Specifically, we sought to connect Wilhelm II's attitudes and policies toward England as an adult to his relationship with his parents as a child and adolescent. Our collaboration resulted in presentations in 1976 and 1977 to the Workshop on Kingship at the Center for Psychosocial Studies in Chicago and contributed to the paper I delivered at the Kaiser Colloquium, a gathering of Wilhelm II scholars on the island of Corfu in fall of 1978. That paper appeared as an article in *Kaiser Wilhelm II: New Interpretations,* edited by John C. G. Röhl and Nicolaus Sombart (Cambridge, 1982). My participation in the Kaiser Colloquium, in the conference "Psychohistorical Meanings of Leadership" at Michael Reese Hospital in Chicago in 1980, and in the panel "Emperors and Ceremonies in Pre-World War I Europe" at the American Historical Association Convention in San Francisco in 1983 helped shift my interest in the Kaiser away from the psychological dimension of his diplomatic activities and toward the psychological dimension of his leadership of the Germans, a shift reflected in my article "Mirror Image of the Nation: An Investigation of Kaiser Wilhelm II's Leadership of the Germans" in *The Leader: Psychohistorical Essays,* edited by Charles B. Strozier and Daniel Offer (New York, 1985).

Ideas originally expressed in those two articles are expressed again in this book. And yet my thinking about the psychological dimension of Wilhelm II's relationship to England and to the Germans has changed since their publication. The transformation of my ideas about the Kaiser is to be attributed in no small measure to the criticisms and suggestions I received from various people. My dissertation adviser at the University of Minnesota, Otto P. Pflanze, was a crucial source of encouragement and a thoughtful and patient critic. Through his teaching and example, Professor Pflanze has done more than anyone to shape my identity as a historian, and for that I will always be in his debt.

A number of colleagues at Williams College offered valuable advice on the manuscript. Of these, I would like to single out Robert G. L. Waite, whose meticulous editing and insightful criticisms improved this book significantly. I would also like to acknowledge the students in my tutorial on Wilhelmian Germany in the spring of 1989, whose interchanges with me during our tutorial sessions helped clarify my thinking about the Kaiser. I am grateful to Irene Etzersdorfer, Kathy Lerman, Peter Loewenberg, Alfred Pfabigan, and Jonathan Steinberg, scholars who provided critical readings of the manuscript that contributed to improving the quality of the final version.

To two historians I owe special gratitude. Over the past decade Peter Gay has been a constant source of inspiration and support. His own prodigious output that is at once scholarly, creative, and, not least, courageous has provided a model of "history informed by psychoanalysis" to emulate. His critique of my manuscript served as a guide in making the final revisions. His encouragement over the last ten years has fostered my development as a historian decisively.

From our first meeting on Corfu in 1979, Lamar Cecil has been a colleague of unsurpassed generosity. During the period that I have been working on the Kaiser, Professor Cecil has been writing his own book on Wilhelm II; indeed, the first volume of what promises to be an important biography of the Kaiser has already appeared. Professor Cecil has consistently shared his expertise with me. He read my manuscript carefully, and, as a result of his criticisms and suggestions, my interpretations have gained in sophistication and historical accuracy.

I want to thank Nancy Lane of Oxford University Press. The quality of the final version of the manuscript owes much to her expert advice, to the copy editing of Rosemary Wellner, and to the help of Assistant Editor David Roll.

The staffs of various archives in Germany and England both facilitated my access to the documents in their collections and helped me to read the documents once they were in my hands. I wish to thank expressly Her Majesty Queen Elizabeth II, who graciously permitted me to make use of her family papers housed in the Royal Archives at Windsor Castle. I am particularly grateful to the Registrar of the Archives, Lady Sheila de Bellaigue, for her scrutiny of the manuscript.

Finally, I would like to express my gratitude to those whose support has been more personal than professional. Actually in the case of my wife, Susan, it is hard to make that distinction, for, in addition to her moral support, whenever I felt stymied by the Kaiser, she and I would figure him out together. I want to thank Lerke Gravenhorst, Tilmann Moser, and the entire Siebeck family, whose kindness and friendship made me feel at home when doing research abroad. And I want to express my affection for Kathy and Tony Lerman. Their friendship was perhaps the best thing to come out of my fifteen-year association with Wilhelm II.

This project was supported by a grant from the German Academic Exchange Service (DAAD) and by a University of Minnesota Doctoral Dissertation Fellowship.

Unless otherwise noted, all translations are my own.

September 1990   T.A.K.
Williamstown, Mass.

Contents

WILHELM II
AND
THE GERMANS

Introduction

I

Although the last few years have witnessed renewed scholarly interest in the Kaiser, for decades historians ignored Wilhelm II while focusing considerable attention on the period of German history that bears his name.[1] Over those same decades numerous popular biographies of the Kaiser appeared.[2] This combination of scholarly neglect and popular interest corresponds to the mixture of irritation and adulation with which Wilhelm II was regarded by his contemporaries. He seemed at once an inept posturer and a dynamic hero. In explaining this paradox, it is useful to distinguish between the two principal leadership functions Wilhelm II was expected to perform, defined by his friend and confidant Count Philipp zu Eulenburg as "the governing statesman and the sleeping Hero-Kaiser."[3] On the one hand, the Kaiser was to be a political leader, a framer and executor of policy. He was to function as a traditional politician, basing his actions on an assessment of what would be to his advantage, to the advantage of those groups on which his power depended, and to the advantage of the nation. In this context "political leadership" is defined primarily in terms of self-interest. On the other hand, the Kaiser was to be a symbolic leader, the spiritual reincarnation of Friedrich Barbarossa, risen from his deep sleep in the Kyffhäuser Grotto to restore, in the words of one contemporary speaking of Wilhelm II, "the German glory which he took down with him into the depths of the mountain."[4] He was to function as the emotional and spiritual personification of the German nation and the German people, giving exalted expression to national ideals and popular aspirations. In this context "symbolic leadership" is defined primarily in terms of public image.[5] Although condemned for incompetence as a political leader, Wilhelm II was able to evoke widespread and intense popular enthusiasm as the personal symbol of the nation.

"The Kaiser," Jonathan Steinberg has written, "was admittedly one of those strange figures in history whose personalities have had more effect on the course of affairs than their deeds."[6] In part that effect is to be attributed to Wilhelm's personality, and in part to his position as Kaiser.[7] The historical significance of Wilhelm II's personality, in other words, was the product of the intersection of his personal needs and the needs of the German people who, in an era of intense nationalism, invested him with symbolic value as the personification of the nation and, through the nation, of themselves. The purpose of this book is to explicate the historical significance of Wilhelm II's personality, to define the impact of that personality on the Germans and the impact of the Germans on that personality. Part I considers Wilhelm II's personal agenda as it was shaped by the history of his childhood, adolescence, and young adulthood, and, through their influence on that history, by the historical forces of the time. Specifically, the process is examined whereby crucial personal issues came to be translated into political terms during the course of Wilhelm's interaction with his parents and the others who influenced his psychological development. Part I traces the politicization of Wilhelm's personality from his birth in 1859 to his accession to the imperial throne in 1888. Part II considers the Kaiser's political and symbolic leadership of the Germans. Specifically, it seeks to explain how, despite Wilhelm's political incompetence, the intersection of his personal agenda and the national agenda of the Germans enabled him to function as the personal symbol of the nation. Part II examines the personalization of political life in "Wilhelmian Germany." It focuses on the period between 1895 and 1909 when Wilhelm consolidated his "personal regime" and impressed his personality most forcefully on the course of affairs. Before 1895, the Reich was dominated by Bismarck and then, after his forced retirement in 1890, by his enormous shadow. After 1908, following a series of international and domestic failures, Wilhelm II's standing with his subjects declined precipitously as the *Daily Telegraph* affair revealed his inability to realize the symbolic value he had promised the Germans and that the Germans demanded of their Kaiser.[8]

Wilhelm II's most significant effect on the course of affairs during this quintessentially Wilhelmian period, his driving support for the development of the German navy, is investigated in some detail. The naval building program is considered as an item on the Kaiser's personal agenda, as an expression of the desire of his subjects that the Reich practice "world politics," and as an important aspect of German policy toward England. On the one hand, Wilhelm's wish to use the navy to pressure England into an Anglo-German alliance favorable to Germany contributed directly to the diplomatic isolation of the Reich and to the rise of the Anglo-German antagonism during his reign. On the other hand, Wilhelm's responsiveness to the nationalistic aspirations of his subjects contributed directly to the fact that the navy became a symbol of national pride and international power behind which Germans could rally together emotionally. Indeed, the construction of the battlefleet represented the apogee of Wilhelm II's leadership of the Germans, at once his greatest political failure and his greatest symbolic success.

This book, then, examines a particular dimension of Wilhelm II from a particular perspective. It is not a biography, and no attempt is made to offer a comprehensive portrait of the Kaiser. For such a portrait, the reader must place this study alongside the many excellent works on Wilhelm II and on Wilhelmian Germany that have appeared recently or will be appearing shortly. Nonetheless, although this book considers only one dimension of Wilhelm II, no portrait of the Kaiser can be complete without it. Only if the interfusion of the personal and the political in Wilhelm II's personality and in his interaction with his subjects is appreciated can the Kaiser's leadership of the Germans be understood and his place in the history of modern Germany be assessed.

II

"The Emperor is like a balloon," Bismarck was said to have remarked less than five months after Wilhelm II's accession to the imperial throne, "if one did not hold him fast on a string, he would go no one knows whither."[9] Conveying Wilhelm's unrestrained grandiosity and inner emptiness, his flamboyant self-aggrandizement and essential superficiality, Bismarck's simile aptly characterized the Kaiser. Raised to rule, kings must perhaps be self-centered personalities, displaying their absolute superiority over the rest of humanity. In self-possessed kings this grandiosity has an authenticity and springs from a self-confidence about who and what they are. By contrast, Wilhelm lacked inner strength and solidity. His grandiosity covered chronically low self-esteem and depression. His exhibitionism reflected a craving for reassurance, recognition, and approval. His outward self-certainty masked insecurity and instability.

The fact that this investigation focuses on Wilhelm II's psyche does not mean that organic damage and heredity bore no responsibility for his intellectual and psychological limitations. During his birth on 27 January 1859 Wilhelm suffered injuries that impaired his physical and possibly his mental functioning. Because the fetus was in a breech position with both arms raised over his head, the uterine contractions of the young mother had little expulsive effect. After a thirteen-hour labor, when the cervix was at last fully dilated, the uterus had become exhausted, and the mother was unable to push the baby out. As a result, the obstetrician, Dr. Eduard Martin, administered ergotamine to stimulate uterine contractions. After the third dose of the drug, the baby's buttocks appeared, and Martin was able to reach in to feel a weak, slow, irregular pulse in the umbilical chord. Concerned that the baby might die, Martin administered general anesthesia to the mother using chloroform. Although it now became possible to effect the delivery, speed was imperative so that the baby could be delivered before the chloroform affected his brain. Quickly withdrawing the legs, Martin reached inside the mother and worked the baby's left arm down to his side, which, due to the narrowness of the birth canal, was achieved, in the words of Martin's report, "not without considerable effort." This maneuver accomplished, the head and right arm were promptly withdrawn. Although at first the baby appeared lifeless, he was immediately revived and began to breathe and to cry and he opened his eyes.

As a result of the traumatic nature of the delivery and, especially, of the speed with which Martin lowered the left arm, the muscles in Wilhelm's left shoulder were crushed, the tendons stretched, and the cervical nerve plexus damaged. The left arm never developed fully, remaining some six inches shorter than the right, and both the arm and left hand were partially paralyzed. Not only was Wilhelm's arm damaged, but the left side of his upper-body, neck, and left ear were also affected, leaving the little boy with an awkward posture and gait. Although Wilhelm was able to overcome his awkwardness, he suffered from frequent infections of the left ear throughout his life. It is also possible that Wilhelm suffered some minimal brain damage during his birth, perhaps through the administration of the ergotamine or the chloroform, rather more likely through a period of reduced blood flow to the brain at the time when Martin detected the low pulse-rate in the umbilical chord.[10]

Nor is it inconceivable, given the history of mental illness on both sides of Wilhelm's family, that the Kaiser had a hereditary predisposition to hypomania.[11] Although there is no direct evidence that Wilhelm suffered brain damage at birth or was manic-depressive,[12] the testimony of his mother strongly suggests that Wilhelm was a hyperactive child.[13] Nevertheless, although constitutional factors must be taken into account in any attempt to determine the source of the Kaiser's psychopathology, this study is not "pathography," a descriptive history of Wilhelm II's mental illness. Rather it is intended as history. The Kaiser's psychological make-up—whatever its source—is of concern only to the extent that it has meaning, meaning in the context of his personal history and in the context of the history of Germany. Therefore the Kaiser will be investigated from a psychoanalytic perspective.

The choice of a psychoanalytic model is based in part upon the conviction that this approach has the greatest relevance for the study of the psychological dimension of the past. In contrast to the psychology of simple (that is, measurable) human experience, psychoanalysis, with its exploration of individuals in their depth and complexity, is fully compatible with the historian's similarly intensive exploration of the human past. Furthermore, psychoanalytic methodology (its mode of observation, conceptualizations, and interpretations) that explains what has been empathically understood is fully compatible with historical understanding and explanation.[14] Finally, both psychoanalysis and history share the fundamental assumptions that human beings are to be understood as developing in interaction with their environment and as products of their past. More important, however, than the general compatibility of approach, method, and premise between psychoanalysis and history in choosing a psychoanalytic model is the fact that such a model would seem to be particularly well suited to the Kaiser.

Walther Rathenau, industrialist, diplomat, and acquaintance of Wilhelm II, argued in his essay "Der Kaiser" that the decisive conceptions of the modern dynast developed in a childhood dominated by his parents. As a result of the dynast's isolated and protected existence, those childhood conceptions were never significantly modified by life experience. "The nursery," Rathenau concluded, "is the nucleus from which the essence of the modern dynasty can never separate, only from the perspective of the nursery can it be under-stood."[15] Although Rathenau's thesis may not apply to other modern dynasts, it applies to Wilhelm II, the dynast Rathenau had in mind. Certainly Wilhelm regarded his parents as decisive influences on his life and, as his volume of memoirs entitled *My Early Life* (New York, 1926) attests, he appreciated the importance of his childhood. Thus a psychoanalytic approach to the Kaiser is appropriate for this contemporary of Sigmund Freud. Indeed, when in margi-nalia, conversations, letters, and memoirs, Wilhelm went into detail about his relationship with his parents and discussed their impact on his personality and development he was already a post-Freudian man, a part of our own psycho-logically minded age.

There are, of course, several psychoanalytic models by which one can order one's impressions of the personality. One can, for example, look to the child's two basic drives, love and aggression, and to the way they are expressed and directed in the child's relationship with the parents. Thus, by focusing on the ubiquitous striving of children during a phase in their development for sexual union with the parent of the opposite sex and for the death or disappearance of the parent of the same sex, by focusing, in other words, on the loves and hatreds of children toward their parents, Freud sought to explain the resultant anxiety-provoking conflicts—between the drives on the one hand and guilt and repression on the other—as they came to be expressed in the adult personality. Although most psychohistory has been informed by this classical psychoana-lytic model, other psychoanalytic theories can, of course, be employed in study-ing the psychological dimension of the past.[16] Indeed, in her book *Emotion and High Politics* (Berkeley, 1982) Judith Hughes explains the Kaiser and a number of his contemporaries at the summit of European politics using object-relations theory.

The present investigation has been informed by various psychoanalytic models, including the classical Freudian model, Erik Erikson's concept of iden-tity, Helene Deutsch's model of the "as-if personality," and, to a somewhat lesser extent, the object-relations theory of W. Ronald Fairbairn and D. W. Winnicott and their colleagues and the separation-individuation model of Mar-garet Mahler and her colleagues.[17] Nevertheless, the most important theoretical influence on this study of Wilhelm II and the Germans has been the psychology of the self. This psychoanalytic approach to narcissism helps explain the impact of history on the Kaiser's personality and the impact of his personality on his-tory. With the aid of this model it becomes possible to reconcile Wilhelm's insubstantiality and his grandeur, his political ineffectuality and his symbolic appeal.

Self psychology differs from the classical psychoanalytic model of the mind, originally articulated by Freud, in two important ways. First, the psychology of the self emphasizes that narcissism—the investment of psychological interest in the self—is not pathological *per se* but is a wholesome and indeed essential feature of the healthy and productive personality when it takes the form of self-esteem, of pride and pleasure in one's mind, body, and achievements. Second, whereas Freud sought to incorporate narcissism into his scheme of psychosexual development, the psychology of the self postulates that the narcissistic investment of the self undergoes its own development in the process of the individual's psychological maturation. Whereas Freud believed that narcissism, which he defined as the investment of sexual energy in the self, was something in effect to be overcome in order to invest energy in others, the psychology of the self is based upon the premise that the development of the self is related to but not a function of psychosexual development. Just as primitive object love develops into mature forms of object love, so primitive narcissism develops into mature forms of narcissism.[18]

The fundamental structure of this psychology of narcissism is the self. The self can be defined as the individual's experience of him or herself as an independent center of initiative, as continuous through time, and as cohesive in space. During infancy the child possesses only a rudimentary self. The mother and her ministrations are not yet experienced "as a you and its actions but within a view of the world in which the I-you differentiation has not yet been established."[19] The infant does not experience the parents as separate and independent entities but regards them in somewhat the same way as adults regard their arms and legs.[20] In theoretical terms, the parents are "selfobjects," objects (others) that the individual experiences as part of the self. The infant experiences the parental selfobjects in two ways. On the one hand, the infant experiences himself as part of perfect and powerful parental figures.[21] The infant's self merges with his idealized image of the parents. On the other hand, the infant experiences the parents as an extension of himself. Here the parents are both an instrument and a reflection of the infant's own perfection and power.

Under optimal conditions these narcissistic relationships are gradually transmuted into enduring psychological structures in the individual. If the parents provide appropriately empathic care, if they allow themselves to be idealized by the child, if they are able to respond to the child's grandiose exhibitionism with affirming and mirroring pride, and if, at the same time, they provide "optimal frustration" of these idealizing and exhibitionistic needs, the child develops a cohesive and well-integrated self, able to deal effectively with narcissistic tension and life's inevitable setbacks and disappointments. Through the gradual and gentle disappointment in the ideal parental figures, the child learns to set up ideals within himself. As the child gradually and gently becomes aware of the limitations on his power and perfection, his grandiosity matures into healthy self-esteem and realistic ambitions.

But if the parents do not respond to the child empathically, if they are unable to tolerate his idealization, if they suppress his grandiose exhibitionism, and/or are unable to provide optimal frustration of his idealization and grandiosity, the individual does not develop a strong and cohesive self. His ideals and ambitions are not fully internalized and integrated in the self. Instead, he remains at a more archaic level of narcissistic development. Therefore, the narcissistically disturbed adult continues to experience other people as primitive selfobjects; like an addict, he continues to crave relationships with others in order to make up for the defects in his self. If the parental figures of early life were unable to respond consistently to the child with affirming and mirroring pride, the individual's infantile grandiosity does not gradually mature into healthy self-esteem. He remains childishly exhibitionistic, vulnerable to real or imagined slights and rejections, to which he responds with shamefaced withdrawal and depression or with outbursts of rage. He craves selfobject relationships with those who will affirm and mirror his grandiosity, who through their praise and admiration can supply the esteem externally he lacks within himself. If the parental figures of early life were unable to allow the child to merge consistently with an adult's calmness, self-confidence, and power, the individual's infantile idealizations do not gradually mature into a well-integrated set of guiding ideals. Instead, he remains unstable and insecure and craves selfobject relationships with those in whom he can find the external strength and security he lacks within himself.

In sum, the psychological substance of narcissistic pathology is disorganization, disharmony, or debility of the self. Like the small child whose self-esteem and psychic equilibrium are maintained via his sense that he is a part of his parents ("idealization") and via his sense that they are a part of him ("mirroring"), the narcissistically disturbed adult experiences himself as part of others and others as part of himself. A hollowness at the center of his personality creates an addictionlike condition in which he craves relationships with people whom he can idealize or who will mirror him and thus affirm his sense of being worthwhile. Without the continuous sustenance obtained from such selfobjects, the narcissistically disturbed individual feels fragmented, weak, and disharmonious. He does not experience himself as a whole, self-confident, and balanced personality.[22]

III

Bismarck was not the only contemporary familiar with the Kaiser to characterize his personality in terms compatible with the formulations of self psychology. Rudolf von Leuthold, Wilhelm's longtime personal physician, denied that the Kaiser had any "*maniaque* features whatever; on the contrary he is if anything too fragmented [*zersplittert*] and changeable [to be] a freak [*Sonderling*]. The only danger was that H.M. might overstrain his nerves and suffer a breakdown."[23] Bernhard von Bülow, Wilhelm's chancellor and friend for many years, was also "often concerned about his psychic balance."[24] "Wilhelm's character was full of contradictions," Bülow wrote in his memoirs. "Prince Guido von Henckel-Donnersmarck [sic] liked to say that the Kaiser reminded him of a dice-box in which the dice rattled against each other. His personality was not cohesive, self-contained, or harmonious; its various aspects did not interfuse as do even stubborn substances and elements during the process of amalgamation."[25] Even casual acquaintances, though dazzled by his position and demeanor, described the Kaiser as lacking psychological coherence. After a lunch with Wilhelm in Londonderry House in the summer of 1891, John Morley noted in his diary: "I was immensely interested in watching a man with such a part to play in Europe. . . . Energy, rapidity, restlessness in every movement from his short quick inclinations of the head to the planting of the foot. But I should be disposed to doubt whether it is all sound, steady and the result of a—what Herbert Spencer would call—rightly coordinated organization."[26] For the historian Hermann Oncken, the Kaiser was a *"zusammengesetzte Persönlichkeit,"* a composite or an assembled personality.[27]

The analogies used by Wilhelm's contemporaries to describe his inner disharmony give a sense of its manifestations. Henckel von Donnersmarck's image of the tumbling dice captures the Kaiser's capriciousness and unpredictability, what Wilhelm's wife described as his "suddenness."[28] Bismarck's balloon simile conveys Wilhelm's lack of self-restraint, the excessiveness that found expression in the exclamation points studding his voluminous marginalia and in his hunting exploits (in December 1902 on Henckel's estate the Kaiser shot 1675 head of game to bring the total number of wild animals he had killed in his career as a hunter to fifty thousand).[29] Dr. Leuthold's characterization of the Kaiser as "fragmented and changable" communicates Wilhelm's emotional volatility, the explosive mood swings that led Philipp Eulenburg to compare the Kaiser to a cloud, "now white, now grey, now black with rain, hail, and storm—and highly charged with electricity."[30]

The central weakness these contemporaries detected in Wilhelm was covered by a display of self-certainty. Unable to admit to ignorance, the Kaiser expressed opinions on almost every subject, and he would commit himself to a position or policy with little or no information about it. He seemed unable to listen to the advice of his ministers, frequently interrupting and monopolizing conversation. Constantly needing to occupy center-stage, he was jealous and resentful when others were the focus of attention.[31] As reflected in his journey to the Holy Land in 1898 and in his effort to cast himself as the savior of Christian civilization ready to launch a modern-day crusade against the "yellow peril" during the Boxer Rebellion in 1900, Wilhelm's belief in himself verged at times upon the messianic.[32] Politically, the Kaiser's display of self-certainty took the form of his frequent claims to rule by divine right. In so doing, Wilhelm reaffirmed the tradition of his Hohenzollern ancestors. Although his father and his grandfather had never explicitly renounced the claim, the passion with which Wilhelm II asserted his sovereignty by divine right recalled the romantic Christian conception of monarchy of his greatuncle, King Friedrich Wilhelm IV of Prussia. On the surface Wilhelm's statement in Königsberg in 1910, "Considering Myself an instrument of the Lord, I go My way without regard for the views or opinions of the day," seems a selfconfident demonstration of virtually unlimited political authority.[33] One gets the sense, however, that its primary psychological purpose, in the aftermath of the *Daily Telegraph* affair, was to shield Wilhelm from his critics and to borrow from God that strength he missed within himself.

In general Wilhelm's self-certainty was self-protective. His vulnerability was such that when he felt unappreciated, let alone condemned, he reacted with icy resentment or uncontrollable anger.[34] Frequently the Kaiser's declarations of sovereignty accompanied his frustration and rage when the Germans failed to support him. Thus in March 1897, as Wilhelm's proposal for a major increase

Wilhelm II in the uniform of the Garde de Corps (1901). Reprinted with the permission of the Ullstein Bilderdienst.

in the size of the navy was going down to defeat in the Reichstag, he burst out
to Admiral Friedrich Hollmann, secretary of state in the Reich Naval Office:
"I know no constitution, I know only what I want."[35] Indeed, Wilhelm's outrage when his subjects refused to obey or appreciate him accounts for his telegram in 1900 to the commanding general in Berlin during a strike of the city's
tram workers that "I expect that when the troops move in at least five hundred
people should be gunned down" and for the complaint of General Gustav von
Kessel three years later that, in the short time he had occupied the post, "H.M.
has already ordered me *twice*, on the most flimsy of pretexts and in *open* telegrams, to fire on the people."[36] Although none of these orders issued in
moments of wrath at his disobedient and ungrateful subjects was carried out,
officials who criticized the Kaiser found themselves unceremoniously dismissed. Thus General Count Alfred von Waldersee, who had been the Kaiser's
close friend and political adviser during much of Wilhelm's young adulthood,
fell out of favor when he publicly criticized Wilhelm during a war games' exercise in 1891. Shortly thereafter, Waldersee, who one year before had been a
candidate to succeed Bismarck as chancellor, was removed as army chief-of-
staff and transferred to Altona outside Hamburg.[37]

The Kaiser not only felt threatened by the negative responses of others to
him, he also felt threatened by his dependence on their positive responses. Wilhelm had the alarming tendency, often remarked upon by his advisers, to adopt
the opinions and goals of the person with whom he had last spoken. His assertions of sovereignty can be understood, then, as an attempt to convince others
and himself of his psychological autonomy. In the final analysis, Wilhelm's
declarations of sovereignty were a defensive facade, behind which he hungered
for approval and reassurance. On close inspection that facade proved to be
painfully transparent. Those like Philipp Eulenburg who knew the Kaiser best
recognized that, although Wilhelm pretended to hold other people in contempt, "he actually feared their judgment of him—without ever being able to
admit that this was so."[38] A report from Alfred von Kiderlen-Wächter, councillor in the Foreign Office, with the Kaiser on his annual Scandinavian cruise,
to Friedrich von Holstein, privy councillor in the Foreign Office, of 25 July
1891, confirms Eulenburg's appraisal:

> I want to recount something to you in strictest confidence that is most charac-
> teristic of the Kaiser. Before we anchored at Torghatten, the plan was that the
> Kaiser, at the urging of Güssfeldt,[39] will go along on the hike up the mountain.
> His [the Kaiser's] only comment was: You go on ahead and I'll follow directly.
>   Now our pilot had his charming wife on the island and had telegraphed
> ahead to her, telling her of our impending arrival. As a result, when we arrived
> a few of the island's inhabitants stood on shore. The Kaiser acted as if he were
> furious: He can be acclaimed in Berlin; in Norway he wants to be left in peace,
> etc., he will remain on board!
>   In Hammerfest and Bodi when there were far more people he was not both-
> ered. In Torgen, however, he was. How could that be? He simply did not want
> to go [hiking], did not want to say so, and thought to himself, I'll find some
> excuse. The people on shore provided him with it at the last minute. By chance

I was able to ascertain that this was the case, in that I learned that H.M. had not ordered his valet—as he always did before walking excursions—to prepare his hiking apparel.[40]

The Kaiser, who claimed to rule by divine right, was afraid to offend his entourage by telling them he did not want to go on a hike. Motivated at bottom by what the misogynistic Eulenburg described as "a feminine tendency to wish to please," Wilhelm II, despite his assertions to the contrary, was a leader keenly sensitive to the attitudes and responses of others and profoundly influenced by "the views or opinions of the day."[41]

Wilhelm's sensitivity to the reactions of others, the product of his vulnerability to those reactions, did not translate into a concern for the feelings of others, however. In early 1905 Chancellor Bülow complained that in his "boundless vanity" the Kaiser had managed to offend one sovereign after the other: the German princes, whose cooperation Wilhelm required in domestic affairs; King Edward VII, by interrogating him about his private life; the king of Italy, by communicating Wilhelm's sense that the king's marriage was a mésalliance and by bringing along enormous adjutants, who emphasized the king's diminutive stature; and the king of Portugal, whom Wilhelm had deliberately snubbed.[42] "I was firmly determined never again to take offense at anything," Prince Chlodwig zu Hohenlohe-Schillingsfürst remarked after only a short time as the Kaiser's chancellor. "If I had done otherwise I should have had to send in my resignation at least once a week."[43]

What Leuthold described as the Kaiser's "fragmented and changable" nature not only resulted in Wilhelm's dependence on external support but also enabled him to adapt to his surroundings in order to elicit the affirmation he required.[44] Eulenburg liked to call him "Wilhelm Proteus" after the legendary Greek prophet who could assume any shape he chose.[45] Princess Daisy of Pless described Wilhelm as "such a good actor, he could make himself do anything."[46] And when asked how she and the Kaiser had gotten along, the French actress Sarah Bernhardt replied: "Why admirably, for are we not both, he and I, fellow troupers?"[47] Bülow marvelled "that the Kaiser, with his spiritual receptivity and versatility, felt himself at home in every country." In Russia, England, Austria, Hungary, Italy, the Vatican, or Sicily, Wilhelm had the capacity to take on the attributes appropriate to the place he was visiting. Although the result was that the Kaiser usually made a favorable impression on his hosts, Bülow understood that Wilhelm's primary purpose was psychological and not political: "For Wilhelm II, it was more the drive to please and to this end to assimilate himself to his surroundings."[48]

Wilhelm's craving for recognition and affirmation was at the source of his excited and unrestrained grandiosity. Never in the history of the Prussian monarchy had a king addressed his subjects more frequently and with greater flamboyance than Wilhelm II. Extremely restless, he became known as the "*Reisekaiser*," the "traveling emperor." In fact in 1894 Wilhelm spent a full two hundred days traveling.[49] As Walther Rathenau recognized, the driven self-display was not a sign of psychological vitality. "There are weak souls in powerful bodies," he wrote of Wilhelm. "Here the weak soul does not manifest itself as tired, dispirited, and depressed . . . rather it is a flame that is kindled, restlessly fanned, boundlessly fed, a cold flame, that shines and consumes but does not warm."[50]

In his private life, the Kaiser's civilian and military entourage provided him with the affirmation that he derived from the state visits, gala receptions, orations, and parades. It is no accident that from his accession to the throne in 1888 until his death in exile in Holland in 1941 Wilhelm surrounded himself with a narrow and relatively homogeneous group of aristocratic gentlemen. Not only did this inner circle share a similar social, political, intellectual, and even emotional outlook, they also seemed to recognize that their principal function was to provide the Kaiser with psychological reinforcement. Like the continuous exposure to new people and new places, the colorful stories of these raconteurs kept Wilhelm entertained. Like the cheers of the crowds, the enthusiasm of the entourage for the Kaiser bolstered his self-esteem.

Philipp Eulenburg appreciated his master's vital need for affirmation. In June 1897 he advised his friend Bülow, as the latter was on his way to assume the post of secretary of state in the Foreign Office, on how best to handle the Kaiser:

> Wilhelm II takes everything personally. Only personal arguments make an impression on him. He wants to instruct others but does not take to being instructed himself. He cannot tolerate anything that is boring. Slow, stiff, or overly serious people get on his nerves and have no success with him. Wilhelm II wants to shine and do everything himself and make all decisions. . . . He loves acclaim, is ambitious, and jealous. In order to get him to accept an idea, one must present it as if it had come from him. You must make everything easy for him. . . . Never forget that now and then H.M. needs praise. He is one of those characters who becomes depressed without occasional recognition from the lips of significant people. You will have access to all your wishes so long as you do not neglect to express recognition of H.M. when he has earned it. He is grateful for it like a good, clever child. Continued silence, when he has deserved recognition, he experiences as a manifestation of ill-will. The two of us will always respect the border between appreciation and flattery scrupulously.[51]

Neither Bülow nor Eulenburg nor the others in Wilhelm's inner circle appear to have heeded this admonition, however, and flattery of the Kaiser reached grotesque proportions during the reign, as when sycophants, knowing of the Kaiser's interest in archeology, scattered "finds" on the beach for him "to discover."[52] Not only did the Kaiser depend upon those around him to assure him of his importance, he also depended upon his entourage to supply him with direction and guidance. And yet the individual members of the entourage could only rely upon the Kaiser's friendship as long as they were in a position to affirm and support him. When they could no longer provide him with the emotional sustenance he required, Wilhelm had few qualms about casting his friends aside.

As a result of the Kaiser's contradictory character, his emotional volatility, his brittle self-certainty, his sensitivity to others' reactions and his insensitivity to others' feelings, his theatricality and adaptability, his restlessness and exhibitionism, his dependence on the affirmation of others, some contemporaries concluded that Wilhelm II was "abnormal"—implying that these tendencies were the product of some hereditary or congenital mental disorder. Bülow did not regard Wilhelm to be abnormal in that sense of the term, however. He reassured Chancellor Hohenlohe that the Kaiser was "perfectly sane." According to Bülow he simply suffered from the hubris that conceals insecurity.

> For Wilhelm II his hubris expresses itself in an addictive self-aggrandizement, that not only arouses antipathy, but also is politically dangerous. It is largely the product of his wish to hide the inner uncertainty, even anxiousness, that the Kaiser more frequently experiences than the world realizes. Fundamentally, he is not a brave but a fearful personality.[53]

As Eulenburg and Bülow recognized, the key to the Kaiser was to understand his central psychological weakness. In Part II of this study the consequences of that inner weakness for Wilhelm II's leadership of the Germans will be examined in detail. Before the historical significance of the Kaiser's psychological weakness can be appreciated, however, it is necessary to consider its origins in Wilhelm's personal history, to understand both the defects in the structure of Wilhelm's personality and the personal and political solutions that Wilhelm developed in attempting to deal with those defects.

Although self psychology has informed the interpretations of Wilhelm II and the Germans offered in this study, it should be emphasized that psychoanalytic theory cannot substitute for traditional historical understanding and explanation. There is no place here for psychological theories that are used to substitute for historical evidence, no place for theories—supported by contemporary evidence—that are used to prove historical interpretations. The interpretations advanced here about Wilhelm II and the Germans must stand on their own and must be convincing on the basis of evidence from the past. Psychoanalytic theory has been presented in the interest of intellectual honesty. It is hoped, however, that, like psychoanalysts who use theory in their clinical practice to promote empathic understanding, organize impressions, and clarify formulations, readers will simply keep the model of self psychology in the back of their minds where it can facilitate a thoroughly historical understanding of Wilhelm II and the Germans.

PART **I**

The Politicization
of Personality

> We have been suffering *morally* a great deal, this winter, I *do* not
> like to put it all on paper,—politics and personal things are so
> much mixed up!
>
> Wilhelm II's mother, Victoria, to her friend
> Countess Marie Dönhoff on 10 March 1887[1]

CHAPTER **1**

The Tragedy of
Friedrich and Victoria

Victoria "looks marvelous and blissfully happy, Fritz also," Queen Victoria wrote of her daughter and son-in-law to Augusta, Princess of Prussia, mother of the groom, three days after their marriage in the Chapel Royal at Windsor on 25 January 1858. "One cannot describe," Queen Victoria continued, "what a wonderful sensation it is for us both [the queen and her husband, Prince Albert] to see these dear children so happy and contented."[1] Despite the couple's happiness on their wedding day, there are few more tragic figures in the long and often unhappy history of European royalty than Wilhelm II's parents, Friedrich and Victoria.

At the time of their marriage, bride and groom had reason to be optimistic about the future. Devoted to his young and vivacious wife, Friedrich was about to become heir to the Prussian throne; and, although there was tension between Friedrich and his father, Wilhelm, it appeared certain that Friedrich would soon become king since his father was already sixty years old. For her part, Victoria, the eldest daughter of Queen Victoria and Prince Albert, loved her "Fritz" and was convinced that together she and her husband could realize the ideal of a liberalized Prussia based upon the model of her English homeland. Thus, although the marriage of Friedrich and Victoria was a love match, it had definite political implications.[2] The marriage of the heir to the Prussian throne and the princess royal of Great Britain implied a union between Prussia and England, diplomatic alliance, and, given the personalities involved, that Prussia should emulate some of England's characteristics.[3]

For various reasons Friedrich and Victoria were unable to realize this ideal, and their lives ended in disappointment and unhappiness. Despite his fame as the victor of Königgrätz (1866) and Wörth (1870), Friedrich was continuously at odds with his father, who (with Bismarck's cooperation) prevented Friedrich from exercising significant influence on the conduct of government. Victoria, increasingly alienated from the Prussian court, society, and political establishment, found herself disliked in Berlin and throughout Germany. Even in their relationship with their children, Friedrich and Victoria experienced disappointment: first, when their two "favorite" children died in childhood; and, second, when the three eldest of the six surviving children turned against their parents. This latter family conflict became a public political humiliation when Wilhelm, the eldest of the three, siding with Bismarck and Wilhelm I, openly denounced his parents' political views. Indeed, even the couple's hope of ascending the throne seemed dashed when Friedrich, at the age of fifty-five, was stricken with throat cancer. After more than a year of physical suffering and bitter controversy, involving his wife, his son Wilhelm, his father, and (through the press) the general public in Germany and England, over the nature and treatment of his illness, Friedrich finally became Kaiser with the death of his father in March 1888. But Friedrich III's reign was brief, only ninety-nine days, and his severe illness prevented him from assuming more than nominal control of the government, which remained in the hands of his adversary Bismarck. With Friedrich's death on 15 June 1888, the dream that a liberalization of Germany, with partnership between Germany and England, might be achieved from the throne seemed certain to die with him. Wilhelm, his son and heir, appeared to be completely under Bismarck's influence, determined to follow in the footsteps not of his father but of his grandfather, Wilhelm I. Until her death in 1901, Victoria remained in lonely isolation outside of sleepy Bad Homburg, ignored by her older children, especially the Kaiser. The hopes and ambitions that she and her husband had shared, for themselves and for Germany, had gone unfulfilled. Within thirteen years Germany and England would be at war.

In understanding the failure of Friedrich and Victoria to achieve their personal and political goals, several factors must be taken into account, not the least of which is the role of historical accident. Although one cannot be certain what would have happened had Friedrich lived longer or his father died sooner, it seems likely, given German political realities and the personalities of Friedrich and Victoria, that the ideal implicit in their marriage could never have been realized.

In the first place, Friedrich and Victoria's political views ran counter to two of the most powerful forces in nineteenth-century Germany. On the one hand, the couple's constitutional liberalism aroused the hostility of those formidable groups (the army, the aristocracy, and to a degree the bureaucracy) that subscribed to the deeply conservative, militaristic, Prussian tradition. On the other hand, Friedrich and Victoria's admiration for English institutions clashed with the heady spirit of German nationalism. Their attempt to tie Germany more closely to England diplomatically was at odds with the popular desire to assert Germany's newly won national greatness in Europe and around the world, for, it was widely believed, colonial, economic, and even military competition with England was inevitable.

Second, the personalities of Friedrich and Victoria and the nature of their relationship contributed to their unpopularity. The two were devoted to one another. "Every time our dear wedding day returns I feel so happy and thankful," Victoria wrote her mother on her third wedding anniversary. "I love to dwell on every minute of that day; not a hope has been disappointed, not an expectation that has not been realized, and much more."⁴ Their affection did not diminish with the passage of years. In 1883, on their twenty-fifth wedding anniversary, Friedrich wrote Marie Dönhoff, a close friend of the couple, "you know well, of course, how my wife and I live through one another and that to work for one another has become our favorite occupation."⁵ Their fondness for each other was a political liability, however. Queen Victoria had reason to warn Victoria that her public displays of affection for Friedrich when coupled with her imperious manner could produce a negative reaction. "I know how you value him and love him," Queen Victoria wrote on 20 August 1861,

> (it would be better, dear, to show it a little less demonstratively before others) and I am sure you will ever try to make him happy. Never, dear, in little things show yourself teasing or willful—don't speak so often of how different everything is here—don't contradict too much, though you do it much less—for it lessens the good you can do in great things.⁶

Indeed, as the years passed, it became widely recognized that Friedrich was dominated by his strong-willed wife. By nature Friedrich was probably somewhat less liberal than Victoria; if left to his own devices, he might have developed political views more acceptable to traditional Prussian conservatives. And yet he became identified with Victoria's political outlook because of her tendency to state her opinions frequently and forcefully and because of his tendency to accommodate himself to her. In fact, his goal in life seems to have been to fulfill Victoria's ambition that he emulate her beloved father, Prince Albert.⁷ Her letter to Friedrich in 1864 testifies to Victoria's success with her husband and reveals something of the nature of their relationship: "You were not, however, sure of, nor versed in, the old liberal and constitutional conceptions and this was still the case when we married. What enormous strides you have made during these years."⁸ The novelist, Gustav Freytag, a close friend of the family, described Friedrich's relationship to Victoria:

> His devotion and subordination to his beloved wife were complete. This love was the highest and most sacred thing in his life, and filled it entirely. She dominated his younger days, the confidante of all his thoughts and his counsellor. The lay-out of a garden, the decoration of a dwelling, the upbringing of the children, opinions on people and events, were all decided by him in conformity with her personal wishes. Whenever he could not go all the way with her, or when his inner instinct discountenanced some particular course of action, he was deeply unhappy and ill at ease with himself.⁹

Depression and weakness were doubtless at the heart of Friedrich's dependence on his wife.¹⁰ "A sort of presentiment of his terrible fate seems to have visited him," Wilhelm wrote of his father. "He was subject to fits of depression, and what he used, laughing at himself, to call *'Weltschmerz'.*"¹¹ This "world-woe" apparently was connected with his vulnerability. Friedrich was constantly on the lookout for slights and insults and would react with anger or brooding when he felt treated with insufficient respect. Preoccupied with questions of protocol, he was ready to see a deliberate snub, a mark of dishonor, in his place at a banquet table or his position in a parade.[12] He became furious when he went unrecognized. "The Crown Prince expects everyone in Berlin to know him by sight," Friedrich von Holstein noted in his diary. "On several occasions he has narrowly escaped being run over, because when he crosses the road he will under no circumstances stand still or hasten his steps to get out of the way of traffic." Holstein described how Friedrich's outrage when he went unrecognized had led to his altercation with a cabdriver, his putting a sentry on report, and his anger at the Portuguese delegate to the Congo Conference.[13] Feeling unacknowledged and unappreciated, Friedrich experienced the respect others received as being at his expense.[14] He openly expressed resentment toward his mother, Kaiserin Augusta, for deflecting public attention away from him and his wife and was quick to regard the advancement of his eldest son as a threat to his own position and authority.[15]

In the powerful personality of his wife, in the strength of her convictions, in the force of her will, Friedrich appears to have found a remedy for his vulnerability and insecurity.[16] In Victoria's enthusiasm for constitutional liberalism and her veneration of her English homeland, Friedrich seems to have discovered a sustaining alternative to the sternness and rigidity of the Prussian court and to the emotional distance and disapproval of his parents.[17] Nevertheless, because of his relationship to Victoria, because he became tainted with her liberal views and English sympathies, he was denied political influence. Indeed, he was viewed with pity and contempt for being openly dominated by the "foreign English Princess."[18]

"My mother was a much more complex character [than Friedrich]," Wilhelm wrote in his memoirs.

> Endowed with a keen and penetrating intelligence, and by no means devoid of humor, she had a remarkable memory, and a singularly well informed and cultivated mind. A woman of unwearied energy, she was passionate, impulsive, argumentative, and had an undeniable love of power.[19]

With her talents, interests, and indomitable and dominating will, Victoria contrasts with her prosaic and passive husband. Whereas Friedrich sought to avoid conflict, Victoria reveled in controversy and confrontation. Opposition did not incapacitate her with self-doubt but served instead to convince her of the correctness of her views which she would state more emphatically than ever.

Victoria also stands in contrast to the women of her time and the aristocrats of her caste in the breadth of her knowledge and political activism and in her disdain for the traditional and enthusiasm for the modern. Fascinated by the natural sciences, she studied the work of the chemist August Wilhelm von Hofmann, was a friend of the physicist, anatomist, and physiologist Hermann Ludwig Ferdinand von Helmholtz, and was attracted to the theories of Ernst Heinrich Haeckel and Charles Darwin. A vigorous opponent of religious dogmatism, Victoria generally preferred philosophy to religion and believed that science, not faith, held the key to man's future. The values and customs of the bourgeoisie were more congenial to her than those of her own class, and she was convinced that European society had entered an age in which the middle class would dominate economically, politically, and intellectually. Befriending artists, scholars, and physicians, visiting mines, factories, and harbors, advocating the development of German maritime interests, Victoria sought to promote the process of modernization.[20]

It was on the political stage that Victoria wished most passionately to perform. With Blackstone's commentary on the English constitution as her political testament, Victoria was certain that parliamentary government was the only rational and moral form of government and the only way to justify and preserve the existence of a hereditary monarchy in the modern world. Upon her arrival in Prussia, the eighteen-year-old princess "set out," in the words of her son Wilhelm, "to create in her new home everything which according to her English education, convictions and outlook was necessary for the creation of national happiness."[21] In fact there seemed grounds for optimism in 1858 that Prussia might be moving in the direction of liberal reform, since the country had just entered the so-called "New Era." Liberal hopes were short-lived, however, and the "New Era" came to an abrupt and acrimonious end with the constitutional conflict and the appointment in 1862 of Otto von Bismarck as Prussian minister president. In the heated controversy between the Landtag and the government, Victoria actively supported the liberal opposition, even writing out an extensive proof that ministerial responsibility should be instituted in Prussia.[22] The capitulation of the Landtag did nothing to diminish Victoria's enthusiasm for the liberal cause. Although Prussia would remain a militaristic and authoritarian state for the next fifty years, she continued to work until her death for the creation of a liberal Germany based on the model of her English homeland.

With the frustration of her political ideals, Victoria grew increasingly intolerant and contemptuous of what she deemed the politically reactionary and culturally unsophisticated character of her new country. She made no effort to understand the historical justification for existing traditions and institutions and, in the words of General von Waldersee, "delivered judgments on everything and found everything wrong with us and better in England."[23] She insisted that she be officially addressed as "Victoria, Kronprinzessin des Deutschen Reichs und von Preussen, Princess Royal of Great Britain and Ireland." On those occasions when German and English self-interest came into conflict, the second half of her title took precedence over the first. "Only today," Holstein noted in his diary on 3 November 1885, "a Secretary of the Legation who had dined with her Imperial Highness told me that he had not known at first what she meant by 'we' and 'our interest'. It could not mean German interests. He soon realized it meant 'the English' and 'England'."[24] As a result of the fact that Victoria "remained an Englishwoman" and exerted "a pro-English influence on her husband," Bismarck became her determined and most effective opponent.[25] It was actually feared that once Friedrich became Kaiser, Bismarck would be dismissed and Germany would be drawn by Vic-

toria into a war with Russia side-by-side with England.[26] "I was born an Englishwoman," she liked to say, "and as an Englishwoman I will die."[27] Indeed,
one of her last requests of Wilhelm II was that on her death she be wrapped in
a British Union Jack and returned to England for burial. Her son ignored his
mother's wishes, however, and Victoria was buried in the Friedenskirche in
Potsdam as a German Kaiserin.[28]

Although frustrated in her efforts to achieve a liberalized, Anglophile Germany, Victoria was somewhat more successful in converting her family to her
political outlook and English way of life. In opposition to the traditional *Prinz-
enerziehung* which sought primarily to prepare the prince for court functions
and service in the army, Victoria promoted liberal values in her children's
upbringing. She selected companions for them "without *any* regard to rank or
family" and sought to give her sons a general education that included the
humanities and the sciences in order to broaden their knowledge, expand their
outlook, and increase their intellectual versatility.[29] Both her choice of a tutor
for her sons and her unprecedented decision to enroll them in a regular gymnasium (where Wilhelm was to be prepared for the university exactly as any
other German young man) were designed to counteract the militaristic and
aristocratic influence of the Berlin court and to expose her sons to middle-class
education and values. The modern prince, Victoria believed, could no longer
isolate himself from the rest of society. He could no longer justify his position
simply on the basis of breeding but needed to be at least the intellectual equal
of the most educated of his subjects. Victoria complemented her effort to give
her sons a liberal education by attempting to instill in all her children the same
devotion to England she experienced herself.[30] By creating an English home
environment, speaking English to them, calling them English names, setting
up the nurseries in the "English way,"[31] providing them with English nurse-
maids[32] and an English tutor,[33] and sending them to England as frequently as
possible,[34] Victoria sought to Anglicize her children. Her ambition in raising
Wilhelm applied equally to his siblings: "to instill our British feeling of independence in him, together with our broad English common sense—so rare on
this side of the water."[35] In so doing, Victoria came into conflict with those
who sought to exert a traditional Prussian influence on her children, and as a
consequence her life was "fraught with *anxiety* of every kind" as she attempted
"alles durchzusetzen which I consider necessary for my children."[36] Despite her
spirited efforts to restrict the influence of clergy, court, and military, Wilhelm
I was able to insure that her children were exposed to the traditions of Prussian
royalty and German culture.

In attempting to understand the intensity of Victoria's wish to recreate her
English home in Germany, both politically and personally, it is helpful to consider her psychological motives. Despite her outward self-reliance, Victoria
remained attached to and dependent on her parents throughout her life. As a
seventeen-year-old bride, Victoria experienced considerable difficulty in leaving her parents and traveling to Berlin with her husband. The princess had
never been separated from her mother for longer than a fortnight in thirteen
years, and Victoria's distress at the prospect of parting from her family was so

Friedrich and Victoria and their children in 1875. From left to right: (standing) Heinrich, Victoria, Friedrich, Margarethe, Wilhelm, and Charlotte; (seated) Vicky, Sophie, and Waldemar. Reprinted with the permission of the Bildarchiv preussischer Kulturbesitz.

acute that she became ill—a pattern, it should be noted, that would often characterize Victoria's reaction when she was forced to separate from those to whom she was emotionally attached.[37] Her parents also found it difficult to allow their daughter to separate from them.[38] Although Victoria's initial homesickness abated, she remained intensely involved with her parents—an attitude that was actively encouraged by her mother. Over the years Queen Victoria frequently wrote her eldest daughter to express her dismay at the ingratitude and lack of devotion of children toward their parents. It seems likely that Queen Victoria's distress reflected her experience with her eldest son, Albert Edward. Victoria took these admonitions to heart, however, and was convinced that in her relationship with her mother it was important that she maintain an emotional investment in her family.[39] Until Queen Victoria's death in January 1901, a half a year before her own, Victoria wrote letters to her mother several times each week containing countless affirmations of her enduring gratitude and devotion. From this perspective, Victoria's tenacious efforts to recreate England in Germany and duplicate the family of her parents in the family she was raising in Berlin become understandable psychologically as an attempt to end her painful separation from her childhood home. If she could reproduce her English home in Germany, she no longer need feel apart from it. This interpretation would seem to be confirmed by the fact that Victoria grew more vociferously "English" and critical of Prussia after the death of Prince Albert in December 1861.[40] When coupled with the political collapse of the "New Era" in Prussia, the loss of her father increased Victoria's dependence on her mother, her longing for her English homeland, and her determination to recreate it in Berlin. In her effort to undo this personal loss and to create champions of her political point of view, Victoria sought to reproduce her beloved father in her husband and sons.[41]

Victoria's attempt to Anglicize her family and adopted country can be interpreted psychologically in another and related way. Just as it is difficult to recognize the dependence that co-existed with Victoria's self-reliance, it is also difficult to recognize the insecurity that accompanied her self-assurance. As was the case with her dependence, Victoria's sense of inadequacy manifested itself in relation to her mother. Holstein noted with some amazement that Victoria, whom he regarded as a determined character, appeared "petrified in Queen Victoria's presence."[42] Victoria's anxiety can be attributed to her sense that what she could achieve on her own would never prove satisfactory either to her mother or to herself. She anticipated that Queen Victoria would find her "exceedingly ugly and uninteresting," interpreted her mother's expressions of concern as reproaches, and was convinced that because she and the family she was raising were not in England neither she nor her children could ever be as important to Queen Victoria as her English relatives.[43] Her English family, her English home, her English motherland were all models of perfection she and Friedrich could never hope to equal in Germany. Therefore, to win her mother's approval and make up for her inadequacy, Victoria sought to recreate in Berlin the environment of the English house and family that she experienced as perfectly protective and nurturant and to recreate in Prussia/Germany the political environment of England that had always been held up to her as ideal. Victoria believed that it was her duty to emulate her mother's English way of life. "I do not know why you should say 'I never took your advice!'—or, your experience went for nothing with me!" Victoria wrote her mother on 10 January 1868. "Have I not *often* proved the *contrary* and asked for written papers—about so *many* things at Home of wh[ich] I considered the arrangement so much better than any I knew? Have I not always held up my Home—as a model?"[44] Any pride Victoria felt in her German heritage, her German family, her position as crown princess of the German Empire, needed to be quickly suppressed. Prussia's unification of Germany, in which Friedrich had played a significant role and which made her husband and eldest son heir to one of the most powerful positions of leadership in the world, did produce an upsurge of pride and pleasure in Victoria. But her statement to her mother on

30 January 1871 that "Fritz and I are equally devoted to Germany and feel ourselves equally German!" had to be accompanied by an affirmation that her head would not "be turned by 'so-called greatness'" because "to my mind an Englishwoman and your daughter is far greater than any foreign crowns though I do not say so here."[45] In the weeks and months that followed, even this tentative expression of German identity and patriotism disappeared from her correspondence and an English identity and patriotism came to dominate her personality and outlook almost completely.[46] The German family which she was raising, the German crown princess which she had become, the German nation to which she belonged did not seem good enough to Victoria or—so she thought—to her mother. Only England or a recreated England in Germany could ever be worthy of approbation.

Because her ideals clashed with Prussian tradition, because she remained an Englishwoman unwilling to understand or accept her new homeland, because of her intolerance and abrasiveness, Victoria was viewed with incomprehension, outrage, and alarm throughout Germany.[47] Perhaps the deepest source of animosity toward her, however, came in reaction to her relationship with her husband and what it seemed to imply for Germany's future. In a land where wives were expected to stay in the background, Victoria's activism met with disapproval. With her courage of conviction, readiness to assume responsibility and take action, she was seen as possessing "masculine" qualities.[48] "According to someone who knows her well," Holstein noted in his diary, "she would endure anything, submit to being called a bad mother and a heartless wife, without turning a hair, but would attack with the ferocity of a tigress, anyone who disputed her political capabilities."[49] Her very dynamism and strength served only to highlight the weakness, the ineffectuality, even the "feminine temperament" of the German crown prince who was her husband.[50] Holstein's diary entry of 1 June 1885 expressed a commonly held view:

> The Crown Princess once said: "Now Bismarck governs not only the German Reich, but also the eighty-eight-year-old Kaiser. But how will it be when Bismarck is faced with a *real* Kaiser?" Her words sound like a jest when one thinks of the Crown Prince's personality. She is the only possible *real* Kaiser.[51]

Victoria was not merely charged with exposing her husband's weakness. The principal indictment was that she was responsible for it. Again Holstein:

> In the opinion of all the initiated, insofar as they are honest, it is absolutely inconceivable that the Crown Prince should ever, no matter what the circumstances, assert his own will in opposition to his wife's. "You only have to look what she's made of him", S[ommerfel]d [Friedrich's private secretary] said recently. "But for her he'd be the average man, very arrogant, good tempered, of mediocre gifts and with a good deal of common sense. But *now* he's not a man at all, he has no ideas of his own, unless she allows him. He's a mere cipher. 'Ask my wife' or 'Have you discussed the matter with the Crown Princess?'— and there's no more to be said."[52]

Victoria stood accused of robbing Germans of their image of a manly, heroic, *German* crown prince and, by implication, of seeking to rob them of their image of a manly, heroic, German nation. The deepest popular concern, in other words, was that Friedrich and Victoria's domestic relationship would be played out upon the national stage. Conservative and nationalistic Germans saw themselves faced with the dismaying prospect that upon Friedrich's accession to the imperial throne this most masculine of countries would be governed by a woman: who, in domestic affairs, would seek to graft an effete and alien system of parliamentary liberalism onto the teutonic, militaristic, Prusso-German body politic; who, in foreign affairs, would seek to tie this proud and powerful and newly unified empire to Britain's skirts as a vassal-ally that would bear the brunt of England's colonial quarrel with Russia.[53] "With the program of Kaiserin Friedrich it was so," Wilhelm II wrote in exile in Holland in 1927, "that she wanted to institute complete English parliamentarianism in Germany and that to a certain extent Germany was to serve as England's *Landsknecht* for continental aspirations."[54]

Maximilian Harden, editor of *Die Zukunft* and *bête noire* of Wilhelm II's reign, expressed the fear of his countrymen that once Friedrich and Victoria ascended the throne their personal relationship would serve as the model for German politics and foreign policy. Because "she wanted to be and remain an Englishwoman," he wrote, Victoria found the concerns of nationalistic Germans intolerable and "saw even with closed eyes the watchful and doubting glances directed at her by the fanatical, primeval Teutons." "Did she not speak English, call herself Vicky, her oldest son William or Willy? Did she not draw to her side English clerics, artists, scholars, and servants? Did she not wear English clothes? Did she not drink tea in the drawing room instead of sitting in the *'Guten Stube'* around the coffee pot according to the custom of the German housewife? And did she not have English cooks prepare cakes, pudding, jam, and pie for her? Even her asparagus had to be served green; and in the whole house a German word was hardly ever heard. And this is the domestic environment of our Fritz, of our blond, blue-eyed Hohenzollern, whom everyone looks upon and says: *made in Germany.*" "In the same way," Harden continued, "she intended to furnish the German Reich in the British style." The traditional Russo-German relationship "would be replaced by the union of two kindred nations in which England would be the ruling head and Germany the strong military arm. . . . Then Victoria, with Friedrich at her side, could rule as a deified Empress over a free and happy people." Concerned only with those people "it hopes to use against Russia," England "blesses" them with "modern institutions" in order "to alienate them" from the Tsarist state. Thus blessed, Prussia "could be England's sword on the continent." In order that this end might be achieved, Friedrich "had to be directed by Anglophiles . . . had to acknowledge publicly his liberal outlook and despite the fact that it clashed with every Prussian tradition had to declare openly his opposition to the measures enacted by his father. He loved splendor and had to appear soberly bourgeois; he was very proud and had to be affable and engaging. For this handsome man, who had the face and the figure of a Germanic warrior-hero, was, in his relationship to his wife, devotedly and lovingly weak." "So she reigned at home," Harden concluded. "And she waited until her sovereign will could expand its dominion."[55]

Of course, Friedrich's illness and death insured that Germans were spared the realization of this nightmarish vision. And yet the forces of conservatism and nationalism had probably already defeated Friedrich and Victoria before the crown prince developed throat cancer. One week after Victoria's death in 1901 the following editorial appeared in the *National Zeitung*, a newspaper sympathetic to the couple's political outlook:

> To be sure it was a tragic loss that these two outstanding people were unable to realize their goal in life. But had not reality already destroyed the luster that had surrounded their highflying hopes for their reign? In the last years of his life, the Crown Prince no longer looked at things with the joy of his youth. . . . The man who had passed his fiftieth birthday was no longer the shining Siegfried we admired in 1871. Even without his creeping illness, the years and the disappointments had undermined his energy and confidence in victory. The Kaiser and the Kaiserin, despite their best intentions, would not have been able to realize the ideal that their imagination had painted for them.[56]

The tragedy of Friedrich and Victoria was not his untimely death. Rather, it was that the ideals—in their personal and political expressions—which meant so much to Friedrich and Victoria and were so integral to their relationship were directly responsible for the fact that their lives went personally and politically unfulfilled.

CHAPTER **2**

The Legacy of Maternal Worry and Disappointment

Prince Wilhelm's childhood and adolescence were characterized by maternal anxiety and paternal neglect. Although the first clear sign of conflict between Wilhelm and his parents dates from after his eighteenth birthday, its roots can be traced to the beginning of his life. Indeed, Wilhelm's public rejection of Friedrich and Victoria and of their ideals in favor of his grandfather, Wilhelm I, and traditional Prussian values after 1877 can be understood as an attempt to solve problems that had developed over the course of his relationship with his parents.

I

The conflicting political traditions and national heritages that would confront Wilhelm II throughout his life were already manifest at his birth on 27 January 1859. Along with the German obstetrician, Dr. Eduard Martin, and the German pediatrician, Dr. August Wegner, a British physician, Sir James Clark, was in attendance at Victoria's delivery, having been sent over by Queen Victoria to observe the condition of her eldest daughter. The British ambassador, Lord Bloomfield, was also present, as were Friedrich's parents. Likewise the names given to the prince, Wilhelm and Victor(ia), after his two reigning grandparents, reflected the task of personal, political, and national integration facing the first-born son of the princess royal of Great Britain and Ireland and the heir to the throne of Prussia.

Like the marriage of his parents, the newborn baby was an expression of friendship and kinship between England and Prussia. Three days after his birth, Queen Victoria wrote Princess Augusta of Prussia, "our mutual grandson binds us and our two countries closer together."[1] Yet Prince Wilhelm was more than a symbol of dynastic affection and Anglo-Prussian friendship. He also embodied expectations about the future of Prussian politics and foreign policy. Those responsible for his upbringing were well aware that how he was raised would determine whether he would realize what was symbolically promised by his birth. On Wilhelm's second birthday, Queen Victoria expressed the wish to her daughter and son-in-law that Wilhelm might "be a blessing and a comfort to you and to his Country!" She reminded the parents that their son "may be born for great deeds and great times" and urged them to "bring him up to be fitted for his position, to be wise, sensible, courageous—liberal-minded—good and pure! He has a fine head, is full of intelligence, and God will bless the endeavours of his dear Parents, if they will be strive [sic] to do their very best to fit him for the task."[2] Victoria responded to her mother three days later:

> Fritz and I think all you say so true and so right that is indeed our task—and mine in particular as I see more of the Children than Fritz does—to do our duty in bringing him up—may he be great and good and wise as Papa is—although he may not be able to be all that Papa is because nobody else is like Papa—yet may he follow his example as much as he can, and be a blessing to this country.[3]

Victoria's choice of Prince Albert as a model in raising her son reflected more than her homesickness and idealization of her father. Prince Albert also seemed appropriate because he was a liberal Anglophile and a German prince. Wilhelm was to be like her father: a German devoted to England and to English institutions. As has been suggested, Albert's death in December 1861, when combined with the ascendance of Bismarck in Prussia, increased the pressure on Victoria to mold her son in the image of her father. "How often I try to trace a likeness to dear Papa in his dear little face," she wrote her mother on 16 August 1864, "but as much as I wish it I cannot find it, but it may come perhaps—may he but remind me of him in mind and in heart and character." Aware of her "great" responsibility and fearful of making mistakes in raising her son, Victoria recognized the importance of taking "the child *itself as it is* . . . instead of making for oneself an ideal of what one would wishes [sic] it to be and what it might be—and then being provoked with the child for not coming up to one[']s wishes." She could even acknowledge that she was "in danger of running into this fault from mere zeal and ambition that he should turn out like dear Papa and become a great man, a second Fredrick [sic] the Great— but one of *another* kind."[4] And yet, despite her intellectual awareness of the danger of trying to force her son to become what he could not, Victoria was unable to follow her own sensible advice. Compelled by ambitions and anxieties, she continued the attempt to recreate her beloved father in her eldest son even though reality would not conform to her wishes: Prince Wilhelm did not have the capacity to be a Prince Albert; and the devoted husband and adviser to the queen of England was hardly a suitable model for the heir to the Prussian throne. Victoria clung stubbornly to her dream during the course of Wilhelm's early life. But she grew frustrated, worried, and disappointed in her son as it became obvious that Wilhelm would never realize the hopes and expectations that had accompanied his birth.

During Wilhelm's infancy, however, Victoria was completely taken with her son. "I feel very proud of him and very proud of being a Mama," Victoria wrote her mother on 28 February 1859.[5] He made her "the happiest person in the world, my little boy is such a darling; he is so pretty and so fair. I think he will be like Papa."[6] As she would with her other children, Victoria delighted in caring for her helpless and dependent baby.[7] "You do not know how dear that child is," she wrote Queen Victoria on 14 May 1859, "I feel so proud of him, and it makes me so happy to carry him about."[8]

Although Victoria entertained doubts about her adequacy as a mother and in particular about her ability to soothe her wildly active (doubtless hyperactive) infant,[9] for the most part she remained proud of him and of herself during the first year of Wilhelm's life. Quick to compare her son to other children, she was "triumphant" when he seemed to surpass other babies in physiological or psychological development.[10] In a correspondence usually devoted to politics, cultural and intellectual issues, or expressions of interest and solicitude about her English relatives, Victoria's pleasure in her son dominated her letters to her mother during 1859.[11] Victoria clearly felt fulfilled by motherhood. Within a very few months Wilhelm had become so much a part of her life that she could no longer understand how she "could do without him before."[12] Simply the thought of her "darling child" made Victoria feel "so happy and thankful, with a heart at peace with all the world, cheerful and determined to do my duty."[13]

Yet even during the first year of Wilhelm's life, Victoria did not always experience this contentment. There were moments when her pride and pleasure in her son were accompanied by distress about the condition of his left arm. Although for the first several months of his life the consequences of the birth injury were hardly noticeable, the damage to Wilhelm's arm became more evident as he developed—as did Victoria's anxiety about it. She wrote her mother on 28 July of the six-month-old Wilhelm: "Baby's arm worries me so much although he is as well as possible and such a dear little pet. He likes to nestle with his downy little head in one's lap—and will go to anyone. He is my whole delight. If only that arm would get well."[14] She grew impatient at the slow rate of the arm's progress and frustrated and doubtful about the medical care it was receiving.[15] By the time Wilhelm was seven months old Victoria was worrying about her son's arm "by day and by night."[16] Just as she had been pleased when Wilhelm seemed to surpass the children of her relatives and friends, Victoria was now correspondingly distressed about what her brothers and sisters might think should they learn of her son's defect.[17] She was greatly upset when she compared Wilhelm with "his poor little arm hanging listlessly by his side without any use in it" with "other children clapping their hands." She feared that rumors about Wilhelm's condition would circulate in Germany and in England and yearned for the advice and support of her father.[18]

With her apprehension about the reaction of others to the son of whom she was proud and perhaps already ashamed, it is understandable that Victoria was especially anxious about showing Wilhelm to her mother, whose judgment she both feared and required. There seemed to be an undertone of relief in Victoria's letters when—despite her expressions of disappointment—various medical factors intervened to prevent Queen Victoria from seeing her grandson during the course of 1859.[19] The fear that had been implicit, became explicit in her letter to her mother of 23 October 1859:

> I am indeed sorry we cannot bring Baby, it would be such an unspeakable delight to me to see him on dear Papa's arm or on your knee,—but he is teething and the weather is so cold, and he is so very well now that it would be a pity to take him from his regular habits. . . . But my notions are not so disinterested. I should not like you to see him with his poor useless arm hanging by his side, although next year it will not be much better, yet perhaps it will not be so very visible as it is now—and it distresses me so dreadfully to see him with other children who have the use of both; forgive me for again plaguing you with my eternal complaints.[20]

Still, Victoria was not always so despairing about her son's condition. There were times when she could see the improvement in his arm, shoulder, and posture, and could "flatter" herself that Wilhelm had "rather a fine bust and figure."[21] In a letter to her mother on 12 December 1859, for example, she emphasized her son's happiness and how unaffected by his defect he seemed to be. Clearly well informed about the nature and extent of the nerve and muscle damage, Victoria expressed pleasure "at the improvement" in his condition and minimized the difference in length between the two arms.[22]

Victoria remained proud of her eldest son after he had reached his first birthday. She missed him when they were apart, and she could see him becoming "intelligent" and "pretty."[23] But "delight" in Wilhelm no longer dominated her correspondence as it had initially; now her pleasure was mixed with a larger dose of disappointment.[24] In December 1859 Victoria had seen the potential advantage of Wilhelm's inability to crawl in that he would "walk all the sooner" for it.[25] Five months later, when he did begin to walk, she could not enjoy his achievement. In contrast to Friedrich, who took evident pride in his son's developmental step,[26] Victoria could only focus on how the arm interfered with Wilhelm's ability to walk further, faster, or stand up on his own.[27] Even when her one-and-a-half-year-old son was able to run "about all our rooms by himself and is very proud of it," Victoria needed to add: "he gets many tumbles and consequently bumps—and not having the use of his left arm is a great impediment to him and continues to be a great distress to me."[28] As she had during the first year of Wilhelm's life, Victoria compared her son unfavorably with other children because of his arm and general appearance and worried about the reaction of others.[29] She was defensive about him to her mother and feared that Queen Victoria would find him unappealing.[30] When news of Wilhelm's condition was finally reported in the German press, Victoria was predictably distraught.[31] One senses Victoria's growing shame at her son's condition and growing conviction that she was somehow to blame for it.[32] "I feel so sore on the subject," she wrote her father on 18 July 1860, "that when other people make remarks about it I wish myself under the ground or in my shoes or anywhere."[33]

The mixture of pleasure and pain, hope and fear, pride and embarrassment, as well as Victoria's sense of responsibility, that constituted her attitude toward her son during his early life is contained in her letter to Prince Albert on Wilhelm's first birthday:

> This day fills me with joyful gratitude! Last year at this time I was in the midst of suffering, and now there is nothing but happiness. . . . Your little Grandchild is a very intelligent little creature very lively—and very violent though merry and good-tempered, and not at all shy. . . . The arm hardly makes any progress, it is a great, great! distress to me, and keeps me often awake at night . . . the idea of his remaining a cripple haunts me . . . I long to have a child with everything perfect about it like everybody else, for I am tired and sick of being teazed [sic] and tormented with questions, which are very kindly meant but which always seem to me like a reproach. I am sure another will never be so dear to me as this one just because of all the trouble and anxiety he has given us. . . . May he grow up to be like *you* in all and *everything* then I shall be the proudest and happiest being in the world and not think about the arm being short or long.[34]

Victoria could not maintain this balance of positive and negative feelings toward her son. Within a year she reported that the arm "in spite of all reasoning torments me continually"[35] and spoiled "all the pleasure and pride I should have in him."[36]

Since Victoria often turned to her father for advice and support in handling her son's disability, it would be logical to assume that Prince Albert's death on 14 December 1861 increased both her determination that her son follow his example and her anxiety that Wilhelm's defect would interfere with his ability to do so.[37] What seems to have exacerbated Victoria's distress most, however, were the various therapeutic measures prescribed by Dr. Wegner, the pediatrician, and later by the surgeon, Dr. Langenbeck. These measures alternately filled Victoria with hope and despair, confidence and uncertainty. During the first weeks of Wilhelm's life, his left arm, which was completely without feeling, was swathed in cool wrappings in order to reduce the swelling produced by the birth injury. This therapy was followed by daily saltwater baths. With the development of the arm and shoulder muscles, Wilhelm acquired some sensation in his arm and some ability to move it. At the beginning of the third month the daily saltwater baths were accompanied by baths in "strengthening spirits"; one month later a regimen of thrice-daily massage and manipulation of the arm was instituted. By the fifth month, Wilhelm could raise his arm, and some movement and sensation could be detected for the first time in the fingers of the left hand. He was still unable to bend the elbow or move the hand itself. Saltwater showers were added in the seventh month as were twice-weekly "animal baths." The latter involved warming Wilhelm's chronically cold arm for half-an-hour inside the body of a freshly killed hare. Although Wegner had no faith in the animal bath and regarded it as a superstition, he decided to continue the practice since it did no harm and was greatly enjoyed by little Wilhelm.[38] During this period Wilhelm's right arm was tied to his side for an hour every day to encourage use of the left arm. There was not much movement in his fingers.[39] After a year, Langenbeck prescribed malt baths and, with Victoria's enthusiastic support, the use of low levels of electric current to stimulate the muscles of the arm and shoulder.[40]

As can be seen from this brief early history of the treatment of Wilhelm's left arm, progress was steady but agonizingly slow. Despite the improvement, the daily therapy, the frequent examinations by Wegner, and the consultations with Langenbeck and with various English doctors kept the issue of Wilhelm's arm in the forefront of Victoria's mind. Every fresh consultation stirred up new fears and made it harder for Victoria to come to terms with the fact of her son's disability.[41] Her distress was intensified by the disagreements that emerged between Wegner and Langenbeck and between the German doctors and the English consultants over the nature of the damage to the arm and its treatment.[42] This controversy, which would be tragically repeated twenty-five years later over Friedrich's throat cancer, was particularly unsettling to Victoria since it transcended the realm of medicine and became an issue involving national loyalty and the superiority of the English or the German way of life.[43] The electrical stimulation of Wilhelm's arm muscles was a source of particular strife, with Victoria—supported by her mother and the English consultants—agitating for its increased use and with Wegner and Langenbeck effectively resisting the extensive use of this therapy, which they believed harmful in large doses to such a young child.[44]

Despite the various therapeutic measures, Wilhelm's arm remained significantly paralyzed, and he did not use it. As a result, the left side of his body was underdeveloped. The neck tendons were also affected, and Wilhelm was increasingly unable to hold his head upright. Concerned that the circulation might be impaired, Wegner contemplated surgery on the neck but first ordered that for an hour a day Wilhelm wear a special brace designed to stretch the muscles and tendons in his neck. The sight of her son in this device filled Victoria with dismay.[45] She was adamant that no one see her son wearing the brace and especially that her brothers and sisters not learn of its existence.[46] Victoria's distress was so acute and her shame so great as to spoil even her memories of Wilhelm's infancy. An event that had originally made Victoria "the happiest person in the world" she now remembered as a painful humiliation.[47] Upon learning of the christening of her sister Alice's baby in the spring of 1863, Victoria wrote her mother:

> How well I recollect how nervous, weak and sad I felt on Willie's christening day and how it went to my heart to see him half covered up to hide his arm which dangled without use or power by his side, and how everybody except the English gentlemen said what a small delicate child he was, and asked me so many questions. He has been a constant source of anxiety ever since he has been in the world. I cannot tell you what I suffered when I saw him in that machine the day before yesterday—it was all I could do to keep myself from crying. To see one's child treated like one deformed—it is really very hard. Of course all that is necessary for his good one must submit to. Doctors are so odd sometimes; they don't mean to be unfeeling I am sure, but they appear so. Wegner said it did not matter if Willie walked about with this thing on; it need not be made a secret of, and the man who made the instrument would be sure to talk

about it in the town. Of course we were horrified and forbid anybody seeing him with it on.

It seems possible that Victoria was more emotionally affected by her son's disability than was Wilhelm himself. While the brace caused her shame and some hypochrondriacal concern that his glands might swell, Wilhelm, according to his mother, was "very good about it."[48] Indeed, from the evidence of Victoria's letters, Wilhelm was able to tolerate his therapies surprisingly well.[49] "William is very good and patient and does not complain," Victoria wrote her father on 31 May 1861. "This morning when I was in his room he said 'nice Mama', 'dear Mama', 'good Mama'; and gave me a great many kisses—he is so affectionate and endearing which makes me very happy as I was afraid the children [Wilhelm and his sister Charlotte] could not be fond of me, but they are both, I am happy to say."[50]

After the spring of 1863 the proportion of elements that composed Victoria's complex attitude toward her son shifted even further in the direction of worry, shame, and disappointment. She remained fond of Wilhelm and attached to him.[51] She could even see the improvement in his overall physical condition. But he had become "a constant anxiety."[52] Disregarding the optimistic assessment of the doctors about her son's progress, Victoria saw no significant change for the better.[53] "I cannot tell you what a distress it is to me,"

Prince Wilhelm on a toy horse. Reprinted with the permission of the Bildarchiv preussischer Kulturbesitz.

she confided to her mother on 26 July 1864, "when I think of him it is never without sadness as that is always uppermost in my mind—to think that the eldest should have anything of a cripple about him."[54] Victoria gloomily saw the defect bringing out a host of undesirable qualities in Wilhelm's character. It increased his helplessness and dependence.[55] It interfered with his intellectual development and caused him to be "backward for his age in all accomplishments."[56] Worst of all was the fact that as a result of his deformity Wilhelm could not achieve the perfection that Victoria had seen in her father:

He is a dear, promising child—lively and sweet-tempered and intelligent; it is a thousand pities he should be so afflicted; he would really be so pretty if it were not for that; it disfigures him so much, gives him something awkward in all his movements which is sad for a prince; though you know I would rather he was straight in mind than in body but I cannot help thinking of dear Papa who was perfect in both, and it is hard that it should be our eldest that has this misfortune.[57]

Disappointed that her son was physically unable to realize her ambition for him (and for herself) and feeling somehow responsible for his affliction, the otherwise domineering crown princess seemed unable to deal with Wilhelm's handicap. Despairing of her own efforts, her own care, the environment of her home in Berlin, Victoria looked more and more to her English homeland during the 1860s. She longed for the advice of her father, intensified her efforts to recreate her childhood English home in Prussia, and sought to send her son to England for treatment and "better food" than she could provide herself.[58] She became more convinced than ever that British medicine was vastly superior, more scientific, "rational, sensible, and skillful" than the "old-fashioned" coddling of the German physicians.[59] With its medical expertise, climate, and way of life, England was simply a healthier country than Prussia.[60]

Even when Anglo-Prussian tension over Schleswig-Holstein in 1864 produced a surge of popular animosity toward Britain and the crown princess and there was talk of war between England and Prussia, Victoria pressured the king to permit Wilhelm to travel to England for his health, insisting that bathing at Osborne in England was far better for the condition of Wilhelm's arm than was bathing in the Baltic as Wegner recommended.[61] "To the [English] sea bath of your son I have no objection," Wilhelm I wryly responded to Friedrich, "since *his* political views are as yet of no value in England. Of course, I would prefer another, closer, continental sea bath."[62] Victoria would not be swayed, despite the king's reluctance, the "outcry" that the decision to send Wilhelm to England would provoke in Prussia, and the fact that "anything that could raise the suspicion of my sympathies being on the english [sic] side—instead of the Prussian would damage Fritz's and my position very much." She was willing to make a slight concession to public opinion by sending Wilhelm's Prussian governess, Baroness Sophie Dobeneck, along with him, because:

He is public property—and we have to consider all these things, particularly as there is such a jealousy about me as a stranger—and such a fear that I have a bad influence and would wish to bring up the children as foreigners—it is very hard and unjust and often makes me very angry. . . . You know best what public opinion is—and one *must* take it into consideration even when it is *not* the most enlightened.[63]

Victoria, then, was not insensitive to the popular mood, but, in this instance as in others, she did not allow it to influence her actions significantly. Although Wilhelm II came to share Victoria's recognition of the power and importance of public opinion, he took it far more seriously. Ironically, in her disregard of public opinion, this self-consciously "progressive" woman was a much more traditional member of royalty than was her son who claimed to rule by divine right.

With Victoria's deepening sense of helplessness and frustration, Friedrich appears to have taken a more active role in Wilhelm's medical treatment: bringing him to England for consultation with various specialists and supervising the electrical stimulation of the arm muscles in November 1865.[64] When, on the first of two occasions, it became necessary to sever tendons in Wilhelm's neck to allow him to hold up his head normally and restore symmetry to his face, Friedrich, recognizing how distraught the crown princess would become, found it judicious to "deceive" his wife about the operation.[65] In contrast to Victoria's obsessive worry, Friedrich appears to have exhibited a steadiness, compassion, and sensible optimism about his son's condition during the often painful treatments.[66] "My father's goodness of heart amounted to tenderness and even to softness," Wilhelm wrote in his memoirs, alluding by implication to his childhood therapy experiences with Friedrich. "He had the most genuine sympathy with any and every form of suffering."[67]

Despite Friedrich's kindness, Wilhelm's memories of childhood were generally unpleasant. There were apparently no other maternal figures to provide him with the emotional sustenance he failed to get from Victoria. Sophie Dobeneck, for instance, the only female caretaker from Wilhelm's early life besides his mother to be mentioned in his memoirs, was described by the former Kaiser as a "gaunt dame of firm character and her method by no means excluded the use of the palm"—hardly a maternal image.[68] Therefore Wilhelm's early life was dominated by his mother and by her uncertainty about him and about herself. All the various medical and gymnastic programs to which Wilhelm was subjected could not alter the fact that in his mother's eyes he was defective. The arm grew only slightly, and, in Wilhelm's words, "the only result was that I was made to suffer great torture."[69]

Although Wilhelm was able to tolerate the therapeutic procedures, it seems clear that he experienced them as humiliating. "Poor Willie is so tormented with all these machines and things that it makes him cross and difficult to manage," Victoria wrote her mother on 23 May 1863.

> Poor child really he is sadly tried. He is so very funny sometimes. He has a sergeant who comes in the morning to make him do exercises, in order that he should be made to hold himself more upright and use his left arm. When he

does not wish to do his exercises he begins to say his prayers and bits of poetry, and the other day he asked the man, before Sophie Dobeneck, who was shocked, "Do you put a nightgown on when you undress yourself to go to bed?"[70]

Feeling shame at having to perform these exercises, Wilhelm turned the tables on his tormentors. This pattern—of humiliating others at those times when he felt humiliated himself—persisted throughout Wilhelm's life. It was at the root of his sarcastic and belittling humor and found its most pathetic expression during the *Daily Telegraph* affair. In the wake of the Kaiser's public humiliation with the publication in October 1908 of remarks he had made to an interviewer, Wilhelm retreated to the estate of his friend Max Egon II Prince zu Fürstenberg in Donaueschingen as he was being denounced in the Reichstag. During his stay, General Count Dietrich von Hülsen-Haeseler, chief of the Military Cabinet, performed dressed as a ballerina in an effort to cheer the Kaiser. Unfortunately the general collapsed and died of a heart attack immediately after his performance. It is striking how Hülsen's ballet performance parallels Wilhelm's remark to the sergeant and Sophie Dobeneck. In both instances Wilhelm sought to make others feel the public humiliation he experienced himself: as a four-year-old, by embarrassing his governess and sergeant; as Kaiser, by having this fifty-six-year-old, six-foot-tall symbol of Prussian manhood dance about dressed as a woman.

II

The year 1866 marked a turning point in the history of Germany with Prussia's victory over Austria at Sadowa in July. Wilhelm's life also underwent a profound change during that year: first, with the death on 18 June of his twenty-one-month-old brother Sigismund; and, second, with the appointment of Dr. Georg Hinzpeter as his tutor.

Sigismund's death was a terrible blow to Victoria. Although her correspondence clearly indicates that Wilhelm had been the child to whom she was most devoted and although she rarely mentioned Sigismund before his death, Victoria now became convinced that she had lost her favorite and most promising child. "A little child does not seem a great loss to other people—but none knows but God how I suffer," she wrote her mother one week after his death. "Oh *how* I loved that little thing, from the first moments of its birth, it was more to me than its brothers and sisters . . . how proud I was of my little one; and just this one my heart's best treasure was taken, and the sorrow seems greater than I can bear." Believing that he was much more intelligent than either Wilhelm or his brother Heinrich, Victoria was convinced that her "little Sigie . . . was going to be like Papa. Fritz and I idolized him—he had such dear, winning little ways, and was like a little sunbeam in the house."[71] Overwhelmed with grief, Victoria appears to have transferred her affection for Sigismund to her infant daughter Vicky, only two months old at the time of her brother's death. The crown princess made wrenching efforts to preserve her little boy in Vicky, going so far as to dress her one year after Sigismund's death in his hat and jacket.[72] The crown princess was never to recover fully from the loss of her little boy, remaining inconsolable eleven years later.[73] The intensity of Victoria's reaction suggests that Sigismund's death confirmed for her that she had been an unsatisfactory mother. She had produced a hyperactive and deformed son and the faults of her other children were painfully obvious to her. Now "little Sigie" had died. In her grief, Victoria did not succumb to depression or lethargy, however. Instead, she determined to change her relationship with her surviving children. Feeling that she had spent too little time with them, she vowed to her mother that she would "not give way."

> I mean to do my duty and neglect nothing—work and occupation are the only things which can restore balance to my mind, not drown my grief or fill the blank in my heart. Oh no, no time can do that, that sweet little face will ever be there and the yearning for it, but I have many and sacred duties to live for—for those other dear children, for my poor dear Fritz![74]

In her relationship with her three eldest children, Victoria's increased involvement took the form of her tenacious effort to influence their lives, indeed to bend the children to her will. In her own life, Victoria had overcome the oppositional tendencies which she and her mother believed were an inevitable part of a child's relationship to its parents. Despite her awareness of the danger of pushing too hard, Victoria was determined that her children would overcome their inherent oppositional tendencies as well.[75] Certainly, the three eldest children looked back on the increased maternal attention after 1866 not as kindly interest and affection but as a stifling and oppressive attempt to mold their personalities and direct their lives—an attempt against which they had ultimately rebelled. Perhaps because of her knowledge of her daughter, Queen Victoria had good reason to warn: "I am sure you watch over your dear boy with care but I often think too great care, too much constant watching leads to the very dangers hereafter which one wishes to avoid."[76] In exile, Wilhelm described his mother as something of a tormentor. Looking back on his early life, he blamed Victoria not only for her own actions but for the actions of others. He attributed the hardships to which he was exposed in the Prussian army (which he entered on his tenth birthday as was traditional for male members of the Hohenzollern family) to his mother, and he held her responsible for the treatment he received at the hands of his governess and for the coldly rational and occasionally brutal educational system of his tutor, Georg Hinzpeter.[77]

By 1866 Friedrich and particularly Victoria had become worried about the influence of the army officers who, by the king's decree, were to play a role in Wilhelm's upbringing. Anxious that "the civilian side should predominate over the military" in their son's education, the crown prince and princess, at the suggestion of the British ambassador, Sir Robert Morier, hired the thirty-nine-year-old Hinzpeter to be the civilian tutor of Wilhelm and his brother Heinrich.[78] Hinzpeter's responsibilities, as Victoria conceived them, were not only to give her sons a broadly based liberal education but also to instill a sense of modesty and self-discipline. Convinced that pride was somehow not an English but a Prussian trait, the crown princess deemed it vitally important to eradicate in her son any tendency toward "Prussian pride" which would inevitably be encouraged by the aristocrats in the army and at court.[79] In seeking to drum pride out of Wilhelm, Victoria was not only acting in accordance with her own worry and sense of dissatisfaction, she was also carrying out the wishes of her mother, who urged Victoria to keep down "that terrible Prussian pride and ambition, which grieved dear Papa so much."[80] "You need not fear that he will be brought up in a way to make him proud and stuck up," Victoria assured her mother, "Willie is very shy by nature and that often makes him look proud. Ladies and gentlemen who tried to nurture a mistaken pride in the idea that it was *patriotic* are no longer about him."[81] In their place was Dr. Georg Hinzpeter.

Hinzpeter sought to use intellectual training to inculcate a sense of abnegation, obligation, and discipline in his charges. The tutor's task was congenial to his Calvinist faith and personality. Described by one contemporary as *"lebensfremd,"* alienated from life, Hinzpeter was evidently austere, bitter, and depressive.[82] He had no use for weakness in others, and he did not tolerate it

Dr. Georg Hinzpeter in 1907. Reprinted with the permission of the Ullstein Bilderdienst.

in himself.[83] He lived a life of self-denial, though not, apparently, without some resentment.[84] Hinzpeter took his duties seriously. Beginning at 6:00 A.M. in summer and 7:00 A.M. in winter, the tutor continued the lessons twelve hours or more a day. Following Victoria's philosophy, Hinzpeter believed that Wilhelm's elevated position could only be justified rationally were he to become intellectually and morally superior to his subjects.[85] A firm believer in classical education as a means of instilling "rigorous intellectual discipline" and a habit of duty, Hinzpeter emphasized memorization, mental problem-solving, and drill. The tutor's instruction was not restricted to the classroom. He gave the princes a thorough and nondogmatic religious training and attempted to broaden their perspective by taking them to museums, mines, and factories.

Hinzpeter pursued his educational and characterological objectives with unremitting severity. He set forth his approach in a handbook for the tutors of royalty:

> It is necessary that the tutor possess extraordinary willpower. . . . For it is the task of the tutor to grasp hold of the soul of his pupil and, overcoming the counterpull of nature, to wrench it along until the pupil has learned to stand and make his way on his own two feet.[86]

Wilhelm II recalled how Hinzpeter put his educational philosophy into practice:

> His educational system was based exclusively on a stern sense of duty and the idea of service; the character was to be fortified by perpetual "renunciation". . . . No praise: the categorical imperative of duty demanded its due; there was no room for the encouraging or approving word. . . . The impossible was expected of a pupil in order to force him to the nearest degree of perfection. Naturally, the impossible goal could never be achieved; logically, therefore, the praise which registers approval was also excluded.[87]

Such a system of instruction, with its denial of praise and absence of basic human responsiveness, would hardly seem appropriate for any child. Furthermore, Victoria's and Hinzpeter's goal of creating a prince who was intellectually and morally supreme was unattainable: it was not possible to create a "modern king" who could justify his position of leadership "rationally" rather than on the basis of breeding and tradition. The tutor's system was singularly ill suited to Prince Wilhelm, however. On the one hand, the little boy's constitutional restlessness made it impossible for him to approach the ideal of obligation, self-discipline, and pertinacity. On the other hand, Hinzpeter's joyless regimen of perpetual dissatisfaction represented a continuation of his mother's fault-finding and can only have confirmed for Wilhelm that there was something reprehensible about him.

The prince's handicap put him at a greater disadvantage. Hinzpeter, for his part, believed that any weakness Wilhelm exhibited as a result of his arm could "only be overcome by unusual energy and ruthlessness."[88] Perhaps the most poignant example of Hinzpeter's educational system was the method by which he taught Wilhelm to ride despite his disability. Hinzpeter described his technique:

> When the prince was eight-and-a-half years old, a lackey still had to lead his pony by the rein, because his balance was so bad that his unsteadiness caused intolerable anxiety to himself and others. So long as this lasted, he could not learn to ride: it had to be overcome, no matter at what cost. Neither groom nor riding-master could do it. Therefore the tutor, using a moral authority over his pupil that by now had become absolute, set the weeping prince on his horse, without stirrups and compelled him to go through the various paces. He fell off continually: every time, despite his prayers and tears, he was lifted up and set upon its back again. After weeks of torture, the difficult task was accomplished: he had got his balance.[89]

Not surprisingly, when Wilhelm looked back on his association with Hinzpeter, he could only lament the "joyless . . . youth through which I was guided by the 'hard hand' of the 'Spartan idealist'."[90]

Compelled by his Calvinist sense of duty and the logic of his system to suppress compassion for the suffering of his charge, Hinzpeter was clearly no sadist, and Wilhelm, perhaps sensing the tutor's inner goodwill, blamed the agonies of his education on his mother. "Hinzpeter was really a good fellow," he remarked in exile to an interviewer. "Whether he was the right tutor for me, I dare not decide. The torments inflicted on me, especially in this pony-riding, must be attributed to my mother."[91] Even worse perhaps than the physical torment was Wilhelm's inability ever to satisfy Hinzpeter and, through him, his mother because of the "logical" denial of praise in the tutor's educational system, because Hinzpeter had concluded that Wilhelm was of mediocre ability, and because the handicap seemed to make it impossible for him ever to live up to his mother's expectations:

> The thought that I, as heir to the Throne, should not be able to ride, was to her intolerable. But I felt I was not fit for it because of my disability. I was worried and afraid. When there was nobody near I wept.[92]

It has become common to attribute Wilhelm II's psychological weaknesses to his birth injury and specifically to understand his grandiosity and bellicosity as efforts to compensate for his handicap.[93] This interpretation can be traced back to Wilhelm's contemporaries. Indeed, Hinzpeter himself ascribed "the Kaiser's powerful inclination to impress others through appearances, to take appearances for reality, to his left arm which had been crippled since birth." The "ugly remarks" of Wilhelm's great-uncle, the famous military leader Prince Friedrich Karl of Prussia, "that a one-armed man should never be King of Prussia," which he had heard as a child, "created the need in Wilhelm to impress his army and his people with the most dashing external demeanor possible, with uniforms and medals, with life-guardsmen as tall as trees behind him, and with his Marshal's baton in his outstretched right hand." Bernhard von Bülow, who quoted Hinzpeter's comments in his memoirs, rejected the tutor's theory. "This verdict is unfair," Bülow asserted. "Among the many good qualities of Wilhelm II . . . was the energy with which he was able to overcome all the difficulties caused him by his useless left arm."[94]

Despite the attraction of Hinzpeter's reductionistic interpretation, despite the importance of Wilhelm's disability in his relationship with his mother, despite the poignant story of his horseback-riding lessons, the dispassionate observer must conclude that Bülow, not Hinzpeter, was correct.[95] Wilhelm II's mastery of his handicap was his greatest developmental accomplishment, perhaps the greatest single achievement of his life. Although his withered arm imposed many limitations on him—he could not dress himself or cut his food—Wilhelm treated his handicap with unself-conscious composure, attempting neither to conceal his deformity nor to evoke sympathy by flaunting it. The Kaiser engaged in activities one might have thought beyond his physical capacities, playing tennis and, using a specially designed rifle, becoming an expert marksman. Most impressive in the present context, however, is the fact that Wilhelm II became an exceptional horseman.[96] It is not surprising therefore that Wilhelm idealized Demosthenes and that the example of the Greek orator filled him "with amazement and admiration" when he learned "in what untoward circumstances he had developed and how he had worked his way up and become the most powerful and famous of orators . . . able to overcome all the obstacles in his path, those connected with his own speech, as well as those placed in his way by his opponents."[97] Like Demosthenes, who conquered his speech impediment by shouting at the sea with pebbles in his mouth, Wilhelm—either because or in spite of his riding lessons—was able to overcome the obstacles placed in his path by his handicap and by the dissatisfaction of his mother and tutor. Testifying to Wilhelm's enduring pride in his achievement was the desk chair in his study—its shape, a saddle.[98]

Others besides Bülow recognized and respected Wilhelm's mastery of his handicap. King Wilhelm I was pleased and surprised at how well the prince carried out his regimental duties despite his disability. "You have done well!" he told his grandson. "I never would have believed it!"[99] Even Hinzpeter looked back on Wilhelm's ability to overcome the consequences of his birth injury as "an eminent moral accomplishment."[100] Victoria was unable to transcend her distress and apprehension to appreciate her son's achievement, however. Because the crown princess experienced her children as reflections of herself, their flaws wounded her own self-esteem. Certain that their shortcomings had been inherited from her, every fault Victoria could detect in them represented an implicit criticism of her care and cast doubt on her ability as a mother.[101] It was thus initially with relief that Victoria shared responsibility for the upbringing of her children with Dr. Hinzpeter and Mlle. Darcourt, Sophie Dobeneck's successor as governess to the younger children. She wrote her mother a few months after Hinzpeter's appointment:

A mother is (as I feel) too apt to be too quick and impulsive, because the children's faults aggravate her much more than other people; she is more ambitious for them and feels responsible for their dispositions—is it not so? How I can feel for you—having had to put up with such a detestable child as I was and yet I loved you so much and the thought that I could grieve you used to give me so much pain! I think you would find me much more gentle and sensible with the children than I was—more patient and forbearing. I have no need of acting the policeman now. I know there are two people about them [Hinzpeter and Darcourt] who watch them and counteract their defects better than I can . . . therefore I do not feel called upon to scold. Not one person in the House has as quick a perception of all the little failings that ought to be prevented from increasing, and my fear of their never being corrected made me perhaps see them in a stronger light than necessary, as my lively imagination dwelt on the consequences which might arise from them.[102]

As revealed in this letter to her mother, Victoria's doubts about her children grew out of her own self-doubt. If she could produce flawless children, her anxiety about her own defects might be relieved. Thus, despite the presence of the tutor and the governess, she was unable to relax what she had described in her letter as her "constant study" of the children, her obsessive search for flaws in them, flaws which had to be instantly and utterly eradicated before they could confirm her worst fears about herself. She wrote Queen Victoria on 19 August 1868:

I tremble when I think of our boys growing up—what they will turn out like. . . . Willy has faults which alarm me often—but he is clever—intelligent, lively and has a warm heart. . . . It is strange how good some children are—and how little trouble they give. . . . I do not wonder at some of mine being so difficult when I think of the trouble I was to everybody. I always tell the governess that I always feel responsible for all the bad qualities as it is certainly only from me they can have inherited them. Still I dote on Willy and think there is a great deal in him. He is by no means a commonplace child; if one can root out—or keep down— pride, conceitedness, selfishness and laziness he may be a fine character some day. . . . I would not speak as openly of our little ones to anybody but you—as it seems cruel and unfair to pick out their little failings but I let my pen move on—and said what makes me anxious sometimes.[103]

As Wilhelm began the transition from childhood to adolescence, Victoria's obsessive worry about him intensified in her anxiety about his future and about the impact that his birth defect would have on it.[104] The bizarre mixture of pride and shame, affection and disdain, hope and apprehension that characterized Victoria's feelings for her son is captured in her letter to Queen Victoria of 28 January 1871:

I am sure you would be pleased with William if you were to see him—he has Bertie's [Victoria's brother, Albert Edward] pleasant, amiable ways—and can be very winning. He is not possessed of brilliant abilities, nor of any strength of character or talents, but he is a dear boy, and I hope and trust will grow up a useful man. . . . I watch over him myself, over each detail, even the minutest, of his education, as his Papa has never had the time to occupy himself with the children. . . . I am happy to say that between him and me there is a bond of love and confidence, which I feel sure nothing can destroy. He has very strong health and would be a very pretty boy were it not for that wretched unhappy arm which shows more and more, spoils his face (for it is on one side), his carriage, walk and figure, makes him awkward in all his movements, and gives him a feeling of shyness, as he feels his complete dependence, not being able to do a single thing for himself. It is a greater additional difficulty in his education, and is not without its effect on his character. To me it remains an inexpressible source of sorrow! I think he will be very good-looking when he grows up, and he is already a universal favorite, as he is so lively and generally intelligent.[105]

It would be a mistake to conclude, as have so many, that the crown princess simply rejected her misshapen son out of hand.[106] Had she done so, Wilhelm doubtless would have turned elsewhere for emotional sustenance. As it was, with Friedrich often emotionally and physically unavailable, Wilhelm and Victoria were intensely involved with one another. There can be little doubt that through Wilhelm's adolescence at least, he remained the child to whom Victoria was most attached and devoted.[107] It would also be a mistake to relate Victoria's disappointment in her son solely to his birth defect, including its effects upon his character. The crown princess was similarly dissatisfied and distressed with the appearance and character of her two other elder children. Her next oldest child, Charlotte, was "*very* difficult to manage—as her capabilities are so few," "backward," "by far the stupidest of the children," "odd," and physically awkward and unattractive to the point of defectiveness.[108] Like Wilhelm, Charlotte was subjected to humiliating therapeutic measures. As a result of fingernail biting, the not yet three-year-old Charlotte was made to sleep with her hands tied together and was forced to wear gloves during the day.[109] Heinrich, her third child, was also "backward," "lazy" and "dull," with a "weak" character, a "poor ugly face" that had "grown if possible much plainer since last year!" about whom she could not "feel very proud."[110] In fact, the same confusion of positive and negative feelings that characterized Victoria's attitude toward Wilhelm marked her attitude toward Charlotte and Heinrich. Witness her description to her mother of Charlotte on 23 May 1874: "Charlotte has greatly improved in every way . . . she is gentle and amiable and . . . I . . . cannot complain of her in any way. Clever she is *not*—and never will be, she has few—or *no* interests—no taste for learning or reading."[111] Or of Heinrich who as a four-year-old was on his way to visit his grandmother in England in November 1866: "I am sure you will like the poor child; he cannot help being so ugly, and he is really not stupid and can be very amusing!"[112]

Deeper than Victoria's distress at Wilhelm's arm was her disappointment that neither he nor his brother had the physical or intellectual capacity to measure up to her ideal of manhood. She had failed, in other words, to reproduce Prince Albert. The crown princess' realization that her sons could never fulfill her life's ambition became a source of bitter sorrow. She wrote her mother on 23 April 1887:

The dream of my life was to have a son who should be something of what our beloved Papa was, a real grandson of his in soul and intellect, a grandson of yours. . . . But one . . . must learn to abandon dreams and to take things as they come and characters as they are—one cannot quarrel with nature, and I suppose it knows best, though to us it seems cruel, perverse and contrary in the extreme. But it ends in one's feeling somewhat solitary at times![113]

During most of Wilhelm's childhood and adolescence, Victoria had not yet reconciled herself (as she apparently had in 1887) to the fact that her eldest son would not realize the dream of her life. Until well into the 1870s, she continued to hope that he might achieve the "perfection" that was her father and to fear that he would not.[114] It was, of course, an unattainable, indeed, illusory goal, even if rationalized in Hinzpeter's educational system. The Albert of Victoria's dreams never existed but had always been the romanticized image of the flawless man who had died at the height of her youthful idealization. That image became the standard by which the crown princess measured her son and herself, measured her success as a mother and as the daughter of Queen Victoria and Prince Albert.

For Victoria, Wilhelm was an expression of her best hopes and worst fears about herself; for Wilhelm, his mother's exaggerated hopes and fears were a psychological legacy that he would have to deal with throughout his life. Wilhelm internalized his mother's confusion about him. Just as Victoria could change her opinion of her son in the space of a single sentence, Wilhelm's mood could change from elation to despair in a matter of seconds. Victoria's dream that her son could attain her image of perfection became Wilhelm's unrestrained grandiosity; Victoria's dismay at his failure to realize her dream became his underlying depression. The inconsistency of his mother's response to him became the inconsistency of Wilhelm's self, his inner disjointedness, his want of "rightly coordinated organization."

Wilhelm's exquisite sensitivity to his environment as an adult was also a product of his mother's emotional unreliability. Seemingly trivial events, slight shifts in the way he was responded to, could affect Wilhelm profoundly. What the outside observer heard as tiny sounds were to the Kaiser deafening echoes of his mother's voice. Wilhelm had not been able take his maternal environment for granted as a child, and as Kaiser he dared not take the world around him for granted either. Given the immanent memory of his mother's precipitous global shifts in attitude, given the ease with which the environment could exhilarate or devastate him, Wilhelm sought to adapt himself to his surroundings or to adapt them to him. The relationship with his hopeful and fearful and dissatisfied mother gave fractured shape to Wilhelm II's personality and left him with a sense of insecurity, anxiety, and self-doubt and a craving for the affirmation and reassurance that had been missing in his early life.

III

Despite the long history of Victoria's dissatisfaction with her son, it was only after Wilhelm had come of age in 1877 and had officially left the house of his parents that the first clear evidence of conflict between them can be discerned.

Indeed, Victoria's attitude toward her son during his adolescence was perhaps more consistently positive and unambiguously affectionate than at any other time since the first few months of Wilhelm's life. With Wilhelm's physical development more or less complete (he appears to have reached puberty at an early age), it finally became possible for the crown princess to reconcile herself to her son's disability, and her letters from these years rarely mention Wilhelm's arm. Victoria's greater equanimity about her son is perhaps also to be attributed to the fact that he and his brother Heinrich spent the greater part of the period from 1874 to 1877 at the gymnasium in Kassel. With her boys under the supervision of the schoolmasters and Hinzpeter, who (along with Wilhelm's military governor, General Walter von Gottberg) accompanied them to Kassel, the crown princess' oppressive sense of responsibility may have lifted, enabling her simply to enjoy them. As her sons left home for school on 6 January 1873, Victoria—like her boys, upset and in tears over the separation—could experience and express how "very proud of them" she was and what "*great* pleasure" she took in them.[115] Throughout Wilhelm's years at the gymnasium, Victoria maintained that pride and pleasure. She was satisfied with his academic and personal progress at Kassel, saw him looking improved physically, enjoyed his vacations, and missed him when he returned to school.[116]

To Victoria's evident surprise, Wilhelm reciprocated her positive feelings. "Willy is as nice as possible," the crown princess wrote her mother during one of her son's vacations, "so affectionate, good and dear to me, which I used to fear he would never be."[117] Indeed, Wilhelm seems to have had a generally happy adolescence, despite the rigors of his life at Kassel, which, with his studies at the gymnasium added to Hinzpeter's own strenuous educational program, involved study from six in the morning until as late as ten o'clock at night.[118] During this period there was no sign of the animosity toward England that Wilhelm would exhibit within just a few years. In fact, he was openly proud of his English heritage and affectionate toward his English relatives, a pride and affection that reached a peak when Queen Victoria bestowed the Order of the Garter on her grandson on the occasion of his coming of age on 27 January 1877.[119]

His eighteenth birthday marked a decisive transition in Wilhelm's life. It came a few weeks after he had passed his exams and graduated tenth in a class of seventeen from the Kassel gymnasium. It brought the retirement of Hinzpeter, Wilhelm's educator, overseer, and companion since 1866. Finally, it marked the official end of Wilhelm's childhood. With his birthday, the prince left the house of his parents, and, accompanied only by a military aide-de-camp, set up quarters in Potsdam where in February he began his duties in the First Regiment of the Guard as ordered by his grandfather, the emperor. It was not without pain that Victoria watched her son cross "the threshold of life."[120] As Wilhelm left the nest, the crown princess looked back on his childhood with satisfaction and self-pity and looked forward to his adulthood with anticipation and trepidation. She wrote her mother on 30 January 1877:

> I felt ready to cry all day on the 27th.—It seemed to me such a giving up of my
> child, and such a wrench though it was *not* so in reality. His life since the day

he was born and I suffered *so* much—seems like one short dream. I spared *no* pains—*no* sacrifice to try and do the *best* for him; had many a tough struggle with the Emperor and Empress about his education, have incurred the censure of everyone—at court and in society from trying to shake off the old Prussian tradition as much as possible, though I could not succeed quite as well in that as I should have wished—still enough to be thought very dangerous and heretical! I bore with Dr. Hinzpeter for these many years—because I respected him and thought him in *many* ways a *great* blessing for Willy—though I knew all the while Dr. Hinzpeter detested me. . . . I feel that Willy will never know how much I have done and suffer for him—but after all—it does not matter if only he becomes good and useful and happy,—he is *very* young, very childish and unformed of his age—but a dear good boy—if he will only remain so. Of course I feel very anxious about him now that he goes out into the world.[121]

For his part, Wilhelm plunged into military life with energy and enthusiasm. Proud of the new responsibilities which kept him very busy, he performed his duties well, earning the praise of his senior officers.[122] Wilhelm's active service in the regiment was brief, however, and in the fall he began his studies at the university in Bonn, where both his father and Prince Albert had studied before him. The young man who took up residence in Bonn in June 1877 was for the first time in his life effectively free from parental, tutorial, or regimental control.[123] He responded to the newfound freedom by indulging in what Lamar Cecil has called a life of "aimless frivolity."[124] Wilhelm took little interest in his studies and spent most of his time in the company of the fellow-members of his Borussia student corps and of various army officers stationed in the area. According to his uncle, the grand duke of Baden, Wilhelm was interested in "pursuing his own pleasures and paid little attention" to the public lectures he attended.[125] The crown princess also deplored her son's lack of studiousness as well as his newfound friends. With the apparent failure of her program to shape Wilhelm's character and intellect, it was her hope that "*life* must now bring out what there is to develop."[126]

Wilhelm's pleasure-seeking student days can be understood in at least three different ways. In the first place, one can interpret Wilhelm's neglect of his education in favor of the comradeship of aristocratic students and Prussian officers as an implicit repudiation of Victoria and Hinzpeter, of their devotion to learning and hard work, of their contempt for aristocratic airs and Prussian militarism.[127] It is also possible that Wilhelm's behavior in Bonn was an expression of simple relief that he had finally escaped from the thankless drudgery of the tutor's system and from the oppressive scrutiny of his worried mother. Finally, on perhaps the deepest psychological level, Wilhelm's student life of "aimless frivolity" can be understood as a response to the sudden lack of structure that until he entered the university had always been provided for him. Whether taking the form of his mother's ambitious involvement, of Hinzpeter's rigid educational system, or of the structure of the Potsdam regiment, Wilhelm's life had always been regulated and directed from without. Partially as a consequence, Wilhelm never developed what his mother and tutor had tried so hard to instill in him: namely, the capacity to regulate and direct himself. Once that outside guidance was gone Wilhelm found himself adrift, able only to wander from one gratification to the next at Bonn.

This latter interpretation accounts for Wilhelm's relief and happiness when he learned that his grandfather had ordered him to return to Potsdam to rejoin his regiment, this time as a second lieutenant, upon completion of his university education in 1879. Victoria had hoped that her son would be able to travel extensively after leaving the university in order to broaden his horizon. Wilhelm gave up this project "with a light heart." He told his mother:

> I can wait; in a year or two it will perhaps be possible. I shall with the greatest pleasure enter my beloved Regiment, *as the Emperor wishes* it; because I long for the dear Potsdam and the life there is so pleasant and nice. And the stern and regular will do me of good [sic], after all the sitting I have gone through. I am to take the command of a company which will be a rather difficult task for me at first; but it will give me ample employment, and besides will be very interesting for me. In fact I look forward to it with great joy.[128]

In the period after Wilhelm had finished at Bonn and before he began his active duty in the Potsdam regiment, Victoria did manage to take her son on a trip to Italy. The prince's heart was not in sightseeing, however. He did not share his mother's enthusiasm for "Churches, Pictures, Galleries, and old Homes." Instead, in every town they visited, Wilhelm was interested only in "looking about for the 'Excercier Plätze' [the military drill grounds]—and the fortifications."[129]

Disregarding the many sermons he had heard from his mother about the stultifying narrowness of the Prussian military mentality, Wilhelm resumed his regimental duties with "delight."[130] In the camaraderie of his fellow officers, in their conviviality, in their praise if not to say flattery, the young man found the emotional sustenance that had been missing in his relationship with his unavailable father and dissatisfied mother. The regimental officer corps, he told his friend Philipp Eulenburg, became his "true home."[131] There he discovered "my family, my friends, my interests—everything of which I had up to that time had to do without."[132] Indeed, in a speech to the Potsdam Guard Regiment on 19 December 1887, Wilhelm again connected military and family life. He told his men: "You are a part of a great Army and of an extended family, whose father is the King and whose nuclear family is your regiment. This will, as far as it goes, take the place of your family, and therefore a Christmas has been prepared for you, as the father in a family does for his children."[133] Taking on the brusque and prideful demeanor he deemed fitting in a Prussian officer and the stridently Anglophobic views of the officer corps, Wilhelm adapted himself to his new masculine "family."[134] "Before I entered the regiment," he explained to Eulenburg, "I had lived through such fearful years of unappreciation of my nature, of ridicule of that which was to me highest and most holy: Prussia, the Army, and all of the fulfilling duties that I first encountered in the officer corps and that have provided me with joy and happiness and contentment on earth."[135]

In the successful performance of structured military duties, Wilhelm experienced, perhaps for the first time in his life, a sense of accomplishment and self-confidence. In the acknowledgment, attention, and admiration of his fellow officers, he experienced a sense of being appreciated, of being worthwhile. In the straightforward obligations, the clear-cut rules, the dependable discipline, and the hierarchical structure that defined military life, he experienced a sense of consistent, reliable external support. The Prussian army offered Wilhelm an alternative to his mother's dissatisfaction and inconsistency. It is not surprising, then, that he "adored" doing his duty or that the acceptance and structure, the self-esteem and order, he experienced in the Potsdam army barracks became associated for Wilhelm with the traditional conservative political values of the Prussian military—values that would bring him into open political conflict with Friedrich and Victoria.[136]

CHAPTER 3

The Legacy of
Maternal Possessiveness

In 1879, while still at the university in Bonn, Wilhelm fell in love with the woman who would become his wife, Princess Auguste Viktoria of Schleswig-Holstein-Sonderburg-Augustenburg. His experience in the regiment and attachment to Dona, as she was known, when combined with his prolonged contact with his grandfather, Wilhelm I, precipitated Wilhelm's personal and political break with his parents. In his regiment, Wilhelm had found the affirmation he had never had at home. In the emperor, he found an admirable and responsive German man to compensate for his weak and largely absent father. In Dona, he found the unequivocal and unwavering devotion that had been missing in his relationship with his mother. To fully appreciate Dona's psychological significance for Wilhelm, however, it is necessary to consider one further aspect of his relationship with Victoria and of her dissatisfaction with him.

I

Wilhelm failed to live up to his mother's ideal not only because of his limitations and her self-doubt, but also because she worked to prevent him from doing so. Victoria wanted him to become strong and capable after the image of her father and at the same time demanded that he remain childlike and dependent on her. Despite her disappointment in them, Victoria was intensely possessive of all her children. She was fondest of them when, as during infancy, they seemed most in need of her; she was most dissatisfied with them when they began to grow up and apart from her.[1] Queen Victoria proved prophetic when she warned in 1870 that Victoria's pleasure in her children would not last: "when one idolises one's children, as you do, what will you suffer when you have quite to give them up and feel how little they care for you and all your care and anxiety! To see one's child totally independent and constantly wishing to go quite contrary to their parents' wishes, convictions and kind advice is very dreadful."[2] In open conflict with her three eldest children in 1886, Victoria echoed the words of her mother: "I quite agree that children are a *very* great anxiety! As long as they are small they are also a very great pleasure. But when they grow up and are not *all* one would wish—it is very bitter and painful."[3]

Victoria's possessiveness probably grew out of her own dependence on her parents.[4] Every step her children took toward maturity and independence doubtless reminded the crown princess of the physical and temporal distance separating her from her childhood home.[5] As has been suggested, Victoria experienced her children as reflections of herself, or, to use her own description of her feelings for Sigismund, as "a part of myself."[6] As they became older and began to establish a measure of autonomy, perhaps she felt as if a part of herself was being torn away. "Sometimes I feel too young for a mother of a son already confirmed and sometimes too old!" Victoria wrote her mother on 1 September 1874 when it came time for Wilhelm and Heinrich to leave for the gymnasium in Kassel. "Another thought grieves me—though one ought not to shrink from a sacrifice! Today is a sort of break up—in two days the boys leave us for school . . . I feel giving them up like this very much!"[7] Once her sons had left, the crown princess' distress increased perhaps to the point of physical illness, and throughout their years at Kassel she found the separation hard to bear.[8] When, as during the summer of 1878, Victoria was again surrounded by all the children, she experienced "an unutterable relief to have them under my wing again—as an old hen should."[9]

Victoria's possessiveness permits a deeper understanding of her effort to maintain exclusive control over Wilhelm's upbringing and her resentment of those who sought to teach her son the traditions of the Hohenzollern family and the culture of the country over which he would someday reign. Beneath the crown princess' resolve that her son would be raised in accordance with her liberal political philosophy and English values lay simple jealousy and the fear that conservative Germans who exerted an influence on Wilhelm would draw him away from her. Despite the fact that she had selected Hinzpeter and that his educational philosophy was generally compatible with her own, Victoria's enthusiasm for the tutor quickly disappeared, and she came to regard him as a rival who sought to turn her sons against their parents.[10]

Victoria bitterly resented Wilhelm I's "interference" in her son's upbringing. She was irritated when her father-in-law sought to determine how Wilhelm's confirmation was to be conducted, indignant when he bestowed a decoration on Wilhelm without her knowledge or consent, and aggravated when he refused to allow her to take her children on trips, particularly to England.[11] Convinced that travel would enable Wilhelm to develop the cosmopolitan outlook he could never acquire in the stultifying and provincial atmosphere of Brandenburg-Prussia, she wrote her mother on 6 May 1865:

> I hope we shall be allowed to send our Willy all over the world but we are in a difficult position as Fritz's parents interfere so much in all we do with the children. The King dislikes all innovations, as most people about Court here do

and think that where the children are born there they are to grow up and never go away for fear of their becoming estranged from their country.[12]

Although the king scuttled her ambitious travel plans for her son, Victoria was able to pressure him to appoint as Wilhelm's military governor not one of the "creatures" of Bismarck and the chief of the Prussian Military Cabinet, but her choice, Lieutenant O'Danne, who, although he could speak only broken English, was at least an Irishman by birth. "You have no idea," she wrote her mother at the conclusion of this episode, "what trouble the reigning party take to put their spies about our court nor to what degree they hate us."[13]

Seven years later, the crown princess again came into conflict with her father-in-law when Wilhelm I insisted that, instead of attending the gymnasium, Wilhelm and Heinrich would "come out" at court and begin active military service following their respective confirmations, as was traditional in the Hohenzollern family.[14] Victoria respected the Kaiser and could at times find him "charming, kind, and amiable." But when he sought to exert his authority in order to direct his grandson down the path traditionally taken by Prussian princes, she was beside herself. "It is just like him!" she wrote in December 1874 when it appeared that Wilhelm I would not permit her boys to go to Kassel. "He has not the faintest idea of education, nor of the requirements of the present day. How should he, he was completely neglected as a child and is one of the most ignorant men alive!"[15] In this instance, as in many others during Wilhelm's childhood, Victoria was eventually able to get her way with the old gentleman. But she was right to fear the influence of Wilhelm I on her eldest son. Once Wilhelm had left Victoria's orbit, the Kaiser would prove a more personally powerful and politically dangerous rival than Hinzpeter had ever been.

Victoria's distress in the controversy with the emperor over whether Wilhelm was to go to court or to Kassel was the product not only of her anger at Wilhelm I's interference in her son's upbringing or of her fear that the Kaiser might convert Wilhelm to traditional Prussian aristocratic and military values. The crown princess was also dismayed because Wilhelm I sought to accelerate her sons' passage into adulthood, thereby ending the period of their dependence on her. The agitation that Victoria experienced when her children made that transition is revealed by her letter of 12 December 1876 to her close friend Marie Dönhoff:

> my nerves have become shaky again as when you saw me last year, I have a perpetual headache, the blood all flies to my heart—and my nights are not good! We have *so* many family arrangements to make and difficulties to overcome, just now owing to our eldest son coming of age in January and having an establishment of his own, and Henry being confirmed at Easter with his sister Charlotte and then going to sea, and Charlotte coming out "dans le monde"—after Easter that I often do not know wo mir der Kopf steht.[16]

The engagement of Charlotte to Bernhard von Saxe-Meiningen in spring of 1877 increased Victoria's distress and left her feeling "knocked up completely.

I have a bad cough and very painful rheumatism in my side and do not feel at *all* well. All the emotions about Charlotte's marriage have bouleverse'd me *very much* indeed."[17] The wedding, one year later on February 20, was traumatic.[18] She wrote her mother the next day:

> I took her to her room after the Crown had been taken off. I helped her to undress and get ready for going to bed, and with an aching heart left her, no more mine now, to care for and watch and take care of, but another's, and that is a hard wrench for a mother. With pangs of pain we bring them into the world, with bitter pain we resign them to others for life, to independence—and to shift for themselves. We bore the one for their sakes and with pleasure—and so must we the other.[19]

Given Victoria's vulnerable state, it should come as no surprise that the first sign of conflict between Wilhelm and his mother appeared after he had come of age. Perhaps the tension derived from Victoria's dissatisfaction with the way Wilhelm had turned out, now that he had officially reached adulthood. Perhaps the strain between mother and son grew out of her displeasure at his enthusiasm for his first tour of duty in the Potsdam Guards Regiment. What is clear, however, is that, with Charlotte's wedding fast approaching and Wilhelm living on his own, Victoria's annoyance with her son in the summer of 1877 was the product of his "neglect" of her.[20] In August, Wilhelm had injured his knee, and Victoria had hoped to care for him. He would not allow it, however. She wrote her mother on 29 August 1877:

> In answer to your kind question about Willy I will only say that he twisted his knee while bathing in the Havel. It is all right again. It was not a bad sprain but we have begged him to take care of it which I trust he is doing but unless I go every day to see him, he does not trouble himself to come and see me, though it is only a drive of 10 minutes and a walk of 25 minutes from his door to ours. I have not seen him since Sunday, and considering that I am going away to the Rhine, and shall not see much of him in the next few weeks and he is going off to Bonn in October, I think he might just drop in for one minute some time or other between 7 in the morning and 10 at night, just to say how do you do, and ask after his Mama, when his Papa is away, but that is a thought which never strikes him and I am not spoilt by marks of attention.[21]

The death of Victoria's youngest son, Waldemar, on 27 March 1879—a tragic event under any circumstances—thus came at a time when the crown princess was already suffering from the loss of her three eldest children to adulthood. As with the death of Sigismund some thirteen years before, Victoria was filled with sorrow at the loss of her ten-year-old son and was convinced that he had been the "dearest and nicest and most promising of my boys."[22] "At first there is but one feeling," she wrote Marie Dönhoff, "the wish to go down into the grave with one's child! Parting from it is too intolerable." But as she had with Sigismund, her despair was followed by the vow "to do one's duty till the end ... I know not how I struggle through one day and one night after another—but I know that my husband and children want me still, and that I must wait until the time comes to lie down by my little Waldemar—and feel no more that he is gone!"[23] Once again the crown princess dealt with the pain of separation from her dead child by increasing her involvement and investment in her surviving children. This time, however, Victoria's surge of possessive feeling occurred just as the three eldest children were trying to establish their independence from her, just as the twenty-year-old Wilhelm was taking his first tentative steps toward manhood.

II

Because of Victoria's possessiveness, Wilhelm was only able to break away from his mother with difficulty. Indeed, Wilhelm's emotional separation from Victoria occurred over a period of years and appears to have been accomplished in three steps: first, through his attachment to at least three older women; second, through his engagement and marriage to Dona; and third, through his relatively sudden and violent rejection of his parents.

Despite his friendship with army officers and lack of studiousness, Wilhelm remained deeply attached to his mother during his years at the university in Bonn. Describing himself "very much grieved" at being apart from her, he kept Victoria's photograph on his desk, and wrote her letters in English recounting his activities, although of course not as frequently as she would have liked.[24] The innocent, childlike quality of Wilhelm's attachment to Victoria is revealed by his letter in English to Marie Dönhoff on 11 December 1878:

> Perhaps in many respects you are happier in Vienna for having no Court restrictions as we have in Berlin, and I am sure the society is much freer than at home. For Xmas I shall go home for a few weeks to that dreadful Berlin! Where the society are so bad towards my poor Mama and where I don't know and don't care for anybody in the least. I can assure you that I never feel happy, realy [sic] happy at Berlin. Only Potsdam that is my "el dorado" and that is also where Mama most likes to live, where one feels free with the beautiful nature around you and soldiers as much as you like. For I love my dear Regiment very much, there are such kind nice young men in it.[25]

Wilhelm's affectionate correspondence with Countess Dönhoff can be understood as an effort to deal with his yearning for his mother.[26] By transferring his feelings for Victoria onto her friend, Wilhelm was able to take a first significant step away from her. As he had with Victoria, Wilhelm regaled Marie Dönhoff with descriptions of the cultural events he had attended: Donizetti's "The Daughter of the Regiment," a piano recital by Clara Schumann, and a performance of Brahms' "Minnelied" that was "something too delicious."[27] The memory of her playing the "Feuerzauber" music from Wagner's "Valkyrie" on the piano for him and his mother in Potsdam was especially important to Wilhelm, perhaps because it reminded him of the connection between him and the two women.[28] "And often, when I feel wearied and tired from work and should like to stop writing," Wilhelm wrote Dönhoff, "then that heavenly 'Feuerzauber' comes into my head; first low, then louder and louder do I hear it, till I begin to sing, and then I feel fresh I take up my work again with vigour. You have done myself a great deal of good by your musik [sic] and I never shall forget those few nice evenings at Potsdam."[29] Marie Dönhoff's photograph joined that of his mother on his desk, and he hung a portrait in oil that Victoria had done of Dönhoff over his bed.[30] She had become the good mother who tucked him in at night and waked him in the morning, "so the last thing I see before I shut my eyes, and the first thing when I open them is your picture."[31]

Through his attachment to Marie Dönhoff, Wilhelm was imitating Victoria's affection for her friend. It also seems possible, then, that he was attempting to stay close to his mother by taking on her attributes. Through his identification with Victoria, he was preserving her in himself.[32] Like his mother, who when depressed longed for the presence of her friend and complained to Dönhoff of her various ailments, Wilhelm missed the countess keenly and described in detail his "severe suffering" from an ear and headache and the "very disagreeable accident" when he reinjured his knee fencing in early 1879.[33] Like his mother, he addressed Dönhoff as "Darling Contessina" and wrote her emotional letters in English. One can hear the voice of Victoria when Wilhelm wrote: "But still more good have you done, by your kind conversation and your excellent advice, and Mama was very right, when she wrote to me that she was very glad I liked and loved you so because I could learn a large deal from you, and form my intellect etc."[34]

By early 1879, however, Wilhelm's ardor for Marie Dönhoff had cooled, in part because of her lack of responsiveness to him and because he had "found and made a new intimate friend, whom I also adore. It is somebody you also love very much: it is Fr. v Schleinitz."[35] In Mimi Schleinitz, the wife of a minister in the Prussian government, Wilhelm found another older married woman, another friend of his mother, even another Wagner enthusiast to help him separate from Victoria. He appears to have used the relationship with her to help him handle his growing attraction to young women. By continuing to focus on a more maternal figure, Wilhelm sought to relieve some of his anxiety about this maturational step away from his mother and toward adult sexuality. "I quite agree with what you say about dear Mimi Schleinitz," Wilhelm wrote to Marie Dönhoff on 20 February 1879, "she is really, I believe, nearly the only lady in the whole of the Berlin society with whom one can talk about other things than dresses and flirtations, and I hope that you know me enough to know that I am a sworn enemy to such kind of thing as well as to such kind of ladies, who want to be flirted with. I think that is something beneath a real man and gentleman; especially I think beneath myself don[']t you think so too?"[36]

During the period when he had established relationships with Marie Dönhoff and Mimi Schleinitz, Wilhelm was also in correspondence with his father's sister, Luise of Baden. Like Dönhoff and Schleinitz, Wilhelm's aunt was an older, married woman. But there the similarity ended. His letters to Marie Dönhoff were romantic. The subject of art and music figured prominently in them. Both Dönhoff and Schleinitz were close friends of his mother, and his letters to Dönhoff contain numerous references to Victoria. His letters to Dönhoff were written in English. By contrast, Wilhelm's letters to Luise of Baden were polite, even deferential, containing expressions of his faith in God and his gratitude for the sober counsel she had given him about his future. Luise of Baden belonged to the paternal side of his family, and his letters to her make solicitous, almost reverent, references to his grandmother, Kaiserin Augusta. The relationship with his aunt—while apparently not as intense as that with the friends of his mother—continued beyond 1880.[37] Wilhelm's letters to Luise of Baden were written in German. His letter of 1 February 1878 is typical. After thanking his aunt for her valuable "guidance on how I can proceed along life's difficult course," Wilhelm continued: "You and Grandmama take a maternal interest in me, and I hope that it will not be in vain but that my success will amply repay your concern."[38] Thus, during 1878 and 1879 Wilhelm attached himself to three maternal figures in an attempt to separate emotionally from his mother. But Wilhelm was living in two different worlds. There was the emotional, cultured, English world of his mother and her friends; and there was the sober, pious, German world of his aunt and grandmother. The same issue— Wilhelm's longing for maternal support and his need to be independent of it— was being worked through in each. But the two worlds remained separate, and their division reflected a division within Wilhelm himself.

Although in February 1879 the prince did not feel ready to take an adult interest in members of the opposite sex, within a few months he had fallen in love with Princess Auguste Viktoria, and on 14 February 1880 they became secretly engaged. To Wilhelm's surprise and delight, his choice of a bride "not only met with no opposition from my parents; but was entirely approved by them."[39] In the days following their son's engagement, Friedrich and Victoria indeed felt "very thankful and much relieved" that Wilhelm had decided to marry Dona, and they actively campaigned to win Bismarck's and the Kaiser's consent for this somewhat problematic match.[40]

It seems likely that the crown princess' initial espousal of the marriage was based on an identification with Dona, on her sense that to the Prussian establishment both she and her future daughter-in-law were outsiders. She had never been fully accepted because of her English heritage. Dona would never be fully accepted because she was not of the high aristocracy and because she was the daughter of the still politically controversial Duke Friedrich von Holstein-Augustenburg, whose claim to the duchies of Schleswig and Holstein had been ruthlessly overridden by Bismarck during 1864–66 in his march to Prussia's unification of Germany. "A brilliant 'parti' in the eyes of the world it certainly is not, and that will wound the inordinate parvenu pride and vanity of the Berlin people who since 1871 think themselves the only great people in the world," Victoria wrote her mother on 13 February 1880. "On the other hand they dislike everything foreign so much, that I fancy they will be better pleased with a Princess bred and born and educated in Germany—and more spite, ill-will, backbiting and criticism of the unkindest sort, she never can have to endure than I have gone through for 22 years." Although Bismarck's campaign against Duke Friedrich might result in popular disapproval of his daughter's engagement to Wilhelm, Victoria was convinced that "this will wear off I am sure when Victoria [Dona] becomes known—for she is so sweet and sensible a girl that she must win all hearts and we shall be there to protect her."[41] When the crown princess' prediction proved accurate and Dona succeeded in charming both the Kaiser and Berlin society, her pleasure at the marriage of her son began to diminish. Dona had been accepted; Victoria remained a foreigner, her political isolation increasing her personal loneliness.[42] "I always feel like a fly struggling in a very tangled web," she wrote her mother, "and feelings of weariness and depression, often of disgust and hopelessness take possession of me."[43]

On the first anniversary of Waldemar's death, the crown princess was overwhelmed by the sense of loss and unable to share her son's happiness. "Congratulations on William's engagement come to me now on all sides," she wrote her mother on 27 March 1880, "it is often a sore trial to speak of joy, happiness and festivities and receive congratulations, when one has an aching void at heart!"[44] As the date of the wedding approached, Victoria grew increasingly distressed.[45] As in the fall of 1874 at the impending departure of her sons for Kassel, Victoria's concerns about becoming old and lonely were mobilized by Wilhelm's maturation. "I am growing very unsightly, have lost almost all my hair and what remains has turned very grey," she wrote Queen Victoria a month before her fortieth birthday and four months before her son's wedding, "my face is full of lines and wrinkles especially around the eyes and mouth, and having no good features to boast of, I really am an annoyance to my esthetic and artistic feelings when I look at myself in the glass! It must be born with equanimity as it is unavoidable, and I comfort myself with the thought that it really matters to no one (except to you) what I look like."[46] That her concern about her age was connected with her son's neglect is confirmed by a letter she wrote to Marie Dönhoff a few weeks later: "My son will come just for *1 day*—my *Birthday* (21. Nov). The thought of being *40* already is rather serious."[47] Filled not with joy but with sadness and nostalgia at Wilhelm's developmental step, Victoria yearned for her little Waldemar, whose loss seemed to sum up the loss of her own youth and of her children—first Sigismund and Waldemar to death, then Heinrich, Charlotte, and Wilhelm to adulthood.[48]

The crown princess' unhappiness was increased by the fact that her son evidently did not share her sadness at the separation and, according to Victoria, deliberately sought to avoid her.[49] "It is the last time we have Willy unmarried in the same house, in his old rooms with us," the crown princess wrote her mother two months before the wedding. "He thinks me absurdly sentimental to observe this and says it is all the same to him in what place, or house, or room he lives. I hate saying the words: 'Good Bye'."[50] Under considerable physical and emotional stress, Victoria looked "very worn and tired" even to Wilhelm who was preoccupied with his own excitement and happiness.[51] The wedding, when it finally occurred on 27 February 1881, was a wearing experience for Victoria, who was preoccupied with her "darling" Waldemar and with her mother. Although the bride looked "lovely" and "all went off very well," the service was "a harangue" and the wedding "exhausting, suffocating and interminable," leaving her "thoroughly tired and knocked up." She barely mentioned Wilhelm in her letters to her mother.[52]

By contrast, the wedding made Wilhelm "a very happy man."[53] He appears to have experienced a mixture of exhilaration and relief at being able to increase his physical and emotional distance from Victoria through his marriage. She exerted a considerable hold over Wilhelm. His ability to separate from her now can be attributed to the fact that in his bride Wilhelm had found a caring, devoted, and loving companion to replace his worried mother. In contrast to the dynamic and domineering crown princess, Dona was generally docile and quietly supportive of Wilhelm, "a submissive blind wife," as Queen Victoria contemptuously described her in 1887 at the height of the conflict between Victoria and Wilhelm.[54] Unlike Victoria, she was a person of limited

Wilhelm and Dona with their engagement official in June 1880. Reprinted with the permission of the Ullstein Bilderdienst.

imagination and few talents. She was no political activist; and her opinions, on those occasions when she expressed them, were conservative, straight-laced, and pious. "Clothes and children are her chief conversation and the only things she thoroughly understands," Daisy Princess of Pless wrote of Dona. "For a woman in that position I have never met *anyone* so devoid of any individual thought or agility of brain and understanding. She is just like a good, quiet, soft cow that has calves and eats grass slowly and ruminates."[55] Even in this caustic description the image of Dona as nurturing and maternal comes through. A more charitable assessment of Dona and of her relationship with Wilhelm came from Bernhard von Bülow: "She sustained the Kaiser; she gave courage to one who so easily swung back and forth between hope and fear."[56] In Dona, Wilhelm had found a woman he could rely on for support, who provided him with emotional stability and stayed in the background, allowing him to dominate the stage.[57]

Despite his wife's devotion, there are indications that their forty-year marriage did not fully satisfy Wilhelm. Aside from reading aloud to his wife, Wilhelm spent little time with his family, and, like his own father, left the care of his seven children in the hands of his wife. Home made him feel, quoting Shakespeare's "Macbeth," "cribbed, cabined, and confined."[58] Not only did Wilhelm's reserve toward his family reflect his confining experience with his possessive mother, it also reflected the fact that in Wilhelm's eyes Dona could never measure up to Victoria. "The Kaiser knew what he had found in his wife," Bülow wrote in his memoirs. "He loved her, to be sure only within the limits of his naive self-absorption [*Selbstsucht*]. He recognized and appreciated her devotion. But, in comparison to his mother, she seemed to him a petty-princess. 'One can always tell,' he remarked to me on more than one occasion, 'that she was not brought up in Windsor but rather in Primkenau.'"[59] Although Wilhelm's marriage and his public rejection of his parents that followed so closely on its heels represented an effort to tear himself away from Victoria's possessiveness, Wilhelm remained deeply involved with his mother. Throughout the rest of his life, in fact, he would struggle against her powerful attraction.

After Wilhelm's marriage, relations with Victoria deteriorated dramatically. Perhaps to insure his separation from her, Wilhelm reduced his contact with his mother as much as possible. He wrote her infrequently and allowed months to pass without sending word.[60] He tried to keep Victoria away from his wife and prevented her from involving herself in the arrangements for the birth of his first child in late 1881, consulting instead her sister, Helena.[61] Nor was his mother allowed to influence the organization of the children's nursery or health care.[62] Rather than turn to Friedrich and Victoria for advice, Wilhelm sought daily counsel from the emperor and empress and did not inform his parents of his plans.[63] Paradoxically, Wilhelm's coolness and distance toward his mother testifies to the intensity of their relationship. Wilhelm's efforts to keep Victoria at arm's length doubtless represented an attempt to protect himself both from her powerful influence over him and from his powerful need to depend on her.

Still mourning her two deceased boys, discouraged about growing old, feeling politically isolated, and suffering emotional and physical anguish over the loss of her three eldest children to adulthood, Victoria was cut to the quick by her son's behavior.[64] It seemed to her that Wilhelm and Dona had simply forgotten "our existence and think it unnecessary to take any notice of us."[65] She experienced the autonomy of Wilhelm, Charlotte, and Heinrich as a failure to appreciate the efforts and sacrifices she had made in raising them, as a repudiation of her, her family, and all that she stood for—their political independence confirming for the crown princess that they had become personally independent of her as well. "My three eldest children give me a good bit of anxiety in one way or another and are not all I could wish," Victoria wrote to Marie Dönhoff in December 1881, "so I miss my Waldie all the more—but my three youngest make up for all by their sweet loving womenly natures. I am afraid I am very weak with them, but they are irresistible little people."[66] Hurt and angry at her eldest for abandoning her, Victoria turned from them and lavished affection on her three "little"—that is, more dependent—daughters.

Perhaps jealous at their mother's preference for their younger sisters, surely hurt and angry at her inability to respond positively to their maturational progress, Wilhelm, Charlotte, and Heinrich joined in opposition to Victoria. The crown princess had given them little choice. She had presented them with two alternatives: dependence or a breakdown in relations. Impelled by their own developmental needs and by the political realities of their environment, they chose the second. As Charlotte later told Count Carl von Wedel, the source of the antagonism between Victoria and her eldest children was that "they would not capitulate to her."[67]

Although political tension between mother and son can already be detected in the fall of 1877 (the period between Wilhelm's first tour of duty with the Potsdam Guards and the start of his studies at Bonn), disagreement over the Eastern Question appears not to have affected their personal relationship.[68] Two years later, however, in a letter in pencil to Queen Victoria of 21 December 1879, Wilhelm made a number of slips and errors in writing that reveal unconscious hostility toward England and his English relatives. One sentence had been originally written: "May the New Year bring good news of success to your arms and of victory of all the dangerous foes" until Wilhelm had changed the victory "of" England's foes to an English victory "over" them. The letter was signed by Queen Victoria's "devoted and respectful nephew," thereby demoting his grandmother to an aunt. Finally, instead of his usual signature, "Your respectful, loving, and dutiful grandson, William," Wilhelm had added "Princ(cz)e [he had originally written 'Prinz' and had corrected it to 'Prince'] of Prussia," thereby asserting his Prussian identity.[69] By August 1880 political conflict with the crown princess was manifest. "Willy is chauvinistic and ultra-Prussian to a degree which is often very painful to me," Victoria wrote her mother on the fifth, "I avoid all discussions—always turn off the subject and remain silent. . . . with my own children I often feel like a hen that has hatched ducklings and it often gives me great pain as one is so wrapped up in them."[70] Although not overtly political, Wilhelm's marriage was not without political significance. Thus, it was not the relationship of Friedrich and Victoria—with its implications for German politics, foreign policy, and the role of women in German society—but the more traditional relationship of his German grandparents that Wilhelm sought to emulate in his marriage to Dona. He wrote his aunt Luise shortly before the wedding: "I hope with God's help together with the incomparable Princess to make a Christian and good house like the one I see and revere of my grandparents."[71]

Within a year of the marriage, the personal split between Wilhelm and Victoria had become openly political.[72] Thereafter personal differences tended to be expressed in political terms. "Sometimes I am so discouraged that I am weary of my existence altogether!" Victoria wrote Queen Victoria on 18 January 1882. "The dear Emperor has gone over to Bismarck completely because he now wants peace with France. . . . Willie and Henry are quite devoted to the Bismarck policy and think it sublime so there we are—alone and *sad;* in the public people say 'Oh the Crown Prince would approve of everything that the Government do were it not for his English wife.'"[73] By mid-March 1882 stories of Wilhelm's insensitivity and rudeness toward his mother were circulating in Berlin.[74] Over the course of the year he openly denounced "our arrogant cousin," "wave-ruling Albion," implicitly attributing Victoria's personal qualities—her supercilious and domineering character—to her English homeland.[75] By the end of 1882, the Hohenzollern family had divided into two factions. In one camp stood the crown prince and princess with their youngest daughters: political proponents of a liberalized Germany allied closely to England. In the other camp stood Wilhelm with Dona, Charlotte, Heinrich, and the Kaiser: traditional Prussian conservatives, allied with Bismarck, inclining diplomatically toward Austria or Russia and implacable opponents of any reorientation of German foreign or domestic policy in the direction of liberal England.[76]

It is a revealing feature of the subsequent history of the relationship between Victoria and Wilhelm that even after he had become her outspoken opponent, she rarely blamed him directly for his antagonism toward her. She was convinced that her son had an unalterably dependent character and attributed his hostility to the influence of others who used him "as a card . . . and a tool" against his parents.[77] Those who manipulated Wilhelm included: Kaiserin Augusta, who "flatters him and twists him round her finger"; his sister Charlotte, who had both Wilhelm and Heinrich in her "pocket" and had turned them both against their sister Vicky; and Kaiser Wilhelm I, under whose "thumb" the two princes were.[78] The principal villain, however, was Bismarck and the ruling "Clique" or "Party" around him which simply "used" Wilhelm "as a tool and instrument against his parents! . . . *These* are all William's friends now, and he is on a footing of the greatest intimacy and familiarity with them! It is easy to see how bad and dangerous this is for him and for us! . . . William's judgment is being wharped [sic] and his mind poisoned by this! He is not sharp enough or experienced enough to see *through* the system nor through the people, and they do with him what they like."[79]

One gets the sense that Victoria's unsparing criticism of her son's reign stemmed in part from her feeling neglected by the young Kaiser. "I think he is simply so wrapped up in himself, his power, his vanity, his plans, his position, that he does not remember my existence," she wrote her mother on 28 March 1889.[80] It particularly rankled that Dona had taken her place and apparently now exerted the influence over her son's life that Victoria so much wanted to wield:

> I am quite away and out of everything and know very little of what goes on at the Schloss. I only meet William and Dona at family dinners, amongst all the others . . . Dona enjoys her position intensely and her whole face expresses the most intense satisfaction. She is convinced that all William and she do and think and say is perfect, and this is certainly a state of beatitude. She meddles in everything the family does, every little trifle is reported to her, and she orders and directs in a way very galling for the others from so young a person.[81]

Victoria's denunciations of her son were a product of her frustrated possessiveness; her complaints about his dependent character masked her underlying need to infantilize him.

And yet, despite Victoria's psychological interest in seeing her son as dependent, her view of Wilhelm was doubtless correct. He was only able to separate from his mother by attaching himself to others: Marie Dönhoff, Mimi Schleinitz, Luise of Baden, Dona, the Kaiser and Kaiserin, Bismarck, and the friends on whom he came to rely after 1881. In part because of her controlling personality, Victoria had been unable to allow her son to grow gradually apart from her, to take step by incremental step toward psychological independence, to internalize a sense of independent strength and initiative. As a result, what Wilhelm achieved through his rebellion against his mother was not true autonomy but rather a diversification of his dependence. Still in need of guidance and support and yet fearing that he would again become enmeshed and controlled, Wilhelm attached himself not to one but to a number of very different individuals. Although he gained psychological support and some sense of independence, since he never relied on any one individual for very long, Wilhelm paid a price for this solution. On the one hand, the support he received was fragmentary; and, as he adapted himself to an ever-changing external environment, his inconsistency increased. On the other hand, his relationships were superficial and transitory, including even that with his wife. He flitted from one dependent relationship to the next, traveling from estate to estate, from town to town, from friend to friend. He preferred, in fact, to be surrounded with groups that could support him and yet by virtue of their size protect him from becoming as dependent on any one individual as he had been on Victoria during his early life.

III

On 7 December 1866 Victoria wrote her mother: "Master Willy said to me this morning in French 'when I am grown up you will be dead. Is that not so?' Very civil was it not? He is continuously occupied with when I shall die, and who will be his Mama."[82] At the risk of overinterpretation, it is possible to see Wilhelm's rebellion against Victoria during young adulthood, his attachments to

Marie Dönhoff, Mimi Schleinitz, and Luise of Baden during his student days in Bonn, and even his relatively precipitous marriage to Dona foreshadowed in these comments to his mother. Perhaps already as a seven-year-old, Wilhelm was convinced that he could not achieve adulthood while his mother was still psychologically alive in him, still able, that is, to exert a pervasive influence over his life. Perhaps it seemed to Wilhelm that to be independent he first had to extirpate Victoria from his psyche: an act of emotional separation he accomplished by attaching himself to substitute mothers and by violently rejecting Victoria personally and politically.

Although it is possible, perhaps, to see Wilhelm's rebellion against his mother signaled during childhood, his motives for it were rather more unambiguously revealed by his actions and opinions as an adult. In raising his children, for example, the Kaiser believed it to be of paramount importance that his sons be separated—forcibly if need be—from their mother's care; and he and Dona, who was deeply attached to her children, came into serious conflict over this issue.[83] The Kaiser's comments about Nicholas II are noteworthy in this context. On the one hand, Wilhelm clearly identified with the Tsar. Thus in exile, Wilhelm asserted that Nicholas' role in planning and preparing the Russo-Japanese war was partially motivated "by desire for personal revenge" for a humiliating incident when he was a child and that the Tsar's marginalia during the war were "very childlike: 'There and there we must strike a blow,' 'destroy, destroy, destroy,' 'everyone must be taken prisoner'."[84] As we shall see, these two criticisms could readily be directed at Wilhelm himself. His political decisions were often made in response to hurt feelings; his marginalia often consisted of childish demands for brutal and thoroughly impossible action. On the other hand, whereas Wilhelm felt that he had succeeded in establishing his independence, he regarded Nicholas with contempt as "an Emperor under the dominion of his mother," and he attributed Nicholas' public shyness, clumsiness, and even helplessness to the fact that "the poor boy was never allowed to go out of the nursery or freed from his mother's apron-strings."[85] Sensing his maturational superiority, the Kaiser continuously offered the Tsar suggestions on how to conduct his personal affairs and govern his country. Nevertheless, despite his patronizing attitude toward his "cousin," Wilhelm was convinced that Nicholas' experience would follow his own. When he learned in 1895 of the ongoing involvement of the Tsar's mother in the life of her son and that of his young wife, Wilhelm predicted Nicholas' violent rebellion against his mother. "That time will come," he declared, revealing far more about himself and about his relationship with Victoria than he did about the Tsar, "and then with elemental force [*Gewalt*]."[86]

Wilhelm's rejection of Victoria can therefore be understood as an attempt to escape from the mother he could never satisfy because of his physical deformity and intellectual and personal shortcomings, from the mother who wanted him to be a Prince Albert and yet sought to keep him dependent and attached to her. Wilhelm's rebellion may have been more than simply an attempt to escape from an impossible situation, however. It may also have been an attempt to win Victoria's esteem, an attempt to demonstrate the very qualities

Victoria so admired and that she had found lacking in him. According to Baron Hugo von Reischach, master of the horse to Wilhelm II and a friend of Victoria, the crown princess "loved argument and went out of her way to provoke it."[87] And Wilhelm himself, reflecting on his mother's personality, wrote in exile: "The Kaiserin had a prodigious passion for debates. She was downright pugnacious. She loved to argue. It was a real treat for her."[88] Victoria had what might be called a contrary personality.[89] After her death, her brother, Edward VII, told Reischach that when in England Victoria always sided with Germany and praised everything German to the skies.[90] Therefore Götz von Seckendorff, Victoria's chamberlain and confidant, believed that only a forceful adversary could win the crown princess' respect. He advised Bismarck in 1885:

> The Chancellor must above all continue to impress her; he must still appear to her as *Jupiter tonans*. What she needs is powerful contradiction. Anyone who handles her with kid gloves is lost. Malet [the British ambassador in Berlin], for example, is in his present scrape because he does not occasionally treat her to a piece of his mind as Ampthill [Malet's predecessor] used to. The Princess responds to rough treatment.[91]

By contending with his contentious mother, by standing up to her, Wilhelm was asserting that he was not dependent and weak, that he did not lack talent or strength of character. Perhaps more important, by breaking away from his parents, by allying with his grandfather and Bismarck, Wilhelm was able to attain a measure of political influence and authority. Wilhelm was demonstrating to his mother and to himself that he was indeed capable of exercising power, that despite his deformity and limitations, that despite his mother's disappointment, he was fit to be a king.

CHAPTER 4

The Legacy of Paternal Weakness and Neglect

In contrast to the voluminous material concerning the intense and vital relationship between Wilhelm and his mother, there is little information about the relationship between Wilhelm and his father. Although the historian must exercise caution in basing a hypothesis on the absence of evidence, the lack of material in Friedrich's diaries or Wilhelm's memoirs gives rise to the suspicion that emotional contact between father and son was limited. This suspicion is confirmed by the evidence that is available. Despite their mutual affection, the relationship appears to have been frustrating for Wilhelm, and he entered adulthood yearning to experience fully what until then had only been tantilizingly promised through his intermittent contact with his father. Wilhelm's rebellion against his parents can therefore be understood not only as an effort to escape Victoria's dissatisfaction and domination but also as an attempt to deal with the psychological consequences of what had been missing in his relationship with Friedrich.

I

To the extent they were in contact, father and son enjoyed an affectionate relationship throughout Wilhelm's infancy, childhood, and adolescence. Friedrich was particularly proud of Wilhelm during the first year of his son's life. From Friedrich's telegram to Queen Victoria after Wilhelm's birth, "my baby is lovely and improves with every hour," through his description of his "indescribable . . . joy" at giving Wilhelm his first Christmas presents and carrying him in to see the Christmas tree, Friedrich's letters to his in-laws expressed pleasure in his first-born infant son.[1] In contrast to the mixture of exaggerated expectation and apprehension that characterized the attitude of his wife toward Wilhelm's future, Friedrich appears to have viewed Wilhelm's development with the uncomplicated optimism already manifest in his initial telegram to

Queen Victoria.[2] Wilhelm responded to his father's fondness for him, and Victoria was convinced that her son actually favored Friedrich. "Fritz adores the child," she wrote her mother on 3 September 1859, "and certainly the baby returns the affection for he is never happy till Fritz has got him on his arm and he never wishes to come to me."[3] It is possible, of course, to attribute this description to Victoria's insecurity about her capacities as a mother. Nevertheless, it seems likely that Friedrich's calmer dispostion may have enabled him to soothe his active infant son, causing Wilhelm to prefer his father to his more agitated and anxious mother.

Although Friedrich's attachment to his son continued beyond Wilhelm's infancy, contact between them diminished rapidly. After 1859 references in Friedrich's diaries and correspondence to Wilhelm and his other children were infrequent. From the outset, Friedrich had left the affairs of the household in the hands of his wife.[4] As Prussia's role in European affairs become more important during the 1860s, Friedrich's involvement in the family was further reduced and Victoria's responsibility for and influence over Wilhelm's upbringing increased.[5] She became, in her words, the "Mater familias." Her letter to Queen Victoria of 5 April 1865 testified to Friedrich's lack of involvement with Wilhelm: "I do not look forward to having a tutor in the house as my authority is then pretty well at an end, but I think it will be quite time that Willy should be in men's hands when he is nearly seven."[6] And yet the men who came to play a role in Wilhelm's early life do not appear to have been satisfactory substitutes for his absent father. Hinzpeter certainly would not do, and the others made little impression on Wilhelm.

Not only did Friedrich's political activities keep him physically apart from Wilhelm, but even when the crown prince was present, they placed him under considerable stress. Only on those rare occasions when he was able to join his family outside of Berlin away from the pressures of court and government could Friedrich, in the words of his son, "give free rein to his inner nature and live with us as a real comrade."[7] With Prussia's unification of Germany, politics intruded into Friedrich's relationship with Wilhelm, causing him to become apprehensive about his son's future. Only days after the creation of the German Empire on Wilhelm's twelfth birthday, the crown prince noted in his diary:

> Thank God there is between him and us, his parents, a simple, natural, cordial relation, to preserve which is our constant endeavor, that he may always look upon us as his true, best friends. It is a truly disquieting thought to realize how many hopes are even now set upon this boy's head and how great a responsibility to the Fatherland we have to bear in the conduct of his education, while outside considerations of family, and rank, court life in Berlin and many other things make his upbringing so much harder.[8]

For his part, Wilhelm appears to have grown disappointed in Friedrich—and not only because he may have felt neglected by him.[9] Certainly after he had left the house of his parents, Wilhelm became aware of the political and cultural values that clashed with those to which he had been exposed through his relationship with his parents and through their relationship with each other. Already as a student at the gymnasium, Wilhelm found admirable alternatives to Friedrich in the historical figure of Friedrich the Great and in his grandfather, the Kaiser, with whom he had, as yet, relatively little contact.[10] Nevertheless, Wilhelm's contempt for his father, clearly in evidence by 1882, is not only to be attributed to Wilhelm's consciousness of the conservatism and misogyny of the Prussian elite, which disparaged Friedrich for his liberalism and subservience to his English wife. Already before leaving home, experiences within the family had led Wilhelm to devalue his father.

Friedrich was devalued in Wilhelm's eyes because of Victoria's obvious domination of the family and of her husband and because of the denigration of Friedrich implicit in her political outlook.[11] With her outspoken contempt for the Prussian military, the crown princess belittled the tradition that Friedrich embodied as the titular commander of Prussian forces in the wars of 1866 and 1870. By surrounding Friedrich with artists and intellectuals instead of army officers, she had transformed the hero of those glorious Prussian victories into a civilian. With her outspoken preference for English over German values, Victoria denigrated her German husband. Thus when Wilhelm told Eulenburg that he had "lived through such fearful years . . . of ridicule of that which was to me highest and most holy: Prussia, the Army," he referred not only to Victoria's political philosophy but also to her implicit "ridicule" of the father of whom he wanted to feel proud. Wilhelm was faced, then, with the task of becoming a Prussian man in the absence of sustained interaction with a strong and secure and admirable father, whose confident pride in himself, in his Prussian heritage and German identity, Wilhelm could internalize as his own securely consolidated masculine German self. Victoria's determined program of Anglicization had undermined Friedrich as an ideal after which Wilhelm could pattern himself in making the transition to manhood.

Victoria explicitly belittled Wilhelm's tentative efforts to establish a masculine Prussian identity. As much as possible the crown princess sought to expose her son to the traditions of the English rather than the Prussian armed forces. She was delighted when Friedrich, in honor of Queen Victoria's birthday on 25 May 1861, dressed Wilhelm in an English sailor's suit. "My joy is great," she wrote her mother, "that he has worn it *before a uniform* which is a great triumph!"[12] She sought, with a success that would have fateful historical consequences, to inspire in her son a love of the sea and ships. "He is so fond of ships," she wrote the queen, "and I wish that to be encouraged as much as possible—as an antidote to the possibility of a too engrossing military passion—which of course is not to be desired."[13]

When Wilhelm was commissioned a lieutenant in the 2nd Pommeranian Regiment on his tenth birthday by the king, Victoria could take no pleasure in her son's developmental step, no pride in his manly display of himself as a Prussian officer like his father and grandfather. "Poor Willy in his uniform looks like some unfortunate, little monkey dressed up, standing on top of an organ," she wrote her mother, "but if I were to say that I should give great offence."[14] The crown princess expressed her dismay to her mother on 26 Jan-

Wilhelm in a Prussian army uniform (ca. 1870).
Reprinted with the permission of the Ullstein
Bilderdienst.

uary 1869 at the prospect of Wilhelm receiving his officer's patent, putting on
the Prussian uniform, reporting to his military superiors, and having "all sorts
of nonsense talked to him—which I have carefully kept from him until now."

> The King and whole family are *delighted*[,] they fancy the child will be quite
> one of *them* from that day forward.
> Of course Willie is as proud and excited as possible to think he is *really* going
> to enter the ranks of the army and have his name put down in the Lists.
> I think of how absurd he looks dressed up in his uniform and all his orders
> etc. . . . [sic] You can imagine that the Household pay him no end of compli-
> ments and. . . . [sic] however it cannot be helped so I must just put on the best
> face I can upon it.[15]

Some months later, when Victoria learned that Wilhelm would parade by his
grandfather, she could only worry about her son's health and speculate about

the deleterious medical consequences of the little boy's excitement and heavy cap.[16] When he marched past again ten days later, Victoria thought "he did it better than the 1st time," but she was convinced that the activity was harmful. "The worst of it is, that it unsettles him so completely his lessons suffer from it and he himself becomes more difficult to manage," she wrote her mother on 15 May 1869.[17] Queen Victoria's response only confirmed Victoria's fears. "I am in despair about dear Willy having to march past," she replied on 18 May, "it is very bad for him morally and physically—and these days above all."[18] Wilhelm's poignant lines to his grandmother about his participation in the parades give a clear sense of his experience:

> There were lately two parades where I marched before the King; he told me that I marched well, but Mama said I did it very badly.[19]

II

Despite the fact that Friedrich appeared to accept his wife's English outlook and way of life completely, there is evidence of underlying tension between Friedrich and Victoria over the question of Wilhelm's national identity. The crown prince was proud of his ancestors and the Prussian military tradition, and he maintained a healthy sense of German national pride.[20] Nine days after the proclamation of the German Empire at Versailles and one day before Victoria described Wilhelm to her mother as "a mixture of all our [English] brothers—there is very little of his Papa or the family of Prussia about him," Friedrich expressed the wish in his diary on 27 January 1871 that Wilhelm would

> grow up a good, upright, true and trusty man, one who delights in all that is good and beautiful, a thorough German who will one day learn to advance further in the paths laid down by his grandfather and father for the good governance of our noble Fatherland, working without fear or favour for the true good of his country.[21]

This tension in Friedrich and Victoria's marriage, compounded by the tension between Victoria and the other Germans who sought to influence her son, came to be reflected in Wilhelm's own conflict and confusion about his national identity: Wilhelm II would become a German Kaiser who at times felt himself to be essentially English.

The lack of integration between the English and the Prussian sides of Wilhelm's personality can be seen in the development of his language as a child. At twenty-two months Wilhelm could not talk at all, according to rumor, "because he hears so much English."[22] Ten days later he had spoken his first words, but, his mother reported, "strange to say only German ones, 'ja' and 'nein'—'artig', 'hinein' but that is all at present."[23] Within three months he had learned to recite English nursery rhymes,[24] but when he spoke his first unprompted sentences in February 1861, they were German: "'Wilhelm heiss

ich'; and 'Soldat ist schöner Mensch'"—both speaking to his developing German identity and his nascent attraction to soldiers, to the military heritage to
which he and his father were heir.[25] As Wilhelm approached his third birthday,
he was speaking a hodge-podge of English and German. Victoria wrote to her
mother on 8 December 1861:

> William comes to me and says—"Nice little Mama, you have a nice little
> face I want to kiss you." Yesterday I was not hungry—and Fritz wished me to
> eat something and said "Iss doch"—William said—["]Pfui Fritz to tease
> Mama, she is not hungry["]—Then he said to Fritz "Essen Sie weiter mein
> Schatz." He is so funny—he always calls after Fritz "mein Schatz" or "mein
> Engel" it sounds so absurd.
> The other day he was playing with Charlotte and said all of a sudden
> "Hobbsy [the nurse, Mrs. Hobbs] let me give Ditta [his name for Charlotte] one
> big slap, only one—I like it, it is so nice."[26]

A good deal of psychological interest is revealed in this letter, including Wilhelm's fondness for his parents, his use of endearments to his father, and his
jealousy of his sister. Important in the present context is what is revealed by
Wilhelm's use of language. Clearly he had been exposed to English and German. It seems likely, from the letter, that Wilhelm had heard English from his
mother and from his English nurse and German from his father: he spoke
English to Victoria and to Mrs. Hobbs; he spoke German to Friedrich. Not yet
three years old, he already had begun to distinguish between the culture and
heritage of his mother and that of his father. Despite the importance for psychological development that linguistic psychologists attach to language, not
every bilingual child develops the fracture that would characterize the structure
of Wilhelm's psyche. In his case, the linguistic difference between his parents
and between his mother and other important caretakers in his life reflected and
grew out of profound psychological, cultural, and political differences. Wilhelm
would never be able to integrate his two heritages either politically or as they
had become transmuted into his personality. But if he would never be able to
speak the same language to both his parents and to those representing their
culture and outlook, what he could do, and was already able to do at less than
the age of three, was imitate and adapt himself to his surroundings.[27] As a child,
he spoke English to his English mother and German to his German father. As
an adult, he became an Englishman in England; in Germany he became a
Prussian.

As Wilhelm's exposure to German influences increased, so too did the Prussian side of his personality. By 1869, having been under Hinzpeter's tutelage
for three years and before that in the care of Sophie Dobeneck and the German
military governors, Schrötter and O'Danne, Wilhelm was speaking almost
exclusively German, and a typically apprehensive Victoria feared that he and
his brother Heinrich had forgotten how to speak English altogether.[28] Although
writing Queen Victoria in English on his birthday in 1871, Wilhelm expressed
his pride at Prussia's unification of Germany: "I am sure you were pleased dear

Grandmama that Germany is united and our dear Grandpapa is its Emperor." He signed himself proudly "William of Prussia."[29] Three years later, on the occasion of his confirmation, Wilhelm, in thanking his grandmother for the portrait of Prince Albert she had sent him, vowed that "I will use my utmost endeavours and do my best to be worthy of being his grandson." But he also explained that he had developed a special interest in learning "what your ancestors and mine in England and Germany did for the Protestant faith." As he had in 1871, he signed himself "William of Prussia."[30] Although Victoria could only see the Prussian side of her son's personality and wrote ruefully to her mother that "he will take more after the Prussian family in tastes and character and in intellect than after ours and is already a regular Hohenzollern,"[31] Wilhelm maintained his pride in his English heritage. He told his grandmother in 1876 of his play "Richard, the Lionhearted," which he had written, produced, directed, and starred in.[32] His letters to his grandmother during adolescence contained frequent expressions of admiration for English naval and military feats, delight in visiting England, appreciation of the beauties of the British landscape, and pleasure in receiving gifts from England.[33] Reflecting his pride in both heritages, he often signed himself "William of Prussia, KG," after Queen Victoria had made him a Knight of the Garter on his eighteenth birthday.[34] Neither his grandmother nor his mother could understand that the signature "William of Prussia" reflected Wilhelm's need to establish and take pride in a Prussian identity. In responding to her mother's complaint about the signature, Victoria wrote: "I cannot imagine what fancy takes Willy to sign himself William of Prussia. He does so to me also, I suppose it is an excuse to put a longer flourish under his name."[35]

The letter Wilhelm wrote as a student in Bonn to Queen Victoria on her birthday in 1878 expressed his divided loyalties. Under pressure from the English side of his family and from that side of his psyche to remain loyal to Great Britain, Wilhelm begged his grandmother to forgive the fact that his letter would not arrive on her birthday, a day "dear not only to millions of Your loving subjects, but also to me, who am proud of beeing [sic] Your grandson and as Knight of the Garter also Your subject. Yes on that day I feel a thorough Englishman and am glad to say it, I am also a Briton." And yet Wilhelm's growing allegiance to Germany was also manifest, and he continued by describing the gift he planned to send his grandmother, "a drawing in pencil of the review Grandpapa held off Travemünde of our ironclads and hope you will like it." The letter was signed "Wilhelm Prince of Prussia, KG."[36]

Thus, as he entered adulthood, Wilhelm had not been able to integrate his two national identities. Instead, he could only shift between the identity of his mother and the identity of his father. Either he was the complete Prussian, or, as on Queen Victoria's birthday, he was the loyal Briton. Nor was either identity established securely enough to dominate his personality completely. For his English self to dominate, it would have to overcome the entire pull of Wilhelm's environment that existed outside of his mother's orbit as well as the pull exerted by his future as king of Prussia and German Kaiser. Ultimately, it was impossible for Wilhelm to have been an Englishman on the German imperial throne. But, as a result of his father's absence, weakness, and domination by Victoria and of her belittling of Friedrich's and his own Prussian identity, Wilhelm's German self was not firmly anchored either.

Despite his efforts to develop the masculine side of his personality, Wilhelm remained substantially dominated by the emotional and political world of his powerful mother before 1879. Propelled by the developmental need to attain manhood and adapting himself to the environment in which he found himself after that date, he soon established idealizing relationships with various Prussian paternal figures and adopted the outlook and demeanor of a Potsdam guard's officer. At the same time Wilhelm was able to observe that his parents' failure to achieve political influence was due in part to their public image, to the unpopularity of their Anglophile political views, and to the fact that they were held in contempt because of their personal relationship. Therefore Wilhelm's rebellion against his parents can be understood as an attempt to become a Prussian man. On the one hand, as in his effort to overcome his mother's possessiveness and his own dependence, he sought to suppress violently the English maternally oriented side of his personality after 1879. Through the repudiation of his parents and attachment to various German father-figures, he attempted to establish a masculine Prusso-German identity. On the other hand, beholding the political consequences of his parents' unpopularity, he sought to distance himself from them publicly, to demonstrate through open rebellion that he was as unlike Friedrich and Victoria as it was possible to be.

III

During his second tour of duty beginning in 1879 in the Potsdam Guards, Wilhelm soon became attached to several men embodying those features of his father of which he was most proud—Friedrich as Prussian military hero—without those features of his father of which he was most ashamed—Friedrich as dominated and devalued by Victoria. The unapologetic, indeed triumphant expression of Prussian military values in the Potsdam barracks had reawakened Wilhelm's need to find a powerful paternal figure he could use as a model in becoming a Prussian man, and he soon established intense admiring relationships with several older officers, including General Count Alfred von Waldersee and Wilhelm's aide-de-camp, Adolf von Bülow. Like Colonel Eduard von Liebenau, who had managed Wilhelm's household in Bonn and became the prince's court marshal after his marriage, these were authoritarian, exaggeratedly masculine personalities who shared an aversion toward England and liberal government and were outspoken opponents of the crown princess.[37] Adolf von Bülow, for example, saw it as his task to overcome the "'mushy' ideas" he ascribed to Wilhelm's English ancestry in order to turn his charge into a proper Prussian soldier.[38] To his parents' dismay, Wilhelm also became an enthusiastic admirer of Bismarck during 1880, adopting the chancellor as his mentor.[39]

The most significant idealizing relationship Wilhelm established during this period was to Kaiser Wilhelm I. Wilhelm had always been fond of his grandfather, but after 1879 the two became constant companions.[40] The Kaiser, Wilhelm declared, was the only member of his family to appreciate his Prussian identity, and, to Victoria's disappointment, he named his first-born son "Wilhelm" after his grandfather.[41] The Kaiser, in turn, was delighted that the crown princess had failed to transform Prince Wilhelm into the "English democrat" that Friedrich had become; he saw not his son but his grandson as Germany's hope for the future.[42] Wilhelm I encouraged his grandson to admire him and follow his example, and the Kaiser became, in Wilhelm's words, "my pattern and my guide."[43] Predictably, Wilhelm's parents were dismayed by these developments. Although Victoria did not blame Wilhelm directly, Friedrich reacted to Wilhelm's attachment to his father with jealous anger.[44] On one occasion, as Wilhelm described the episode to Luise of Baden, Friedrich made a "scene," his pent-up resentment erupting in wrath at his son. Wilhelm attributed the outburst to "envy and mistrust over the increased intercourse with the grandparents" and reported proudly that, in contrast to his father, he had reacted "with complete coldness and calm and allowed the storm to pass over."[45]

The anguish of Friedrich and Victoria was increased when the Kaiser, with Bismarck's cooperation, sought to promote his grandson's Prussian orientation by entrusting him with various diplomatic responsibilities.[46] Already hurt by the Kaiser's obvious preference for Wilhelm, Friedrich feared with some justification that his son was being used to supplant him.[47] The evident success with which Wilhelm performed his new duties made Friedrich even more insecure. The prince's visit to Tsar Alexander III in 1884 exceeded the expectations of Bismarck who sent him to St. Petersburg as the Kaiser's personal representative. The chancellor's son, Herbert, reported triumphantly to his father that the Russian foreign minister, Nikolai Karlovich de Giers, was delighted with the visit and that the normally taciturn Tsar apparently could not stop talking about the young prince.[48] On his return to Berlin he was received enthusiastically by Bismarck and the emperor, who, in Wilhelm's words, "hugged me so warmly that I was thoroughly embarrassed."[49] By contrast, Friedrich and Victoria could take no pleasure in their son's accomplishment, and Wilhelm "met with a surly reception from both of his royal parents, who asked him nothing about his experiences."[50]

When, two years later in August 1886, Bismarck and the Kaiser again wished to dispatch Prince Wilhelm to meet the Tsar, this time in Skiernewice, Victoria and Friedrich were "horrified" and dreaded the political consequences because "Wilhelm is as blind and green, wrong-headed and violent on politics as can be."[51] Friedrich, when he learned of the visit in the newspapers, wrote the chancellor to insist that because of Wilhelm's "lack of maturity and inexperience" he should not be permitted to make the trip. The crown prince was also appalled because he had heard from his son that Bismarck and the Kaiser planned to allow Wilhelm to work in the Foreign Office on his return. Friedrich urged the chancellor to send him in Wilhelm's stead.[52] With Herbert von Bismarck suspecting that the crown prince's suggestion had originated in England and with Wilhelm I and Otto von Bismarck concerned that Friedrich would not accurately represent German policy to the Tsar, the Kaiser and the chancellor refused to change their plan.[53] "Because of the Crown Prince's liberalizing tendencies," Wilhelm I told Undersecretary of State in the Foreign Office Count von Berchem, "Tsar Alexander is not sympathetic to him. Prince Wilhelm on the other hand had made a favorable impression on the Tsar and had even convinced him of the necessity of [reviving] the Holy Alliance."[54] Friedrich proved similarly unsuccessful in his effort to prevent his son from working in the Foreign Office. Again he complained to Bismarck that he had not been consulted and expressed his "decided opposition" to the decision. "The lack of maturity as well as the inexperience of my eldest son," Friedrich wrote on 28 September 1886, echoing his words of the previous month, "when coupled with his tendency toward presumptuousness and conceit makes it, in my estimation, *dangerous* for him to become involved so soon with foreign affairs."[55] But the Kaiser refused, in his words, "to respect the opposition of my son," believing that the current crises in foreign affairs would protect his youthful grandson from premature judgments.[56]

The fulfillment Wilhelm experienced in successfully carrying out his duties contrasted with his experience in the house of his parents, where his sensitive father and domineering and disappointed mother either prevented Wilhelm from taking on responsibilities or were dissatisfied with the way he performed them. Resentful of his father's attempts to interfere with his development, Wilhelm pointedly refused to ask the crown prince's permission before taking up his exciting responsibilities—even when, as in the state visits to the Tsar, they clearly implied taking Friedrich's place.[57] According to Friedrich von Holstein, Wilhelm "actually complained to his grandfather about his father, because the latter constantly felt offended."[58] Friedrich's opposition not only antagonized Wilhelm, but its futility confirmed Wilhelm's impression of his father as weak and ineffectual and of his grandfather as powerful and authoritative. When Victoria upbraided her son in December 1886 for working in the Foreign Office over the objections of his father, Wilhelm replied: "The only thing that matters to us Princes is the Kaiser's command. And it's the Kaiser who pays me, not my father."[59] In exile Wilhelm still had not changed his attitude. The conflict with Friedrich and his relationship with Wilhelm I he attributed to the fact that as a prince he was materially dependent not on his father but on his grandfather. "My father," he concluded, "never once gave me a single penny."[60] These sentiments seem crass. If translated from the language of money into the language of emotion, they become more understandable, however. From his powerful grandfather Wilhelm received the support, confidence, and responsibility that his father had been unable to provide.

And yet, doubtless in an effort to preserve his image of an admirable father, Wilhelm rarely blamed Friedrich directly for the tension that had developed between them. Instead, Wilhelm blamed others, especially Victoria, for his disappointment in Friedrich. "My father did not treat me very well," he conceded in exile. "Nevertheless, Papa could be very sweet to me when we were alone. But as soon as others were around, including my mother, this changed immediately."[61] During the conflict with his parents, Wilhelm was more explicit in attributing the tension with Friedrich to Victoria. "Now I cannot talk to my father at any time in an open and relaxed manner," he told Herbert von Bismarck in the fall of 1886, "because the Crown Princess *never* leaves us alone for even 5 minutes for fear that my father—ultimately having recognized how honest my intentions toward him are—would come under my influence."[62]

Wilhelm's tendency to blame his mother for the breakdown in his relationship with his father increased with his awareness of Friedrich's public image. Already in the regiment in Potsdam he learned that his father was viewed with contempt by the Prussian officers because of his relationship with Victoria. "Nothing appears to an officer more degrading than the tyranny of women," one of Wilhelm's commanders wrote who disliked the crown princess because of her domination of her husband. "A lash of the whip offends him hardly less than the reproach *'Weiberknecht'* [slave to women]!"[63] The obvious implication of this barrack's misogyny was not lost on the prince, and he became convinced that Friedrich's public humiliation would end if he could gain influence over his father. It was his hope that, given the crown prince's dependent personality, he could persuade Friedrich to follow the course he had charted himself: a course away from Victoria and her domination, away from Anglophile liberalism, toward the assertion of masculine strength and traditional Prussian military values.[64] He told Herbert von Bismarck in 1886:

> With my mother I will never come to an understanding; she is not a German but rather has contempt for us as the true daughter of the petty, bitter, Anglomaniac Sharpshooter King of 1848—that is, of Prince Albert.... The two of us—my mother and I—come, in other words, from two completely different worlds. With my father, who has a soft heart and is so unable to stand on his own feet that one might even say that he is helpless in domestic affairs, I could not only get along well, but I could even exert influence over him were it not for the intrigues.[65]

By mid-1884 Wilhelm had apparently concluded that his father could be saved politically only if he could win Friedrich away from Victoria by breaking up his parents' marriage. During his trip to St. Petersburg Wilhelm "stated quite openly" that because his mother had "never become a Prussian" but had "always remained an Englishwoman" it was "almost inevitable" when Friedrich ascended the throne that "a crisis" would occur "between her and the Chancellor—not merely Bismarck, but any other *German* Chancellor. The Kaiser, ie., the present Crown Prince, might even feel obliged to 'be separated from his wife.'" Holstein, who recorded these comments in his diary on 6 June 1884, believed "the remark sounded as if the threat of imprisonment lurked in the background." Although unable to imagine how "this weak man, now completely under his wife's thumb," could "be brought to such a decision" and certain that Bismarck would never instigate such an action, Holstein concluded that "Prince Wilhelm himself might. He is said to be heartless, fiercely determined, obstinate and cunning, and moreover penetrated with the idea that *every* personal consideration should be subordinated to the interests of the state. The Crown Prince is afraid of his son already; if this fear increases it may render possible much that seems inconceivable at present."[66]

Frustrated at Friedrich's failure to assert himself, at his inability to grasp the reasons for his political weakness, at his unwillingness to trust his son and come under his influence, Wilhelm began to hope for a crisis that would force Friedrich to face the reality of his position. Perhaps then he would become the father Wilhelm craved: a powerful German crown prince, a hero in the eyes of the nation and of his son. "Nothing will change until my father has experienced a catastrophe in his house," Wilhelm told Herbert von Bismarck in early October 1886, "a catastrophe which cannot possibly be avoided: only *then* will he seek to rely on me, and I will always be there for him to have as soon as *he wants* to and does not reject me and treat me with undignified mistrust."[67] A catastrophe would in fact occur. But Friedrich's throat cancer was not the one Wilhelm had imagined, and its results were very different from those Wilhelm had anticipated in the fall of 1886.

IV

Wilhelm wanted a strong and domineering father and a tender and compassionate mother. Instead, his father was compassionate and his mother was domineering. Of course not all children need their parents to fill these roles. In the culture of Imperial Germany, however, it was expected that parents play the parts appointed by tradition and, Germans were convinced, by biological function. It was particularly important that the family of the crown prince present an image faithfully reflecting or even exaggerating relationships in which the various family members played the roles deemed appropriate for men and women by German culture. Clearly, the male-centered values of Imperial Germany proved more powerful to Prince Wilhelm than the example set for him by his parents. He sought to force Friedrich and Victoria into their traditionally appointed roles. In his own family, he ostentatiously rejected their relationship.

Wilhelm made certain that the public image of his marriage would be very different from that of his parents. "In his youth," Bernhard von Bülow wrote in his memoirs, "Wilhelm had often heard grumbling that in the house of his parents the wife dominated the husband and held the power in her hands. He did not want that said of him, and he kept, as he told me once, his 'henhouse' orderly and at a respectful distance."[68] Wilhelm's mother and wife could hardly have been more dissimilar. In contrast to Victoria, Dona seemed the embodiment of the ideal Prussian royal wife. She gave little public indication that she was interested in politics; Princess Marie Radziwill was convinced that the Kaiserin never read newspapers and was completely ignorant of political matters.[69] Actually, in the course of her marriage Dona became politically active, albeit inconspicuously. As a devout Protestant (who abhorred Catholics, atheists, and socialists), she devoted herself to the defense of public morality: building churches; having the director of the Berlin theaters dismissed for allowing a "scantily clad" actress to appear on stage; and preventing the performance of Richard Strauss' opera *Salomé*.[70] She also sought, without much apparent success, to exert a conservative influence on her husband. "A German through and through," according to Bülow, Dona particularly disliked the English, regarding them as "egotistical and brutal hypocrites," and she surrounded herself with ladies-in-waiting who shared her Anglophobia.[71] In domestic politics she tended to favor the agrarian party, seeing it as the defender of orthodox Protestantism. In choosing a woman who was nearly the antithesis of Victoria to be his wife, Wilhelm demonstrated to the Germans that he was not like Friedrich and that he would not repeat his father's personal or political mistakes.[72]

Observing that his parents' unpopularity was due in part to their opposition to Bismarck and Kaiser Wilhelm I, Wilhelm accommodated himself to those two powerful individuals and adapted himself to the conservative political realities of the Berlin court. By openly rebelling against his parents and particularly by defying his mother and broadcasting his opposition to her—as he did to Herbert von Bismarck in 1884 and 1886 and through him to his father, Otto, and the other members of the Prussian establishment—Wilhelm sought to demonstrate that he was not dependent and weak, liberal and Anglophile, like his father. In a sense, Wilhelm's rebellion against his parents was a propaganda campaign designed to convince the court, the country, and, most of all, Wilhelm himself that he was strong, that he was independent, that he was German.

Wilhelm presented himself as inevitably in conflict with his mother because he was a Prussian while she had remained an Englishwoman. This version of Wilhelm and Victoria's relationship was quickly accepted in Berlin and soon spread across Europe. Shortly after Wilhelm's accession to the throne, Herbert von Bismarck told the Tsar that, despite a superficial cordiality, an unbridgable antagonism actually existed between mother and son. In confidence Herbert explained to Alexander III that Victoria "felt herself to be a complete Englishwoman," that she was not sympathetic to Germany, and that "she had never given my present master what one in normal life understands by maternal love." Wilhelm had told him, Herbert continued, that he and Victoria were bound to be in conflict since the two "came from two completely different worlds, my mother remains ever the Englishwoman and I am a Prussian, how are we then to become reconciled?"[73] In effect, the younger Bismarck was assuring the Tsar that the new Kaiser was compelled psychologically to pursue policies different from those of his parents, was compelled, that is, to be a friend of Russia and an enemy of England. Already during his tenure in the Foreign Office, Wilhelm gave out that he had taken the place of his father because Friedrich was not sufficiently Prussian.[74] A myth had been created, in no small measure by Wilhelm himself, that he was in conflict with his parents because he was personally and politically different from them.[75] It was a myth that suited Wilhelm's purposes and the purposes of the Prussian elite. It was an effective myth because the myth was partially true—certainly Wilhelm and the elite wished it to be.

Already by the end of 1882, following a view popular in army circles, Wilhelm publicly voiced his regret that the British, who had occupied Cairo in mid-September, had not "taken a beating in Egypt."[76] In fact he even expressed his perplexity to Bismarck that Germany had adopted such a "friendly attitude" toward England in the Egyptian question. Although the prince accepted Bismarck's explanation that—given the Reich's interest in preventing an Anglo-French entente—the German position had been calculated to drive a wedge between the two countries, Wilhelm still took every opportunity to express "his aversion toward everything English and his preference for the stern, rigidly Prussian, conservative way [*Wesen*]."[77]

To his English relatives, Wilhelm expressed different sentiments. When Queen Victoria reproached him for not congratulating her on the English success in Egypt and questioned whether he liked England anymore, Wilhelm heatedly denied that he was Anglophobic. Blaming "some scoundrel, who wishes to sow dissension in the Royal Family," he declared "I know that I have never said or done anything to hurt or injure any Englishman's feelings during the whole time. On the contrary, I have been a silent and attentive observer of everything and admired—as a soldier ought—the gallant way in which the Highlanders struck the final blow at Tel-el-Kebir."[78] Wilhelm wrote a similar letter in April 1884 to the British military attaché in Berlin, Leopold Swaine. As Swaine reported its contents to Sir Henry Ponsonby, Wilhelm complained "that he had been seriously misrepresented and that he is believed in England to possess anti-English feelings; that he is supposed to have made inimical and disparaging remarks about our military institutions, campaigns, etc., which he strongly and emphatically denies and begs me in every way in my power to refute." The prince, Swaine was convinced, had never displayed "a sign of any such feeling."[79]

Wilhelm's conflicting expressions over the British in Egypt were probably the product less of duplicity than of confusion. Adapting to the environment in which he found himself, the prince was sympathetic to England when he spoke or wrote to English men and women, and he was unsympathetic when he was in the company of Germans. Wilhelm's inner tension over England and his attempt to resolve it is revealed in his letter to Queen Victoria of 15 February 1884 in which he analyzed the situation in the Sudan:

> Had Mr. Gladstone been less filled with Utopian ideas of "no responsibility" and of humanitarian wishes not to shed blood, and if he had shown more courage and energy in grappling with the Mahdi, the moment he was *first* heard of, he would not have to answer for all the blood of Hicks Pasha, Moncrieff, Baker Pash and their slaughtered hosts, now lying at his door. . . . I am sure that a good round British infantry Division . . . under command of HRH the Duke of Connaught would be quite sufficient to beat any numbers of ever so brave Arabs, and to pitch the Mahdi, Osman Digma, etc. into the Blue or White Nile whichever is preferred.[80]

A certain hostility is evident in Wilhelm's letter: the British losses to the Mahdi are described with gusto. And yet that hostility was directed not at England generally or at his English relatives but at Gladstone. The prime minister was condemned for being weak, idealistic, and humanitarian. As a tough, realistic Prussian soldier, Wilhelm offered his grandmother advice on how to deal forcefully and effectively with the Egyptian problem. Throughout his reign, Wilhelm felt comfortable when he was able to adopt this stance with the English. But when he felt forced into a position in relation to England and his English relatives reminiscent of his father's subordinate relationship to his mother, he reacted with Anglophobia.

Wilhelm's increasingly strident public hostility toward Britain was complimented by the conservatism of the Prussian army barracks in German domestic politics, and during this period Wilhelm and his wife began patronizing the right-wing, anti-semitic, Christian-socialist preacher Adolf Stoecker.[81] Wilhelm, it appeared, could hardly have been more exaggeratedly Prussian. And yet some observers recognized that all was not what it seemed with the young prince.[82] Baron Robert Lucius von Ballhausen, for example, one of Bismarck's intimate associates, was not entirely convinced of the authenticity of Wilhelm's manifest antipathies and partialities. He recorded in his diary on 16 December 1882: "Nonetheless, in my opinion, he has a great predilection for England—an unconscious predilection."[83]

Symptomatic of Wilhelm's confusion was a photograph Wilhelm had distributed in February 1883 showing him dressed in the Royal Stuart tartan of the Scottish Highlanders and bearing the inscription in English: "I bide my time." When news of the photograph reached London, it was regarded as a portent of the hostile policy toward England Wilhelm would pursue as Kaiser.[84] Almost certainly that was the message Wilhelm wished to convey to his Anglophobic friends in the army and at court. The origin of this photograph reveals a rather more complex attitude, however. In the first place, Wilhelm had received the Highland dress from Queen Victoria. Moreover, Wilhelm had gone to considerable lengths to get the costume exactly right and had written to the Prince of Wales, in December 1882, asking him to send a claymore so that the outfit could be completely authentic. He also asked Albert Edward's advice about what he should have in order to appear at a costume ball in the war apparel that the Highlanders wore during the Middle Ages. "Nobody," he told his uncle proudly, "has ever seen a real Highland dress here."[85] Finally, the photograph of Wilhelm in Highland dress that he distributed with the provocative English inscription in February 1883 must be understood in the context of his letter to his grandmother of the previous month in which he had expressed his silent admiration for the Highlanders' military success in Egypt. At the same moment he was to all the world thumbing his nose at the British, he was also secretly identifying with them, wearing their uniform, speaking their language.[86]

Although Ballhausen and a few others recognized the element of artificiality in Wilhelm's denunciations of England and rejection of his parents' values, most of Wilhelm's contemporaries took him at his word. The prince's father could not penetrate beneath the surface of his son's public utterances. "See how life treats me," he lamented in early 1883. "Just look at my son, the complete Guard's officer."[87] Regarding Wilhelm with increasing "disapproval and sus-

Wilhelm in the dress of the Scottish Highlanders (1883). Reprinted with the permission
of the Bilderdienst Süddeutscher Verlag.

picion," Friedrich finally became so "upset" at "the sorrow" his son was causing him and seemed likely to cause him in the future that he apparently "burst
into tears" in front of General Emil von Albedyll.[88]

Wilhelm's image now stood in marked contrast to that of a weeping and
dominated German crown prince circulating through Berlin society. "Prince
Wilhelm is said to have a determined character," Holstein noted in his diary
on 6 January 1884; "at any rate he is self-willed, devoid of all tenderness; an
ardent soldier, anti-democratic, anti-English. He shares the Kaiser's view on
everything and has the greatest admiration for the Chancellor."[89] "Obstinate

and heartless," Wilhelm "may be a good ruler some day," Holstein con-
cluded.[90] It was believed that Victoria actually feared her son, and Count von
Seckendorff predicted in February 1883 that "in less than five years' time
Prince Wilhelm will exert a decisive influence on his parents—both of them.
He knows what he wants, is very self-willed, and one could even say hard."[91]
In the spring of 1885 not just the Prussian elite but, Holstein reported, the
general populace also preferred Wilhelm to his father:

> I am told that expressions such as the following can often be heard among the
> ordinary folk lately: "The Crown Prince won't make a good ruler. We want
> Prince Wilhelm; *he'll* be a second Frederick the Great."[92]

V

It was the Battenberg affair that crystalized Wilhelm's personal and political
opposition to his parents.[93] In 1883, Friedrich and Victoria's daughter Vicky,
"attracted," according to Queen Victoria, by the "English element" in him, fell
head-over-heels in love with Alexander of Battenberg, the reigning prince in
Bulgaria since 1879.[94] For various reasons, the crown princess became a vigorous proponent of the marriage. It is possible that diplomatic considerations
motivated Victoria: the marriage between her daughter and Battenberg would
serve British interests by tying Bulgaria under Battenberg to Germany, thereby
making it more difficult for Russia to depose the prince and make Bulgaria a
satellite. But political factors were probably only secondary in Victoria's support for the marriage project. In fact there were rumors that the crown princess
actually hoped Alexander would be driven off the Bulgarian throne. He could
then come to Germany, Holstein noted with a keen appreciation of Victoria's
possessive nature, "be put in command of a brigade of Horse Guards here and
can then live with his wife under his mother-in-law's wing, just like von Meiningen," Charlotte's husband.[95] Most important to the crown princess, however,
was her unusually intense commitment to the happiness of her daughter, perhaps because Victoria connected Vicky psychologically with Sigismund, the
son she had lost.[96]

Until the discovery of Friedrich's throat cancer in early 1887, the Battenberg marriage project was Victoria's constant preoccupation. The intensity of
her espousal of the match only increased when powerful members of the Prussian establishment, including Bismarck and Wilhelm I, prevented its realization. They were convinced that the marriage would harm German interests by
poisoning relations with Russia, which viewed Battenberg with alarm and
wanted nothing more than to remove him from power in Bulgaria. In the face
of these formidable opponents, the crown princess enlisted the aid of her
mother and eldest brother, both of whom campaigned actively on behalf of
Battenberg.[97] By May 1884, battlelines had been drawn: with Friedrich and
Victoria, their three youngest daughters, and Victoria's English relatives on one
side; and with Prince Wilhelm, Charlotte, and Heinrich allying themselves with

Bismarck and Wilhelm I on the other. "Alas! we have many disagreeables on account of poor Sandro," Victoria wrote of Alexander of Battenberg to her mother on the 16th. "Willie behaved most unkindly and spoke in terms of Sandro which made it difficult for his Papa to keep his temper. He said he could not imagine how such a person could dare to think of his sister—the Emperor's granddaughter—how impertinent everyone thought it, and then he repeated all the usual accusations . . . I own I could hardly contain myself. Then I had the same story over again from Henry and from Charlotte. They quite cut poor Vicky; and range themselves on the Emperor's side."[98]

That Wilhelm joined the German camp in this dispute is not surprising. There seems to have been a particular virulence to Wilhelm's opposition to his sister's marriage, however, which had not characterized his previous interaction with his parents. That virulence can probably be attributed to the fact that Friedrich had initially been negative about Battenberg himself. Perhaps for a time the crown prince was able to recognize that the marriage was simply not in the national interest. What is certain is that Friedrich, with his sensitivity to precedence and protocol, at first deemed Prince Alexander, the descendant of a morganatic marriage between a Hessian prince and a Polish countess, unworthy of his daughter.[99] As so often in the past, Friedrich was unable to resist the will of his wife, however. Her influence proved more powerful than his political judgment or even his social snobbery, and he soon joined her in advocating the match.

The alacrity with which Friedrich conformed to his wife's wishes and abandoned his opposition to Battenberg only increased his unpopularity and the perception that he was more likely to represent English than German interests.[100] Because of Victoria's domination of Friedrich, fears grew about her power once he became Kaiser. For the moment she was held in check by the Kaiser, Bismarck, and her widespread unpopularity.[101] But it was hoped that even after the death of Wilhelm I, the combination of Prince Wilhelm and the chancellor would prove stronger than Friedrich and Victoria.[102] Were it necessary to thwart the Battenberg marriage, Holstein believed, Bismarck could always incite public opinion against Victoria:

> He has the nation behind him in this question more than in any other. The Crown Princess knows it too, and is aware of her unpopularity. She will never like Bismarck, so it is better that she should fear him. She must be made to realize the "a bas l'étrangère" is the most dangerous rallying cry in a revolution.[103]

With Bismarck, the emperor, the court, German public opinion, and her three eldest children ranged against her over the Battenberg marriage, Victoria's sense of alienation from her adopted country reached a new high. "The moral atmosphere of the Court, the political and official world seem to *suffocate* me!" she wrote Marie Dönhoff on 21 October 1885. "The ideas—the tastes and feelings and habits are so totally different from mine, that I feel the gulf between me and them deepen and widen—and bitterest and hardest of all is that my son William and his wife stand on the *other* side of this gulf!"[104] Already by the beginning of the year, Victoria's relationship with her eldest son had deteriorated markedly. "Willy behaves as badly to us especially to me as you can imagine, is rude[,] ungrateful[,] etc," she wrote her sister-in-law, the duchess of Connaught on January 2. "It nearly drives me mad! Of course his wife thinks all he does and says charming and infallible." Thinking himself better informed than his father "on every subject," boasting loudly that he was the "favorite" of the Kaiser and Bismarck, and fancying himself "the head of the Junker . . . Party," Wilhelm had become so personally and politically disagreeable to Victoria that she was, in her words, "quite thankful when I do not come across him!" In addition, Wilhelm had turned Heinrich against his parents and his sister Vicky. As a consequence, Victoria wrote, "I often sit down in my room and have a good cry! How I spent *so* much care and love and affection and time on these naughty boys that they should become what they are!—stuck up—vain, proud, narrow minded, insolent and oh *so* ignorant! My 2 own pet boys are in their graves! How Waldy loved me and now he is gone!!"[105] In frustration, the crown princess abandoned what loyalty to the German Empire she once experienced and adopted completely the perspective of the Englishwoman it was long suspected she had remained. "They are so inflated here with self[-]sufficiency[,] pride and vanity that they will burst some day!" she wrote her mother on 30 December 1884 in urging her to build up the size of the Royal Navy in order to check Germany's colonial ambitions. "It is a Lesson for our own dear Country to keep her eyes *open*. 3 years ago we ought to have taken New Guinea!"[106]

Bewildered by his parents' unwavering support for whom he called the "damn Polack" and by what seemed their glaring lack of patriotism, Wilhelm denounced the marriage as a British plot to drive a wedge between Germany and Russia and as a disgraceful mésalliance that threatened to stain the family honor.[107] Furious at his father for disappointing and humiliating him, furious at his mother for failing either to respect his judgment or to subordinate her personal feelings and English partisanship to the interests of the nation to which he and his father were heir, furious at Queen Victoria, whom he denounced to Herbert von Bismarck as the "old hag," and at his uncle Albert Edward for failing to take account of his position in Germany and political realities there, and eager to distance himself from the unpopular position of his parents, Wilhelm could not praise Russia or condemn England sufficiently. "Caeterum censeo," Wilhelm proclaimed in 1885, "Britannia [sic] esse delendam."[108] He vowed "to pay home with interest [*heimzahlen*] what we have had to suffer from across the channel. One day the British will hear from me and will long remember me."[109] Yet even in this most angry and manifestly threatening outburst, "Wilhelm's unconscious predilection for England" was still evident beneath the surface. England was still a "home." And he still yearned to be listened to and remembered, perhaps not so much by his mother now as by her English homeland.[110]

Although with hindsight one can sometimes detect Wilhelm's unbroken attachment to England beneath his most Anglophobic utterances, his contemporaries, including his parents and English relatives, were convinced of Wilhelm's unshakable hostility toward England. In February 1885, Queen Victoria expressed the wish that "he could get a good 'skelping' as the Scotch say (flogging) and seriously a good setting down."[111] In October, the queen indicated that she would not welcome a visit from her grandson during that year, and she refused to acknowledge a military plan Wilhelm had sent for the relief of General Gordon at Khartoum.[112] Wilhelm was mystified and hurt by Queen Victoria's failure to understand his position, telling his father that he "was much aggrieved and offended at his visit to England being prevented; and that no one could understand it!"[113]

Despite Wilhelm's inability to understand the reaction of his English relatives, his correspondence with the Tsar would certainly have justified their anger had they known of its existence. During his meetings with Alexander III in May 1884 and September 1886, Wilhelm had assured the Tsar of his and the Kaiser's opposition to Battenberg and asserted that the emperors of Austria, Russia, and Germany should band together in a reactionary alliance.[114] Between the meetings, Wilhelm, in a number of letters, sought to increase the Tsar's suspicion of England, the English royal family, and Friedrich and Victoria. In May 1884 he warned Alexander III not to "trust the English uncles!" and urged his "dear cousin" not to be "frightened by things you will hear from my father," whom he described as being "in the hands of my mother, who in turn is led on by the Queen of England and makes him see everything through 'English lenses.'" Wilhelm assured the Tsar that he, Bismarck, and the Kaiser were as one in their desire "to consolidate and maintain" the Holy Alliance in defense of "the monarchy and Europe against the waves of anarchy; and this is precisely what England fears most of all." The prince concluded his letter by assuring the Tsar that he would warn Alexander should "something important happen on the political scene here."[115]

True to his word, one month later Wilhelm instantly reported to the Tsar "some worrisome things" his father had said about Alexander of Battenberg. In Wilhelm's account, Friedrich, "accused the [Russian] Government of lying, of treason, etc.; there was no hateful adjective that he did not use to paint you black." According to Wilhelm, he had risen to the Tsar's defense, proclaiming, in his words, "that 'lying' was a word that I could not tolerate as relating to You and Your government." Whereupon Friedrich allegedly denounced Wilhelm as a "Russophile" and declared that Battenberg had been placed on the Bulgarian throne by Disraeli and the Powers in order to thwart Russian ambitions in Turkey. Wilhelm concluded that Battenberg "'by fair means and foull [sic]' has put my mother in his pocket and my father also of course. The mission of the Prince of Wales has yielded and continues to yield extraordinary fruit, which will continue to multiply with my mother's guidance and that of the Queen of England." "But," Wilhelm declared in closing his letter to the Tsar, "these English happen to have forgotten about me! And I swear to You, my dear cousin, that all I can do for You and Your country I will do, and what I swear to do, I shall hold to it!"[116]

A year later, Wilhelm again warned his "beloved Cousin" about the Prince of Wales, "with his false and intriguing disposition," who was coming to Berlin in order "to do a little 'politiking [sic]' behind the scenes with the ladies" on behalf of the Battenberg marriage. He told the Tsar that he had given the Russian military attaché in Berlin, Prince Dolgoruki, "some interesting little notes concerning the number and names of the Indian and English regiments which are being concentrated at Rawul-Pindi to be reviewed by the Emir, the 24th of this month." Assuring the Tsar that he would keep Dolgoruki informed and that "I shall do everything I can to be useful to You and Your country," Wilhelm urged the Tsar to see these events as well as a cartoon in *Punch* as part of an organized English plot against Russia. "'Reader please note'," he concluded ominously.[117] In subsequent letters Wilhelm sought to convince the Tsar that the Prince of Wales was seeking to destabilize the Russian currency and warned Alexander about British military and naval preparations for war with Russia and about the general popularity of such a conflict in Britain.[118] Although Friedrich was denounced in Germany for representing the interests of another country, it was actually Wilhelm who, in his correspondence with the Tsar at least, acted like the agent of a foreign power.

Ironically, Wilhelm's warnings to Alexander appear to have backfired. In Berlin it was believed that the Tsar had given in to the British demands over Afghanistan when he became suspicious that Germany was trying to push Russia into a war with England.[119] Wilhelm's correspondence with Alexander III also increased the Tsar's fear that Friedrich, once he became Kaiser, would not be able to withstand English pressure on him to launch a German attack on Russia.[120] It also became necessary to reassure the Austrian emperor Franz Joseph that Wilhelm's apparent predilection for Russia did not indicate an impending abandonment of the Austro-German alliance.[121] Not surprisingly, the British government also grew worried about Wilhelm's intentions, particularly with the rapid deterioration of Friedrich's health during 1887. Lord Salisbury, the British prime minister, became so concerned, in fact, that he took the extraordinary step in November 1887 of seeking Bismarck's assurance that, with Wilhelm's accession to the throne apparently imminent, there would not be a radical transformation of German policy in the direction of hostility toward England.[122] Indeed members of the Anglophobic Prussian elite had already become alarmed at the intensity of Wilhelm's hatred for England and at its consequences for German foreign policy. Philipp Eulenburg, for example, who advocated an anti-English shift in German policy, felt obliged when he was with his friend "to struggle against his antipathy against England."[123] Finally in February 1888, with the death of his grandfather and father imminent, Wilhelm in a speech before the Brandenburg Provincial Diet felt it necessary to reassure his listeners that despite rumors of his bellicosity he was not about to start some foreign adventure or war when he ascended the throne.[124]

The Tsar was worried about German foreign policy under Kaiser Friedrich III; the Austrian emperor and the British prime minister were worried about German foreign policy under Kaiser Wilhelm II. With personality and politics inextricably bound together, the family dispute between Wilhelm and his parents had come to trouble the leaders of Europe.

VI

With the discovery of Friedrich's illness, Wilhelm's wish, expressed to Herbert von Bismarck in October 1886, for a "catastrophe" that would enable him to win his father away from his mother seemed to have been fulfilled.[125] The first sign that anything was wrong with Friedrich came in January 1887 when he developed a persistent hoarseness that by early March had left him without a voice. Initially diagnosed as "chronic catarrh of the larynx," it was thought that by scraping off the vocal chords every morning a cure could be anticipated within ten days.[126] By the emperor's ninetieth birthday on 22 March, Friedrich's condition had not much improved, and his hoarseness was noticeable in the speech he delivered on that day. When a brief sojourn in Ems failed to effect significant improvement, the celebrated surgeon, Ernst von Bergmann, was called in to examine the crown prince in mid-May.

Bergmann suspected that the growth on Friedrich's larynx was malignant and recommended surgery through the neck to remove the tumor. Before proceeding with such a radical procedure, however, Bergmann suggested that the noted Harley Street throat specialist, Morell Mackenzie, give his opinion on the crown prince's condition. Victoria was appalled by the prospect of surgery for her husband. "I was more dead than alive with horror and distress when I heard this," she wrote her mother on 17 May 1887, "the idea of a knife touching his dear throat is terrible to me." In order not to exacerbate her husband's depression about his infirmity, she kept Friedrich in the dark about Bergmann's diagnosis and sought unsuccessfully to prevent the news from getting to her eldest children, the emperor and empress, Luise of Baden, and the other members of the German royal family.[127]

Predictably Victoria leapt at Bergmann's recommendation that Mackenzie be brought in to examine Friedrich. She did so not only because of her faith in British medicine but also because she favored anything that might protect her husband and herself from the radical surgery proposed by Bergmann.[128] Victoria was aware that public opinion demanded that the suggestion of Mackenzie not come from her "as it would alarm the public unnecessarily in the first place, and as many are so benighted, that they would blame *me* for suggesting a foreigner," and she asked Queen Victoria to send Mackenzie as her personal emissary.[129] Nevertheless, the myth spread that the crown princess had demanded the consultation with the British physician over the objections of the German doctors.

When Mackenzie arrived on May 20, everything was prepared for surgery should he deem it necessary. Mackenzie was optimistic about Friedrich's condition, however, and he recommended that a biopsy be performed before any radical measures were taken.[130] When the first biopsy proved inconclusive, a second biopsy was performed to be examined by the noted German pathologist Rudolf Virchow.[131] Although Virchow's report was favorable and Mackenzie thought the condition of Friedrich's throat improved, Bergmann and the other German doctors remained convinced that the growth was malignant and continued to recommend surgery.[132] The Prussian elite also assumed the worst about the crown prince and lined up on the side of the German doctors against Mackenzie and Victoria.[133]

The crown princess' efforts to keep up the chin of her depressed husband and to deny to herself the seriousness of his condition were taken as manifestations of unconcern and increased her unpopularity dramatically. All that seemed to interest her was the marriage of her daughter to Battenberg. Holstein believed she would experience the death of her husband "as the gateway to freedom," and the rumor spread in elite circles that Victoria was "*completely* indifferent" to her husband's fate because she was having a love affair with Count von Seckendorff.[134]

Although aware of her unpopularity, the crown princess could not change her stripes. She insisted that Friedrich accompany her to England for the queen's golden jubilee so that he might receive medical treatment from Mackenzie while there. Again, she recognized that this idea should not be seen as coming from her "as it would annoy the people here and make them angry with me."[135] She was even aware that medical risk was involved. Despite Virchow's favorable pathology report, the condition of Friedrich's throat had deteriorated, and Wegner, now his personal physician, feared that increased swelling might make an emergency tracheotomy necessary. There was also concern that the ninety-year-old Kaiser might die with the crown prince in England. For the first time, Victoria entertained doubt about Mackenzie's diagnosis. "I am struggling between hopes and fears," she wrote her mother on 3 June 1887, "I *cannot* bring myself to believe that the German doctors are right!!—People torment me with questions someday;—it would be *my fault* if anything happened to Fritz in England etc!"[136] Although Victoria had managed to keep Friedrich in the dark about the controversy over his illness, even he was aware that "local patriotism" and the reputation of the Berlin doctors made it unadvisable politically that he travel to England for treatment. Still he insisted that his father permit him to go.[137]

Like the Prussian elite, Wilhelm immediately concluded the worst about his father's condition and felt that his mother was taking the situation too lightly.[138] He also sought to use Friedrich's infirmity to increase his power and responsibility by taking his father's place at Queen Victoria's jubilee. Without Friedrich's permission, Wilhelm had his grandfather appoint him the Kaiser's official representative. Naturally, Friedrich and Victoria were outraged.[139] Although they calmed down somewhat when the Kaiser agreed to let them travel to England, Queen Victoria refused to be mollified.[140] In fact she was so "furious" at her grandson's "shocking" and "pompous" conduct that her daughter urged her not to "be angry with William! He did not mean to be impertinent,—it is only his *rashness* his want of reflexion and tact . . . which make him do such foolish things."[141]

Although Wilhelm and his wife and Friedrich and Victoria all attended Queen Victoria's golden jubilee in London on 21 June 1887, their attendance at the festivities increased the polarization in the family. On her arrival in

England, Victoria expressed her delight in again being "on what will ever remain for me the right side of the Channel."[142] Her mother snubbed Wilhelm and Dona at the jubilee, receiving them rarely and then with minimal courtesy. Dona was always seated behind the queen of Hawaii.[143] As a result Wilhelm grew more heated in his public denunciations of his mother and England on his return to Berlin.[144] As if to confirm Holstein's suspicion that "English influences" were behind Mackenzie's optimistic pronouncements on the crown prince's condition, Queen Victoria, at Friedrich's urging, bestowed a knighthood on the doctor.[145]

Having stayed in Britain for two months, the crown prince and princess returned to the continent, where they immediately traveled to Toblach in the Tyrol. With Victoria continuing to deny the seriousness of Friedrich's condition, the rumor gained credence that she was actually eager to be rid of him so that she could take up with Seckendorff. Her unwillingness to alter the family routines to accommodate her husband's weakened condition was widely interpreted as an indication of her callousness toward him.[146] "Judging by all I have heard in recent months, I am tempted to call her a degenerate or corrupt character," Holstein noted in his diary on 28 September 1887. "She has always despised her husband. She will greet his death as the moment of deliverance."[147]

Holstein's condemnation of Victoria makes it easier to understand Wilhelm's public behavior toward his mother. In the prevailing environment of suspicion, fear, and hatred, Wilhelm adopted both the Prussian position on his father's illness and the Prussian manner of espousing it. Although he was, in his mother's words, "nice, amiable, and friendly" when he visited his parents in Baveno in Italy in October 1887,[148] he wrote Eulenburg, with a certain gusto one senses, that a consensus now existed confirming the opinion of the German doctors. Still, the medical consensus did not signify a change in Friedrich's treatment. "Here too," he concluded, "Britannia must play an evil trick on us! Mackenzie remains the only one allowed in [to see the patient]."[149]

On his return from Baveno, Wilhelm described the crown prince's condition as having deteriorated markedly. With the entire larynx now affected, the slightest irritation through activity, excitement, or cold threatened to produce a general infection. Friedrich had become more depressed and irritable than ever and was easily angered, according to Wilhelm. Only his parents, the prince concluded, remained convinced of Mackenzie's competence.[150] As word of Friedrich's deteriorating condition spread, the German newspapers began to denounce Mackenzie's treatment of the crown prince. In October the *Kölnische Zeitung* condemned Mackenzie, asserting that "the vast majority of the German people" demanded that greater responsibility be given the German medical specialists.[151] By November it was being suggested in Berlin that Victoria was to blame for the presence of the British doctor and for taking Friedrich to an English instead of a German house in Italy.[152] The Berlin correspondent of the Viennese *Politische Korrespondent* wrote on 14 November:

There is no longer a compelling reason not to state openly what must be obvious to every observer of public opinion, namely: that along with the deepest sympathy for the fate of the beloved and respected Crown Prince, *a deep bitterness* has taken root, which goes to the extent of *open outbreaks of passionate rage against the English doctor.*

A sudden swelling of the larynx during that month shook the confidence of Mackenzie and Victoria. For the first time, Mackenzie expressed fear that he had underestimated the seriousness of the illness and that the growth on Friedrich's vocal chords might indeed be malignant. Victoria was forced to call in two German specialists and to inform her children, the Kaiser, and Bismarck about the gravity of the situation.[153] As a result, Wilhelm rushed to San Remo against his mother's wishes.[154]

The contrast between Victoria's and Wilhelm's accounts of his arrival is striking and significant. The crown princess wrote her mother:

> You ask how Willy was when he was here! He was *as rude*, as *disagreeable* and as impertinent to me as possible when he arrived, but I pitched into him with, I am afraid, considerable violence, and he became quite nice and gentle and amiable (for him)—at least quite natural and we got on very well! . . . William came with the intention of *insisting* on this *terrible* operation being performed . . . and to carry us off to Berlin for that purpose! It would simply have assassinated Fritz. William is of course much too young and inexperienced to understand all this! He was merely put up to it at Berlin! He thought he was to save his Papa from my mismanagement!![155]

In Wilhelm's almost romantic account of his arrival in San Remo in his memoirs, the young prince heroically overcame the interference of his mother in order at last to effect a tender reconciliation with his father.

> When on the evening of the 9th of November, I entered the Villa Zirio . . . my arrival gave little pleasure to my mother. . . . Standing at the foot of the stairs, I had to allow the flood of her reproaches to pass over me, and had to hear her decided refusal to allow me to see my father. . . . Then I heard a rustling at the top of the stairs, looked up, and saw my father smiling welcome to me. I rushed up the stairs, and with infinite emotion we held each other embraced, while in low whispers he expressed his joy at my visit. During the heavy days that followed we came in spirit very close to one another.[156]

Wilhelm was present two days later when the doctors presented their unanimous verdict to the crown prince that he was suffering from cancer. Again mother and son experienced this episode differently. Although Victoria had feared that the shock of the news would be too much for her husband, since some time before when Mackenzie had suggested he might have cancer "it depressed Fritz so frightfully that he shed the bitterest tears and had a heartbreaking outburst of grief," she was greatly relieved that he now did not understand the import of the doctors' diagnosis. "He listened quite calmly to them, but he did not realize exactly what they meant!" She told her mother that she had no use for those who sought to speak plainly to her husband about his condition. "You know how sensitive and apprehensive, how suspicious and despondent Fritz is by nature! All the more wrong and positively dangerous (let alone the cruelty of it) to wish him to think the *worst!*"[157]

For Victoria, Friedrich was an uncomprehending invalid. For Wilhelm, Friedrich was a hero. He wrote Queen Victoria on the 11th:

> The final decision of the Doctors has been taken this morning, and the fearful hour has at last after all arrived! They told Papa everything and he received the news like a Hohenzollern soldier, upright, looking the Doctor straight in the face. He knows that he is irretrievably lost and doomed! And yet he did not move an inch or a muscle, they were immensely moved by this splendid display of character. His great and noble heart did not flinch and he is serene, composed and calm, like a brave captain, who knows that in leading his forlorne [sic] hope he will fall with his brave men, he holds up his head and even tries to cheer us up when we all of us broke down after the doctors had left.[158]

On the same day he wrote to Hinzpeter:

> This morning the doctors, assembled together informed him of this [that he had cancer]. *Standing erect, and looking the spokesman straight in the face, he heard his sentence. Without a tremor and without betraying even a trace of emotion,* he thanked them for their efforts and for their care, and then dismissed them.
> Silent and astonished, they left the hero, *filled with admiration for his character, which designated him as a true Hohenzollern and a great soldier.*
> When we were with him afterwards, it was he who consoled us with a calm smiling face, while we could no longer control our tears. *What a man!*[159]

Wilhelm's pride and joy at having finally found a strong, heroic, Hohenzollern father speaks out of every line of his letters and testify to the strength of his wish to admire Friedrich. Wilhelm's pleasure in his father was shortlived, however, and came to an abrupt and acrimonious end within a few days with the news that Kaiser Wilhelm I had made his grandson his official deputy. Regarding the appointment as an attempt to force him to renounce the succession, Friedrich flew into a rage that aggravated his condition, and it was only with considerable difficulty that Victoria was able to pacify him.[160]

The crown prince's fears were not entirely groundless. On the day the verdict of cancer was announced, Holstein expected that an attempt would be made to force Friedrich to renounce his claim to the throne since "under the present conditions his wife could do all manner of mischief in a few months."[161] Members of the establishment thought to perceive sinister motives behind Victoria's determined efforts to deny the doctors' verdict and her unwillingness to contemplate surgery for her husband. The suspicion grew that the crown princess "and her democratic adherents" hoped that she could "destroy or severely damage the monarchy" if her husband came to power and were therefore spreading lies about the crown prince's condition in order to defeat the efforts to get him to renounce his succession.[162] Sensationalism, rumor, intrigue, and anxiety were rife. San Remo was inundated with newspaper reporters, and the correspondence in and out of the crown prince's house was read by both German and French authorities.[163]

The history of the controversy over the nature and treatment of Friedrich's illness changed little over the next five months. The participants remained the same, as did the issues over which they came into conflict. Only the tone became more strident as the controversy involving the two royal families, the feuding camps of doctors, the political establishments of Germany and England, and, through the press, public opinion in both countries became increasingly hostile, intolerant, even vicious.

Despite the pressure of her eldest children, the Kaiser, the German doctors, the Prussian establishment, and German public opinion, Victoria maintained control over her husband's treatment, keeping him in the hands of the two British doctors, Mackenzie and Mark Hovell, and the German-Jewish doctor, Hermann Krause, and successfully resisting efforts to take Friedrich to Berlin for the laryngotomy.[164] She blamed Bergmann and the other German doctors for the deterioration in her husband's condition, and she blamed Wilhelm for their continuing intervention.[165] Defensive about her conduct, she grew increasingly angry at her eldest children.[166] Still, as in the past, she ultimately forgave them and attributed their disloyalty to the machinations of Bismarck; as before, Queen Victoria was less willing to excuse the conduct of her grandson.[167] Encouraged by Mackenzie's optimism, the crown princess continued to deny that her husband was dying and to assert that conclusive "proof" was still lacking that the growth on Friedrich's larynx was cancerous.[168] Victoria's denial reached its pathetic climax when the swelling in the crown prince's throat became so great that it was necessary on 9 February 1888 to perform the tracheotomy that had long been expected and feared by the German doctors. Everyone except the crown princess appeared upset about the procedure. While Dr. Bramann performed the tracheotomy with a pistol in his pocket to use on himself should the operation fail, Victoria went about *"smiling as if nothing had happened,"* according to Radolinski, a member of the crown prince's entourage.[169]

In contrast to his mother, Wilhelm remained a hard, Prussian "realist" about his father's condition.[170] He continued to associate with the political enemies of his parents—Waldersee, Herbert Bismarck, the other members of the "Court party," and the social-religious movement of Adolf Stoecker—and to blame his mother for the suffering of what he described to Eulenburg as "my poor, much deceived father . . . surrounded by lies, deceit, intrigue, and machinations." The difficulties encountered during Friedrich's tracheotomy he attributed to the malpractice of his mother's British and Jewish physicians; the success of the operation, to the heroic conduct of his father and the German doctors. Although his memoirs indicate that he recognized his mother's denial for what it was, he denounced Victoria to his friends. The tracheotomy was typical, he wrote Eulenburg. "So it goes here every day. Racial hatred, Germanophobia to the edge of the grave, pereat Germania! Fiat voluntas mea is the motto there."[171]

Although by the end of November some members of Friedrich's entourage had finally come to recognize that Victoria's seeming indifference was designed to protect her husband and herself from the truth about their desperate situation, the Prussian establishment and Berlin society showed no such understanding.[172] Nor did the German press, which attacked the medical treatment the crown prince was receiving and reported that a regency under Prince Wilhelm was near.[173] "Of course I am tongue-tied," Victoria wrote her mother on 26 February 1888, "I dare say *nothing* against this *infallible* wisdom of the German medical authorities or I should be torn to pieces."[174]

To Victoria's dismay, on the 2nd of March Wilhelm arrived in San Remo as the Kaiser's representative to reconcile the feud between the doctors.[175] Victoria need not have worried about the effect of her son's presence on her husband's treatment. Embarrassed by his deteriorating condition, the crown prince hardly saw his son.[176] Instead he wrote a few firm lines telling Wilhelm that he would brook no interference in his affairs, and the visit passed without incident.[177] As he had throughout their married life, Friedrich remained his wife's staunchest ally.[178]

One week later, on 9 March 1888, in this atmosphere of animosity, incomprehension, and suffering, with German newspapers condemning the conduct of the British doctors and British newspapers condemning the conduct of the German doctors, Wilhelm I died.[179] The long and illustrious reign of the *"weise Kaiser,"* the wise emperor, had ended. The short and pitiful reign of the *"leise Kaiser,"* the silent emperor, had begun.

VII

The ninety-nine days of Kaiser Friedrich III were an interregnum, a time of waiting for the next reign to begin.[180] "I think people in general consider us a mere passing shadow," the new Kaiserin wrote her mother less than a week after her husband's accession to the throne, "soon to be replaced by *reality* in the shape of *William*!!"[181] The principal accomplishment from a progressive point of view was the dismissal of a single reactionary minister, Robert von Puttkamer. Yet even this modest change was unpopular outside of liberal circles in and of itself and as an indication of what Victoria could accomplish should her husband long survive.[182] Indeed from the beginning of Friedrich's reign the powerful forces of the Prussian elite and conservative and nationalist opinion were mobilized to frustrate the couple's attempts at political reform. Wilhelm acted and was treated as if he were already Kaiser, while Bismarck continued to take responsibility for the conduct of government.[183] Friedrich was so politically powerless that he was unable to bestow decorations on progressive politicians close to the royal couple or to prevent any of the "1000 things" of which he disapproved.[184]

Victoria was equally unsuccessful in pursuing the Battenberg marriage for her daughter. Bismarck still stood in the way of the realization of her most cherished wish. If the Kaiser should even receive Battenberg, the chancellor wrote Friedrich on 4 April 1888, "one would—in order to account for such an otherwise inexplicable break with the long tradition in the royal family of putting personal interests behind the interests of the country—come to the suspicion that here not exclusively German interests prevail but that English interests have produced this unexpected shift in our foreign policy. One would conclude that the impulse for encouraging Prince Battenberg came from Queen Victoria. . . . since it serves the interests of *English* foreign policy to sow dissension between Germany and Russia." If the German people were to believe that peaceful relations between Germany and Russia were being jeopardized "in order to please England and out of personal and dynastic motives, then," Bismarck continued, "it would be difficult to calm the not unjustified outrage that would arise as a result."[185] Two days later, the *Kölnische Zeitung,* a newspaper with connections to the Foreign Office, reported that the chancellor intended to resign if the Battenberg marriage was pushed through against his wishes, the wishes of Wilhelm I, and those of the German people.[186] Prince Wilhelm also played a part in putting an end to the marriage by threatening Battenberg that if he married Vicky, Wilhelm, upon becoming Kaiser, would banish both from the country, and he would disown his sister.[187] "Today the Kaiserin is reaping what she formerly sowed with her ostentatious contempt of everything that is German," Holstein concluded not without sympathy for Victoria's plight. "But the people who are now gratuitously insulting the Kaiserin will get their own back under Wilhelm II; he will show them what a monarch is. That is the nemesis of history."[188]

As before Friedrich's accession to the throne, debate raged on between the British and German doctors and in the English and German press.[189] British newspapers and journals defended Mackenzie and were echoed in the liberal German press.[190] Conservative and nationalist German newspapers and medical journals denounced Mackenzie.[191] The tone of the press debate is revealed by the accusation of *The Weekly Dispatch* that Bismarck and the German doctors had conspired to prevent Friedrich from ascending the throne, by the nonclusion of the liberal *Berliner Volkszeitung* that if the German doctors had had their way Friedrich would have been long dead, and by the *Kölnische Zeitung,* which asserted on 26 April 1888 in the context of the debate on Mackenzie's treatment of Friedrich: "The German Kaiserin is an Englishwoman by birth and has undoubtedly remained an Englishwoman in her tastes, her outlook, and her habits. That is *fons et origo mali.*"[192]

The actions of Friedrich and Victoria did nothing to still the public controversy. Instead the ostentatious gifts and decorations they and Queen Victoria bestowed on now Sir Morell Mackenzie turned up the volume of debate.[193] Preoccupied with the futile Battenberg marriage project and her husband's deteriorating health, Victoria, in an all too familiar litany, could only bewail the influences on her son, his retrograde politics, and his autocratic airs. She devoted herself to isolating her husband from the tumult as best she could, and she tried to keep anyone, including her eldest children, from seeing him.[194] Wilhelm described these efforts in his memoirs:

> I soon noticed that difficulties were being put in the way of my visits to my father, that attempts were being made to cut them off, and, indeed, to prevent them altogether on the most flimsy pretexts. I had the feeling that efforts were being made to erect an invisible wall between my father and myself. Then I learned that spies were posted who gave timely notice of my arrival at the palace, whereupon I was either received by my mother or greeted at the door with the information that the Emperor was asleep and that my mother had gone out for a walk. It was clear that I was to have no speech with my father without witnesses being present.

Victoria remained the barrier between Wilhelm and his father; as before Friedrich's accession, the prince was convinced that if that barrier could be removed, all would be well between the two of them. When Wilhelm finally managed to see Friedrich, the Kaiser told his son that Wilhelm's "presence was welcome to him at anytime."[195]

Like Victoria, Wilhelm would not be deflected from his course. He continued to denounce all things British, including his mother, Mackenzie, and his English relatives, and to broadcast his conservative, Prussian character. He wrote Eulenburg on 12 April 1888 from Berlin:

> What I have lived through here during the last 8 days simply cannot be described. Even the thought of it mocks me! The strongest feeling is that of shame at the sunken image of my royal house, a house that once stood so high and so inviolable! I regard it as a test for me and for us all, and seek to bear it with patience! That our royal family escutcheon has been besmirched and the Reich brought to the edge of ruin by the English princess who is my mother, that is the most horrible of all![196]

He continued to emphasize the difference between his father, whom he portrayed as completely helpless, and himself, whom he portrayed as vigorous and decisive. After a lunch with Wilhelm, Carl von Wedel reported that the crown prince had told him that "it was scandalous how the Kaiser, sickly and unable to offer resistence, was unconscionably exploited. The correct thing would have been to devolve responsibility to him, the son, and to give the Kaiser only a few merely ceremonial activities." Eager to take his father's place, Wilhelm declared that he intended to take up where his grandfather had left off.[197] It would be as if Friedrich's reign had never been.

Queen Victoria, too, remained outraged at the "dreadful" conduct of her grandson and his two eldest siblings, and she urged her daughter to be firm with them.[198] "I have *no* words to express my *indignation* and astonishment at the conduct of your 3 Children," the queen wrote her daughter on 31 March 1888. "This *must not* be *allowed* and *if* it is not exaggerated by *repetition* I think you *ought* to send for them and to threaten strong measures if it *goes on*. Wilhelm with his odious ungrateful wife should be sent to *travel*. Send them or at least him to India . . . or to Canada to see the world."[199] Denouncing her grandson's "double game" in continuing to oppose the Battenberg marriage, Queen Victoria concluded: "it is impossible for us honest straightforward English to understand. Thank God! we *are* English!"[200]

Queen Victoria was so hostile toward Wilhelm in fact that members of both governments were concerned lest an unfortunate incident occur when Queen Victoria visited Friedrich and Victoria in Berlin in late April, and efforts were made on both sides of the channel to insure that neither party antagonized the other.[201] Fortunately, the visit went off smoothly, and Wilhelm and his grandmother behaved graciously to one another. The queen and Bismarck had an audience which both parties deemed successful, and Bismarck again assured the queen that Wilhelm, as Kaiser, would not be able to follow any impulses other than those that served the interests of the Reich.[202] Wilhelm expressed his pleasure at being able to converse with his grandmother again, and Holstein hoped that the cordial atmosphere of the visit would "somewhat lessen the Prince's foolish hatred of England."[203] Even Queen Victoria was somewhat more forgiving of her grandson.[204] In general, the cloud of mistrust and anger that had darkened relations between the two royal families and the two countries appeared to have dissipated slightly.

Immediately after the visit of his grandmother, Wilhelm adopted a view popular the previous fall in army circles that now was the time for Germany to launch a preemptive strike against France and Russia.[205] The prince wrote a series of marginal comments to reports from and to the German ambassador in Vienna expressing his approval of this plan as advanced by the Austrian foreign minister Gustav von Kálnoky and certain officers on the General Staff in Berlin. Russia now appeared to Wilhelm to be Germany's inevitable enemy who was dealt with better sooner than later.[206] Bismarck was appalled at Wilhelm's bellicosity. As he had when Friedrich threatened to antagonize Russia over Battenberg, Bismarck once again contemplated submitting his resignation.[207] Before taking such a drastic step, however, he sent Wilhelm a letter in which he spelled out the military and diplomatic implications of the crown prince's proposal and informed him that he was abandoning the political path laid out by his late grandfather.[208] In a letter of 10 May 1888 Wilhelm responded to the chancellor's admonitions. Declaring that he did not mean to depart from traditional German foreign policy, a somewhat chastened Wilhelm asserted that he was merely making the point in his "ominous marginal comments" that, since Russia and France could not be kept apart for long, now was the time from a purely military point of view to strike at both countries before Germany was threatened by an alliance of pan-Slavs and republicans.[209]

How is one to account for this shift in Wilhelm's attitude toward Russia? The easiest response is simply to attribute it to Wilhelm's capricious personality. Although he was and would continue to be unstable and unpredictable, it is possible to speculate about the meaning behind Wilhelm's marginalia. In the first place, by advocating a preemptive strike against France and Russia, Wilhelm was adopting the view held by members of the military high command, especially by his friend and confidant, General von Waldersee.[210] He was continuing, that is, to display what his father described as his "barracks' mentality," his proud identification with the Prussian military and his adoption of the "realistic" attitude toward war he deemed appropriate in a Prussian officer. Moreover, it cannot be coincidental that Wilhelm's marginal comments were written immediately following his grandmother's visit to Berlin. Under the impact of his friendly interaction with Queen Victoria, it seems possible that Wilhelm's English sympathies reasserted themselves, and he adopted an attitude in keeping with the interests not only of a Prussian officer but also of the English government.[211] And, finally, it is possible to understand Wilhelm's shift in attitude as an attempt to maintain his autonomy. Just as Wilhelm sought to avoid becoming as dependent on any one person as he had been on his mother by surrounding himself with groups and traveling from one friend to the next, his comments to Bismarck represented a first tentative step toward independence from the chancellor. Anyone aware of Wilhelm's fear of becoming overwhelmed by another powerful personality might have predicted that sooner or later he would have to break with Bismarck.[212]

It was shortly after this episode that the end for Friedrich III finally came. By June 12, the cancer had eaten its way through the Kaiser's esophagus, and he could only take in small amounts of nourishment. He was vomiting, had a high fever, and was very weak.[213] Two days later Friedrich had his final interview with Bismarck. Gesturing that the chancellor should join Victoria at his bedside, the Kaiser took Bismarck's hand and for a long time pressed it into the hand of his wife.[214] Shortly thereafter, just past 11 A.M. on the 15th of June 1888, Friedrich died. Victoria wrote her mother: "Oh! my husband, my darling, my Fritz!! So good, so kind, so tender, brave, patient and noble, so cruelly tried, taken from the nation, and the wife and daughters that did so need him."[215] Queen Victoria was similarly distraught. She telegraphed to Wilhelm on the same day: "I am brokenhearted. Help and do all you can for your poor dear Mother and try to follow in your best, noblest, and kindest of father's footsteps."[216] She also communicated similar concern over the fate of Victoria to Bismarck through the British ambassador, who reminded the chancellor of her words to him during their interview at Charlottenburg: "Stehen Sie meiner armen Tochter bei." Stand by my poor daughter.[217] The spirit of reconciliation manifested in Friedrich's touching gesture and Queen Victoria's communication to Bismarck was evidently not shared by Wilhelm. On the night of June 14, as his father lay dying, he ordered that a military cordon be drawn around the palace to prevent anyone from going out or coming in.[218]

VIII

For at least four months Wilhelm had been planning to seal off the Royal Palace.[219] As Wilhelm told an interviewer in exile, he had taken this dramatic action in order to prevent "state or secret documents being conveyed to England by my mother. . . . That even these measures were insufficient is shown by the fact that important State papers did reach England and were made public there, to the detriment of the German Reich."[220] Although it may not have justified this particularly public humiliation of Victoria, there was some basis for Wilhelm's suspicion that she might seek to smuggle sensitive documents out of the country. In an atmosphere in which Bismarck could readily admit to Victoria that he was reading her correspondence with her mother, Victoria and Friedrich had taken steps to secure their papers.[221] While still in Italy, Friedrich burned numerous documents, and in early June of 1887 Victoria asked her mother whether she and her husband could secrete their personal papers in Buckingham Palace.[222] When they attended Queen Victoria's golden jubilee later in the month, the crown prince and princess transferred documents to England for safekeeping. In May 1888, after Wilhelm had openly threatened his mother to surround the royal palace on his father's death in order to search anyone who sought to leave, Victoria sent a box of personal papers and two volumes of Friedrich's diary to London.[223] It seems likely that the trunk seen carried by Dr. Mark Hovell to the British Embassy and conveyed from there to London on May 14 contained these documents.

At first it appeared that a particularly nasty personal scandal and international incident might take place. The British ambassador, Sir Edward Malet, vowed to stand by the Kaiserin should Wilhelm carry out his threat to search the palace.[224] Herbert von Bismarck and two other emissaries of the chancellor, surprised at finding so few papers in Friedrich's rooms, voiced their suspicion openly that Victoria had sent important documents abroad.[225] Although she had not sent official documents abroad, Victoria was terrified lest the whereabouts or the contents of the personal papers stored in England become known.[226] In June, Wilhelm made inquiries of the Prussian minister of justice, Heinrich von Friedberg, about his right to search the effects of the doctors; and in August, he ordered Friedberg to request information from Victoria about the missing papers and to demand their return.[227] Yet, in the end, no search was made and no official inquiry was launched. Indeed, by 20 July 1888, with the incident apparently over, Victoria's papers were returned to her in Germany.[228] Perhaps, as Malet suspected, Friedberg had convinced the Kaiser that it would be unwise to begin his reign with an act of doubtful legality, or perhaps Bismarck had convinced him that these few papers were not worth an international incident.[229] Or perhaps it was that Wilhelm had accomplished his mission. Even if the missing documents had not been recovered, Wilhelm had demonstrated to the world that he was not like his father and that it was a powerful and independent and German Kaiser who wielded power now.

The official account of Friedrich's death in the *Norddeutsche Allgemeine Zeitung* on June 15 also conveyed the message of Wilhelm's power and independence. The newspaper reported that, after Mackenzie had determined that Friedrich was dead, "the Kaiserin collapsed with loud cries of anguish onto the body—the son, the Kaiser, led his mother out of the death chamber." Wilhelm's order that Victoria vacate Friedrichskron and move to Bad Homburg, despite her pleas and those of her mother that she be allowed to stay in the palace where she and Friedrich had lived in Berlin, served the same purpose.[230] As Mlle. de Perpigna, lady-in-waiting to Kaiserin Friedrich, observed, Wilhelm's treatment of his mother was an expression of his "strong, youthful desire to show his power."[231] Personally, the young Kaiser wished to assert his independence from his mother and his power over her. Politically, he wished to demonstrate that independence and power to the German people. Not Victoria but Wilhelm II—he reminded his subjects, his mother, and himself—was sovereign in the royal family and in the German Reich.

Almost immediately after ascending the throne, instead of mourning Friedrich, Wilhelm began what his mother described as a "whirl of visits, receptions, dinners, journeys, parades, manoeuvers, shooting and entertaining."[232] He also made a series of state visits to various European courts, despite the warning of Queen Victoria that such activities would be unseemly so soon after Friedrich's death.[233] Wilhelm's response to his grandmother's reproach emphasized the contrast between him and his father. Wilhelm was not infirm but youthful, active, and vigorous. He could not reply to her sooner, he told the queen, because he had first to "work nearly night and day to get rid of" the "enormous amount of work" resulting from the "complete stagnation which had set in during the second half of Papa's time."[234] Nor was he Anglophile or tainted with liberalism, opposed to Bismarck or willing (as Friedrich had been in the Battenberg affair) to place the happiness of his family over the interests of the nation.[235] As if to mark the contrast with his father, Wilhelm, one week after becoming Kaiser, changed the name of the royal palace from "Friedrichskron" back to the "Neues Palais," the New Palace.

Wilhelm found an ally in his effort to distance himself publicly from Friedrich in his former tutor, Georg Hinzpeter. Shortly after Wilhelm's accession, Hinzpeter published a tract in which he reassured Germans that their new Kaiser was unlike their old. Wilhelm, he asserted, was above all an independent character able to resist all external influences and to set his own course: "In the truest sense of the word his nature is *sovereign,* for the essence of sovereignty lies in independence from every foreign influence, in self-determination, and self-command."[236] The Kaiser was a thorough German, Hinzpeter concluded, imbued with a deep sense of "German national identity" and filled "with an enthusiasm for German life and sensibility."[237]

In general, Wilhelm presented himself as the heir not of his father but of his grandfather. According to Bernhard von Bülow, the new Kaiser regarded Friedrich's reign to have been an "intermezzo," and it was Wilhelm's wish that his father would be remembered by history and by the German people simply as "the Crown Prince."[238] Wilhelm's first speech from the throne on 25 June 1888 confirmed Bülow's observation. He told his subjects that he was determined "to follow the same path as that taken by my late Grandfather which had won the trust of his allies, the love of the German people, and benevolent appreciation abroad."[239] The British noted with concern that Wilhelm expressed his friendship for Austria, Italy, and Russia in the speech but made no mention of England, a "symptom," Queen Victoria believed, of "a leaning towards Russia."[240]

Despite his efforts to portray himself as the the executor of the legacy of his grandfather, the new Kaiser, through his demonstrations of activity and authority, presented himself as the leading representative of a younger and more vigorous generation of Germans. They and their youthful and vigorous Kaiser had grown up in a Reich that was already unified and rapidly industrializing. They and he were not content to rest on the laurels of the past or simply to carry on the traditions of their grandparents. They and he would bring the era of Wilhelm I and Bismarck to a close.[241] Wilhelm II and the Germans who identified with him had a new political style and a new political agenda. The Kaiser and the Germans who dominated the stage of Wilhelmian Germany along with him were unwilling to see Germany remain a "satiated power." He and they were too dynamic for such modest ambitions. Together they would establish the German Reich as an empire in the truest sense of the word, a thoroughly modern nation, economically and militarily, a world power.

IX

Although his first acts as Kaiser were designed to demonstrate that Wilhelm had become the proud and powerful and "sovereign" German man whom he and influential sectors of the German public wished Friedrich had been, the conflict that errupted in the summer of 1888 between Wilhelm and his uncle, Albert Edward, reveals that, despite his repudiation of his father, Wilhelm II still wished to preserve an idealizable image of Friedrich for himself and for the Germans. There had already been tension between Wilhelm and his uncle over the Battenberg affair. The Prince of Wales provoked his nephew's fresh aggravation by urging him to look favorably on the candidacy of Ernst August, Duke of Cumberland, for the Hannoverian throne during his visits to Berlin for the wedding of Wilhelm's brother Heinrich in May and for the funeral of Friedrich III in June.[242] The Prince of Wales aroused the Kaiser's outrage, however, when he apparently suggested that, had he lived, Friedrich might have returned Alsace and Lorraine to France in an effort to achieve a reconciliation with that country. Wilhelm's anger at his uncle's suggestion found expression in a speech he delivered on 16 August 1888 in Frankfurt an der Oder.[243] The idea that "the Crown Prince" would have returned Alsace and Lorraine to the French, he told those gathered to celebrate the unveiling of a memorial to Prince Friedrich Karl (who, like Friedrich, had commanded an army corps in the Franco-Prussian war), was "an insult to the memory of my father." He assured his listeners that Friedrich "had the same thoughts as we, that nothing from the conquests of that momentous time can be given up." "Not one stone," he concluded, "will be relinquished of that conquered by my father and Prince Friedrich Karl."[244]

The Kaiser doubtless experienced his uncle's suggestion as an attempt to rob him and the German people of all that remained to admire in Friedrich: the image of the victorious commander of the wars of German unification. Wilhelm's anger at this final humiliation of his father by his English relatives was so great that he urged Kaiser Franz Joseph of Austria not to show the Prince of Wales sensitive military documents during the latter's visit to observe the Austrian army's fall manuevers in 1888 because his uncle posed a security risk to the Triple Alliance.[245] Wilhelm also went out of his way to avoid meeting the Prince of Wales, although both were in Austria during this period.[246] When Albert Edward learned that "it would *not* be agreeable to the Emperor William to meet his uncle at Vienna," he experienced the "utmost surprise and . . . *great pain*," according to General Arthur Ellis, equerry to the Prince of Wales. Ellis reported that the prince was mystified at his nephew's behavior because "he was under the impression that they were now as heretofore on the most friendly terms and he was looking forward with greatest pleasure to their meeting."[247] Lord Salisbury concluded from the Kaiser's conduct that Wilhelm was "a little off his head."[248]

This episode, which soured the Kaiser's relations with his uncle for some time, is typical of the incidents that would create tension between Wilhelm II and his English relatives and, to a degree, between Germany and England as well. Albert Edward's conduct reveals him to have been out of touch with the personal sensitivities of his nephew and with the political sensitivities of Germans in an era of intense nationalism. He failed to appreciate that what he surely perceived to be a complimentary portrayal of Friedrich as moderate and magnanimous would be perceived by the Kaiser and his subjects as an unwanted reminder of Friedrich's weakness and domination and as an unwarranted meddling in German affairs. By the same token, the prince failed to recognize that his earlier attempt to advise Wilhelm by proposing that Hannover be returned to the Cumberland family would have offended the Kaiser. As the British prime minister, Lord Salisbury, astutely observed to Queen Victoria, Wilhelm was upset because "the Prince [of Wales] treated him as an uncle treats a nephew, instead of recognising that he was an emperor who, though young, had still been of age for some time."[249] Queen Victoria was unable to understand Salisbury's interpretation of Wilhelm's anger, however. The suggestion that her son had offended the Kaiser by treating him like a nephew and not like an emperor was "really too *vulgar* and too absurd . . . almost *to be believed*," she replied to the prime minister. "We have always been very intimate with our grandson and nephew, and to pretend that he is to be treated *in private* as well as in public as 'his Imperial Majesty' is *perfect madness! . . .* The Queen will not swallow this affront."[250]

Like her son Albert Edward and her daughter Victoria before him, Queen Victoria was sensitive neither to Wilhelm's need to protect his fragile psychological "sovereignty" against the influence of personalities more powerful than his own nor to German political realities. By treating the Kaiser as a relative, all three members of British royalty were encumbered by a view of monarchy that was increasingly incompatible with the politics of mass nationalism. In late nineteenth-century Europe, the monarch was becoming less a member of a transnational caste connected by heredity and more the leader of a cultural and political nation. In the same way, the model of kinship was losing its relevance as a way to define the relationship between ruler and subject. In a mass industrial society, emotional identification bound leader and led together. The Kaiser was less a paternal figure whose country was his personal possession and whose subjects were his personal responsibility, and more the personal symbol of people who shared a common cultural and political identity. Wilhelm II saw himself not as the son or the grandson or the nephew of his English relatives nor as the father of his subjects. Instead, he was the symbol of the German people and the personification of the German nation.

Wilhelm's ostentatious snub to his uncle in Austria in a sense continued his order to surround the royal palace after the death of his father. In both instances the Kaiser sought to demonstrate that he was a force to be reckoned with, a sovereign to be listened to and respected. To be sure, Wilhelm's actions toward his mother and his uncle were doubtless motivated primarily by his need to be treated with respect and to preserve and enhance his fragile psychological autonomy. And yet in asserting his sovereignty, Wilhelm, as German Kaiser, also fulfilled the national political agenda of those many Germans who demanded that their newly unified Reich be treated with respect, as an independent power, as a sovereign nation, as an equal among the other European world empires.

CHAPTER 5

Wilhelm II
and His Parents

Wilhelm's effort to come to terms with issues growing out of his relationship with Friedrich and Victoria and out of their relationship with each other would continue after he became Kaiser. Even when his parents were no longer physically a part of his life, they exerted psychological influence over him. Indeed, already in his rebellion as a young adult, Wilhelm was struggling not only with Friedrich and Victoria as separately experienced individuals but also with features of their personalities that had become incorporated in himself. Therefore, by way of concluding this investigation of Wilhelm's development, let us consider his personality in light of the personalities of Friedrich and Victoria.

I

Wilhelm yearned to have an idealizable father with whom he could identify in becoming a man. Despite his disappointment in Friedrich, Wilhelm still patterned himself after his father, adopting those of Friedrich's interests and personality traits he found admirable. Like his father, Wilhelm was attracted to romantic literature and had, in his words, "a hobby for costumes."[1] Perhaps because Friedrich asserted himself in matters of court etiquette and social standing, Wilhelm attached great importance to decorations and protocol and shared with his father a love of ceremony.[2] It is likely that Friedrich's calm compassion for his son's suffering as a child as well as the example of fortitude he set during his own illness laid the foundation for Wilhelm's courage as an adult.[3] In assuming a Prussian identity, Wilhelm emulated his father; his affiliation with the military was not merely a rejection of Victoria's ideals but also an association with Friedrich at the peak of his glory, as the victor in the wars of 1866 and 1870.

And yet what was present in the relationship between father and son, as manifested by the interests and attributes Wilhelm acquired from Friedrich, was probably less psychologically consequential than what was missing in their relationship. To be sure, there were moments when his father provided Wilhelm with strength and sympathy, as during the painful and humiliating treatments of Wilhelm's left arm; and there were moments when his father appeared heroic in Wilhelm's eyes, as on Friedrich's return as the triumphant military leader.[4] But these were infrequent and fleeting and ultimately unsatisfactory. Unable to internalize a secure sense of masculine strength through sustained interaction with a powerful father or other paternal figure during childhood, Wilhelm yearned throughout his life for relationships with men who would make him feel powerful and masculine.

To compensate for what he lacked internally, Wilhelm constantly wore uniforms and surrounded himself with soldiers, symbols of male strength. Like his ancestor, King Friedrich Wilhelm I of Prussia, he selected bodyguards and adjutants who were tall and imposing.[5] As a little boy, Wilhelm had been fascinated with soldiers and reassured by their presence.[6] As an adult, the company of soldiers gave him a sense of stability and security; the command of his troops gave him a sense of confidence and power.[7]

Because the Kaiser felt enhanced by the presence of soldiers, his military entourage gained considerable political influence over him. Since the nature and consequences of that influence have been examined in several excellent studies, no purpose would be served by going over that ground again here.[8] Nonetheless, one feature of Wilhelm's relationship to his entourage noted by a number of scholars deserves attention in the present context: the homosexual component of the bond connecting Wilhelm to some of his companions.[9]

Wilhelm II with his men at the end of the fall maneuvers in 1905. Reprinted with the permission of the Bilderdienst Süddeutscher Verlag.

Although there is no credible evidence that Wilhelm was actively homosexual, his contemporaries, in remarking on the feminine quality about him, implicitly raised questions about his sexual inclinations.[10] He enjoyed pinching men on the cheek, slapping his male friends on the behind, tickling them, and squeezing their legs.[11] A significant number of the Kaiser's friends were suspected of homosexuality, and his closest friend, Philipp Eulenburg, was an active homosexual, who was ultimately disgraced publicly.[12] It would oversimplify Wilhelm II psychologically to explain his complex personality as emerging in defensive reaction against latent homosexuality. Instead, Wilhelm's homoeroticism is better understood within the context of his need to make up for the psychologically absent father of his childhood by getting close to men as an adult.[13]

Similarly, the Kaiser's preference for male companionship, his disparagement of women, his contempt for "ladies' men," and the distance he maintained in his marriage can be understood as arising in response to his relationship with his mother and to his experience of the relationship of his parents.[14] Wilhelm's animosity toward Victoria for undermining Friedrich as an idealizable father and for belittling his own efforts to achieve a masculine identity helps explain these attitudes. From the fate of his father and from his own experience with Victoria, Wilhelm had learned of the psychological and political dangers awaiting men who became too attached to women or allowed themselves to be dominated by them. Ironically, despite the severe prohibitions against homosexuality in Imperial Germany, the misogyny, the contempt for men who were seen as dependent on women, and the glorification of the *"Männerbund"* prevalent among the Prussian elite fostered homoeroticism.[15]

When he was a child, Wilhelm received a present from his father of which he was especially fond: "two terra-cotta statuettes of Achilles and Patrocles in complete armour; I was never tired of looking at them."[16] Perhaps because of the connection with Friedrich, Achilles became a figure of importance to Wilhelm. When, in 1907, he purchased the former summer residence of the Austrian empress, Elisabeth, on Corfu, he renamed the palace the Achilleion. To this day the gardens are dominated by a gigantic, semi-nude statue of Achilles. The relationship between Achilles and Patrocles serves to define two ways Wilhelm related to men during his life. On the one hand, Wilhelm yearned to be a Patrocles to an Achilles and sought relationships with powerful men he could look up to. Wilhelm's attachment to Wilhelm I, Bismarck, and Waldersee can be seen as expressions of that desire. But perhaps because these forceful personalities came to remind Wilhelm of his mother and of her domination, he usually could not tolerate such relationships for long. On the other hand, Wilhelm yearned to be an Achilles to a Patrocles and sought relationships with men who would look up to him as a powerful man. In general, Wilhelm's entourage came to perform the part of the admiring male cohort surrounding the heroic warrior-king.[17] When Wilhelm became Patrocles, he derived strength from the mighty warriors around him. When he became Achilles, the admiration of his men confirmed him as the mighty warrior.

II

The attempt to make up for what was missing in his relationship with Friedrich helps to explain Wilhelm's most intimate friendship with a man, his friendship with Philipp Eulenburg. There can be little doubt about the intensity of Eulenburg's affection for the Kaiser. Perhaps it is not too much to say that Eulenburg was in love with him. Numerous letters to Wilhelm and others testify to Eulenburg's passion for the Kaiser and idealization of him.[18] Eulenburg's devotion and adoration creates a problem for the historian, however. Clearly, Eulenburg saw what he needed and wanted to see in the Kaiser. Thus caution must be exercised in accepting Eulenburg's description of the relationship between Wilhelm and his wife in the fall of 1900. According to Eulenburg, in a series of letters to Bülow, Wilhelm's efforts to distance himself from Dona had caused her such distress that both he and Eulenburg feared she might suffer a "nervous breakdown." Eulenburg intimated that tension had become so great that Wilhelm, to get the rest and peace he required, was contemplating a separation from his wife.[19] But, as Bülow suspected, it seems likely that this crisis in the royal household was more the product of Eulenburg's wish to remove a rival for the Kaiser's affection than it was an accurate depiction of Wilhelm's marital relations.[20]

Not only Eulenburg's testimony about Wilhelm must be accepted with caution but also that of the other members of the entourage. With their careers and social standing dependent on the Kaiser's favor, these men developed strong positive and negative transferences to Wilhelm. Thus Bülow's statement to Eulenburg in March 1902, "I often think of Achilles, with whom our master has much in common, and of whom Homer says: 'His glory seeking heart knows neither fear nor flight,'" and Eulenburg's "complete agreement" with this characterization of the Kaiser reflected the wish of both men to be in the thrall and in the service of a powerful, heroic personality.[21] Similarly, many of the unflattering descriptions of Wilhelm by the members of the entourage reflected their disappointment and anger when Wilhelm failed to live up to the idealized image they wished to have of him.[22]

Therefore, although Eulenburg's letters reveal his love for Wilhelm and express his wish that the Kaiser love him back, it is more difficult to define the nature of Wilhelm's feelings for Eulenburg.[23] There is considerable evidence suggesting that Wilhelm's affection for Eulenburg rivaled Eulenburg's for him. In 1889, near the beginning of their relationship, Wilhelm described Eulenburg to Hinzpeter as "my bosom friend . . . the only one I have."[24] In July 1892, while together on a Scandinavian cruise, Wilhelm and Eulenburg drank a toast of brotherhood; the Kaiser thereafter addressing his friend as *"Du,"* an intimacy he shared with almost none of his other confidants.[25] Acquaintances of the two men were convinced of Wilhelm's attachment to his friend and either sought to use Eulenburg's influence on the Kaiser to advance their careers and policies or worried about the consequences of that influence. Indeed, concern about the spell Eulenburg was apparently able to cast over the Kaiser led Maximilian Harden to accuse Eulenburg and Kuno von Moltke of homosexuality in *Die Zukunft* in 1907.[26] Those accusations, and the libel suits that came in their wake, brought about Eulenburg's disgrace and fall from imperial favor.[27]

At first glance, Wilhelm's dramatic collapse immediately following Harden's acquittal on 29 October 1907 in a libel suit brought by Kuno von Moltke (whose correspondence with Eulenburg had formed the basis of Harden's accusations against both men) appears to confirm the intensity of the Kaiser's feelings for Eulenburg. When faced with the public substantiation of the homosexuality of his best friend, Eulenburg, and of his former aide-de-camp, Moltke, and, possibly, with his own homosexuality, Wilhelm, in his words, suffered a "complete collapse! Also brought on by my dreadful mental depression; as well as by the complete lack of sunshine on my body in this terrible year of rain; since I need the sun so much"—perhaps referring not only to the Berlin weather in the fall of 1907 but also to the loss of Eulenburg's emotional warmth.[28] Because of his condition, Wilhelm concluded, it was necessary to cancel the visit to England he was scheduled to make in the second week of November.[29] But when the British foreign secretary, Sir Edward Grey, suggested that the Kaiser might be canceling the visit out of embarrassment at the "sad things" happening to his friends (a view shared by Edward VII and Wilhelm's court marshal, Count August von Eulenburg), Wilhelm denied that the Eulenburg affair had precipitated his collapse.[30]

> That had nothing directly to do with it! I just have a sharp bronchial catarrh, with coughing and sneezing; which, through debilitation, led to the fainting spell, something I have never had before! Kings, after all, are just plain human beings and can also sometimes be ill![31]

It seems, in fact, that Wilhelm's "complete collapse!" was actually a spell of dizziness he used as a pretext to avoid traveling to England.[32] Over the course of 1907 Wilhelm had become increasingly hostile toward Britain as a result of the Anglo-German naval rivalry, which had taken on a new intensity with the construction of Dreadnoughts on both sides of the channel. He professed bewilderment at England's alarm over the pace of German naval construction and suspected the British of seeking to isolate Germany. He believed that his uncle, Edward VII, was intriguing against him and his nation throughout Europe. Although the British government and the German Foreign Office hoped that a state visit to England by the Kaiser might improve relations between the two countries, Wilhelm displayed a marked lack of enthusiasm for the idea. Nonetheless, unable to resist the pressure of his advisers, Wilhelm had reluctantly agreed to the trip.[33] Harden's acquittal, then, appears to have presented Wilhelm with an opportunity to back out of the visit at the last minute. The Eulenburg scandal undoubtedly contributed to Wilhelm's fainting spell and to his sense that he could not possibly travel to England. Embarrassed and hurt by his friend's disgrace, Wilhelm probably felt that he lacked the strength to face the English and his uncle. But the Harden verdict, rather than overwhelming Wilhelm psychologically, was used by him in order to extricate himself from an unpleasant situation, and he dramatized his "complete collapse" to get out of the trip without antagonizing his advisers, his uncle, or the English.[34] Once he thought he had achieved his objective and had canceled the trip, he apparently experienced a miraculous recovery.[35] In the end, Wilhelm's attempt to exploit his condition failed; he yielded to the pressure of his aides and traveled to England. Although the visit passed off successfully, the Kaiser would later have reason to regret it. During his stay in Britain he gave an interview to Colonel Stuart Wortley at Highcliffe Castle. That interview, published a year later, produced the worst scandal of his reign, the *Daily Telegraph* affair.

It is difficult therefore to reconcile the evidence of Wilhelm's deep affection for Eulenburg with this transparent attempt to use his friend's humiliation as a pretext to avoid another potentially embarrassing experience.[36] It is even more difficult to reconcile Wilhelm's evident devotion to Eulenburg with the fact that he was able to drop Eulenburg without apparent difficulty after the latter's disgrace. Finally, as far as their correspondence is concerned at least, the relationship between the two friends, even during the best of times, flowed mainly in one direction: from Eulenburg to the Kaiser.[37] And yet to conclude that Wilhelm's affection and devotion were fraudulent would also be unwarranted. Ever dependent on his environment to maintain equilibrium, Wilhelm was attached to Eulenburg when their relationship bolstered his self-esteem and self-confidence; and he dropped Eulenburg with relief when it became apparent after the scandal broke that their relationship would only upset his psychological balance. Like the entourage generally, Philipp Eulenburg was important to Wilhelm II less as a separately experienced individual and more as a source of stability and security. Although it was his fondest wish to serve the Kaiser, Eulenburg, one suspects, would have been appalled to learn that in relation to Wilhelm he was not so much a "bosom friend" as he was a psychological function.

Eulenburg's importance to the Kaiser can be understood as an outgrowth of the shallowness of Wilhelm's relationship with his father. By virtue of being a Prussian and adopting generally Anglophobic attitudes, the twelve-year-older Eulenburg bolstered Wilhelm's German identity and supported the Kaiser's independence against the powerful influence exerted on him by his English relatives and by his own English inclinations. As Friedrich had been, Eulenburg was deeply concerned about any pain—whether physical or spiritual—that Wilhelm might suffer; but, in contrast to Friedrich's occasional compassion, Eulenburg offered Wilhelm sustained sympathy. Keenly sensitive to the feelings of his friend, Eulenburg reassured the Kaiser when the latter felt overwhelmed by the pressures of office.[38] Thus, in December 1896, Eulenburg "remained alone" with his "beloved Kaiser" after breakfast as "a stream of complaints" was poured over him. Lamenting that he "could no longer govern" with a chancellor, Hohenlohe, and a secretary of state in the Foreign Office, Baron Adolf Marschall von Bieberstein, who were South Germans, Wilhelm angrily declared that "Prussia would founder under such leadership, which completely *misunderstood* the duty of Prussia and of the Prussian King." Eulenburg concluded:

He suffered greatly—the poor man! I could only grasp his dear hand and say to him that Prussia was still strong enough not to suffer any real damage. My action brought the flow of his wrath to a sudden halt—he felt right away that I understood him completely! And it reduced his distress. He became calmer.[39]

Eulenburg saw it as his duty to soothe his anxious and agitated master. After another episode in which he had successfully performed that function, Eulenburg wrote Bülow: "I had only one wish in my heart, always to be able to wipe his cares away."[40]

The emotional Eulenburg also enabled Wilhelm to express his own emotionality. Like Friedrich, Eulenburg was a romantic, fascinated not with the Middle Ages but with Nordic legends, and the two friends could vent their romantic enthusiasms over subjects ranging from the world of art to the world of spirits.[41] In the fervor of Eulenburg's devotion, Wilhelm could openly express his fondness for his friend and could describe his activities in unembarrassed, even glowing terms, certain that Eulenburg would passionately affirm his successes.[42] Only months after the beginning of their friendship, Wilhelm was able to tell Eulenburg what he found so attractive about him:

> When I first meet people my instincts generally tell me quickly about the spiritual essence of the person I have encountered, and they have rarely betrayed me. With you it did not take me long to see that you are a sympathetic, warmly emotional character, such as one rarely encounters in the world, and whom princes in particular need so very badly.

He then proceeded to boast about the decision of Bismarck and Wilhelm I to let him work in the Foreign Office, anticipating with some glee the aggravation this news would cause his parents and English relatives.[43] Eulenburg's enthusiasm for the Kaiser, then, stood in marked contrast to the tendency of Victoria to belittle and of Friedrich to resent Wilhelm's successes. Eulenburg's passion also provided relief from the stiffness and formality that characterized many of the responses to Wilhelm as Kaiser.[44] And, finally, Eulenburg's genuine affection and idealization contrasted with the flattery of those who sought (often successfully) to advance their careers by currying favor with the Kaiser.

Sensitive, devoted, and caring, spontaneous, demonstrative, and passionate, Eulenburg could provide emotional sustenance that Friedrich had never been able to offer. Thus, it was perhaps not coincidental that Wilhelm made Eulenburg a privy councillor of distinction on the tenth anniversary of Friedrich's death. "For your true and active friendship I thank you from the bottom of my heart," the Kaiser wrote Eulenburg in informing him of the honor. "May you, who strives in accordance with ideals, always remain preserved to strengthen my own strivings. That is my daily prayer."[45]

More important than the strength Eulenburg lent his friend, however, was Eulenburg's weakness which enabled Wilhelm to feel self-confident and powerful. Eulenburg's primary psychological function, in other words, was less to play the role of Achilles and more to allow the Kaiser to play that part himself. Seemingly constantly ill with various nervous and physical ailments, unable to tolerate loud military music or the salvoes of guns, Eulenburg would regale

Wilhelm with detailed descriptions of his distress.[46] Two tennis matches Wilhelm and Eulenburg played against members of the entourage became occasions for Eulenburg to complain about his "slightly lame arm" and "lame fingers" resulting from his exertions on the tennis court—complaints that can only have reminded Wilhelm of the silent courage with which he mastered the authentic lameness in his left arm and hand.[47] Similarly in 1896, on Wilhelm's return from a hunt in which he had fired off 1600 rounds of ammunition, Eulenburg exclaimed that he "would have been made very anxious by this unheard of mass of shots." Wilhelm replied manfully: "I feel absolutely nothing and have slept splendidly without a swollen cheek or headache."[48] Just as the Kaiser enjoyed being the only sober person surrounded by tipsy and childish companions, so Eulenburg's delicacy, fussiness, and hypochondria enabled Wilhelm to feel stronger and more masculine.[49]

Wilhelm's humor served the same function. Perhaps out of embarrassment at his deformity, it amused the Kaiser to make fun of other people's anatomical abnormalities.[50] In a letter to Eulenburg, for example, he described with relish the impression created by King Dom Louis of Portugal through his "quite colossal rear end which was advantageously set off by a short English hussar's jacket," and he liked to refer to Victor Emmanuel III of Italy, once in the presence of a German-speaking Italian officer, as "the little dwarf" because of the king's short stature.[51] Even Wilhelm's most harmless anecdotes involved, at their core, someone having made a fool of himself.[52] In the summer of 1890, Kiderlen-Wächter reported one such anecdote told by Wilhelm with great effect during the annual Scandinavian cruise. According to the Kaiser, after a banquet in his honor in Bremen, at which the mayor of the city had consumed too much wine, a panorama of New York was shown so that the viewer seemed to be standing on a moving ship. Wilhelm recounted the following dialogue:

> Mayor: "Ah, yes, the panorama is revolving."
> An obsequious senator: "No, Your Honor, the panorama is not revolving."
> Mayor (after a pause): "Ah, I see, the ship on which we are standing is revolving."
> Senator: "No, Your Honor, the ship is not revolving."
> Mayor (again after a pause): "But Your Majesty, *surely something* is revolving!"[53]

Wilhelm's humor, then, temporarily relieved his chronic insecurity: the jokes and stories that belittled others allowed Wilhelm, for a moment at least, to feel better about himself.

The members of the entourage were especially favored butts of the Kaiser's wit. Indeed, it became one of their primary functions to bolster Wilhelm's self-esteem and self-assurance not only through their admiration and deference but also by allowing themselves to be belittled for his amusement in a series of pranks, practical jokes, and staged entertainments. It was in the relaxed and intimate atmosphere aboard the royal yacht that Wilhelm gave his humor free rein. There he liked to tickle his often elderly traveling companions and to slap them on the behind. He also took pleasure in observing the exertions of these gentlemen during morning gymnastic exercises on deck and, on one occasion, in cutting the suspenders of an old general with scissors.[54] Eulenburg reported that Wilhelm "baptized" new members of the party by pouring champagne on their heads and having them carried around on a block of ice.[55]

Instead of expressing revulsion at these juvenile antics, members of the entourage participated in them enthusiastically. Georg von Hülsen, for example, described how he and Count Emil von Schlitz genannt von Görtz could divert the Kaiser when he visited Eulenburg's estate in 1892:

> You must be paraded by me as a circus poodle!—That will be a "hit" like nothing else. Just think: behind *shaved* (tights), in front long bangs out of black or white wool, at the back under a genuine poodle tail a marked rectal opening and, when you "beg," *in front* a fig-leaf. Just think how wonderful when you bark, howl to music, shoot off a pistol or do other tricks. It is simply *splendid!!* ... In my mind's eye I can already see H.M. laughing with us.[56]

To be sure, this vulgar entertainment provided the Kaiser and the mostly Prussian aristocrats around him with a measure of relief from the stiffness and formality of court life and from the prudery of official society.[57] Still, these pranks could be malicious, as when Wilhelm made an elderly Prussian general, Remus von Woyrsch, imitate Bülow's dog by having him jump over a stick.[58] This crude and, for the participants, demeaning way to amuse the Kaiser reached its pathetic climax in 1908 with Dietrich von Hülsen-Haeseler's fatal ballet performance in Donaueschingen. Although the general's performance no doubt represented an effort to cheer Wilhelm up at the height of the *Daily Telegraph* affair, Hülsen had frequently danced in a tutu for the Kaiser. Indeed, because Wilhelm always laughed himself "half to death" at seeing men perform in women's clothing, cross-dressing was a frequent form of imperial entertainment.[59] Certainly there was a homosexual component to Wilhelm's enjoyment of these performances; and yet a pronounced sadistic streak found expression here as well. Wilhelm derived strength not only by being close to powerful and imposing men but also by seeing them degraded. Their foolishness bolstered his self-confidence. Their humiliation bolstered his self-esteem. Their feminization bolstered his masculinity.

Although steadfastly refusing to participate in these activities, Eulenburg nevertheless fulfilled their primary psychological function by flaunting his frailties to the Kaiser. It was in the area of health that Eulenburg's weakness confirmed Wilhelm's strength most dramatically. Never robust at the best of times, Eulenburg's physical condition deteriorated after 1897.[60] In April 1902, following the death of his beloved mother, Eulenburg became so distraught and unwell that he resigned as ambassador to Vienna and withdrew from political activity.[61] Throughout their relationship, Wilhelm's communications to his friend contained solicitous references to Eulenburg's health.[62] And on those not infrequent occasions, as in October 1903, when Eulenburg was ill while with the Kaiser, Wilhelm, in the words of his friend, "could not have displayed greater consideration, sympathy, friendliness." Assuming responsibility for Eulenburg's care, he organized the routines of the household so as to speed his friend's recovery and paid frequent visits to the invalid each day.[63] One month earlier, a bed-ridden and feverish Eulenburg had, as he recorded it, the following conversation with Wilhelm:

> I: "I am suffering greatly because I fear that instead of providing social entertainment I have become a burden to Your Majesty."
>
> Kaiser: "Please don't take it so tragically! It's good, after all, that you are receiving here trustworthy care. That's the main thing. . . . So, now you'll get better!"
>
> I: "Not much. For the time being I'm only a ghastly parcel. There is absolutely nothing more to be expected from my wretched body—and I have reconciled myself to my condition as good as it may get."
>
> Kaiser: "Such episodes don't mean much."
>
> I: "They are the links of a chain. But I don't complain about it."[64]

This interchange took place less than a month after Wilhelm had developed persistent hoarseness, reminiscent of the onset of Friedrich's throat cancer, about which the Kaiser's personal physician was deeply concerned.[65] Eulenburg's melodramatic suffering and self-pity allowed Wilhelm to overcome anxiety about his own health by playing the role of the stronger, more courageous friend who offers encouragement and support.[66] It also led later in their conversation to Wilhelm's self-confident assertion of his imperial authority and capacity to take responsibility for unpopular decisions made by others in the government.[67]

"Regarding my health, H.M. is *moving*," Eulenburg wrote Bülow on 24 July 1901. "It obviously matters to him to know that I am well. He tries to make everyone whom he knows or suspects is close to me . . . responsible for my adopting a healthy lifestyle. A few days ago I had a serious discussion about my health [with him] and asked H.M. 'to be my doctor', since he knows me so well, better than most people. . . . H.M. declared that he did indeed want to be my doctor."[68] It is striking and significant that this letter was written less than two weeks before the death of Wilhelm's mother. As Victoria lay dying of cancer in Friedrichskron outside Bad Homburg, Wilhelm was aboard the royal yacht tending to Philipp Eulenburg. Perhaps as he was about to lose his mother, Wilhelm became especially concerned about the health of the friend who was so important to him. Perhaps as he was faced with the death of the mother who was herself a devoted caretaker of the helpless and the infirm, Wilhelm took on her caregiving role, thereby preserving a feature of her personality in himself.[69] Perhaps, given the intensity of Wilhelm's attachment to Victoria and the intensity of his conflict over that attachment, Eulenburg served as a stand-in for the dying Victoria, whom Wilhelm could nurse without ambivalence. We will never know the precise meaning of this episode for Wilhelm of course. Still, when set within the context of his tendency to adopt a caretaking, even maternal, role with Eulenburg, this episode reveals, as do so many other events in

Wilhelm's life and aspects of his personality, that, despite the longstanding tension in their relationship and his public hostility toward her, Victoria remained for Wilhelm as Kaiser what she had been for Wilhelm as a child: the single most important person in his life.

III

Contemporaries remarked on the similarity of mother and son. "The same character as his mother, but with a greater contempt for mankind," the acerbic Holstein noted, as the tension between Wilhelm and his parents mounted in 1884.[70] And Count von Seckendorff, well acquainted with both Victoria and Wilhelm, told Bülow on one occasion: "There are not two people who are more alike than the Kaiserin and her eldest son. The only difference is that the latter wears pants and goes about with an unbuckled saber, while the mother goes about in long dresses wearing a veil."[71]

Some evidence that would seem to link Wilhelm to Friedrich, his association with the German armed forces, for example, on closer scrutiny reveals an underlying connection to Victoria. Instead of associating with the army, as was traditional in the Hohenzollern family, the branch of service in which his father had won his glory, Wilhelm affiliated himself with the fledgling German navy, England's traditional armed force. Whereas Wilhelm, like his own father, neglected his children, leaving them largely in their mother's care, he still insisted that his sons be brought up, as he himself had been, in a harshly demanding atmosphere.[72] At the height of their conflict, Wilhelm had told his mother: "Girls are useless creatures, he did not want one and far preferred to be without."[73] Yet of his children, it was only with his daughter, Viktoria Luise, that Wilhelm developed a warm and affectionate relationship.[74] Like his mother, Wilhelm sought to give his children's upbringing an English orientation. Indeed, "given the strong English sympathies of the Kaiser and his wish that his son in every way take root in England," members of the entourage considered it "a blessing" that the Kaiserin exerted a German counter-influence on the children.[75] Even in attempting to liberate his father from his mother's influence, Wilhelm used the same reasoning as Victoria had in trying to free him from the influence of Bismarck and Wilhelm I. Just as Victoria rarely blamed her son directly for the breakdown in their relationship and attributed Wilhelm's hostility to his dependence and the intrigues of the Bismarck circle, so Wilhelm attributed his lack of emotional contact with his father to Friedrich's helplessness and the interference of his mother.

Those familiar with mother and son attributed a host of the Kaiser's traits to Victoria. Bernhard von Bülow, for example, saw Wilhelm sharing his mother's ability to grasp things quickly, lack of snobbery, natural demeanor, openness, vivacity, and charm as well as some of her less desirable qualities, including obstinacy, moodiness, overestimating the importance of sovereigns, and being "clever but not wise."[76] To be sure, the efforts of Bülow and others to ascribe negative features of the Kaiser to an English woman reflected the self-interest of Germans in an age of nationalism and of men in a misogynous Prussian society. Thus, it was convenient for Carl von Wedel, the Kaiser's general adjutant, in his anger over Wilhelm's dismissal of Eduard von Liebenau as court marshal, to blame Victoria for the conduct of her son: "Like a lackey he drives him out of the house, like a worn out glove, he throws him away!—My God, the English blood has brought nothing good into the Hohenzollern family, for this heartlessness the young master has his mother to thank!"[77] Likewise Holstein believed that Wilhelm had inherited insincerity from his mother, a view shared by Eulenburg, although he was of the opinion that Victoria had endowed her son with the ability to lie innocently.[78] Indeed, Eulenburg thought that the Kaiser's lies were so convincing because, "like Kaiserin Friedrich who also believed firmly in her tears—as long as she was crying," Wilhelm, in the moment he uttered his falsehoods, was convinced of their veracity himself.[79]

Victoria and Wilhelm not only had similar characters, they also shared many of the same interests. Both were early risers and devotees of "fresh air."[80] Both enjoyed tennis and were passionate horseback riders.[81] Like Victoria who sang and painted still lifes and landscapes in her spare time, Wilhelm was an amateur composer and artist who sketched warships and fleets. Many of his closest friends, like Eulenburg, composed, sang, or painted.

Wilhelm admired and respected his mother.[82] The Kaiser's childhood playmate, Poultney Bigelow, recalled that as a little boy Wilhelm was in awe of her:

> I noted that William was particularly proud of his mother's accomplishments. One day he told me as a great secret that the cake we were eating was of her making. Another day he took me surreptitiously into a room of the palace where his mother had her studio, and there he made me admire her watercolors.[83]

Although Victoria's worry and disappointment cast a shadow over Wilhelm's childhood, their relationship had its good moments. "I remember happy hours spent in the studio of the Crown Prince's Palace," Wilhelm wrote in his memoirs, "my mother sitting at her easel, while I read aloud to her from some English tale, and how she every now and then dropped her palette to enjoy a hearty laugh."[84] By reading aloud, Wilhelm was able to get one of the few positive responses from Victoria, and it remained a favorite activity throughout his life.[85] One of the most striking features of the Kaiser's personality, his facility of expression and love of public speaking, can perhaps be traced back to these "happy hours." Openly disappointed in Wilhelm physically and intellectually, Victoria's positive response to his reading may well be the source of the Kaiser's faith in the power of his voice.

Another striking feature of Wilhelm's adult personality—his love of the sea and ships—was also associated with Victoria. Already as children, Wilhelm and his brother Heinrich were, in Victoria's words, "mad about ships," something she feared they had "inherited" from "their foolish Mama."[86] According to Eulenburg, the Kaiser's obsession with the development of the German navy

Wilhelm reading to his mother (ca. 1875). Reprinted with the permission of the Ullstein Bilderdienst.

was only to be understood as "*the inheritance of his English mother,* who loved the ocean and ships so much, that she (constantly seasick, like her son) would have herself bound to the deck when it was stormy because she wanted to experience the glory of the raging sea: giving vent both to her rapture—and to her dinner."[87] Indeed, Wilhelm himself proudly asserted in his memoirs that his "peculiar passion for the Navy . . . sprang to no small extent from my English blood on my mother's side."[88]

Even the antagonism between Wilhelm and Victoria was attributed by contemporaries not to their differences but to their similarity. In November 1888, at the height of the conflict, Holstein noted of Victoria in his diary that "she speaks, curses, sulks, as if she were still dealing with her husband, instead of her son, who resembles her too much to put up with such treatment."[89] Or as Eulenburg explained the hostility between Wilhelm and Victoria: "He was so similar in character and temperament to this unusually clever, highly educated, and interesting woman, that these two headstrong individuals with their autocratic outlooks simply *had* to collide with one another."[90] Bülow reached the same conclusion: "They resembled each other like two billiard balls which also mutually repel on contact."[91] Even Wilhelm ascribed the conflict with Victoria to their similarity. One year after ascending the throne, he told the British ambassador, Sir Edward Malet:

> My mother and I have the same characters. I have inherited hers. That good stubborn English blood that will not give way runs in both our veins. The consequence is that, if we do not happen to agree, the situation becomes difficult.[92]

Therefore the most dramatic chapter in Wilhelm's life before he ascended the throne—his rebellion against his parents and, particularly, his repudiation of Victoria—was attributed by Wilhelm, and by some contemporaries, to his psychological identity with her. A similar sense of contention based upon essential alikeness characterized the Kaiser's view of the relationship between Germany and Victoria's mother country.[93] Indeed, there are a number of parallels that can be discerned between Wilhelm's attitudes and actions toward Victoria as a youth and his attitudes and actions toward England as Kaiser— parallels that will be considered in Chapter 10. It should be stressed at this point, however, that to conclude that Wilhelm simply equated England with his mother and treated that country as if it were Victoria would be reductionistic and unsophisticated. Clearly, the Kaiser's policies toward England were the product of numerous factors unrelated to his psychology. And, just as clearly, Wilhelm's personality was the product of many psychological influences; his development did not cease with his break away from his mother. Nevertheless, the parallels between the way Wilhelm dealt with his mother and the way he dealt with England were not historical or psychological accidents. On the one hand, the same social and political forces that pushed Wilhelm into conflict with his mother were present after 1888 to direct and constrain his policies toward England as Kaiser. On the other hand, Wilhelm II was the product of his personal history. His past influenced the way he felt, thought, and acted in the present, and the basic patterns of response laid down in the first thirty years of Wilhelm's life continued to define his responses in the last fifty. Of course, those patterns were altered by his experiences after 1888, and the responses themselves were influenced by the circumstances he faced. And yet the ways that Wilhelm dealt with the issues confronting him in his relationship with his parents tended to be the ways he dealt with the issues confronting him as an adult. Wilhelm did not simply equate England with his mother, but the approaches Wilhelm adopted in relation to her tended to be the approaches he adopted in relation to her homeland. Literally and figuratively, they were familiar to him.

IV

A primary purpose of this book is to begin to explain how Friedrich Naumann, during the *Daily Telegraph* affair, could proclaim to the German people that the Kaiser they were vilifying was in fact their "mirror image" and how Walther Rathenau, in the aftermath of the Reich's collapse and the Kaiser's abdication, could describe Wilhelm II and Wilhelmian Germany as reflections of one another.[94] The second half of this book is devoted to those questions, to understanding how, despite its contribution to his political incompetence and symbolic fiascos like the *Daily Telegraph* affair, Wilhelm II's personality allowed him to function as a national symbol and, in that capacity in an age of nationalism, to inspire the enthusiasm of the Germans.

It has been argued here that, because of his development, Wilhelm II's psychological equilibrium was unusually susceptible to the responses of his environment. The German nation and the German people were an environment on which Wilhelm depended psychologically. To be sure, "a nation" and "a people" cannot be defined explicitly, and in the case of Wilhelmian Germany—given its ethnic, social, political, and religious divisions—these concepts become even more problematical. Although these concepts may seem ambiguous to the historian, the Kaiser was in no doubt about their meaning. He had a definite sense of "his nation" and "his subjects": they were an integral part of his emotional life.

As a result, his fortunes and those of his country were indistinguishable for Wilhelm II. On the one hand, increases in the military or economic power of the Reich, expansions of Germany's diplomatic influence, even cultural or scientific advances, enhanced Wilhelm's self-esteem and self-confidence. International setbacks for Germany increased his anxiety and self-doubt. On the other hand, blows to Wilhelm's pride increased his sense of the vulnerability of the nation. And when he was more confident about himself, he felt confident about Germany's international status as well. In the same way, Wilhelm was vulnerable to the responses of his subjects: their adulation increased his self-esteem; their reprobation reduced it. Because of his vulnerability to those responses, Wilhelm developed a sensitivity to public opinion as it was reflected in the press. That sensitivity enabled Wilhelm to adapt himself to the popular mood as he perceived it and, on a few notable occasions, to adapt the popular mood to him. But German public opinion as reflected in the press was neither itself consistent nor the only German environment to which the Kaiser was psychologically susceptible. There were many Germanys and many Germans with whom the Kaiser had to contend and to whose responses he was vulnerable. Indeed, in adapting to the other environments on which he was also emotionally dependent, Wilhelm could flagrantly disregard press and public opinion. The Kaiser's adaptation to a multiplicity of German environments, then, increased his instability and inconsistency. Nevertheless, Wilhelm's disjoint-edness enabled him to respond to the variety of often contradictory interests confronting him as Kaiser and to reflect back the diverse natures and aspira-tions of the Germanies and the Germans that made up his environment.

Wilhelm's driven need to find the affirmation as an adult that had been missing in his childhood and to find the security and stability he had been unable to acquire from his parents enhanced his symbolic appeal to the Ger-mans. The Kaiser's boastful and bellicose rhetoric and dramatic gestures pro-duced no substantive domestic or foreign political achievements and only con-tributed to the Reich's diplomatic and military isolation. And yet, as the personification of Germany, Wilhelm's grandiosity was frequently not per-ceived to be a sign of underlying depression but was seen as an appropriate expression of the greatness and power of the Reich. The Kaiser's demand that he and his country be recognized and appreciated was in tune with the need of his subjects in an era of intense German nationalism to see their nation and, by extension, themselves treated with respect and admiration.

Similarly, the Kaiser's inner weakness and incoherence contributed to the erratic course of German foreign and domestic policy during his reign. His political inconsistency was increased not only by his adaptation to an environ-ment that was itself inconsistent but also by his efforts to overcome his pow-erful dependent longings as he shifted from one source of strength and guidance to another. And yet, as the personification of Germany, Wilhelm's flamboyant assertions of personal sovereignty were frequently not perceived to be a sign of underlying self-doubt and insecurity but were seen as appropriate demonstra-tions of power by the leader of this newly unified nation. Nor were the Kaiser's efforts to increase his autonomy and strength by increasing the autonomy and strength of the nation frequently perceived to be part of a struggle against underlying dependency and weakness but were seen as appropriate efforts to secure the independence and increase the power of an empire that aspired to be a true *Weltreich.*

Before proceeding to a detailed consideration of these issues, one question relating to Wilhelm's psychological development is appropriately raised first, although it presumes what Part II of this study seeks to demonstrate. How could a king, perhaps the most atypical individual in the realm, have become Naumann's "mirror image" of the Germans? Or, put another way, how could Wilhelm II, who grew up in an environment so unlike that of any of his sub-jects, have become Rathenau's "symbolic individual" who personified an epoch of German history?

Before this difficult and important question can be addressed it must be stated immediately that features of Wilhelm II's personality cannot be con-nected to the Germans, although they are not the focus of this study of the Kaiser's leadership. Moreover, it is important to acknowledge the possibility that features attributed here to Wilhelm may have represented popular myths about him. As considered in relation to Eulenburg and the other members of the entourage and examined again in Part II, the Kaiser was a transference figure for his subjects. Germans close to Wilhelm, like Eulenburg, and those whose knowledge of the Kaiser came secondhand saw in Wilhelm what they wanted and needed to see. In part because of the nature of his imperial office and in part because of the nature of his personality, Germans came to project their hopes and fears about themselves onto Wilhelm II. Finally, it must be conceded that because of the Kaiser's receptivity to external influences and his adaptability, some of the attitudes he shared with his subjects were the expressions of what Eulenburg called "Wilhelm Proteus."

And yet, as the preceding pages have presumably made clear, Wilhelm II was not a blank screen, with no identity—or identities—of his own, with no aspirations or ideals. And presumably sufficient evidence has been presented, from various sources, to demonstrate that the identities, aspirations, and ideals ascribed here to Wilhelm II were not simply popular fictions unrelated to his actual person. What was so striking to Naumann and Rathenau about the relationship between Wilhelm II and the Germans was that so many of his identities, aspirations, and ideals were in tune with the identities, aspirations, and ideals of so many of his subjects during his reign. This convergence can be attributed to simple historical accident, of course. Nevertheless, one factor can be identified which helps to explain how it came to be that Wilhelmian Germany had such an appropriate ruler in Wilhelm II. That factor is the integral role played by German politics in Wilhelm's psychological development. To the extent that Kaiser Wilhelm II became the mirror image of the Germans, he did so in significant measure because of the thoroughgoing politicization of his personality.

Ironically, this point can be most clearly illustrated in considering the origin of that feature of the Kaiser's personality perhaps most tenuously connected to the Germans: Wilhelm's profound sympathy for England, indeed, his partial English identity. Even here German politics contributed to the development of the English side of Wilhelm II's personality. Various historians have considered the role played by Great Britain in German domestic politics in the second half of the nineteenth century.[95] England represented liberal political tradition in Germany during this period. For leftwing German Liberals, Progressives, and Democrats, the British political system was the model to be emulated.[96] In fact it was only a matter of time, these liberals believed, until Germany adopted a form of government similar to England's because, as the British example had apparently revealed, parliamentary democracy was in the natural order of an industrializing and modernizing nation's political development.[97] Many conservatives shared this—what was for them a fatalistic—vision of historical development. They viewed England with hostility and trepidation as the symbol of the potential decline of their political power and tended naturally to favor autocratic Russia.[98] After the unification of the Reich in 1871, as Germany's imperialist ambitions grew along with its industrial might, England came to represent not only liberalism but empire. Germans of various political persuasions came to view England with a mixture of admiration and envy as the model imperial power that stood in the way of the creation of a German world empire.[99]

Thus, when Wilhelm II ascended the throne in June 1888, his attitudes toward England, although obviously more intense than those of his subjects, were not unlike attitudes toward England then prevalent in the German population. Wilhelm's admiration for England and for English institutions, his wish that Germany emulate certain of Britain's characteristics, especially her imperial power, and perhaps even his desire to forge an alliance with England in which Germany would be the dominant partner in the relationship were sentiments shared by many of his subjects. Similarly, the Kaiser's jealousy of England and of his English relatives, his anger at the English for treating him and his country with insufficient respect, his hostility toward Britain for obstructing Germany's imperial ambitions, and his fear of Britain's naval and imperial power were also fundamentally in tune with German public opinion.[100]

To be sure, this congruence can be partially attributed to the fact that Wilhelm and the Germans were reacting to the same historical circumstances and to Wilhelm's sensitivity to public opinion and his willingness and ability to adapt himself to it. And yet, as the foregoing consideration of the relationship between Wilhelm and his parents should have demonstrated, Wilhelm's attitudes toward England were developing from the beginning of his life and were rooted in the depths of his psyche. How then is this congruence to be explained? Part of the answer at least lies in the fact that the Kaiser shared not only a common present with his subjects but a common past as well. The political experiences that shaped the attitudes of Germans toward England after mid-century were for Wilhelm personal experiences that shaped his personality and world view. Because of the politicization of his personal life, the history of German attitudes toward England was played out in the history of Wilhelm's family.

Personal and political motives were interfused in Friedrich's decision to marry Victoria. Although his father approved of his bride and even encouraged the marriage for dynastic reasons, Friedrich, given what England represented in Germany in the 1850s, implicitly turned away from the conservative, Prussian political philosophy of his father and from the more traditional German marriage of his parents by marrying an English princess with strongly held liberal political views and a forceful personality.[101] By taking the political action of marrying a liberal English princess, Friedrich made a personal statement to his father.[102] By taking the personal action of marrying Victoria, he made a political statement to the Prussians.[103] The nature of his personal statement to his father was influenced by the politics of the day: contemporary German politics set the options for personal action. The nature of his political statement to the Prussians was influenced by his personality and relationship with his father: personal motives determined which political option he decided to take.

By the same token, Friedrich and Victoria's love for one another was at once a personal and a political affection, and politics played an important role in their relationship. The Germans were right, in other words, to see the relationship between Friedrich and Victoria as a potential model for Germany's foreign and domestic relations during the reign of Friedrich III. Not only did the personal dimension of the relationship between Friedrich and Victoria have political consequences for the Germans, the political dimension of their relationship had personal consequences for both the royal couple and their eldest son. Therefore, German politics, through their influence on Friedrich's personal action, played a role in giving the future German Kaiser an English mother and a partial English identity.

It can be said, then, that the politicization of Wilhelm II's personality had begun even before his conception. Politics not only played a role in Wilhelm's creation, they were present in his life from the instant of his birth, in the form of those in attendance at the delivery: his mother and father, the English and German doctors, the British ambassador, the ladies-in-waiting, Friedrich's parents, and the crowds of Berliners to whom the baby was displayed from the palace balcony. Wilhelm's personality would be shaped by the politics of those who influenced his psychological development. For Wilhelm, their personalities and their political views were inextricably bound together. Furthermore, as a result of the efforts of his parents to acquaint him with a wide range of views (including especially the bourgeois political philosophies Victoria so admired) and of the political realities of mid-century Prussia, Wilhelm was exposed to the politics and the personalities of a host of very different individuals, including his parents and other relatives, nurses, tutors, governors, soldiers, teachers, brother-officers, and friends. Wilhelm internalized aspects of these, in many cases, incompatible personalities and political philosophies and as Kaiser was able to reflect back features of the various personalities and political philosophies to which he had been exposed. Since radicals and radicalism, socialists and socialism, as well as certain regional and ethnic groups were not included in the influences on Wilhelm, he never internalized their personal and political outlooks and, as Kaiser, was generally ineffective in reflecting back their aspirations and ideals. But many Germans and many German political philosophies (including those of the Junker and liberal aristocracy, the military, the industrial and commercial classes, the educated bourgeoisie, and even, through the no doubt distorting mediation of some of these groups, sections of the peasantry and the working classes) did exert an influence on Wilhelm, and, as Kaiser, he was frequently effective in reflecting back their contradictory aspirations and ideals.

In sum, German politics influenced Wilhelm II's psychological development and came to be incorporated in his psyche. Of course every human being is shaped by the political and social forces of the day. In Wilhelm's case, the influence of those forces was not small but extensive. Not only did the fragmentary state of the political environment to which he was exposed contribute to the fragmentary state of Wilhelm's personality, politics helped to determine the composition of those fragments. In attempting to fulfill his inner program—or programs—of action, Wilhelm II in a way fulfilled the political programs of the Germans, or at least of those Germans and their representatives who had given shape to Wilhelm's fractured self and had helped set the psychological agenda for his life.

The first half of this study has considered the politicization of Wilhelm II's personality. The second half considers the consequence of that politicization:

the personalization of politics in Wilhelmianism. Part II seeks to explain how Wilhelm II functioned as what Friedrich Naumann called the "mirror image" of the Germans. Part I has sought to explain why he was able to do so. Put another way, Part II seeks to demonstrate that, as Walther Rathenau believed, it was fitting that the troubled history of Germany from 1890 to 1914 should bear the name of the Kaiser. Part I has sought to demonstrate that the fit was not simply an accident of history.

PART

The Personalization of Politics

This Kaiser, about whom you are in an uproar, is your mirror image!

Friedrich Naumann's admonition to
the German people in January 1909[1]

Never before had a symbolic individual been so completely reflected in an epoch, an epoch in an individual.

Walther Rathenau on Wilhelm II in 1919[2]

CHAPTER

The Kaiser, the Press, and Public Opinion

"In politics no one does anything for another," Otto von Bismarck wrote in 1857, "unless he also finds it in his own interest to do so."[1] With this statement, nineteenth-century Europe's master of pragmatic politics summed up what he believed to be the "fundamental rule of all political behavior," according to one biographer of the statesman. For Bismarck, the rational pursuit of self-interest was natural to individuals, groups, and states; indeed, it was part of God's divine order. As a result, the statesman was morally compelled to define the interest of state and to dedicate himself to its fulfillment.[2] On the basis of this principle, the chancellor treated political parties not as advocates of any political or social ideology but as interest groups, both in themselves and as representatives of their self-interested constituencies.[3] Similarly, in foreign affairs Bismarck understood "the only sound basis" for the conduct of the nation-state to be "its egoism and not romanticism."[4] Personal feelings, the wishes of elites or political parties, popular opinion, all were to be subordinated to the interest of state. They were to be manipulated in the service of the rational conduct of policy; they were never to shape it.

To Bismarck it seemed nearly inevitable that the state would follow a course based upon its rational self-interest. In November 1887 when the German ambassador in London, Count Paul von Hatzfeldt-Wildenburg, reported that the British were worried that Prince Wilhelm's accession to the throne would bring an anti-English shift in German foreign policy, Bismarck noted in the margin of the ambassador's report that such a shift would be "impossible" since it was not in Germany's interest.[5] Several days later Bismarck assured Lord Salisbury in a personal letter that no individual, be he Kaiser or chancellor, could steer the ship of state off its predetermined course. You need not be concerned, Bismarck wrote the prime minister, that Prince Wilhelm will pursue an anti-English policy. "Neither this nor the opposite would be possible in Germany." Whoever is Kaiser will and can only be influenced by the interests of the German Empire. The path that must be taken in order to uphold these interests is so urgently prescribed that it is impossible to depart from it. . . . Therefore German policy is compelled to steer the course dictated by the European political situation, and neither the temperament nor the temperamentality of a monarch or leading minister can cause it to change.[6]

Unfortunately, Bismarck's prediction about the future of Anglo-German relations was mistaken, and his optimistic conception of the rational nature of political behavior proved to be out of tune with the mass politics of the twentieth century. Following the accession of Wilhelm II in June 1888, *"Realpolitik"* gave way to the politics of symbolism. The reassuringly logical politics of rational self-interest became submerged by the politics of emotion, impulsive reaction, and public relations. When Bismarck retired in anger to Friedrichsruh in 1890—dismissed by a headstrong Kaiser who wished to steer the ship of state himself—Germany's course was no longer self-evident either domestically or internationally. Nor was Wilhelm II able to define his personal aims and ideals. What was certain was that both the youthfully impetuous Kaiser and his youthfully impetuous nation wanted the speed increased, the ship's screws turned up. Germany had entered the Wilhelmian era.

I

The transformation of German political life from *Realpolitik* to the politics of symbolism was dramatically represented in the shift in style of leadership from Bismarck to Wilhelm II, from the chancellor's efforts to realize the interest of state to the Kaiser's attention to public image and popular opinion.[7] Indeed, Wilhelm's advisers who were products of the Bismarckian school of politics could not understand the Kaiser's preoccupation with his relationship to his subjects. They were particularly perplexed and dismayed by the time Wilhelm devoted to the press. "Complaints from everyone that H.M. dodges political reports," longtime privy councillor in the Foreign Office Friedrich von Holstein wrote shortly after Wilhelm's accession to the throne. "At the same time he reads thirty to forty newspaper clippings one after the other and makes marginal comments on them. A curious personality."[8] To a man like Holstein, steeped in the Bismarckian tradition of political leadership, the assiduous reading of newspaper clippings seemed an eccentric and wasteful occupation. Even Eulenburg, with a character and outlook far closer to the Kaiser's, found Wilhelm's absorption in the press, at the expense of careful attention to the tightly reasoned memoranda of domestic and foreign policy experts, to be a sign of laziness.[9]

The time and energy Wilhelm devoted to newspaper clippings, noted by his disgruntled advisers, reflected his sense that public opinion played a crucial role in determining the political behavior of nations. In 1895, during the Armenian crisis, the British military attaché in Berlin, Colonel Leopold Swaine, complained to Wilhelm that an article in the Russian paper *Grazhdanin* was symptomatic of a fundamental Russian antipathy toward England that was preventing rapprochement between the two countries. The Kaiser's telling response was that *Grazhdanin*

> like the press in Russia generally has no appreciable influence on account of its limited circulation; certainly nothing like the influence of the press in other countries, particularly in England. It is precisely this press and British public opinion dominated by it that we have to thank for the whole sorry scandal of the Armenian question.[10]

Wilhelm II did not attribute the bloody Near Eastern crisis to the actions of the Turks and Armenians or to the policies of the European world powers actively seeking to defend and promote their national interests in the foundering Ottoman Empire. He did not even blame the British government directly for attempting to hasten and exploit the process of Turkish collapse, as did many in the German Foreign Office. Instead the Kaiser blamed the English press, because of its influence on public opinion in a generally literate, well-educated country. By the same token, he discounted the influence of the Russian press. Because of its limited circulation, *Grazhdanin* had no impact on the illiterate mass of the Russian people. The fact that newspapers were read by the educated elite that determined and directed the foreign policy of the Russian government seemed irrelevant to the Kaiser. For him, in this instance at least, it was mass public opinion and the press, insofar as it influenced mass public opinion, that determined the nation's course and defined the nature of its leadership.

International conflicts for Wilhelm II were not the product of conflicting national "egoisms" or of incompatible military, political, or economic interests. They were attributable to emotional discord between peoples. In fact, when incited, public opinion could cause states to act in ways contrary to their rational self-interest. The tension that characterized Anglo-German relations during most of the Kaiser's reign was therefore very often understood by him in terms of public opinion. "There is no denying the fact that the political relations between the two countries had little by little become charged with electrical fluid to an extent, that its discharge might have created endless woe to both," he wrote Edward VII in 1906. "In both countries newspapers as well as individuals, some actuated by political some by personal motives, worked the public feeling to such a degree that both nations began to mistrust each other, thereby causing an immense amount of mischief, and the seeds of discord to grow. Cui bono? Who was to benefit by this nefarious work? Certainly as far as I can see, neither of our two countries has gained even the slightest advantage by this."[11]

Therefore good relations between nations were not to be achieved or preserved simply by agreements, treaties, or government contacts, according to the Kaiser, but also by the attitudes of the respective populations. Despite his tendency to regard sovereigns as decisive political actors, Wilhelm was not reassured by Edward VII's declarations of his peaceful intentions and friendship for Germany in 1903. Edward's statement at a banquet given by the king of Portugal, "Je ne veux pas la guerre . . . c'est la paix que je désire," prompted Wilhelm to write: "Mais la 'Times'!" referring to the influential and Germanophobic British paper.[12] To the news that his uncle had singled out the German representative for a long discussion in front of the king of Portugal, a gesture interpreted by the representative as a mark of Edward's friendship for Germany, Wilhelm responded: "Correct, that is doubtless the opinion of the *King,* but his *minister?* Certainly *not his press* and his *subjects.*"[13]

Therefore the activities of politicians and diplomats were important not only in their own right but also because of their impact on public opinion. Wilhelm's response in April 1900 to the report of the German ambassador in London was characteristic. To the news that influential members of the British cabinet and London society had given their private assurance that the conduct of the German government and particularly that of the Kaiser during the Boer War was greatly appreciated, Wilhelm angrily declared: "Confidential communications are completely useless! They should proclaim it loudly to everyone in London!"[14] In general the Kaiser had little patience or understanding for leaders who were unable or unwilling to influence public opinion or who failed to appreciate its importance. Throughout his reign he urged the British government to pressure the English press to print articles favorable to Germany. Thus, to Arthur Balfour's statement in 1905 that "no sane person in England wishes to have a quarrel with Germany," Wilhelm responded "then why let the quarrelsome tone of Press and literature go on?" And when the prime minister conceded that the popular mood in Britain was very bitter toward Germany at that moment, largely because of the naval race between the two countries, Wilhelm replied that the bitterness existed only "because absolutely nothing is being done at the top to change the mood."[15]

Because the Kaiser believed that the modern leader's actions must be based upon an appreciation of public opinion, it became one of his principal obligations to follow the press, both foreign and domestic. As medium between ruler and subject, the press occupied a critical position, simultaneously influencing and reflecting public opinion. He ascribed such major political developments as the growth of Anglo-French diplomatic and military cooperation by early 1906 to the fact that the German press had "scolded" the two countries "together."[16] With its influence on popular opinion in France and England, the German press, Wilhelm believed, had produced a decisive political change— one quite to Germany's disadvantage. As a reflection of public opinion, however, the press indicated future political change. In 1896, for example, Wilhelm, in the aftermath of his telegram to President Krüger, anticipated that the English would soon seize Germany's colonies because "the newspaper expectorations from England[,] which announce the steady increase in anti-German feeling, demonstrate that the antipathy is more deep-seated than has hitherto been believed."[17]

In a way that many of his advisers did not, Wilhelm II recognized that public opinion had become a decisive political factor in Europe by the end of the nineteenth century.[18] Unlike Bismarck, Wilhelm did not regard public opinion as simply another political instrument to be manipulated in accordance with the reason of state. Although his rule as a monarch was theoretically justified "by the grace of God," although he could proclaim and at times believe that he was above "the views or opinions of the day,"[19] he sensed that his position and power depended upon popular support. He expressed that recognition in December 1896 to the British ambassador in Berlin, Sir Edward Malet. During the course of the discussion, Wilhelm learned from the ambassador that Lord Salisbury had rejected the Kaiser's suggestion that the prime minister issue a statement to the press denying that England was engaged in subversive activities in Germany (and specifically was not attempting to foment labor unrest) as beneath the dignity of the British government. Wilhelm insisted that such a statement was necessary in order to reassure German public opinion, because, despite his personal desire to promote Anglo-German understanding, he simply was "not able to act in opposition to the interests and wishes of the German people."[20]

II

The Kaiser's recognition that he must be a "modern monarch," sensitive and responsive to the needs of his subjects, his belief in the importance of public opinion in foreign and domestic politics, and his perception of the power of the press as a mediator between ruler and subject reflected both his past experience and the structure of his adult personality. From his parents' unpopularity and failure to achieve significant political influence, Wilhelm had learned the peril of disregarding public image. Indeed, the successes he achieved in the 1880s were due in part to his sensitivity and accommodation to the popular mood. And yet, the importance that Wilhelm attached to public relations was not simply a product of his experience and awareness of the importance that press and public opinion had assumed in contemporary political life. His preoccupation with the "interests and wishes of the German people"—often to the neglect of the interests of the state—was also a result of his vulnerability to popular responses to him. Because public opinion played such an important role in his personal life, Wilhelm appears to have naturally assumed that it played an equally important role in political affairs.

Lacking inner purpose, Wilhelm generally relied on his environment to help him define his attitudes and direct his activities. It was difficult, perhaps impossible, for the Kaiser to develop a position on his own. Like iron filings which only assume a recognizable pattern in the presence of a magnetic field, Wilhelm formed his opinions in reaction to the opinions of others. At times the Kaiser simply adopted the views of those around him as his own. But even on those not infrequent occasions when he adopted a view diametrically opposed to that of the person with whom he was speaking, Wilhelm needed the structured position of another to which he could impulsively react in defining his point of view. He did not have the capacity for solitary contemplation. The impulsiveness, the tactlessness, the indiscretion so lamented by his advisers were for Wilhelm a psychological and intellectual necessity.

The intense reactivity that characterized Wilhelm's conversations was also evident in the other principal ways the Kaiser developed and articulated his ideas: that is, in letters, telegrams, and marginal comments to reports and newspaper articles. Lacking the thoughtfulness, patience, and persistence necessary for sustained correspondence, Wilhelm preferred telegrams to letters in communicating with friends, relatives, and advisers. Like his impulsive need to blurt out his reactions to the opinions of the person with whom he was speaking, Wilhelm felt compelled to respond immediately to the discussions he had had and to the reports, letters, and articles he had read.[21] It is significant in this context that so many of the Kaiser's telegrams and letters were essentially accounts of his conversations with others, his point of view only formulated in his descriptions of his own replies. But most often, Wilhelm made his positions known to his advisers by circulating newspaper clippings and government reports covered with marginal comments. As his court marshal for many years, Count Robert von Zedlitz-Trützschler, recognized, these marginalia were a manifestation of Wilhelm's reactive personality. Zedlitz noted that the Kaiser, as he was indiscreet in conversation, was also "unable to read a report, a newspaper, or a book without making marginal comments in pencil. Since these marginalia are totally the product of his feelings of the moment and since there is no warning voice enjoining him to caution, they will one day provide the historian with a rich if very thought-provoking source."[22]

In the present context, the marginalia reveal just how many newspaper clippings Wilhelm read. Because his ideas were frequently formed in reaction to newspaper articles, the press and public opinion (to the extent it was reflected in the press) can be described as having participated in the development of the Kaiser's opinions. Nevertheless, Wilhelm's absorption in the press and his preoccupation with public opinion usually did not translate into policy. Instead, the principal function of press and public opinion for Wilhelm was to offer the external affirmation he required to make up for the affirmation and approval he had never received as a child. In relation to press and public opinion, the Kaiser was like an actor who derives little satisfaction from his performance until he hears the applause of the audience, who waits anxiously for the reviews of the critics, who only feels emotionally alive in the positive responses of others to him. First as secretary of state in the Foreign Office and then as chancellor, Bernhard von Bülow had ample opportunity to observe Wilhelm's intense gratification at being the focus of popular attention. "In the course of my time in office I seldom went anywhere with the Kaiser," Bülow wrote in his memoirs, "when he did not declare after his ceremonial entrance that it had been the most lovely reception of his life. So it was in Peterhof and in Windsor, Budapest and in Vienna, in Constantinople and in Venice, in Rome and in Jerusalem, in Naples and in Palermo, in Damascus and Beirut, at every visit, at every maneuver."[23] The pleasure Wilhelm experienced on such occasions influenced his actions. In June 1904, for example, the cheers of a French crowd of *'Vive l'Imperatrice!'* and *'Vive l'Empereur!'* at a car race transformed the Kaiser's attitude toward France. Before the race, it was only with difficulty that Bülow had prevented Wilhelm from using the dedication of a war memorial at Metz or Saarbrücken to fire a verbal salvo at France. Indeed, during the course of the spring, the Kaiser had talked incessantly about the possibility of war with that country.[24] After the race, it was only with difficulty that the chancellor prevented Wilhelm from sending an overly friendly and conciliatory telegram to French President Émile Loubet.[25] Wilhelm's political behavior was even more profoundly affected by the reactions of the British, and he sought to pursue pro-English policies whenever he felt supported and appreciated by press and public opinion in Britain.[26] But if the Kaiser felt uplifted by the positive response of the French or British, he was dependent upon the sustaining responses of his own subjects. As he needed oxygen to breathe, he needed to feel popularly affirmed and in harmony with "the interests and wishes of the German people."[27]

To a significant degree the Kaiser was at the mercy of the Germans' responses to him.[28] Just as he could feel exhilarated by the cheers of the crowds upon entering a city, as he could feel gratified by favorable newspaper reaction to one of his speeches, he could feel correspondingly devastated when he felt himself unappreciated, undermined, or criticized by his subjects. When projects important to the Kaiser, like the expansion of the navy, were not greeted with popular enthusiasm or were rejected by the Reichstag, Wilhelm reacted, as he did after the defeat of the naval bill in 1897, with outbursts of rage and a public display of "icy coldness."[29] Similarly in August 1899 Wilhelm took the defeat of a bill to build canals between Dortmund-Rhine and the Central German Canals in the Prussian Diet as "a personal affront." In fact the Kaiserin was moved to write Bülow of her concern about Wilhelm's "great anxiety and depression" in the hope that he might be able to calm the Kaiser.[30] When, as a result of widespread antipathy toward England during the Boer War, Germans failed to share Wilhelm's grief at the death of Queen Victoria, he angrily denounced his "blockheaded louts of countrymen."[31]

Because his psychological balance depended on his standing with his subjects, articles relating to Wilhelm or his family were, by imperial decree, collected and preserved—the Kaiser's customary "very good" scrawled at the bottom testifying to his sense of satisfaction at the favorable press coverage. All of Wilhelm's activities were recounted in the press, and Wilhelm took an active part in maximizing and managing his exposure to his subjects. "It is remarkable," Zedlitz noted in his diary in 1904, "how sensitive the Kaiser is to the press. In of themselves harmless inaccuracies and untruths about his life can greatly upset him when they are reported to him or when he comes across them in his own reading."[32] Wilhelm's distress at the publication of misinformation about him can be attributed to his concern lest his subjects develop misconceptions about him that could skew the popular responses on which he depended. On those occasions when his aides, for reasons of political or diplomatic self-interest, acted to suppress information about Wilhelm or censor his speeches, he reacted with annoyance and disappointment.[33]

Ironically Wilhelm's annoyance when aides sought to withhold his views from his subjects may have contributed to the *Daily Telegraph* affair, the most serious crisis of his reign before 1914 and precipitant of the most famous of the "nervous breakdowns" that he suffered as Kaiser.[34] Knowing of Wilhelm's tendency to become angry when told that his remarks could not be made public, Chancellor Bülow passed the text of the interview the Kaiser had given to Colonel Stuart Wortley during his visit to England in 1907 on to the Foreign Office for screening. There, the officials who received the document, probably anxious to avoid upsetting Wilhelm, suggested only superficial changes in the text. As a result, the interview was published essentially in its original form in the *Daily Telegraph* in late October 1908. The publication of the Kaiser's remarks, in which he claimed, among other things, to be the Anglophile ruler of Anglophobic subjects, produced widespread indignation in Germany and a precipitous drop in Wilhelm's standing with the Germans. Wilhelm's reception of Count Ferdinand von Zeppelin on 10 November, the day the Reichstag began debating his interview, reveals the degree to which the Kaiser's psychological balance had been upset by the national uproar. Embracing the inventor of the dirigible three times and bestowing on him the Order of the Black Eagle, the Kaiser proclaimed Zeppelin to be "the greatest German of the twentieth century"—after only nine years of the century had elapsed—and described the day's events as constituting "one of the greatest moments in the development of human culture."[35] The crisis reached its peak a few days later with the Reichstag's demand that restraints be placed on the Kaiser's conduct. With the shocking death of General Hülsen three days after the Reichstag debates, the anxiety and depression that Wilhelm had been experiencing since the publication of his interview increased to the point that Freiherr Martin von Jenisch, councillor à la suite to the Kaiser, telegraphed Bülow that Wilhelm was "in a very vulnerable condition and obviously suffering emotionally."[36] Using similar language, the Kaiserin described her husband as "completely broken," and several days later, with the Kaiser considering abdication, she told the chancellor that Wilhelm had suffered a nervous "collapse" and had taken "to bed with a fit of shaking and convulsive weeping."[37] Nearly a month after the publication of the interview, the Kaiser, able only to take short walks and care for his dogs, still contemplated abdication.[38] Although his physical health gradually improved, Wilhelm remained depressed and unstable at least until the end of the year.[39]

One of Wilhelm's first, if less dramatic, nervous breakdowns occurred after he was roundly criticized for an inflammatory speech to the Brandenburg Provincial Diet on 26 February 1897. As it was becoming apparent that the naval bill was going down to defeat in the Reichstag, the Kaiser struck a bellicose pose for the mostly Junker aristocrats in the audience. Implicitly denigrating Bismarck, Wilhelm mythologized and glorified his grandfather, Wilhelm I, and called, allegedly, for the "rooting out" of the "plague" of social democracy "down to the stumps."[40] The Kaiser expected that his forceful remarks would be met with acclaim, thereby bolstering his self-confidence at a time when he was already feeling vulnerable as a result of the naval bill's impending defeat.

Instead, the speech produced an outcry throughout Germany. As Bülow recalled Wilhelm's reaction, "the Kaiser was so disappointed by the failure of his speech, which could not be kept from him, that . . . he suffered a nervous collapse."[41]

It is not enough to say that the Kaiser simply felt criticized. On this occasion, and to a degree on all occasions when he felt out of tune with his subjects, the intensity of Wilhelm's reaction indicates that he experienced the response of the Germans as a denigration of something he had proudly created and displayed for popular approval, as a devastating rejection where he had expected, indeed counted on, popular acclaim to support him emotionally. It is difficult to know how these breakdowns would be characterized in the terminology of contemporary psychiatry or what their precise precipitants may have been. They were doubtless the product of various intersecting factors. Nonetheless, these incapacitating episodes of anxiety and depression demonstrate that the supporting and sustaining responses of the Germans were essential to the Kaiser's personal and political functioning.

III

The importance that Wilhelm attached to public opinion and its impact on him personally placed the Kaiser in a difficult position. The dilemma confronting Wilhelm was manifest in his letter to Tsar Nicholas II of 9 May 1909. In the aftermath of the *Daily Telegraph* affair, the Kaiser wrote that he felt "blamed" for the tension in Europe following Austria's annexation of Bosnia-Herzogovina in October of the preceding year. "Especially the Press in general," he complained, "has behaved in the basest way against me." Despite the inaccuracy of the newspaper attacks against him, they should be taken seriously, Wilhelm believed, since "the fact must be taken note of that the papers mostly create public opinion." He concluded:

> As sovereigns who are responsible to God for the welfare of the Nations entrusted to our care it is our duty therefore to closely study the genesis and development of "public opinion" before we allow it to influence our actions. Should we find that it takes its origin from the tarnished and gutterlike sources of the above named infamous press our duty will and must oblige us to energetically correct it and resist it.
>
> Personally I am totally indifferent to newspaper gossip, but I cannot refrain from a certain feeling of anxiety, that if not corrected at once, the foul and filthy lies which are freely circulated about my policies and country, will tend to create bitterness between our two people by virtue of their constant and uncontradicted repetition. Public opinion wants clear information and leading.[42]

The Kaiser's contradictory letter to the Tsar expressed the paradox inherent in his position as a monarch in an age of mass political participation. As a sovereign he was above newspaper criticism, yet he was obviously susceptible to it politically. He was theoretically accountable to God, and yet he recognized that his leadership rested ultimately on his standing with his subjects. Wilhelm was confronted with the task of reconciling the facade of sovereignty that seemed necessary to his political functioning with his appreciation of the decisive role played by press and public opinion in modern politics.[43]

The contradiction in Wilhelm's political position was inevitable given the changing realities of monarchical rule in turn-of-the-century Europe. The dilemma confronting the Kaiser also had to be faced by all the European hereditary sovereigns of his era. If Wilhelm's success in coming to terms with this dilemma did not match that of Edward VII perhaps, he certainly was far more successful in reconciling monarchical leadership with the exigencies of modern political life than was, for example, his unhappy "cousin" Nicholas II. But though Wilhelm's political predicament was not unique, he was faced with a personal dilemma more threatening than his political discomfiture. The Kaiser needed to reconcile his need to experience himself as autonomous, as psychologically sovereign, with the fact that he was profoundly dependent on and vulnerable to the responses of his subjects. He had to reconcile his need to appear "totally indifferent to newspaper gossip" with his need to devote so much energy to the reading of newspapers.

In an effort to deal with his political and personal dilemma, the Kaiser demonstrated an interest in swaying public opinion unprecedented for a hereditary monarch of his era.[44] Wilhelm sought to overcome his sense of helplessness in relation to his subjects by attempting to control their feelings and opinions through the press. As he stated so emphatically in his letter to the Tsar: "Public opinion wants clear information and leading." For if Kaiser and country were in fundamental agreement, Wilhelm was not confronted with the paradox of his political and personal dependence on popular support, since it was only when he and his subjects were out of step that the Kaiser realized that it was they and not he who set the pace. The fact that Wilhelm was sensitive and responsive to his subjects and tended to match his step to theirs does not mean that the Kaiser was without inner promptings, without ambitions and ideals of his own, that he never attempted to set his own pace. Rather, Wilhelm II was a man whose inner promptings propelled him in different directions, whose ambitions and ideals were incoherent, whose feet became entangled when he attempted to march on his own. For the most part Wilhelm, in his confusion about himself, relied upon his environment to direct his activities—an environment that included his entourage, his official political advisers, his relatives, his friends, the person with whom he had last spoken, the press and public opinion. Nevertheless, there were areas in which the Kaiser did have a sense of where he wanted to go. The most significant of these concerned England and the navy. Unlike Friedrich and Victoria, he could not function in opposition to the wishes of the German people. He lacked the political and psychological strength to accomplish that. Instead of disregarding public opinion as his parents had or simply adapting himself to it, Wilhelm sought to "lead" the Germans to adapt themselves to his attitude toward England and to his burning desire for naval construction. In this matter, as in several others that were important to him, Wilhelm sought, primarily through the press, to bring his subjects to his way of thinking and especially to his way of feeling.

In its crudest form, Wilhelm's "leading" of public opinion involved the effort to prevent the publication of articles he deemed inappropriate, inaccurate, or malicious. As he wrote to Nicholas II, it was necessary to correct "the foul and filthy lies" circulated by the press before they could corrupt the popular image of Wilhelm or of his policies. The Kaiser was particularly worried that foreign governments were manipulating public opinion in ways calculated to harm the Reich.[45] "Aha, agent provocateurs are among us and the Ruble has been at work on our press," Wilhelm scrawled on the report of the first secretary of the German Embassy in St. Petersburg, Heinrich von Tschirschky-Bögendorff, on Russian interest in the state of German public opinion in the fall of 1899. "Now these honest men want to observe the cuckoo eggs hatching that they have laid here! Therefore doubled vigilance over our press and every impertinent article against England must be squelched immediately!"[46] Wilhelm constantly put pressure on his ministers to suppress articles he deemed damaging to the domestic and especially to the foreign policies of the government. Thus, during the Boer War, after the *Dresdener Nachrichten* had published an article hostile to Britain and sympathetic to the Boers, Wilhelm ordered that the minister of the interior and of foreign affairs of the Kingdom of Saxony, Georg von Metsch-Reichenbach, "most urgently be reminded to keep his press in order and to reprimand the Dresdener Nachrichten. Since its conduct has a deleterious effect on relations with a great power with which we are on friendly terms!"[47] Despite his ability to suppress articles and prosecute "hostile" editors, Wilhelm was irritated that there were limits on the government's authority to censor the press.[48]

When it was not possible to prevent damaging articles from appearing, the Kaiser sought "energetically to correct" popular misconceptions by publishing government denials or bulletins in the two official press organs, the *Norddeutsche Allgemeine Zeitung* and *Wolffs Telegraphisches Bureau;* and by using leaks, friendly persuasion, or pressure to get his point of view expressed in papers sympathetic to the government.[49] In 1904, at the height of the Anglo-German naval race, Wilhelm reacted angrily to an article by Count Ernst von Reventlow in the *Münchner neueste Nachrichten* of 18 August 1904. The former naval officer turned journalist blamed the visit of a German naval squadron to Plymouth earlier in the year for contributing to the mood for naval increases in the British Parliament.[50] Since it had been Wilhelm's idea to have Edward VII invite the squadron to England, he was predictably outraged, writing in the margin of the article: "This impertinent boy needs a good spanking! Through the Norddeutsche."[51] Annoyed at the publication of articles in Germany critical of the English royal family, the Kaiser, in January 1902, ordered that with the forthcoming visit of the Prince of Wales "our press must in the last 8 days before his arrival print only amicable articles about his trip."[52] Not only was the prince to be spared embarrassment, but the German people were to share Wilhelm's enthusiasm for the visit. In general, during those periods when the Kaiser felt favorably disposed toward England, he sought to foster mutual goodwill on the part of the German and English people.[53] When articles friendly toward Germany were printed in the English newspapers, Wilhelm ordered that they be translated and reprinted with approving commentary in the German press, and he had government officials, academics, and journalists write articles (often under assumed names) expressing the myriad economic, cultural, diplomatic, and military advantages for Germany of closer ties with England.[54] Likewise, the Kaiser had Anglophile German articles distributed to the English papers.[55] And he urged English friends, such as Lord Lonsdale, "to inspire" Germanophile articles in the British press.[56] He encouraged organizations with vested interests in improved relations between the two countries, like the Hamburg Chamber of Commerce, to hold rallies and meetings to promote Anglo-German friendship.[57]

On several notable occasions the Kaiser attempted to manipulate public opinion through a press campaign discreetly orchestrated by the government. In 1895, for example, he sought both to use the government's press campaign against the socialists to strengthen the identification of his grandfather with the nation and to use his grandfather as an instrument to turn the German people against social democracy. He instructed the chancellor to order the minister of the interior, Ernst Matthias von Köller, to continue the press campaign against the socialists with unremitting vigor. "The point to be emphasized over and over again in these debates," the Kaiser telegraphed Chancellor Hohenlohe on 31 August 1895, "must be the personality of Kaiser Wilhelm the Great. Each and every depreciation of his memory, criticism of his person or of his deeds must be presented as an insult to the entire nation, which, through skillful management, should be brought to rise up itself in defense of the old gentleman or to demand that the government do so."[58] On the one hand, the press campaign would serve the causes of dynasty and national unity. The nation was to be identified with Kaiser Wilhelm I and, through him, with the Hohenzollern dynasty. Wilhelm's attempt to tie Reich and monarchy together through the campaign against social democracy can be seen as part of his ongoing effort to glorify his grandfather and to use him as a symbol that could strengthen German national identity. On the other hand, the press campaign would also attack social democracy. Not only was national sentiment to be mobilized against international socialism but a personal symbol, a revered—and, it should be added, a deceased and hence relatively inviolable—personality was to be used as a weapon against an abstract ideology.

Although the Kaiser's "leading" of public opinion is not in evidence, his interest in doing so is reflected in one of the most closely studied and hotly debated events in the history of Imperial Germany: the so-called *"Kriegsrat"* or "war council" of 8 December 1912.[59] Despite the time and energy historians have devoted to the *Kriegsrat* in the effort to assess responsibility for the outbreak of the First World War, comparatively little attention has been focused on the extensive discussion of press and public opinion at the meeting. According to the diary of Admiral Georg Alexander von Müller, chief of the Naval Cabinet, the conference, attended only by the leaders of Germany's armed forces, opened with an appraisal of the international situation by the Kaiser in which he asserted that a war between Russia and Austria, which he regarded as inevitable, would also make war for Germany unavoidable. Thereupon the chief of the General Staff, Helmuth von Moltke, made the oft-quoted statement: "I regard a war to be inevitable and the sooner the better." Moltke continued immediately: "We should, however, prepare better through the press for the popularity of a war against Russia in the sense of His Majesty's presentation." According to Müller's diary, the Kaiser confirmed Moltke's suggestion and "ordered the State S[ecretary in the Reich Naval Office, Admiral von Tirpitz] also to use his press resources to work in this same direction."[60] After the meeting Müller sent the following message to Chancellor Theobald von Bethmann Hollweg:

> During a consideration of the military-political situation, H.R.H. ordered that through the press the people are to be enlightened as to the great national interest that Germany, too, has at stake in a war emerging out of the Austro-Serbian conflict. The people should not be placed in the position at the outbreak of a great European war of having to ask themselves what are the interests that Germany has to fight for in this war. The people must rather already have been made familiar with the idea of such a war beforehand.[61]

To be sure, German governments had sought to prepare their citizens for war before 1914 or 1912.[62] Particularly when war demanded national mobilization, logic suggested that steps be taken beforehand to secure popular support for the war effort. Today it is axiomatic that public opinion is a factor of decisive political and military significance—and not only in democratic countries. And yet, in 1912, in the German *Kaiserreich*, with a sovereign theoretically accountable to God, at the crucial moment when the question of war or peace, of *"sein oder nicht sein,"* was being debated and perhaps decided, the leaders of Germany, the military and naval leaders and their commander-in-chief, were centrally concerned with German press and public opinion. That fact is attributable not only to the importance that press and public opinion had assumed in modern life but also to the recognition of that importance, indeed the preoccupation with it, by the sovereign theoretically accountable to God.

It is no accident that the two key advisers who were put in place in 1897 to execute the Kaiser's personal regime, Bernhard von Bülow and Alfred von Tirpitz, were keenly aware of the important role that press and public opinion had come to play in German politics. Under their direction, the Foreign Office and the Reich Naval Office devoted considerable time and energy to monitoring and controlling public opinion as it was reflected in the press.[63] The two state secretaries also had able assistants who were responsible for the day-to-day management of press policy. Otto Hammann directed the press bureau in the Foreign Office; Captain Alfred von Heeringen, the press bureau in the Reich Naval Office.[64] All four of these advisers belonged to a new, post-Bismarckian generation of leaders. In their sensitivity to public opinion as it was reflected in the press and in their skill at manipulating public opinion through the press, they were indeed the Kaiser's men.

The effort to engender popular support for a policy or position of the Kaiser by influencing the press and organizing public demonstrations found its clearest and most effective expression in the propaganda campaign directed by Wilhelm II and Admiral Tirpitz to create widespread enthusiasm for the development of the navy. Although both sought to mobilize the German people in support of naval expansion, each understood the purpose of the navy and the campaign on its behalf differently.[65] Whereas Tirpitz sought to manipulate public opinion in order to achieve relatively well-defined political objectives, the Kaiser's approach in attempting to influence his subjects was less calculated and more emotional. At heart he was motivated by the need to make them feel what he himself experienced: they were to share and affirm his enthusiasm for the navy.

That the Kaiser's efforts at "leading" public opinion were ultimately designed to create political and emotional identity between Wilhelm and the Germans is revealed by his order of early February 1896 that an article in the English newspaper *The Speaker* be translated and printed in the German press. The article was a critical account of the British campaign against the Ashanti in West Africa. It concluded with the statement: "The most powerful nation in the world had crushed a naked African savage, and had celebrated its victory by treating him, his family, and his envoys considerably worse than it would have ventured to treat a party of pickpockets." To this passage, Wilhelm had written in English in the margin "as it treats everybody."[66]

At first glance it seems incomprehensible that the Kaiser would want this article, on a subject apparently irrelevant to German concerns, circulated throughout the country. Wilhelm's reaction to the article and his desire that it be reprinted becomes understandable, however, in the context of the events following the Krüger telegram. On 3 January 1896, a month before the Kaiser's order regarding the article in *The Speaker,* Wilhelm had sent a telegram to President Paul Krüger of the South African Republic congratulating him on the Boer defeat of a band of British irregulars led by Leander Starr Jameson. The publication of the Kaiser's telegram produced a storm of anti-German feeling in England. Wilhelm was personally criticized by his English relatives and condemned in the British press. There were calls for an anti-German alliance between England and her traditional enemies, France and Russia. Wilhelm was unprepared for the British reaction. He felt hurt and angry and even feared that, because Germany did not possess a powerful navy, the English might be planning a surprise attack. Wilhelm felt vulnerable and, as his marginalia to *The Speaker* indicates, treated with contempt by "the most powerful nation in the world," a phrase Wilhelm had underlined in the article. At such a time it was especially important for the Kaiser to have the support of his subjects. By exposing his subjects to *The Speaker* article about the Ashanti campaign, he hoped that their reaction would mirror his. If the Germans could share his experience of being treated with disdain, they might also conclude that only a mighty navy could bring England to accept and respect Germany as a world power.

CHAPTER 7

On the Imperial Stage

I

Wilhelm's craving for approval and his ability to adapt in order to get it gave him the incentive and the capacity to play roles he sensed his subjects wanted him to perform.[1] Three years into the Kaiser's reign, the Portuguese diplomat and author Jose Maria Eça de Queiroz wrote of him:

> In this sovereign what a variety of incarnations of Royalty! One day he is a Soldier-King, rigid, stiff in helmet and cuirass . . . regarding the drill-sergeant as the fundamental unity of the nation. . . . Suddenly he strips off the uniform and dons the workman's overalls; he is the Reform-King . . . determined to go down in history embracing the proletariat as a brother whom he has set free. Then all unaware he becomes the King by Divine Right . . . convinced of his infallibility, driving over the frontiers all who do not devotedly believe in him. . . . [Then he becomes the] Courtier-King, worldly, pompous, thinking only of the brilliancy and sumptuosity of etiquette. . . . The world smiles and presto! he becomes the Modern King . . . treating the past as bigoted . . . regarding the factory as the supreme temple, dreaming of Germany as worked entirely by electricity.[2]

This versatile theatricality, when coupled with his broadly based education and ability to grasp and retain vast amounts of information, enabled the Kaiser, in private as in public, to engage his subjects in an immediate and individual way.[3] Although he recognized that "the Kaiser's solicitude was not free of solicitation," Walther Rathenau found that Wilhelm's "conversation had substance, his question showed genuine concern. He empathized, he spoke differently with each person."[4] As a result, Wilhelm could relate to a wide range of people and converse intelligently with them about their interests and activities. Presenting himself to his subjects in a variety of occupational roles, the Kaiser was composer, painter, art historian, anthropologist, archeologist, historian, theologian, engineer, military strategist, sea captain, naval architect, uniform designer, businessman. He had the capacity, it seemed, to be all things to all people.

Similarly in his countless, usually unprepared, public speeches, Wilhelm, impelled by the need to win popular acclaim, was able to establish an identity of outlook with a wide range of audiences. Given his love of speaking, his excellent memory and presence of mind, his gift for the stirring phrase and the heroic pose, the Kaiser, as even his critics conceded, was an impressive orator. "Nowhere else," Rathenau observed, "did his heraldic sensibilities, his Wagnerian apparatus strike so precisely the nerve of the Prusso-mechanical population as in his speeches which . . . almost always were delivered to those of a like mind."[5] What enabled Wilhelm to reach audiences drawn from every region of the country and every social class was not what he said but how he said it. As the historian Karl Lamprecht described one of Wilhelm's speeches: "A full, sonorous voice flowed wide and wider throughout the enormous room, and before long there commenced an ever more lively play of expressions, a gesticulation that rose to the point of fullest activity. The Kaiser was a speaker from head to toe. . . . What did the content matter, then?"[6]

Like his travels through Germany, which gave his subjects the opportunity to see him face to face, the diversity of his interests and "the variety of his incarnations of royalty" strengthened the link between ruler and subject and intensified the Germans' sense that the Kaiser represented them personally.[7] Nevertheless, the fact that Wilhelm played a great many parts does not mean that his performances were equally successful. The "Soldier King" was certainly one of Wilhelm's favorite and most effective parts, surpassed only perhaps by his enactment of the "Sailor King." As reflected in his bourgeois occupational roles and fascination with and friendship for wealthy businessmen, the Kaiser was also successful in representing the interests, attitudes, and aspirations of the German middle classes. Indeed, in his very versatility Wilhelm can be seen as embodying the new breed of Wilhelmian German, the aggressive bourgeois parvenu, who regarded versatility to be an essential attribute of the modern, successful man.[8] Although Eça de Queiroz described the Kaiser in workman's overalls, the "Reform King" was not one of Wilhelm's better parts, however. Conspicuously absent from the professions adopted by the Kaiser were those of the working class. Perhaps because he had not been exposed to working-class influences during the course of his development, Wilhelm was comparatively unsuccessful in understanding, articulating, or embodying the ideals and aspirations of the German proletariat, despite his conciliatory policy toward labor in the first years of the reign.[9]

Reflecting the fact that his adaptability was a manifestation of instability, a response to insecurity, and a consequence of his exposure to incongruous influences early in life, Wilhelm could not maintain or integrate his incarnations of royalty; his knowledge lacked depth, his interests proved ephemeral. Although his versatility was impressive, those who knew Wilhelm recognized him to be a dilettante. According to his longtime chief of the Naval Cabinet, Admiral Georg Alexander von Müller: "No thoughtful observer from this period can be in any doubt that the Kaiser understood much, very much very superficially, that he was very self-absorbed and believed that he could give judgments about things that he actually neither could nor needed to make judgments about."[10]

For Wilhelm, success was measured in flamboyant display, not substantive achievement. Thus, as commander during the fall maneuvers in 1893, the Kaiser sacrificed significance for spectacle. Count Bogdan Hutten-Czapski noted that the grand cavalry attack designed and directed by Wilhelm "certainly offered the spectators a splendid picture but was sharply criticized at home and abroad as a piece of worthless military theater." Count Alfred von Schlieffen, judge of the maneuvers, was placed in an uncomfortable position since he could not praise the Kaiser's assault and yet felt unable to criticize Wilhelm who was so obviously pleased with his performance.[11] After many years experience with the Kaiser, the British statesman, Sir Edward Grey, was convinced that Wilhelm's versatility was a sign not of strength but of weakness. Reginald Viscount Esher noted in his diary in 1908 that Grey "is not an admirer of the German Emperor. He thinks him not quite sane, and very superficial. This has always been my opinion. That he is picturesque, and has a certain gift of language, is true, but he is not 'a consistent or persistent thinker.'"[12]

In *Der Untertan,* Heinrich Mann's brilliant satire of Wilhelmian Germany, Wilhelm II was presented as an actor presiding over a generation of actors which together with the Kaiser produced history that was theater.[13] Writing between 1912 and 1914, Mann concluded that despite all the fanfare, the celebration and the criticism, Wilhelm II had actually accomplished little during his reign. He had achieved few real successes for his admirers to applaud, and he had committed few real crimes for his detractors to denounce. Both the Kaiser's celebrants and critics fastened on his utterances, and directed their admiration or their indignation at his performances on the imperial stage.[14] At one point in *Der Untertan,* Wolfgang Buck, a character in the novel recognizing the artificial, absurd, and destructive nature of Wilhelmian Germany, told Diederich Hessling, Mann's quintessential Wilhelmian German:

> "I suppose you do not know whom history will designate as the representative type of this era?"
> "The Emperor," said Diederich.
> "No," Buck replied. "The actor."[15]

II

In keeping with his theatricality, the Kaiser made dramatic use of symbols in communicating with his subjects. As with his appreciation of the significance of press and public opinion, Wilhelm sensed the power of symbolic communication with his subjects because symbols affected him so powerfully. For the Kaiser, symbols were not symbolic. They were tangible and enduring expressions of recognition that could at least momentarily satisfy his constant need for reassurance. On a personal level, the many honors and titles he bestowed on others and were bestowed on him were not mere formalities but important statements of appreciation. Politically, the state visits and the obligatory decorations and tributes exchanged between heads of state did not merely represent the state of relations between countries, but, like public opinion on which they exerted so much influence, themselves determined the state of relations between countries.[16] Although seven years had elapsed since the conclusion of a formal alliance between France and Russia, Wilhelm's fear of the two countries became most acute during the Tsar's visit to France in 1901, and he demanded that more forts be built along the Rhine, more garrisons be sent to Posen and West Prussia, and the size of the German navy be increased.[17] In the same way, the Kaiser regarded the cancelation of Edward VII's visit to Berlin in June 1908 as a portent of war. He vehemently denied Edward Grey's assertion that his uncle sought to preserve peace: "Wrong! He wants war! Only someone else is to wage it for him, and I am to instigate it so that he does not have to bear the odium!"[18]

As with Wilhelm's preoccupation with press and public opinion, the Kaiser's advisers could not understand the importance he attached to what seemed insignificant symbolic gestures.[19] Regarding it not as a formal honor but as a commission of political and military significance, Wilhelm reacted with pleasure and excitement at being made an English field marshal.[20] After Queen Victoria had made him an admiral in the Royal Navy in 1889, Wilhelm told Bismarck that "he now had the opportunity and right to intervene directly in the construction, organization, and administration of the English Fleet."[21] And intervene the Kaiser did—to the dismay of his advisers and the indignation of the British.[22]

Wilhelm's interventions, although designed to reduce political tension, usually had the opposite effect, like that produced by his letter to the first lord of the British Admiralty, Edward Tweedmouth, in February 1908. It came at the critical moment during the Anglo-German naval rivalry when the British Admiralty was to submit its estimates on German naval construction during Parliament's consideration of the naval budget. In a private letter the Kaiser assured Lord Tweedmouth that Germany intended no challenge to British naval supremacy. He complained that the Admiralty estimates about the German navy as they had been reported in the newspapers were erroneous, and he justified his direct involvement in this sensitive matter by virtue of the fact that his letter was written "by one who is proud to wear the British Naval Uniform of an Admiral of the Fleet, which was conferred on him by the late great Queen of blessed memory."[23] Wilhelm had not informed Chancellor Bülow, Secretary of State in the Foreign Office Baron Wilhelm von Schoen, or Secretary of State in the Naval Office Tirpitz about his letter, and they were appalled when they learned of the Kaiser's action.[24] As rumors of the letter's existence spread, the German press became alarmed. The *B.Z. am Mittag* of 6 March 1908 expressed concern that Wilhelm did not appreciate sufficiently that even the private correspondence of a crowned head of state had the potential to do political damage. The article concluded: "Indeed, the suspicion cannot be repressed that the Tweedmouth letter is real and that it is but the newest link in a chain of our Kaiser's *impulsive actions.*" The British press reacted with anger and suspicion. *The Times* was uncertain neither about the existence of the letter nor about its significance: "If there was any doubt before about the meaning of the German naval expansion, none can remain after an attempt of this kind to influence the minister responsible for our navy in a direction favourable to German interests, an attempt, in other words, to make it more easy for German preparations to overtake our own." The paper concluded: "If the complimentary title of Admiral of the Fleet is held to warrant a foreign Potentate in interfering in our domestic affairs by secret appeals to the head of a department on which the national safety depends, the abolition of dynastic compliments of this kind is an urgent necessity."[25] When the German ambassador in London, Paul von Metternich, reported British outrage to Berlin and expressed his concern that the letter would increase tension and mistrust between the two countries, the Kaiser reacted with disbelief. "I do not share Metternich's fears," he wrote in the margin of the ambassador's telegram. "The English have not yet become so totally crazy."[26] Still smarting from his uncle Edward VII's rebuke that the letter to Tweedmouth represented "a new departure," Wilhelm could only attribute *The Times'* editorial to the king, "who is worried that the letter makes such a calming impression."[27]

Many of the Kaiser's actions ostensibly serving political purposes were primarily symbolic statements of grandeur and importance. His notorious "Hun" speech in 1900, his dramatic alliance with the Tsar at Björkö in 1905, and his messianic journey to the Middle East in late 1898, to cite three examples, were theatrical epics whose political significance was limited to the negative reaction they produced in foreign capitals. Wilhelm's ostentatious demonstrations of German military, diplomatic, and cultural authority can be understood psychologically in several different ways. In the first place, they may have served a defensive function for the Kaiser. The bellicose statements, the bold political initiatives, the heroic journeys were, from this perspective, attempts to mask Wilhelm's chronic insecurity. That, at least, was Bülow's interpretation. "The Kaiser," he wrote in his memoirs, "through loud speeches and strong words sought to deceive others and himself about his inner uncertainty and anxiousness."[28] The exaggerated bellicosity of Wilhelm's speech of 27 July 1900 to the German troops embarking for China during the Boxer Rebellion appears to confirm Bülow's hypothesis. The Kaiser urged his men to avenge the murder of the German envoy in Peking:

Show yourselves Christians, happily enduring in the face of the heathens! May Honour and Fame attend your colours and arms! Give the world an example of virility and discipline! . . . *Anyone who falls into your hands falls to your sword!* Just as the Huns under their King Etzel created for themselves a thousand years ago a name which men still respect, you should give the name of German such cause to be remembered in China for a thousand years that no Chinaman, no matter whether his eyes be slit or not, will dare to look a German in the face.[29]

It can also be argued that Wilhelm simply lacked the unity of purpose to for-mulate clear-cut policies and the inner strength to tolerate the tension and uncertainty that accompany the realization of distant political objectives. The Kaiser could only produce sudden bursts of dramatic action designed to effect immediate political change. And yet it seems likely that on the deepest level the political displays were yet another manifestation of Wilhelm II's need for recognition. That these theatrical performances were ultimately designed to attract attention and elicit admiration, to give the Kaiser epochal significance, and to portray himself as fulfilling a divine mission is revealed by his letter to Bülow of 25 July 1905 in which he described how he had secured the Tsar's signature on the Björkö treaty.

The Kaiser recounted that, after brooding for several days on how best to serve Germany and the monarchical principle, he finally raised his "hands to the Lord who reigns over all of us, and entrusted everything to Him." Praying that "He direct and lead me where He will," Wilhelm vowed to make himself "simply a tool in His hands," determined to "do whatever He asks of me no matter how difficult the task." Thereupon the Kaiser's "will and resolve became ever firmer and directed"; he would "'carry it through no matter what the cost'!" Wilhelm proudly related how he had chosen the most propitious moment to present the Tsar with his proposal for a Russo-German alliance. As Nicholas read the document, the Kaiser, looking out across the water to the royal yacht, saw "the Imperial Standard on her fluttering in the morning breeze. I was just reading the words 'God with us' inscribed upon its black cross when I heard the voice of the Tsar say next to me 'that is quite excellent. I quite agree'!" After both rulers had signed, Wilhelm's "eyes filled with shining tears of joy," sweat streamed down his back, and he felt the spirits of his ancestors close at hand. He concluded his letter to Bülow: "Thus has the morning of 25 July 1905 off Björkö been a turning point in European history, thanks to the grace of God. The situation of my dear Fatherland has been greatly relieved as it now will be freed from the terrible grip of the Franco-Russian vice."[30] We shall never know, of course, what actually transpired at Björkö or whether Wilhelm actually experienced the divine aura he described in his letter to Bülow written later in the day. What can be clearly discerned in Wilhelm's letter, how-ever, is his attempt to impress Bülow, to convince the chancellor, himself, and, ultimately no doubt, all of humanity of his world-historical significance.

Wilhelm's assessment of Björkö proved mistaken, however, and the treaty was quickly scuttled by the two governments—each recognizing that it simply was not compatible with either the Russian or the German national interest. In fact, Bülow, whom Wilhelm had hoped to impress, threatened to resign should the Kaiser insist on the treaty's validity. On this occasion, as on others when his performances miscarried or were misunderstood, the Kaiser reacted with surprise, anger, anxiety, and depression. Kuno von Moltke reported to Bülow that the Kaiser had "completely lost possession of himself." "He now not only fears that Russia will turn against him but also expects an English attack." According to Moltke, Wilhelm's "initial excitement was soon followed by a deep depression and physical exhaustion. . . . He sits at his desk with an unhappy expression, drops of sweat forming on his brow. He is very pale." The adjutant feared a "complete collapse."[31]

Moltke brought a second letter from Wilhelm for the chancellor whose melodramatic pathos offers a counterpoint to the melodramatic grandiloquence of his earlier communication. He had assumed, the Kaiser wrote, that Bülow would welcome his actions since "it has always been my aim to pave the way for you, to help you. . . . I had thought that I was working for you and that I had accomplished something special. And then you send me a few cool lines and your resignation!!! Allow me then to tell you of my mental condition, my dear Bülow. To be treated in this way by my best, my most intimate friend . . . has given me such a dreadful shock that I have completely fallen apart, and must now fear a serious nervous breakdown!" Although refusing to concede that the treaty had been a mistake, Wilhelm agreed to Bülow's demands. Convinced that he had scored a great personal triumph and unprepared for the rejection of the treaty, Wilhelm's confidence in himself and in his judgment was shaken. At a time when his dependence on others for direction had been so dramatically demonstrated, the Kaiser became frightened at the prospect of losing his chancellor's advice and support. As he would seek to use his "collapse" after Harden's acquittal to avoid traveling to England in 1907, he now threatened Bülow with nervous breakdown, even suicide, to keep him at his post. "I call upon your friendship for me and ask you never again to let me hear anymore about your intention to resign. Telegraph your response to this letter that it is 'Allright!' [sic], then I will know that you will remain! Because the morning after you request your resignation will find the Kaiser *no longer alive!* Think of my poor wife and children. W."[32] Bülow withdrew his resignation.

Perhaps Wilhelm's most grandiose symbolic action was his pilgrimage to Palestine in 1898, during which he variously presented himself as the representative of German Protestants and of Christians generally and as the eternal friend of the three hundred million Moslems of the Ottoman Empire.[33] In a poem in *Simplicissimus* entitled "In the Holy Land," Frank Wedekind, under the pseudonym "Hieronymous," satirized the Kaiser's messianic self-display. The last two verses read:

So therefore welcome once again,
And let us consecrate to you our reverence most great,
Since from the Holy Land you've removed the stain,
Of your not having visited to date.
Millions of Christians with pride you fill;
Likewise too Golgotha's hill,
That once from the Cross the final word
From you today the first has heard.

Mankind's thirst for deeds can thus be quenched,
But to admire is its thirst immense.
Since you are able both to slake,
Be it in uniform for tropic clime,

In sailor's suit or purple cape,
In rococo costume of silk most fine,
In hunting dress or sports' attire,
Welcome to the Holy Land most noble Sire![34]

The poem appeared in an issue of the magazine entitled "Palestine." The title page by the artist Thomas Theodor Heine depicted the ghosts of two medieval crusaders in Palestine, Gottfried von Bouillon and a derisive Friedrich Barbarossa, looking at a pith helmet. The caption beneath the picture read: "Gottfried von Bouillon: 'Don't laugh so scornfully, Barbarossa! After all, our crusades had no purpose either.'"[35] As a result of Wedekind's poem and Heine's title page, the "Palestine" issue of *Simplicissimus* was confiscated and its editor Albert Langen, Heine, and the unknown author of the poem were charged with lese majesty. Langen fled into exile only to return to Munich in 1903 after paying a fine of thirty thousand gold marks. Heine was sentenced to six months' fortress detention. And once his identity had been discovered, Wedekind, having briefly fled the country himself, was sentenced to seven months' detention.[36] The government's harsh response to the authors of the "Palestine" issue testifies not only to the effectiveness of their satire and to Wilhelm II's personal vulnerability to criticism. The confiscation and the indictments also reflect the susceptibility of the Kaiser's symbolic leadership to parody. The epics performed upon the imperial stage could survive opposition, but their symbolic effect was destroyed when the performer was made to seem ludicrous.

III

While with the Kaiser on board the royal yacht in 1903, Philipp Eulenburg wrote Bülow that Wilhelm's tendency "to regard and to evaluate *all* things and *all* people solely from a personal point of view" was becoming increasingly obvious. "Objectivity is lost completely," he continued, "and subjectivity rides on a biting and stamping charger." Thus, according to Eulenburg, the failure of the German South Pole expedition was a personal humiliation for the Kaiser: "With his tendency to take everything personally, the poor man experiences this expedition as an *insult,* and material is being collected in order to crush the unfortunate and utterly blameless Professor [Erich von] Drygalski," the expedition leader.[37] Identifying with the fortunes of the nation he led, Wilhelm was "crushed" by the failure of an expedition he had anticipated would enhance German national pride and, by extension, his own self-esteem.[38] In the same way, ten years later, Wilhelm attributed delays in completing the construction of the steamer *Imperator* to the fact that "the chaps have held a big strike so that the ship would not be finished for *my* trip. It was arranged by the Reds [*Sozen*] as a personal insult to me." A mechanical failure marring the vessel's test run was attributed to the fact "that the Reds have thrown a boothook into the turbine in order to ruin *my* ship that bears my title."[39]

Wilhelm's rearing subjectivity was not without impact on the policies of the government of the Reich. When by 1894 it had become clear that the policy of social welfare introduced by Wilhelm at the beginning of his reign had failed to either reverse socialist electoral successes or reduce labor unrest, the Kaiser denounced his working-class subjects as ingrates who had failed to appreciate the benevolence of their sovereign. Experiencing the socialist votes and the industrial strikes as a personal affront, Wilhelm decided to abandon his policy of conciliation toward the proletariat in favor of coercion. He instructed Chancellor General Leo von Caprivi to prepare anti-socialist legislation similar to that sought by Bismarck in 1890. Like Bismarck, the Kaiser was prepared to suspend the constitution should the Reichstag fail to pass the legislation. What in 1890 had been grounds for Bismarck's dismissal now led to the resignation of his successor, when Caprivi refused to countenance the draconian measures favored by the Kaiser. Although the anti-socialist legislation was put in abeyance and the plan for a coup d'état dropped, Wilhelm's abandonment of his policy of social welfare in the fall of 1894 was a direct result of the Kaiser's sense that his subjects had rejected him.[40]

The Kaiser's tendency "to take everything personally" also influenced the functioning of government. Anyone who has glanced through the published political correspondence of this period will be astonished at the amount of time and energy devoted by the Kaiser, his chancellors, and advisers to what was known as *Personalpolitik,* their absorption with personal matters and matters of personnel.[41] Of course personality always plays a role in political life, but the conclusion seems unescapable that the concern of the leaders of Wilhelmian Germany with promotion, scandal, and intrigue at the expense of policy analysis and political debate was extraordinary.[42] Even without access to the voluminous correspondence of the ruling elite, contemporaries aptly characterized the atmosphere within the government as Byzantine. To a considerable extent the prominence of *Personalpolitik* can be attributed to the structure of Wilhelmian government. Given what Hans-Ulrich Wehler has called the "polycracy of competing centers of power" and the absence of a readily discernible hierarchy of authority, it was logical that personal influence should have played an important role in political discourse and activity.[43] The fact that an emperor theoretically possessing final authority presided over this system increased the degree to which political life within the Wilhelmian government was personalized. Indeed, a degree of complexity and confusion was built into the power structure in order to preserve the sovereign's authority and freedom of action.[44] That the sovereign was Wilhelm II only increased the role played by personality in the functioning of government. Thus, even without significant formal authority, a crucially placed individual like Philipp Eulenburg was able through his friendship with the Kaiser and his personal connections to place his friends in the key positions of power and impress himself firmly on the course of German history.[45] Individuals favored by the Kaiser, such as Waldersee, Eulenburg, and Bülow, rose to positions of great power, and, when they had managed to offend Wilhelm, fell from both imperial favor and political office.[46]

The Kaiser's tendency to understand politics in terms of personalities was even more obviously manifest in his foreign policy. In part because of their personal authority, in part because of their impact on public opinion, the Kaiser believed other leaders and especially other sovereigns to be politically decisive.[47] He was convinced that their policies, like his own, were determined primarily by personal considerations. Thus, in March 1907, Wilhelm was sure that Edward VII, motivated by hatred of his nephew, was "intriguing" against him throughout Europe. Georges Clemenceau himself, the Kaiser asserted, had told the German ambassador in Paris that he feared English efforts to foment war between France and Germany. "In other countries, however," Zedlitz reported Wilhelm to say, "the King was working with equal diligence against him. Actually the entire press, including the American press, had been manipulated against him with English money. It is unbelievable how much personal hatred is manifested in the conduct of his uncle." "He is a Satan," Wilhelm concluded, "one cannot believe how much of a Satan he is."[48] Two years later the Kaiser again attributed Anglo-German tension to the animosity of his uncle toward him, and he therefore defined as the aim of German foreign policy: "Stop the King! That is now our most urgent task."[49]

Consistent with his personalized view of politics, Wilhelm regarded countries as if they were living, breathing, and above all emotional individuals.[50] From this perspective, policies were the organized expression of feeling, and it was the duty of the leader to pursue a course compatible not with the national interest but with the national character. In conducting foreign policy the statesman was confronted with the task of reconciling the feelings of his own people with the feelings of foreign peoples. In a discussion with Joseph Chamberlain in late November 1899, the Kaiser described the national character of the Germans and advised the British colonial minister on how best to deal with them. Bülow reported the contents of this conversation to Holstein:

> His Majesty added that it would be to the advantage of the English to treat the sensitive, obstinate and rather sentimental Germans with caution, not to make them impatient, but to show them goodwill in little things. The German is "touchy." The more this fact is borne in mind on the English side, the more useful it will be for the relationship between the two countries.[51]

It is striking and significant that the Kaiser's description of the Germans was a description of himself. Thus, he experienced blows to German national pride as blows to his own self-esteem. Upon learning that two German missionaries had been murdered in China in 1897, Wilhelm demanded reprisals "that, with total severity and if necessary with the most brutal disregard for the Chinese people, would finally demonstrate that the German Emperor will not allow himself to be trifled with and that it is ill-advised to have him for an enemy."[52] Wilhelm ordered that Germany occupy Kiaochou as compensation for the murders. "Hundreds of German businessmen," the Kaiser telegraphed Bülow, "will exult in the knowledge that the German Reich has finally secured a foothold for itself in Asia. Hundreds of thousands of Chinese will tremble when they feel the mailed fist of the German Reich pushing down on their necks.

And the entire German nation will rejoice that its government has done such a manly deed." He concluded: "May the world once and for all learn the lesson that my motto is: 'Nemo me impune lacessit.'"[53] By the same token, for Wilhelm, insults to him were insults to the nation. According to Bülow, he regarded the possible cancelation of the visit of the Prince of Wales to Germany in 1902 "as a slight directed against Him personally," and he threatened "to recall the German Ambassador in London."[54]

Wilhelm's letter to Queen Victoria of 22 May 1899, in which he denounced the British prime minister, Lord Salisbury, for his treatment of Germany over Samoa captures perhaps as well as any single document Wilhelm II's conception of politics and foreign policy. Although the Berlin Act of 1889 had provided for joint supervision of Samoa by Britain, Germany, and the United States, tension over the islands continued. The crisis that provoked the Kaiser's letter to his grandmother grew out of a conflict involving various Samoan factions and the three Western powers over the successor to the king of Samoa who had died in August 1898. With Germany backing one of the candidates for the throne and Britain and the United States another, civil war broke out, during which British and American naval forces became involved. At one point in the fighting, the German consulate in the capital Apia was struck by an American naval barrage, and plantations on the islands owned by German nationals were damaged.[55]

German press and public opinion were aroused by these events, and when Queen Victoria wrote her grandson on 18 May 1899, Wilhelm took the opportunity of his reply to vent his anger over the conduct of Lord Salisbury in the Samoan affair.[56] The importance the Kaiser ascribed to press and public opinion, the importance he attached to symbolic action, his understanding of politics as the play of personalities, his blurring of the distinction between himself and his nation, his tendency to attribute political tension between states not to conflicting self-interest but to hurt feelings, all are expressed in his letter to his grandmother. Specifically and most significantly perhaps, the letter reveals that the guiding principle of Wilhelm II's conduct of foreign policy was not political but psychological: namely, the need to uphold the honor of the German nation and of the German Kaiser. Indeed, Wilhelm's anger and, according to him, that of his subjects was not occasioned so much by the fact that Britain had sided with the United States in the question of the Samoan succession or even by the naval bombardment of the German installation and plantations. Instead it was Salisbury's failure to respond promptly to a German proposal for a resolution of the Samoan crisis and even more his failure to express regret over the damage done to German property that so outraged Wilhelm and his subjects.[57]

"I think it is my duty to point out," the Kaiser wrote, "that public feeling has been very much agitated, and stirred to its depths by the most unhappy way in which L[or]d Salisbury has treated Germany in the Samoan business." This, after all the actions he, Wilhelm, had taken to improve Anglo-German relations in recent months, including: the Anglo-German agreement over the disposition of Portugal's colonies in southern Africa in August 1898, signed by the German government over the opposition of colonial circles; the military demonstration at Waterlooplatz in Hannover in September 1898 where the Kaiser had announced the British victory over the Dervishes at Omduram and had led the assembled troops in a cheer for the queen of England; his visit to Malta in November 1898 which "was a sign of affectionate interest in your fleet and your Flag, of which I am so proud to be an Admiral"; and, finally, in the face of a hostile German public, his reception of Cecil Rhodes in Berlin in March 1899.[58] With the exception of the colonial agreement with Britain, none of these actions can be described as possessing political substance. Instead, they were symbolic statements, which for Wilhelm were significant demonstrations, undertaken by him at the risk of public disfavor in Germany, of his respect and appreciation for the British nation and the British people. For the Kaiser these symbolic statements were the stuff with which effective foreign policy was made; for Lord Salisbury they were evidently empty gestures. And in return for what the Kaiser deemed courageous and important acts of friendship, the prime minister treated Germany with gross lack of civility and respect. An out-raged German public was the result:

> This way of treating Germany's feelings and interests has come upon the People like an electric shock and has evoked the impression that L[ord] S[alisbury] cares for us no more than for Portugal, Chili [sic] or the Patagonians, and out of this impression the feeling has arisen that Germany was being despised by his Government, and this has stung my subjects to the quick. This fact is looked at as a taint to national honour and to their feelings of selfrespect. Therefore I am most sorry to have to state that popular feeling is very bitter on England just now, and . . . it is the same with the simple people as with their Princes, it is unanimous.

Unless Salisbury ended his "highhanded treatment of Germany," Wilhelm continued, "bad blood" between the two countries would inevitably result. The Kaiser was particularly distressed because all his work

> to make the two countries understand each other and respect each others [sic] wishes and aspirations, was destroyed by one blow by the highhanded disdainful treatment of ministers who have never even come over to stay in or to study Germany, and hardly have taken the trouble to try to understand her People! . . . And all that on account of a stupid Island which is a hair-pin to England compared to the thousands of Square miles she is annexing right and left every year unopposed.

According to Wilhelm there was a simple solution to the Samoan tangle and to the Anglo-German antagonism of which it was a part.[59] "The Government of L[ord] S[alisbury] must learn to respect and to treat us as equals; as long as he cannot be brought to do that, Germany's People will always remain dis-trustful and a sort of coolness will be the unavoidable result."[60]

It was the fundamental aim of Wilhelm II's foreign policy that the German Reich and the German Kaiser be treated with "respect" and "as equals" by the other European powers, especially by Britain with its world empire. Despite the efforts of the Kaiser's advisers to wrap it in the rational interest of state, the realization of this essentially emotional objective underlay not only Wilhelm's foreign policy but also, to a not insignificant degree, that of the Reich. The Kaiser was right to see Samoa as essentially irrelevant to Germany from an economic, strategic, or political point of view. The relevance of Samoa to the Reich lay, as Wilhelm expressed it in his letter to his grandmother, in the realm of national prestige and public opinion.[61] The rise in the Anglo-German antagonism during Wilhelm II's reign must be ascribed in part to the differing conceptualizations of foreign policy so clearly manifest in the Kaiser's letter to the queen and in her angry response of 12 June 1899 in which she expressed astonishment and outrage at Wilhelm's letter and in Lord Salisbury's accompanying memorandum in which he described the Kaiser's complaints as "quite unintelligible."[62] To be sure, national pride motivated British foreign policy, and the rational interest of state motivated the foreign policy of the German Empire. And yet, on balance, it would seem that the British subordinated national pride to the rational interests of state more often than did the Germans and that, as in the Samoan affair, the Germans subordinated the rational interests of state to national pride more often than did the British. Perhaps Wilhelm II was right to attribute the rise in the Anglo-German antagonism to misunderstanding and ignorance. Even beyond the fact that Britain possessed a world empire and Germany only aspired to do so, to a significant degree the foreign policies of the two countries had different priorities and were based upon different assumptions.[63] That Wilhelmian foreign policy, and more specifically *Weltpolitik,* was designed ultimately to enhance German national pride and rested, therefore, on an emotional foundation is not least to be attributed to the important role played by emotional factors in motivating Wilhelm II and more specifically to the Kaiser's insistent demand, voiced in his letter to his grandmother, that he and his nation be treated with "respect and . . . as equals."[64]

Although it is difficult to define the Kaiser's impact on the day-to-day practice of German foreign policy precisely, it seems clear that Wilhelm's personalization of politics contributed to the emotionally reactive conduct of the government during his reign. Certainly what frequently passed for foreign "policy" in Wilhelmian Germany can be attributed to the "touchiness" of the Kaiser and to the "touchiness" of his advisers and subjects, as they and he reacted to what were experienced as blows to the fragile honor of Kaiser and Reich. Wilhelm's typical response to such "insults" was anger followed by the effort to restore the self-esteem of Kaiser and country through some bold and dramatic action. When Wilhelm learned in June 1900, for example, that his envoy in Peking, Clemens von Ketteler, had been killed during the Boxer Rebellion, he demanded joint European action against the Chinese. He insisted that German troops play the leading role, however.[65] "The German representative will be avenged by my troops," he telegraphed the secretary of state in the Foreign Office. "Peking must be razed."[66] The news that the situation in China was being brought under control without any glorious German victories, before the German commander of the European forces had even arrived on the scene, "completely upset His Majesty," Eulenburg reported. "He spoke in the strongest possible terms about Russia and England, who had 'betrayed' him, had not even spared his own advisers." Wilhelm demanded that Eulenburg "send a telegram to the Foreign Office ordering the immediate conclusion of a defensive and offensive alliance with Japan, a country which until that time he had held in the utmost contempt."[67] It was only with difficulty that Eulenburg was able to persuade the Kaiser to drop the idea. It seemed to Wilhelm that Germany had lost the opportunity to redeem its honor and restore its strength in the eyes of the world. Feeling exposed and threatened, he reacted with the desperate demand for a new ally to support and strengthen his country and himself.

Only four years after Bismarck's dismissal, Eulenburg was convinced that the confusion in the conduct of German foreign policy was to be attributed to the Kaiser. "Unity of command is lacking [in the Foreign Office]," Eulenburg wrote, "because H.M. has no unity in himself."[68] Lacking the psychological unity necessary to define a coherent self-interest either for himself or for his nation, Wilhelm's course was determined by the buffeting seas around him. Reflecting the reactive and dramatic personality of the Kaiser, German foreign policy during his reign was punctuated by sudden bursts of activity. There seemed to be no single long-range purpose or clear program of action. Convinced that the Kaiser wielded considerable power, foreign governments were uncertain where he stood or what he would be likely to do in the future. Partially as a result, they came to mistrust and fear both him and his country.[69] After reading Eyre Crowe's famous "Memorandum on the Present State of British Relations with France and Germany" of 1 January 1907, Lord Fitzmaurice, parliamentary undersecretary of state for foreign affairs, noted that "there was at least method in Prince Bismarck's madness; but the Emperor is like a cat in a cupboard. He may jump out anywhere. The whole situation would be changed in a moment if this personal factor were changed."[70] Sir Edward Grey's characterization of the Kaiser suggested a greater capacity for destruction. "The German Emperor is ageing me"; he wrote during the *Daily Telegraph* affair, "he is like a battleship with steam up and screws going, but with no rudder, and he will run into something one day and cause a catastrophe."[71]

CHAPTER

Personal Symbol
of the Nation

Upon Wilhelm II's accession to the imperial throne, Germany had been in existence seventeen years as a united and independent nation.[1] Without benefit of longstanding national unity, the Kaiser's subjects were still attempting to answer such basic existential questions as: What is Germany? How is it to be governed? Where does Germany fit in with the rest of the world? What does it mean to be German? At the same time Germans were confronted with the economic, political, social, and psychological dislocations brought on by the rapid industrialization that transformed Germany after 1871. As a result of the suddenness, recency, and impact of unification and industrialization, Germans found themselves in fundamental disagreement over their state and society.

Tradition, rather than promoting consensus, tended to promote disunity. Threats to the Reich's fragile cohesion included: tension between the forces of centralism and those of particularism (Germany was made up of twenty-five heterogeneous states); the heritage of the Austro-Prussian dualism; tension between the state militarism of Prussia and the more liberal political traditions of the southern and western parts of the country; tension between authoritarian government and middle-class constitutional aspirations; among diverse economic interests, tension between the agrarian East and the industrial West; tension between Protestants and Catholics; tension between the German majority and Polish, Danish, French, and Alsatian minorities; sharp divisions and antagonisms among the various social classes and castes. Furthermore, despite efforts to establish its historical legitimacy, the imperial monarchy that Bismarck had created along with the nation in 1871 had then not been allowed to function by him during the first twenty years of its existence. Only with Wilhelm II's dismissal of the chancellor in 1890 did the Kaiserdom established in theory in the Hall of Mirrors at Versailles actually come into being.[2] Although most Germans during Wilhelm's reign were convinced that they belonged together in something called the German Reich, that empire was a very recent and, to a degree, even an artificial creation.[3]

I

Wilhelm II was sensitive to the solidity and durability of the Reich. Regarding it as his task to increase German unity, Wilhelm, despite his Hohenzollern ancestry and his Prussian crown, presented himself "as the symbol of the Reich and the embodiment of the national tradition."[4] In so doing, he provoked the hostility of the Prussian establishment, which, according to the South German secretary of state in the Foreign Office, Marschall, found Wilhelm to be "too little the King of Prussia and too much the German Kaiser."[5] Despite his criticism of the Kaiser, Alexander Hohenlohe, another South German and son of the chancellor, recognized Wilhelm's importance in preserving the German character of the Reich against the Prussian influence of the ruling elite. "I hope that they will not succeed in realizing their Prussian particularist ideas," he wrote his father on 18 December 1898. "They will get little sympathy from the Kaiser, however; since he is despite everything very German."[6] An even harsher critic, the diplomat Count Anton Monts, found his "love for Germany and for the Germans" to be "perhaps the most redeeming feature of Wilhelm II's character. As longtime representative in Munich, I had the opportunity to ascertain that Bavaria was just as close to him as his traditional Prussia, that he sought to penetrate the thought-processes of the South Germans, and that he truly strove to be the Kaiser of all the Germans."[7] In fact the opposition of several of the federal princes to Wilhelm II can be partially attributed to their fear that his determined nationalism and presentation of himself as a national leader would compromise the federal character of the Reich.[8]

As in other areas of his activity, the Kaiser sought to promote national unity through symbolic action.[9] From the monuments to his grandfather he had erected all across the Reich to his efforts to reform Germany's educational system in order, in his words, to transform students into "young, national Germans," Wilhelm attempted to strengthen national consciousness.[10] Sensing that his subjects needed to have their German identity grounded in a sense of historical legitimacy and seeking to wed that identity to the monarchy, Wilhelm worked to establish a tradition of a national monarchy that included features of the medieval Hohenstaufens, the Holy Roman emperors, and the Prussian Hohenzollerns. In contrast to his grandfather, Wilhelm I, who regarded himself primarily as king of Prussia, and to his father, Friedrich III, who thought of the imperial monarchy in romantically medieval terms, Wilhelm, as he would stress over and over again, was first and foremost the *German* Kaiser.[11] Where no German imperial tradition existed, the Kaiser attempted to create one by glorifying the military victories against the French in 1870–71 and the "pantheon" of national heroes. Despite the fact that Wilhelm I had only assumed the imperial crown with reluctance and had been deeply averse to the subordination of his title of king of Prussia to the imperial title, his grandson glorified "Wilhelm the Great" as German emperor and sought to elevate him to the level of Luther and Goethe to form a holy "Trinity of modern Germans."[12]

Occasions such as the centenary of Wilhelm I's birth were used to celebrate the German character of Reich and monarchy. Uncomprehending advisers like Chancellor Hohenlohe argued that Wilhelm I's centenary was far less significant than his accession to the Prussian throne. The Kaiser telegraphed back angrily on 6 December 1896:

> The celebration of the one-hundredth anniversary of the birth of the first *German* Emperor of a *German* national Empire from the *German* House of Hohenzollern has a completely different significance for Germany and the whole world than does the coronation of the King of Prussia in 1861.[13]

To commemorate the one-hundredth anniversary of the birth of Wilhelm I, his grandson wished to distribute a medal to every soldier, sailor, and civil servant in the realm since "the memory of the Kaiser is the best way of collecting the parties which support the State together in a patriotic decision."[14] Although the cost of this symbolic gesture proved prohibitive, Wilhelm was successful in using his grandfather's centenary to bestow a black-white-red cockade on the army as a "symbol of the unity achieved under Wilhelm I."[15] The cockade bearing the German national colors was controversial. Opposition centered around the fact that the cockade appeared to compromise the theoretical independence of the contingents from the individual German states which together made up the army of the Reich.[16] Those powerful circles that upheld the Prussian character of monarchy and army also strongly opposed the imposition of a national symbol. Nevertheless, overcoming legalistic and particularistic objections, the Kaiser ultimately was able to have the cockade made a permanent part of the German army uniform. Count Hutten-Czapski, an astute political observer and confidant of Hohenlohe, greeted the introduction of the "German cockade" with nationalistic fervor. In a letter to the chancellor on 22 March 1897 he described the cockade as "the most telling measure that has been undertaken in the military-political sphere since 1870."[17] Hutten-Czapski's enthusiasm did not diminish with the passage of years. "Here the Kaiser proved to have a feeling for what was psychologically appropriate and effective," he wrote in his memoirs. "It did not take long until the position of the black-white-red cockade over the cockade of the German states had become naturally accepted and a self-evident imponderable of the idea of the unity of the Reich."[18]

Despite his dismissal of Bismarck in 1890 and anger at the chancellor in retirement for his vindictive criticisms, the Kaiser sought to use Bismarck in the establishment of an heroic national tradition. When Bismarck died on 31 July 1898 Wilhelm hoped to have him buried with great patriotic fanfare in the cathedral in Berlin in a sarcophagus to be presented by the Kaiser.[19] Because of the opposition of the Bismarck family, however, this symbolic act could not be carried out, and the chancellor was buried on a little hill at his estate in Friedrichsruh.[20] A year later, after the publication of the first two volumes of Bismarck's memoirs, Wilhelm refused to respond publicly to what he regarded as the chancellor's attacks. Only after his own death, Wilhelm told Eulenburg, would the reasons for Bismarck's dismissal be revealed, since "I neither can nor wish to rob the German people of their ideals."[21]

The Kaiser also used Germany's international position to increase national unity. By communicating his own vulnerability to international "insults," Wilhelm contributed to the climate of anxious and indignant tension in Germany, to the popular perception that Germany was treated with disdain by the other European world powers who were systematically frustrating Germany's rightful foreign political ambitions. As England drew closer to France and Russia in opposition to Germany, Wilhelm and his subjects began to feel encircled by hostile powers. Although genuinely alarmed, the Kaiser sought to use the Reich's growing isolation to awaken the Germans to the need to increase domestic unity along with military preparedness.[22] Thus in 1898 he ordered Bülow to issue the following directive to the Foreign Office which was to guide its public pronouncements:

> As long as we do not possess sufficient naval power, our weakness in this area must be compensated for through the formation of a united front on the part of the parties, the popular representatives, and the nation in all major foreign policy issues. Never has there been more reason to turn our attention away from petty party squabbling and away from less significant internal issues and to focus on the decisive and world-historical problems of foreign policy.[23]

The effort to win mass support for the German naval building program was also designed to increase national cohesion. Through a propaganda campaign that emphasized Germany's international vulnerability, the general populace was to rally together behind the effort to create a navy able to preserve national independence and uphold national honor in a hostile world.

These themes all found expression in Wilhelm's Royal Message of 18 January 1896 on the occasion of the twenty-fifth anniversary of the founding of the German Empire. "With God's help," the Kaiser began, the vow passed down by "Our never-to-be forgotten Grandfather to his successors . . . to protect with Germanic fealty the rights of the Reich and of its parts, to preserve peace, to defend the independence of the Reich, to increase the strength of its people" had "thus far been fulfilled." In keeping with that vow not only was it now necessary to expand Germany's armed might so as to defend "the independence of the Fatherland," but "in order to follow dutifully the example set forth by Our Grandfather who rests in the Lord, an example We have so recently praised, We make the Imperial demand on all members of the people to place divisive party interests behind them and to join with Us and Our noble allies in placing the welfare of the Reich in the forefront, in placing themselves with Germanic fealty in the service of the whole, thus working together to increase the greatness and good fortune of the beloved Fatherland."[24]

II

As a more consistent leader could not, Wilhelm II was able to personify the often contradictory national aspirations of his subjects. In what Eça de Queiroz called his "variety of incarnations of Royalty," Wilhelm symbolically represented many different Germanies which were only united in the national figure of the Kaiser. Specifically, Wilhelm saw it as his task to integrate for the Germans the conception of a glorious past and a traditionally authoritarian system of government with modern mass industrial society. "I have been placed in an infinitely difficult period of history," he told Eulenburg in 1903, a period that required "the reconciliation of traditional society with modern times."[25]

In private and in public the Kaiser sought the "reconciliation" of the "traditional" with the "modern." Therefore, despite his interest in spiritualism, Wilhelm, according to Eulenburg, sought "ostentatiously to toss [it] overboard" because he recognized that mysticism was incompatible with the image of the modern Kaiser he wanted to project.[26] Wilhelm designed the education of the crown prince to make his heir a leader able to harmonize the old and the new. "On the one hand, the Kaiser wants to make the Crown Prince into a modern ruler," Eulenburg wrote Bülow on 26 September 1901; "on the other hand, [he] wants to know that traditional customs are preserved." But Eulenburg was not confident about Wilhelm's chances of success with his eldest son: "Modern mankind expresses itself as much in artistic and fashion trends, however, as in support for the great world-, commercial- and communication-movement. A mixture of feudal sensibilities and commercial passions the Crown Prince will never develop."[27]

Wilhelm II sought to use occasions of symbolic significance like the celebration of the beginning of the twentieth century to promote the unity of the Reich through the integration of Germany's past with its present and future. He decreed, therefore, that *Die Meistersinger* be performed on New Year's Day at the Royal Playhouse in Berlin. Musically innovative and yet romantically conservative, composed relatively recently (1867) and yet dealing with medieval Nürnberg, Wagner's opera was an apt choice for Wilhelm to have made. With its theme of the reconciliation of traditional and modern art and of bourgeois and aristocratic classes in a passionate celebration of German national culture under the aegis of the great integrating leader, acceptable to both populace and elites, *Die Meistersinger* symbolized Wilhelm's goals as Kaiser and his vision of his imperial role. In designing those New Year's ceremonies in which he was a direct participant, the Kaiser used the army, the Reich's great armed force of the past, and the navy, the Reich's great armed force of the future, as powerful symbols of the integration of the old and the new. "Traditions and confidence in the future came together here," Michael Salewski has written in his study of New Year's 1900 in Germany, "and the German Kaiser left no doubt about the fact that he grasped that he was the symbol and guardian of these highest cultural values."[28]

Although the outside observer might conclude that the Kaiser's various personae were integrated within a harmonious total self, those who knew Wilhelm

The Kaiser, flanked by heralds, escorted across the Marienplatz in Munich.

II recognized his discordancy. Philipp Eulenburg, for example, detected an admixture of the old and the new in Wilhelm's psyche. "The Kaiser represents within himself, more than I have ever observed in any other person, two totally different natures," Eulenburg wrote to Bülow in 1896: "the knightly—in the sense of the most beautiful period of the Middle Ages with piety and mysticism—and the modern."[29] Walther Rathenau identified three conflicting tendencies in Wilhelm: "the indeterminate Prusso-German tendency toward power; the inherited dynastic tendency toward self-preservation; and in hidden contradiction to these two, a general tendency toward modernism, particularly in the technical-mechanical, occasionally in the social sphere. The ideal conception to which the realization of such inclinations would have led is unimaginable: a type of electrical-journalistic Caesarian popery."[30]

Given his inner disjointedness, Wilhelm II generally dealt with the task of "reconciliation" by pointedly manifesting features of past and present in his personality and behavior. On occasion the Kaiser would tangibly identify with the past by dressing in the costumes of Friedrich the Great and other rulers of Prussia. The glorification of his Hohenzollern ancestors, the court galas, the monumentality of the Siegesallee in Berlin, the restoration of medieval castles, the spectacular military parades and maneuvers, even his claims to rule by divine right, all testified to Wilhelm's reverence for a romanticized past.[31] At the same time, he was the spokesman of his own self-consciously progressive Wilhelmian epoch. In every area of modern life the Kaiser attempted to set the tone and direction. Writing in the four volume *Deutschland unter Kaiser Wilhelm II* that was published in 1913 to celebrate Wilhelm's silver jubilee, Friedrich Wilhelm von Loebell proclaimed:

> When we give the name Kaiser Wilhelm II to the period since the death of Kaiser Friedrich, this signifies more than simply the labelling of an historical era with the name of the monarch. Indeed, the first quarter-century of the government of our Kaiser gives lie to that political theory which no longer recognizes the influence of a leader on the character and goals of his age. . . . The German people, this most profoundly monarchical of all people in Europe, has been transformed from the people of Kaiser Wilhelm I to the people of Kaiser Wilhelm II. In our Kaiser the spirit of the new era expresses itself and in the era the spirit of our Kaiser.

No matter how stark the contradictions in the nation or how violent the clashes in parliament and public, Loebell continued, "it remains an unshakable fact that the Kaiser and the vast majority of the German people are united behind the goals of the nation." Indeed, "precisely in those developments of epochal significance," particularly the shift from continental to world politics and, accompanying that shift, the supplementation of Germany's army with a battlefleet, "it was the Kaiser who won the nation over to his point of view, who taught the nation to believe in his ideas." Also in other areas of contemporary German life—in the social, agricultural, commercial, industrial, transportational, artistic, archeological, scientific, technological, medical, and educational spheres—Loebell claimed that the Kaiser had been the leading force. Although conceding the difficulty in ascribing advances in these areas to either Wilhelm or the Germans, Loebell concluded: "No matter how diverse the achievements in the individual areas of national activity may be, the last 25 years have a unique character, and that character could hardly be more aptly conveyed than with the name Kaiser Wilhelm II."[32]

Wilhelm saw nothing incongruous about wearing the traditional Prussian spiked helmet to the opening of an institute of technology in Breslau and, even more significantly, neither did his subjects. The liberal historian Friedrich Meinecke was rather more critical of the Kaiser than Loebell, former head of the Chancellery under Bülow. Nevertheless, Meinecke declared, also on the twenty-fifth anniversary of Wilhelm's accession to the throne, that the Kaiser

> combines the intense actuality, the sharp purposefulness of the modern man with a glowing veneration of the national past. The grand figures and memories of his forebearers, his state, and his people are transfigured into colorful, gleaming symbols of lasting value. One who focuses on the individual features of his being tends to find a contradiction between his determined modernism and romantic traditionalism. In truth, his historical ideals and symbols are the spiritual tools he uses to inspire the energies of his contemporaries and to keep the surging flow of modern life within wholesome limits.[33]

On the same occasion another historian, Hermann Oncken, reached a different conclusion about Wilhelm's ability to integrate the traditional and the modern:

> His personality wanted to be more than heir to a name and bearer of an institution and strove to become nothing less than a true leader of the nation. And yet his personality appeared in itself not to embody the self-contained unity of the constitution of the born leader but rather embraced in a peculiar mixture modern and traditional features; a world of contradictions.[34]

Looking back, it seems clear that Oncken and not Meinecke was correct. Wilhelm's features were contradictory, and he was unable to fuse the modern with the traditional. He did, however, incorporate elements of both in himself and reflect them back to his subjects—integrated only insofar as they were fragments of the same incoherent personality.

III

In his restless search for confirmation, Wilhelm II was driven to display himself throughout Germany. His perpetual traveling with spectacular receptions everywhere he went and his countless speeches to enthusiastic audiences kept him continuously—either directly or through the press—in the public eye. "At every step," Rathenau wrote of Wilhelm's life of incessant celebrity, "salvoes are fired, bells ring, drums beat, horns blow, trumpets sound, flags wave. . . . Every day there is some festivity, every hour a solemn occasion is celebrated somewhere. As is said: festivals are held (fast) [*es wird festgehalten*]: photographically, cinematographically, telegraphically, journalistically, by way of a protocol. World history rolls off a cylinder."[35] Although such an existence might seem unimaginable, what was truly unimaginable, Rathenau believed, was the demand of the Germans that their Kaiser lead such a life. "Unbelievable, unbelievable appears only one thing: that year in and year out, with great seriousness, a serious and profound people should not only have accepted these things, but should indeed have extolled and sworn by them; and that anyone who dared to doubt their necessity, their definitive and God-given nature, was mocked, scorned, and persecuted."[36]

"Fundamentally, the populace *wished* to see itself represented in a proud and magnificent fashion," Thomas Mann wrote in 1905 of the relationship between ruler and subject in his allegorical critique of Wilhelmian Germany *Königliche Hoheit*.[37] Indeed, it seems clear that in the grandeur of the Kaiser's self-display a widespread yearning for national greatness found expression. Despite their limited political benefit, the Kaiser's symbolic demonstrations were greeted with popular enthusiasm. The sumptuous banquets, the memorable state visits, the impressive parades, the imposing military maneuvers, the decorations and uniforms, all conveyed a message of national power that Germans readily understood and appreciated. The spectacular journeys, the fiery speeches, the dramatic diplomatic initiatives, all proclaimed the importance of Germany's place in the world to the excited applause of Wilhelm's subjects. Ludwig Thoma, a leading South German liberal and co-founder of the journal *März*, recognized that the Kaiser's glorification of himself served to affirm the glory of the Germans. He wrote in 1908:

> It was precisely the remarkable penchant for the operatic that brought our loyal citizenry to see in Wilhelm II the embodiment of its ideal. What epic emotions were unleashed by the monarch's every pleasure cruise. What lyricisms have been written and spoken when he did nothing more than participate in a parade. There was no room for sobriety and nothing could occur in silence. Even the simplest thing took place in a Bengal light. The imagination of the bourgeoisie was inspired and aroused daily by the personality of the Kaiser. In every popular court of judgment on him, Wilhelm never found himself opposed, even in those places where he actively searched for opposition.[38]

If, psychologically, Wilhelm can be described as having blurred the distinction between himself and the Germans, the Germans can be described as having blurred the distinction between themselves and their Kaiser.[39] In an age of nationalism people define themselves to a greater or lesser degree in terms of the nation to which they belong. Thus a nation's defeat or victory may be experienced with a sense of personal humiliation or exhilaration by its citizens even though that defeat or victory does not affect them directly. Defining themselves as part of that collective identity called Germany, Germans were emotionally invested in their country's fortunes and invested in the personal symbol of that collective identity. In an age of nationalism, in other words, Wilhelm II was experienced by his subjects as an extension of themselves.[40]

To be sure, the Kaiser had his critics. Socialists and other political radicals, Jews, and South Germans were less enthusiastic about Wilhelm II than were Prussians, the literati, and the bourgeoisie. Nevertheless, even the Kaiser's detractors, some of whom are quoted in these pages, bore reluctant witness to his popularity with their fellow Germans. Of course, that popularity fluctuated during the course of the reign, and, with the passage of years, the Kaiser's reputation began to suffer as he proved unable to match his symbolic promises with political achievements. Thus Wilhelm's popularity declined after 1905/1906, when the Algeciras Conference and the growing Anglo-Russian rapprochement revealed—instead of the promised respect and influence—Germany's increasing international isolation and ineffectiveness. Nevertheless, the Kaiser's standing with his subjects declined most precipitously when his increasingly obvious political incompetence began, finally, to have a negative symbolic effect, as his political blunders gave lie to the image of the Hero-Kaiser, the ruler whose grandeur and glory reflected the grandeur and glory of the people he personified.[41] Thus the Kaiser's popularity suffered its most grievous blow before the end of the war when the publication of his *Daily Telegraph* interview in 1908 presented Germans with a symbol not of majesty and strength but of irresponsibility and instability.[42] And yet, although the passage of years enabled Germans to recognize Wilhelm's grandiose posturing for what it was, for almost two decades most were willing to disregard the political failures and even the occasional symbolic debacle in order, in an intensely nationalistic era, to believe themselves represented by a dynamic and heroic national leader. Thus despite his political blunders and increasingly obvious superficiality, the Kaiser, the qualitative evidence suggests, remained broadly and deeply popular with his subjects.[43] It was only the collapse of the Reich in 1918 that brought about the final collapse of Wilhelm II's popularity with the Germans.

Perhaps the clearest example of the intersection of the Kaiser's need for personal self-aggrandizement and the need of his subjects for national self-aggrandizement was Wilhelm's constant travel throughout Germany during the course of his reign, the centerpiece of which was his ceremonial entrance into German villages, towns, and cities.[44] For Wilhelm, the life of driven self-display relieved his sense of inadequacy. Entering a city at the head of a column of soldiers, the Kaiser could experience himself as the powerful and heroic ruler to whom adulation and homage are due; the cheering crowds lining the city

Wilhelm II and his sons, Crown Prince Wilhelm (2) and Prince Oskar (3), entering Posen in 1913. Reprinted with the permission of the Bilderdienst Süddeutscher Verlag.

streets confirmed him in that role. But despite the pleasure and excitement the entrances provided, they could not sustain the Kaiser, and he was impelled to move on to the next city, the next parade, the next speech, the next reception.

Wilhelm recognized that his life of perpetual motion served a psychological function for him. In an interview in 1906 with the popular author Ludwig Ganghofer, Wilhelm praised the optimistic spirit of Ganghofer's books and the virtues of an optimistic philosophy of life. "In politics it is no different," Ganghofer reported the Kaiser to say. "The German people do indeed have a future, and there is a word that always hurts his feelings whenever he hears it: that word is *Reichsverdrossenheit* [national malaise]. 'What advantage is there to be had from *Verdrossenheit?* Better to work and be optimistic. I work without malaise and believe that I do in fact make progress.'" The Kaiser went on to describe his workday "and how the profusion and weight of the duties and labors that storm over him are often exhausting. At such times the need always rises up in him to relax and again see a new part of the world, to again meet new people, who again are so stimulating." After describing the "calming and refreshing effect" of his travels, Wilhelm concluded:

> Everything which oppresses Me is gone within a few weeks, and that which gives Me such pleasure that other people take amiss frequently. I know that I am called the *"Reisekaiser,"* but I have always regarded that with amusement. . . . I believe that through travel the feeling of belonging together [*Zusammengehörigkeit*] is strengthened. . . . Such refreshing trips are especially necessary in My serious profession, doubly necessary because one has to fight against many misunderstandings.[45]

The interview with Ganghofer reveals the pressure Wilhelm experienced in his imperial office. The stimulation of travel—the exposure to new people and impressions, displaying himself to adoring crowds—soothed Wilhelm and allowed him to overcome his underlying depression, the *Verdrossenheit*, he was so anxious to deny and allay.[46] Traveling, then, increased not just the national *Zusammengehörigkeit* of the Germans but also the psychological cohesion of their Kaiser.

As he indicated in his interview, Wilhelm saw his travels as part of a campaign against *Reichsverdrossenheit* and national fragmentation. Through his ceremonial entrances, the Kaiser symbolically enacted the infusion of national spirit into communities all across Germany. His physical presence concretized the feeling of the local inhabitants that they were German, and it was assumed that the contact of the townspeople with the living symbol of the nation would strengthen their German national identity. "The Saxon people will always remember the Imperial visit," the Prussian representative in Dresden wrote approvingly following the Kaiser's visit to that city in 1889, "and it will contribute substantially to strengthening their consciousness that they belong to the German Reich."[47]

Germans were to develop a sense of national *Zusammengehörigkeit* not only through their exposure to the Kaiser as passive onlookers but also through their active participation in the ceremony of his entrances. In the masses that gathered to welcome Wilhelm, individual distinctions and identities were submerged. Through the common ceremonial expression of enthusiasm for the personal symbol of the nation, Germans were to develop a national group identity bridging the regional, social, political, and religious divisions that so often kept them apart. Furthermore, the very number of the Kaiser's ceremonial entrances, the range of his travels, symbolically expressed and reinforced the notion of the pervasiveness of national spirit. What one writer has called the Kaiser's "omnipresence" concretized the omnipresence of the national idea.[48]

Elisabeth Fehrenbach has written that lacking a tradition of nationhood the Germans yearned for symbols to give concrete expression to the idea of the Reich. The Reichstag could not serve that function. "Owing to constitutional impediments to parliamentary government and the consequent perception which the parties had of their role, [it] was seen more as a forum for the representation of vested interests than the expression of national unity." Instead the Germans came to see the Kaiser as "the embodiment of the whole spiritual personality of the nation."[49] Wilhelm "became the visible and real symbol of the nation-state by virtue of his personal conspicuousness. . . . The Kaiser made possible the escape from the labyrinths of mass society; he concentrated people's gaze on the great man, the gifted individual, the embodiment of an

Kaiser Wilhelm II entering the city of Münster at the head of the Flag Company of the XIII Infantry Regiment.

historical mission."[50] As a figure continuously celebrated, Wilhelm became the cynosure of nationalistic strivings, the brilliant symbol of a proud, glorious, and united Germany. Through what Walther Rathenau described as the "sacral, uninterrupted spectacle, the epopee" that was Wilhelm II's existence, the Kaiser held up a mirror to his subjects in which was reflected an image of themselves that was larger than life.[51] It was, for very many Germans, an image they very much wanted to see.[52]

IV

"The German," the Kaiser told Eulenburg in the summer of 1903, "wants to be led."[53] Indeed the popular demonstrations of enthusiasm for the Kaiser testified to the depth of the nation's faith in monarchical rule.[54] To Friedrich Naumann, the Kaiserdom, instead of becoming increasingly anachronistic, seemed to be growing ever more rooted in the national soil, ever more entwined with the national destiny. He wrote in 1900:

> In present-day Germany there is no stronger force than the Kaiser. The very complaints of the anti-Kaiser democrats about the growth of personal absolutism are the best proof of this fact, for these complaints are not pure invention but are based on the repeated observation that all policy, foreign and internal, stems from the will and word of the Kaiser. No monarch of absolutist times ever had so much real power as the Kaiser has today. He does not achieve everything he wants, but it is still more than anybody would have believed possible in the middle of the last century. That century, whose middle years echoed with the dreams of a German republic, ended with more power in the Kaiser's hands than even Barbarossa possessed.[55]

Wilhelm's harshest critics testified to the popularity of his "personal regime." Only five years after the beginning of the reign Ludwig Quidde launched a vicious assault on the Kaiser in an article in the journal *Gesellschaft* entitled "Caligula—eine Studie über römischen Cäsarenwahnsinn." Although (to escape censorship) ostensibly about the Roman emperor Caligula, Quidde's article was immediately recognized as an attempt to brand Wilhelm II a dangerous megalomaniac. A year later, in 1894, Quidde's study was reprinted under separate cover, and for a brief period enjoyed extraordinary popularity, going through more than twenty-five printings in the first year.[56] Quidde denounced Caligula-Wilhelm as a man motivated only by ambition and the wish to be publicly acclaimed, a man driven to do everything and be everywhere. The emperor's "Casaerian madness" manifested itself in six specific symptoms, according to Quidde: "a boundless addiction to pomp and extravagance"; "a burning desire for military triumphs" that took the form of maneuvers and war games; "the fantastic idea of conquering the oceans of the world" and "a predilection for the sea that was so distorted as to be a sickness"; "a theatrical strain" that took the form of dressing in costumes and delivering orations; a flaunting of power and authority; and a messianic view typical of all megalomaniacs, "who think that they have a mission to fulfill, who feel that they have a special relationship to God, who regard themselves as having been chosen by Him, and finally who demand that they be worshipped like a god themselves."[57] Given his position, the emperor had few restraints placed upon his conduct and could put his deranged ideas into practice. But what alarmed Quidde most was the combination of the megalomaniacal ruler and subjects predisposed to monarchical leadership:

> Surely—and it provides the indeed disgraceful and wretched foundation of the entire Casaerian existence—such [megalomaniacal] notions come together often in the most dangerous manner with the outlook of the masses and the ruling classes of those peoples who are imbued with actual monarchical sentiment. How else could Alexander have laid claim to deification, how else could deification have been claimed for Caesar?[58]

The most "disgraceful and wretched" aspect of the Kaiser's personal regime, Quidde implied, was that it was proving so popular with the Germans.

Although many Germans "imbued with actual monarchical sentiment" came to share Quidde's outrage over the Kaiser's personal regime, the historian Hans Delbrück believed that Wilhelm's personality could not be separated from the institution of the imperial monarchy.[59] "The true German monarchy, also in modern constitutionalism," he wrote in 1891, "is something personal and therefore also strongly subjective. Whoever wants this monarchy must also accept the subjectivity even when it takes a somewhat less agreeable course."[60] In 1913, Delbrück's colleague, Friedrich Meinecke, confirmed that the person of Wilhelm II was the vital link connecting the Germans to monarchy and nation. "The destiny of our Kaiser is our destiny," Meinecke told those gathered at Freiburg University on June 14 to celebrate the twenty-fifth anniversary of Wilhelm's accession to the imperial throne.[61] Over the course of the one hundred years since the German resistance to Napoleon, leader and nation had become indistinguishable.[62] The identification between Kaiser and Germany was especially important, Meinecke declared, because those one hundred years had also witnessed the emergence of numerous divisions within the German nation. The Kaiserdom under Wilhelm II had come to be the force for national integration, not only bringing past and present together, but also reconciling the various religious confessions and social classes in forms that were compatible with national brotherhood and Germany's position of power in the world.[63] Indeed, Meinecke concluded, the person of the Kaiser had become essential to the unity of the nation:

> That is the first thing we call out to our Kaiser today, that we regard the national monarchy as the untouchable foundation and cornerstone of our national life. The national monarchy is valuable to us not for reasons of simple rationality but as an irreplaceable feeling. As boldly as he may fly into the realm of ideas, the German can only first open his heart when he encounters a living personality as the bearer of the idea. We are not content with the awareness that our

nation is a great spiritual total personality, but we demand a leader for that personality for whom we can go through the fire.[64]

A similar, if more uncritical, appreciation of the emotional basis of the monarchy was expressed, also in 1913, by Eugen Fischer, whose views are reminiscent of the Kaiser's own as he expressed them to Eulenberg in the summer of 1903. Fischer criticized those intellectuals, like Meinecke, who argued that it was necessary to limit the power of the monarchy in order to preserve it. Such ideas were out of touch with "modern sentiment" Fischer asserted. The feeling that attached subject to monarch "wanted nothing to do" with such ideas. Indeed, Fischer was convinced that contemporary popular sentiment "wanted, as does Wilhelm II himself, that the king live up to his name and set an example of his life and beliefs for the people to follow." Like Meinecke, Fischer offered a justification of the monarchy that reflected the mass politics of the twentieth century. Now the popularity of the monarchy provided the basis of its continued existence. Now the king ruled "by the grace of God" not because he did in fact but because his subjects wanted him to; his declarations of contempt for public opinion were actually an appeal to it. The German people desired that their Kaiser exercise authority; and "that is why Wilhelm II's conception of kingship has the power to elevate the political life of the Germans," Fischer concluded.[65]

For that reason alone it was important for Wilhelm II to dismiss Bismarck in order to become his "own Chancellor."[66] In 1899, in an article entitled "The Legal Position of the Kaiser in Contemporary Germany," the law professor Karl Binding wrote triumphantly: "'We no longer have a presidial authority— we have a Kaiser!' The difference may perhaps 'not be clearly understood, but rather deeply experienced.'"[67] Or as Bülow put it to the Reichstag on 21 January 1903: "The German People do not want a Shadow Kaiser, the German People want a Kaiser of flesh and blood."[68]

Although Wilhelm's declarations of his sovereignty masked chronic insecurity, contemporaries took him at his word, and many—both inside and outside Germany—believed the Kaiser to be the single most powerful leader in the world. The charismatic and commanding Cecil Rhodes, for example, was fascinated by Wilhelm and thought to recognize a kindred spirit in him. After meeting the Kaiser in 1899 he wrote the Prince of Wales: "The Emperor is really Germany, at least it appeared to me to be so when I was in Berlin, Ministers doing just what he desired and the Reichstag most docile."[69] The political reality of Wilhelm II's sovereignty was rather more equivocal of course, and the historian of Wilhelmian Germany is confronted with the dilemma of trying to reconcile a Kaiser who could be attacked as a Caligula, the tyrant who appointed his horse Consul of Rome, with a Kaiser who could feel "tyrannized" by his octogenarian chancellor, Hohenlohe.[70] In fact, historians have long debated the question of Wilhelm II's "personal regime" and have until recently tended to play down his political authority and significance.[71]

Within the limits of the present investigation it is not possible, of course, to provide anything approaching a definitive answer to this complex question.

Still it can be said that the Kaiser's positive political influence was in practice rather limited. No useful purpose would be served by going over again the various features of Wilhelm's personality that reduced his political effectiveness. His restlessness and impulsiveness when combined with his efforts to be in charge of everything usually meant that Wilhelm could only interfere in the affairs of state. Unable to have knowledge in depth about those myriad areas over which he claimed competence and authority, Wilhelm's sovereignty often took the form of sullen resistance to the plans and programs of his advisers. Many of his more impetuous orders were never issued, as aides would delay sending them off until the Kaiser's impulse had passed or he could be persuaded to change his mind. Given Wilhelm's obstinacy, considerable time and energy had to be expended by bureaucrats, ministers, and chancellors in "managing" the Kaiser. Wilhelm's self-will, Eulenburg wrote, "is unusually strongly developed and the spirit of contradiction is so powerful in him that those around him have accustomed themselves to present their requests to him in such a form that they request approximately the opposite of that which they actually wish to achieve."[72] Despite the difficulties involved, however, Wilhelm's advisers were generally able to manipulate him. The most common approach, used with particular success by Bülow, was to flatter the Kaiser into adopting their positions as his own.[73] Ministers and chancellors, particularly Hohenlohe, also used the threat of resignation to get their way.[74] On those occasions when Wilhelm had a clear sense of what he wanted, he was not always able to overcome the opposition of his advisers. One of the most telling examples of the Kaiser's weakness was his inability to either convince or compel the chancellor and other top officials to accept the dismissal of Marschall, whom Wilhelm despised, from his position as secretary of state in the Foreign Office for almost four years.[75]

In general, it would appear that Wilhelm's impact on the functioning of government was negative. By asserting his right to exercise authority, the Kaiser tended to impede the conduct of government. In addition to reducing their efficiency, the Kaiser's impulsiveness and "touchiness" made it difficult for his advisers to formulate or implement consistent policy. Indeed, in at least one important area, the policy emanating from the Kaiser was different from the policies pursued by his key advisers. Instead of resolving their differences, they simply pursued these incompatible policies simultaneously. Thus, there was not one but at least three German policies toward England.[76] One gets the sense that the attempt to achieve consensus was avoided by the Kaiser's aides in order to preserve their freedom of action from the sovereignty theoretically possessed by their monarch and by Wilhelm II in order to avoid exposing his personal weakness. Afraid to tell members of his entourage that he did not want to accompany them on a hike, he was even more anxious about having to contradict his advisers on matters of political, diplomatic, and military policy. By keeping things vague, the Kaiser's advisers avoided exposing the political limits of their authority and Wilhelm avoided exposing the personal limits of his—at the price of consistent policy.

Although the Kaiser was far from being a forceful and authoritative political leader and although his political impact was generally negative, it would be wrong to dismiss the observations of Rhodes, Naumann, and Quidde. The "personal regime" was not an illusion. To the extent it was believed, the myth of the Kaiser's sovereignty lent him significance. Although foreign governments recognized that Wilhelm exercised less authority than he claimed for himself, they still believed him to be a political factor of decisive importance. Interpreting his conversations, speeches, and displays as revealing the irresponsible and dangerous character of German foreign policy, they came to regard the Reich as a threat to world peace.[77] Believing—wanting to believe—that the Kaiser possessed great political power, Germans invested the Kaiser with emotional authority. As the symbol of Germany, as the "embodiment of the whole spiritual personality of the nation," as "the leader" for whom Germans "would go through the fire," Wilhelm II was indeed sovereign in the Reich.

The Kaiser sought to focus attention on himself as a symbol of national strength and unity. The royal "standard waves high in the breeze," he wrote his mother in October 1898, "comforting every anxious look cast upwards; the Crown sends its rays 'by the grace of God' into Palace and hut, and—pardon me if I say so—Europe and the world listen to hear, 'what does the German Emperor say or think.'"[78] Through subjugation to and identification with the Kaiser, Germans were to develop a national group identity bridging social divisions. "*Everyone*, without class distinction," Wilhelm told Eulenberg, "should stand behind me, should fight beside me for the interests of the Fatherland! No matter what class they belong to. . . . On me, no one exerts any influence; and no one will be permitted to exert any influence on me. *I* am to command."[79] Wilhelm's assertion of sovereignty not only bound Germans together by virtue of the fact that all were subject to his authority, that all, in his words, stood *behind* the Kaiser; but also through their shared identification with the Kaiser, through their sense of fighting *beside* him, Germans felt their own grand fantasies about themselves played out on the stage of world history. Traditionally, the Hohenzollern dynasty had occupied the first position, with the people standing behind the king of Prussia. The role of rulers like Friedrich Wilhelm I and Friedrich II was predominantly that of the wise and trusted and powerful father who watched over his subjects and looked after the welfare of an essentially agrarian society. Even Wilhelm I, although ruler of a country that became industrialized during his reign, still conceived of himself as the traditional Prussian king to whom children-subjects looked for protection and guidance.[80] By contrast, the imperial monarchy under his grandson primarily occupied the second position, with the people standing beside the German Kaiser. Wilhelm II was less a paternal figure than he was the narcissistic object (selfobject) of a mass industrial society.[81] He was not the venerable "Sire" but the imperial "Highness," the youthful and vigorous personification of the German nation, the mighty and glorious extension of the German people. The Kaiser's speeches, parades, maneuvers, and entrances were demonstrations of power designed less to make his subjects feel safe and secure than to overcome *Reichs-*

verdrossenheit, national malaise, by increasing the Germans' sense of national pride, power, and enthusiasm. The cheering crowds identified with the Hero-Kaiser. In their cheers for Wilhelm II, the Germans were also celebrating themselves, celebrating the dynamism, independence, and strength of the Reich.[82]

There is an unforgettable moment in Heinrich Mann's *Der Untertan* when Diederich Hessling, the protagonist of the novel, saw the Kaiser for the first time. In describing Hessling's ecstasy at encountering his ideal, Mann sought to account for the Germans' attachment to authority in Wilhelmian Germany. What attracted Hessling to the Kaiser was not some tendency toward servility or masochism imbedded in the German character. What filled Hessling with passion upon seeing his master was less the pleasure in being dominated and more the joy in identifying with the dominator. Even as he was being subjugated, in other words, Hessling was able to participate vicariously in the power of authority. In the very moment of degradation, Mann concluded, the self is elevated and enhanced through merger with power:

> An intoxication . . . raised his [Hessling's] feet off the ground and carried him into the air. He waved his hat high above all heads in enthusiastic madness, in a heaven where our finest feelings move. There on the horse rode Power, through the gateway of triumphal entries, with dazzling features, but graven as in stone. The Power which transcends and whose hoofs we kiss, the Power which is beyond the reach of hunger, spite and mockery! Against it we are impotent, for we all love it! We have it in our blood, for in our blood is submission. We are an atom of that Power, a diminutive molecule of something it has given out. Each one of us is as nothing, but massed in ranks . . . we taper up like a pyramid to the point at the top where Power itself stands, graven and dazzling. In it we live and have our being, merciless towards those who are remote beneath us, and triumphing even when we ourselves are crushed, for thus does power justify our love for it.[83]

As was the case with Wilhelm's need to appear to know everything (the Kaiser's omniscience) and his need to appear to be everywhere (the Kaiser's omnipresence), so was his need to appear omnipotent fundamentally in tune with the need of Germans to feel themselves defined and represented by a leader firmly in control of the national destiny. For Walther Rathenau, the basis of the "attachment" of the Germans to the Kaiser was that they "saw him as the paragon of the national being, the expression of the national character." He was, Rathenau concluded, "the most German man in whose features everyone finds his own image enhanced."[84]

The heroic poses that masked Wilhelm's inner uncertainty, the self-display that reflected his craving for attention and approval were not understood by many of his subjects—or at least not understood for a long time—to be the manifestations of a weak and needy personality. Instead they took the Kaiser at his symbolic face value and experienced him as a powerful and glorious and dynamic personal symbol of their nation and themselves.

V

According to Maximilian Harden, editor of *Die Zukunft* and one of Wilhelm II's fiercest and most effective opponents, "enlightened" critics of the Kaiser were prepared to tolerate his erratic and impulsive conduct in return for the benefits Germany derived from the fact that "the Kaiser is his own Chancellor."

> All the important political decisions of the past twelve years have been made by him. Changes in trade policy, the build-up of the fleet, the belief in the German Reich achieving *Weltmacht* on an enormous scale, the friendly relations and secret treaties with England, the military campaign in China, all that and a lot more besides is his work. His objectives have been correct almost without exception but his chosen ways and means have been unfortunate.[85]

In general, even the most committed adversaries of Wilhelm II tended to direct their criticism at the Kaiser's methods and not at his aims.[86]

According to Harden's definition, Max Weber should be counted among the Kaiser's "enlightened" critics.[87] Weber was outspoken in his denunciations of the clumsiness and unsteadiness, the theatricality and braggadocio of Wilhelm's "personal regime." What Weber condemned with particular vehemence was that in the conduct of government and especially in the conduct of foreign affairs appearance had replaced substance, the passion for prestige and popularity had replaced the politics of rational self-interest, and the Kaiser's personal emotional agenda had replaced the reason of state.[88] And yet, although Weber was a vociferous opponent of the style of Wilhelm II's leadership, he was an even more vociferous proponent of its goals. For Weber, as for the Kaiser, the nation possessed the highest value, taking precedence over all other moral and political considerations.[89] Weber, like the Kaiser, believed that it was Germany's "historical duty" to practice "*Weltmachtpolitik*," a policy of world power, and that Germany was obliged to become a "*Machtstaat*," a power state, if, echoing Wilhelm's very words, its "voice was to be heard in the decisions affecting the history of the earth."[90] Weber, like the Kaiser, was convinced that Germany's survival as a nation depended upon the acquisition of a world empire, and he was an enthusiastic advocate of the construction of a battlefleet as a means to that end.[91] In fact, Weber, like the Kaiser, believed that a mighty German navy could be created without antagonizing the British, and he, like Wilhelm, hoped that an Anglo-German understanding could ultimately be achieved.[92] Finally, like the Kaiser, Weber anticipated that the practice of world politics would integrate German society and lead to a national regeneration.[93]

Thus, with the exception of Weber's veneration of the recently dismissed Bismarck, the Kaiser would have greeted the sociologist's famous inaugural address at the University of Freiburg in 1895 (in which many of these ideas were already expressed) with the same excitement and enthusiasm with which so many of his subjects responded to Weber's remarks.[94] "We must grasp," Weber proclaimed in the speech's most frequently quoted passage, "that the unification of the nation was but a youthful prank played by the nation on its bygone days and which, on account of its costliness, would have been better left undone should it be regarded as the conclusion and not as the starting point of a German policy of world power."[95]

Despite Weber's admiration for Bismarck and for the politics of rational self-interest, it would be difficult to characterize the goals that Weber shared with Wilhelm II or those acclaimed by Harden's "enlightened" critics of the Kaiser as constituting circumscribed political objectives in the Bismarckian sense of the term. These objectives were not based upon an appreciation of Germany's rational self-interest but were by and large ill-defined and at bottom motivated by the essentially emotional wish that Germany take its rightful place in the world, that it be accorded the international respect that a proud and powerful nation deserved. Indeed, according to Wolfgang Mommsen, Weber's political biographer, Weber's enthusiasm for *Weltpolitik* was not simply the result of sober economic and political calculation but was to a significant degree the product of "nationalistic pathos," of his passionate desire to see an increase in German prestige and power in the world—the very *Renommiersucht* that Weber found so deplorable in Wilhelm II.[96]

For needlessly antagonizing the British and as a vivid example of Wilhelmian politics, the Krüger telegram earned Weber's special reprobation. "The first, with long aftereffects, serious, and furthermore wholly unnecessary defeat suffered by German policy . . . was brought about by the foolish politics of feeling [*Gefühlspolitik*] in the Boer question," Weber wrote in 1916. And yet, he was forced to concede, not the Kaiser but the Germans were to blame for the fiasco: "The nation . . . *not diplomacy* made the mistake. It was a completely aimless policy of feeling which brought that upon us. And it was only one of numerous cases."[97] Although ill advised politically, the emotional gesture of the Krüger telegram was, as Weber acknowledged, extraordinarily popular in Germany. Even a seasoned diplomat like Anton Monts, despite his criticism of nearly everything about the Kaiser's reign, could write Bülow one month later: "The only thing that is going well is our foreign policy. The Krüger telegram has my complete approval. If only one doesn't back down."[98]

It would be difficult, however, to describe the telegram to President Krüger as constituting part of a foreign "policy," let alone part of a policy of rational self-interest. Rather, as Weber recognized, it represented an outburst of emotion. Wilhelm's sense of triumphant satisfaction at the English defeat by the Boers was shared by Monts and many other Germans. Feeling themselves treated with insufficient respect by the British and the other European world powers and envious of England's mighty empire, the Kaiser and his subjects appear to have identified on some level with the tiny Boer Republics' act of heroic defiance.[99] Wilhelm's telegram gave dramatic expression to this identification with the Boers. It was a symbolic defiance of the British that paralleled the military defeat of Jameson's raiders.[100]

As World War I approached, many Germans became convinced that the future held only two alternatives for the Reich: international respect or national humiliation. Echoing the words of Max Weber uttered nearly twenty years before in the same location, Friedrich Meinecke expressed the anxiety coupled with the insistent demand for international respect so characteristic of the Wilhelmian era. He told his listeners at Freiburg University in 1913: "A new epoch of world history is beginning that will place the nations of the world on a scale to decide whether they are capable of helping to determine world history and of contributing creatively to world culture or whether they are to be condemned to a dependent and stagnant land-locked existence [*Binnenexistenz*]."[101] Despite the domestic crises and scandals, despite the foreign policy fiascos, despite the fact that *Weltpolitik* and naval expansion had led to Germany's virtual diplomatic and military isolation, Meinecke, one year before the beginning of the war that would bring about the collapse of Kaiserdom and Reich, contended that Wilhelm II—particularly through his expansion of German military and naval power—had tipped the scale in the direction of international respect.[102] Under the leadership of the Kaiser, Germany had moved further away from the humiliating *Binnenexistenz* that Britain had sought to impose upon the Boers and had moved closer to the status of a world power, independent, strong, and deserving of respect.

According to Heinrich Mann, Germany under the Kaiser was like Diederich Hessling. Both exhibited the brash arrogance and the anxious insecurity of the recently wealthy and the suddenly powerful—wealth and power, it should be added, that they had not achieved themselves but had inherited from their ancestors. Lacking the self-assurance derived from a tradition of the responsible exercise of economic and military power, Wilhelmian Germany, like the parvenu Hessling, was uncertain of its position in the world, eager to assert its newly acquired wealth and power and yet "touchy," ever ready to see a denigration of its status in the slightest rebuff. For Mann, that power and insecurity when combined with a hierarchical disposition of authority made for domestic oppression, as those with political power and social status ostentatiously sought to assert themselves over those beneath them in the hierarchy, and for international disaster, as the newly unified and industrialized Reich ostentatiously sought to assert its economic power and military might over the other nations of the world.

Looking back after the war on the history of the period through which he had lived and to which he had contributed, Walther Rathenau also concluded that German foreign policy under Wilhelm II reflected the emotional needs of an immature, *nouveau riche* country, uncertain of its status and eager to show off its wealth and importance.

One had become rich, one had become powerful, and wanted to show it to the world; and like the neophyte traveler in a foreign country who is critical, loud, and authoritative, so one wanted to conduct oneself in world affairs. A policy of telegrams and sudden decisions lay in this direction. Set on technology and so-called achievements, greedy for festivals, for the astonishing, for parades, and noisy nullities, for those things which the Berliners had invented the mocking names of *Klimbim* and *Klamauk*, an overheated big city life that was hungry for deeds demanded a representation that could unite Rome and Byzantium, Versailles and Potsdam on a single salver.[103]

The Kaiser was that representation; the Krüger telegram, the campaign in China, the naval building program, the drive to become a *Weltmacht* were all that policy of *Klimbim* and *Klamauk*, all expressions of the demand of this economically and militarily powerful yet internally divided and uncertain nation that it be recognized, appreciated, and respected.[104]

Harden's "enlightened" critics were correct to attribute these aims to the Kaiser. Wilhelm II's inner disunity and uncertainty drove him to demand that he be recognized, appreciated, and respected. That goal ultimately formed the basis of his leadership of the Germans. He told Eulenberg in 1903:

> I have never thought about autocracy, but I have long ago made my program of *how* I wanted to be German Kaiser, how I conceived of the German Kaiser: Deep into the most distant jungles of other parts of the world, everyone should know the voice of the German Kaiser. *Nothing* should occur on this earth without having first heard him. His word must have its weight placed on every scale. Well—and I think I have generally held to my program! Also domestically, the word of the Kaiser should be *everything!*[105]

The program for the man had become fused with the program for the nation. It was hoped that the national voice of the Kaiser would submerge the discordant babble of German voices all speaking at once on behalf of their own narrow interests. Foreign affairs provided the principal escape from the domestic din. In this fragmented country, in this recently and insecurely consolidated nation, the emotional goal that the voice of Germany, of the German Kaiser, be listened to throughout the world was perhaps the only goal that Germans could agree upon.

CHAPTER 9

The Kaiser, the Navy, and *Weltpolitik*

The wish that the German Kaiser and the German people be listened to in every corner of the world found expression in the burning ambition to practice *Weltpolitik*, to practice world politics. Events during the reign of Wilhelm II that otherwise seem unintelligible or unrelated become comprehensible and consistent if they are understood as manifestations of the demand that the Reich be accepted and respected as a great world power: the founding of the Pan-German League in 1891 and of the Naval League in 1899; the Krüger telegram in 1896; the German occupation of Kiaochow in 1897; the Kaiser's visit to the Holy Land in 1898; the Samoan tangle and the Samoan treaty in 1899; the conflict over the construction of a *Mittellandkanal* in 1899; the reaction to the Boxer Rebellion in 1900; the Bagdad railway; German conduct in the Moroccan crises of 1905 and 1911; the deterioration of Anglo-German relations; and the building of a German battlefleet. So perplexing from the perspective of Bismarckian *Realpolitik*, German naval development becomes readily intelligible if world politics are understood from the perspective of *Gefühlspolitik*, the Wilhelmian politics of feeling.[1] It was appropriate, therefore, that the Kaiser regarded the construction of a high seas' fleet to be his grandest achievement. Bringing his subjects to share his feeling that a mighty navy represented national strength and would therefore secure international recognition for the Reich was the culmination of Wilhelm II's symbolic leadership of the Germans.

If in most areas of foreign and domestic policy the Kaiser's influence was less than he claimed for himself or was ascribed to him by contemporaries, his contribution to the development of the German navy and to the mobilization of the German people behind naval development was decisive. Nevertheless, Admiral Tirpitz has usually been credited both with devising the plan to increase and modernize the navy and with executing the mass political action that enabled the plan to be put into practice. Without taking away from Tirpitz's role in designing the Tirpitz plan or manipulating public opinion, the

Kaiser must be regarded as the moving force behind the creation of a mighty German navy and the transformation of Germany from a continentally oriented country, proud of the achievements of its armies, to a nation that thought of itself in global terms and dreamed of grandeur on the high seas.[2]

I

From the first, ships and navies were associated with strength and stability for Wilhelm.[3] In exile, he told an interviewer that on board ship "one lived as though on an island; nobody bothered you, but you could send your orders by telegram wherever and whenever you wished."[4] Connected to the outside world and yet insulated from its demands and soothed by the movement of the boat, Wilhelm experienced relief from what he described to Ganghofer as the "misunderstandings" he had to endure as Kaiser and from his tendency toward "*Verdrossenheit*."[5] Like the military entourage, which enabled Wilhelm to merge with its masculine strength, ships, particularly naval vessels, increased his sense of security; like entering a town at the head of a column of soldiers, command of a naval flotilla increased his self-confidence.[6] Since ships were associated with power and stability, Germany's lack of an imposing fleet became connected with insecurity and instablity for the Kaiser. Without a mighty navy, Wilhelm's authority and prestige were diminished and the Reich was exposed to hostile naval action and international humiliation. It is not surprising that when Wilhelm felt threatened or belittled he clamored for an increase in naval strength.

The Kaiser's sense of vulnerability in the absense of a powerful navy helps to account for the significance of the Krüger telegram in the history of German naval development.[7] Although Wilhelm had long favored naval increases, his humiliation, impotence, and fear in the face of the outraged British reaction to his telegram to President Krüger gave his demand for naval expansion a desperate urgency and transformed German naval policy. Before the Krüger telegram, it had been the navy's mission to defend Germany and promote the commercial and diplomatic interests of the Reich. German strategic planning assumed a war with France and Russia and allowed for the possibility that the Triple Alliance (Germany, Austria-Hungary, and Italy) would have the assistance of Britain's Royal Navy in the event of such a conflict.[8] Naval development centered around the construction of cruisers. After the Krüger telegram, Alfred Tirpitz became the Kaiser's key adviser on naval affairs, a man who believed that only by challenging Britain's naval supremacy with a battlefleet could the Reich secure its status as a world power.[9] England became the focus of strategic thinking and construction planning, and a war with that country in the North Sea became the basis of both. Battleships took priority over cruisers and coastal defenses.[10] The naval authorities became directly involved in the formulation of a foreign policy that focused more sharply on England, and the navy assumed new importance in the thinking of the leaders of the Reich.

Unnerved by the violence of the British reaction to his telegram, the Kaiser—fearing an imminent English attack—urged that legislation be introduced to increase the size of the navy. Events in the Transvaal had demonstrated, he wrote Chancellor Hohenlohe on 7 January 1896, "that the ever more shriveled-up[11] navy has too few vessels to justify Germany's position as a world power." Now was the time, Wilhelm concluded, to use the excitement in Germany to increase the naval budget.[12] When it became clear that such an increase would not pass the Reichstag, the Kaiser grew depressed.[13] He ordered the *Kaiser*, the navy's largest cruiser in the China Sea, back to Germany to defend the Reich in the event of an English attack, and justified recalling the vessel to the secretary of state in the Foreign Office by telling him "that since the Reichstag feels so little the notion of our Fatherland vis-à-vis England and since no one is enthusiastic about or interested in the navy, I cannot weaken the Home Fleet anymore—given the uncertain prospects of this coming spring." He further ordered that German vessels stationed off the coast of South Africa be withdrawn "since I do not want them to be present when the English concentrate their naval forces."[14]

With the passage of months, the Kaiser, rather than regaining self-confidence and composure, grew more agitated. In a telegram to Hohenlohe on 25 October 1896, he expressed the fear that Britain would seize Germany's colonial possessions, an act the Reich would be powerless to prevent since "our fleet is to be regarded as amounting to a handful of peas." Reflecting Wilhelm's tendency to understand politics in emotional terms, he was not so much concerned with the loss of Germany's colonies or even with the economic, military, or diplomatic consequences of such a disaster. Instead, what he feared most was the loss of prestige that the seizure of the Reich's overseas empire by England would entail: "It would, in other words, be an easy way to give us a box on the ears and to discredit us before the world." Therefore he ordered the chancellor to open negotiations with Russia and France for the mutual protection of the respective colonial empires in the face of the British naval threat, negotiations that came to naught when Germany's allies, Austria and Italy, not to speak of Russia and France, repudiated the idea of a continental league against England.[15] The Kaiser concluded that the Krüger telegram had demonstrated Germany's foolishness in acquiring colonies before having constructed a fleet to defend them. Indeed, because of "our complete powerlessness on the seas," the colonial empire had become an "Achilles heel" that for the first time made the Reich vulnerable to British attack.[16]

In 1899 Wilhelm was still preoccupied with the Krüger telegram and with the opportunity that had then been missed to check England's colonial ambitions. On 29 October he telegraphed Bülow an account of a conversation he had at a party the previous evening with the French ambassador in Berlin. With evident self-satisfaction the Kaiser described how he had told the ambassador that the Fashoda crisis had revealed that the British were in the process of establishing a great colonial empire on the African continent. "*Now*," he had asserted, "nothing more can be done to *prevent* it. Now if the English are in any way disturbed in their work, all they have to do is make a slight movement of the elbow[17] to push all of us on the periphery of Africa effortlessly into the

sea without our being able to do the least thing about it. In the year 1896," he
continued, "the English fleet would not have been prepared and was weaker by
a third and as a result of My telegram the country was completely taken aback.
If at that time all the states had joined us, something could have been done."
Now England's navy was equal to any coalition, and Germany was as good as
without a fleet. He, the Kaiser, must therefore maintain a position of strict
neutrality until a navy had been acquired. "In twenty years," Wilhelm proclaimed, "when that fleet is ready, then I will speak a different language." He
concluded his telegram to Bülow, and presumably his remarks to the French
ambassador, with the following analogy:

> In short the same phrase can be used in regard to our naval situation that my
> late-father once called out to his brother-in-law, the Grand Duke of Hessen,
> during a trip when the latter sought to enter a very small toilet stall in the
> Cologne railway station that my father was just then using, whereupon Papa
> called out to him: "Pas encore ready."[18]

Like his telegram to Hohenlohe three years before, Wilhelm's telegram to
Bülow reveals the importance he attached to the Krüger telegram and his fear
of British naval power. His extraordinary association to his father, caught literally with his pants down, reveals the degree to which Wilhelm felt exposed
and humiliated in the absence of a mighty German navy. And finally the telegram to Bülow reveals the psychological source of those feelings. Without a
navy, the Kaiser and his nation were in the same demeaned position in relation
to England that Friedrich had occupied in relation to Ludwig IV, the Anglophile grand duke of Hessen (married to Alice, Wilhelm's English aunt), the
same position that Friedrich had occupied in relation to the powerful and domineering Victoria. As a child and adolescent, Wilhelm had experienced the personal consequences of that position for his father and for himself; as a young
adult, he had observed the political consequences of that position for Friedrich.
He did not want to occupy that position as Kaiser. He saw the creation of a
mighty German navy as the way to extricate him and his nation from it, the
way to be strong and independent, the way to insure that Kaiser and Reich be
treated with respect, the way to end Germany's "time of shame."[19]

As manifest in his demand that the *Kaiser* return to defend Germany
against possible British attack, Wilhelm flaunted the weakness of the navy to
convince his advisers and subjects of the need for its expansion. Although prevailed upon to leave the *Kaiser* in the Far East, Wilhelm used his concession
to pressure the Foreign Office (which had opposed using the Krüger affair to
submit an increased naval budget to the Reichstag) to support his campaign on
behalf of the navy. He had Admiral Eduard von Knorr, chief of the Naval High
Command, inform Hohenlohe on 3 February 1896 that, "despite our weakness
in battleships stationed in home waters and despite the fact that, of the few
modern cruisers designated for duty in home waters, half are being used in
foreign service," Wilhelm would not recall the *Kaiser*. "Therefore," Knorr concluded, "it must be our aim that an unavoidable precondition for the use of

ships in foreign service is that several more warships be built beyond the number required for service in home waters."[20] Again and again the Kaiser clashed with chancellor and Foreign Office and even on occasion with the Admiralty over the issue of dispatching naval vessels to trouble-spots around the world.[21] The ships were always too few, too small, and too old according to the Kaiser. Again and again he argued that their presence would only expose Germany's naval inferiority and humiliate the Reich.[22]

In February 1897 Hohenlohe begged the Kaiser to order the frigate *Stein*, stationed in Naples, to Crete where violence between Greeks and Turks had broken out. Given the importance of the revolt on Crete for the Eastern Question, the governments of Russia, France, England, and Italy were strengthening their naval presence off the island. Germany was not represented by a single naval vessel, and the few German nationals on the island had been forced to seek refuge on board an Austrian ship. Although his request was doubtless based upon an appreciation of the consequences of the crisis on Crete for the stability of the entire region, Hohenlohe used an argument calculated to appeal to the Kaiser. Order the *Stein* to Crete, he pleaded, since "it is in the interest of the Reich's honor and its status among the European powers to protect German subjects itself and to be present off the coast of Crete during the incident there." Wilhelm was not convinced by this appeal to Germany's "honor" and "status," however. "No!" he scrawled angrily in the margin of the chancellor's letter. "Training vessels are not to be used for serious political purposes. The Reichstag must first perceive our naval shame."[23] The following month the Kaiser reacted with angry satisfaction to the news that, because the Powers had failed to take the decisive naval action against Greece that Wilhelm had advocated, the government in Athens was now apparently ignoring their demand that Greece withdraw its ships and men from Crete. "Out of all this one sees again how greviously Germany feels the *lack* of a *powerful navy*, since it is not able to assert itself effectively in the Concert. . . . Therefore nothing was done in the end, and the one who cancels out all plans, paralyzes[24] all energetic action and to whom therefore in the end attention is paid is England! And why? *Because it has the strongest navy*! Our 1,000,000 grenadiers are thereby of *no use* to us!"[25]

A year later the Kaiser expressed similar sentiments, this time in connection with the effort of the German government to use the Anglo-Portuguese negotiations over the disposition of the Portuguese empire to exact colonial concessions for the Reich. Wilhelm's anger at Lord Salisbury, which would culminate in his acrimonious correspondence with Queen Victoria of the following spring, was already evident in July 1898.[26] When he learned that the British prime minister had responded negatively to a German proposal because of the need "to take account of the mood in Australia," the Kaiser was outraged:

The conduct of Lord Salisbury is frankly jesuitical, monstrous, and impudent! As he has to take the mood of his colonies into account, I have to take account of the mood of the German people; and for *me*, it is the decisive factor. From this we once again see how the noble Lord plays and trifles with us simply because he has no fear of us since *we have* no fleet as a result of the doltish Reichstag's having constantly threatened its development during the 10 years of my reign. Furthermore I stand upon my rights and make *no further concessions.* In agreement with the view of Mr. v. Bülow that it is better to allow the unavoidable to befall us and to use it to build the navy.[27]

Wilhelm used every opportunity to make his subjects experience the indignation he felt at Germany's naval inferiority, and he commanded that documents highlighting this national disgrace be circulated "in order to create a mood for naval increases."[28] Even the visit of the British Home Fleet in 1905 was to be used to shame and frighten the Germans into supporting the navy. "It would be advisable," Wilhelm telegraphed the Foreign Office on 15 August 1905, "if—through skillful press releases and the publication of railroad time-tables with the possible addition of extra trains with reduced fares—large numbers of Germans from inland could have the opportunity to view the English 'Home Fleet' anchored off Swinemünde with their own eyes. The view would do much to clarify the evaluation of our own naval situation and would be most valuable politically. Please take the discreet steps necessary to bring this about."[29]

In seeking to bring the Germans to share his sense of the navy's importance, Wilhelm set the tone and determined the direction of a propaganda campaign which, in the words of the author of the definitive study of the public relations effort, Wilhelm Deist, "was the first . . . attempt to realize a military-political program through the systematically and continuously practiced manipulation of public opinion."[30] Already in late 1893/early 1894 the Kaiser set forth the principle that would guide the campaign that resulted in the passage of the German Navy Law of 1898. Instead of attempting to get naval increases through the Reichstag by lobbying the recalcitrant deputies, Wilhelm instructed the Naval High Command and the Reich Naval Office to devote their energies to the "enlightenment" of the general public to the need for naval development. The expansion of the German navy, then, would be pushed through the Reichstag less by government pressure from above and more by popular pressure from below.[31] As early as 1894, he commanded that diplomatic dispatches and the reports of navy commanders stationed abroad be distributed to the press in order to increase popular awareness of the loss of prestige resulting from German naval weakness, a practice that would be supplemented a few years later by the unprecedented use of the reports of naval attachés to "give the German public a picture of the development and significance" of the fleets of the Reich's potential adversaries.[32]

Following the Krüger telegram Wilhelm sought to use the tension with England over South Africa to engender popular support for the navy. In May 1896 a Royal Cabinet Order decreed that the naval officer corps agitate for increases in the naval budget particularly through contact with popular organizations supporting naval development. Industries that stood to gain from naval construction were to be encouraged to participate in the campaign with their financial and political resources. Finally, the circulation of information about maritime issues was to be increased and those sections of the press sympathetic to the navy were to be promoted. According to the Order, these measures were to achieve three objectives:

I. The instruction and guidance of broad segments of the population about the new national mission which the development of our maritime interests must sustain.

II. The understanding, especially in educated circles, of the development of naval power, which on the one hand forms the only healthy basis for the Empire's maritime interests and on the other promotes German economic strength and the flourishing of public welfare, in the broadest sense beneficial.

III. The comprehensive and continuing increase of the already partially mobilized popular trend for further development of our maritime interests and naval power.[33]

Traditional politicians like Chancellor Hohenlohe, Secretary of State in the Foreign Office Marschall, and Secretary of State in the Reich Naval Office Admiral Friedrich Hollmann had little understanding or sympathy for the attempt to rouse German public opinion, however.[34] Hohenlohe interpreted it as a symptom of Wilhelm's instability. "For the Chancellor," his friend Hutten-Czapski reported, "this movement with its noisy vehemence was politically uncomfortable and unwelcome. He regarded it more as a boiling up of a pretentious politics of feeling [*Gefühlspolitik*] rather than a serious politics of realism [*Realpolitik*]. In his gentlemanly and objective manner, he expressed himself in approximately this sense to the Kaiser in order to prevent further royal 'suddennesses.'"[35] Thus, even if the principles of a broadly based propaganda campaign had already been set forth in May 1896, the energies of the government on behalf of the navy remained focused on the Reichstag. In March 1897 after that body's defeat of the naval bill, the Kaiser, although contemplating a dissolution of the Reichstag and toying with the idea of a *Staatsstreich*,[36] continued his effort to transform public opinion. To a report in March 1897 that the middle class was coming to recognize that German commerce could not flourish without a powerful navy, Wilhelm ordered: "This mood must be methodically exploited and strengthened by the press. At the same time the people must be oriented and incited against the Reichstag."[37] When, under pressure from the Kaiser, Hollmann submitted his resignation as secretary of state in the Reich Naval Office, Hohenlohe noted gloomily in his diary:

Hollmann's departure is a catastrophe for the navy. Without the Reichstag H.M. can't make a navy. For the Reichstag, Hollmann is at present irreplaceable. If H.M. wants to proceed without the Reichstag, then comes conflict and dissolution. From that follow measures involving force.[38]

The chancellor could hardly have been more mistaken. In Hollmann's replacement, Alfred Tirpitz, the navy and the Kaiser found an effective proponent of naval development. Through mass political action, Wilhelm and Tirpitz were able to achieve what traditional political lobbying had failed to accomplish. In conjunction with powerful industrial and commercial circles, the Reich Naval Office manipulated the press, abetted popular naval and colonial leagues, and generally spent vast amounts of financial and political capital to produce a groundswell of popular support for the development of the German navy. Within a year the Reichstag had passed a naval law setting forth the long-range expansion and modernization of the navy. What the Kaiser had described as the "struggle for the fleet" had been won with astonishing ease.[39]

II

As naval vessels increased Wilhelm's sense of strength, harmony, and cohesion, so he assumed that the construction of a powerful navy would increase the strength, harmony, and cohesion of the Reich. World and naval policy would enhance national self-esteem and establish a national agenda.[40] "The people must have goals," he told Bülow in 1897, "without goals, without achieving something, without our voice being heard, morale [*Stimmung*] is not to be achieved."[41] For Wilhelm, the "struggle for the fleet" was enobling, sustaining, and integrative: bringing together North and South, Protestant and Catholic, capitalist and worker, aristocrat and farmer.[42] The navy was modern and liberal: it served the economic interests of industry and to a degree the middle class as a whole and had been a favorite liberal cause since 1848. The navy was authoritarian: it was the weapon of a conservative and militaristic state. The navy was imperialist: it was an instrument of colonial expansion. The navy was "*kaiserliche*": it embodied monarchical-imperial power. As the integration of the Reich would be increased by focusing popular attention on the person of the Kaiser, Germans would be brought together in their support for the construction of this massive, mighty national symbol.[43] Wilhelm told the British prime minister Arthur Balfour in 1902:

> Whereas England forms a political totality complete unto itself, Germany resembles a mosaic in which the individual pieces are still clearly distinguishable and have not yet blended together. This is manifested by the army which, though inspired by the identical patriotic spirit, is still made up of contingents from the various German states. The young German Reich needs institutitions in which the unitary idea of a Reich is embodied. The navy is such an institution. The Kaiser is its only commander. The Germans from all counties trend toward it, and it is a constant living example of the unity of the Reich. For this reason alone, it is necessary and finds a warm supporter in H.M.[44]

In part because the navy served the cause of national integration, Wilhelm insisted that Tirpitz be appointed an active member of the Prussian State Ministry following the passage of the Navy Law in March 1898. Wilhelm would have nothing to do with Hohenlohe's suggestion that Tirpitz be made an honorary Prussian state minister. The Kaiser demanded that Tirpitz have full voting and seating privileges and rejected the concern expressed by members of the Ministry that Tirpitz's appointment as an active member could lead to a subordination of Prussian interests to the interests of the Reich. For Wilhelm this was a development to be welcomed rather than feared, and his conduct in this episode, as in others involving the conflict between national and particularist interests, was guided by the principle that placed the German before the Prussian, the national before the federal character of the Reich.[45]

Consistent with Wilhelm's sense that naval development promoted national cohesion was his concern with the fleet's symbolic impact, with "the harmony and homogeneousness" of its impression.[46] Since the navy was a modern institution, the fleet was to be up-to-date and technologically advanced. Since the navy was an expression of imperial aspirations, it was to be vast and imposing. Since the navy was a national institution, foreign nautical terms were ordered Germanified by the Kaiser on 1 January 1899. Since the navy was a monarchical institution, he forbade any other federal prince to affiliate with it, declaring that he "wants to be the only German prince to wear the naval officer's uniform."[47] Only the imperial German flag was to be raised on naval vessels. The standards of the German states, including that of the king of Prussia (that is, of Wilhelm himself), could only be raised with the Kaiser's expressed permission.[48]

Wilhelm's preoccupation with the symbolic value of the fleet helps explain his position in the debate that raged in naval circles until 1897 over whether the future German navy should be primarily composed of cruisers or battleships. Initially, in opposition to Tirpitz, Wilhelm advocated the construction of a vast fleet of high-speed cruisers.[49] The Kaiser's position in this controversy can be attributed in part to the persuasiveness of the arguments of the French naval strategists of the *Jeune École*, who believed that cruisers either operating independently or stationed along world shipping lanes could be used during wartime to destroy enemy merchant vessels only to steam away with the appearance of the larger but slower enemy battleships. According to these strategists, victory at sea would be achieved less through armed confrontation and more through a kind of maritime guerila warfare in which the commercial lifelines of the enemy would be cut. The Kaiser's advocacy of cruiser construction was probably based on more than strategic considerations, however. On the one hand, with his own congenital restlessness, Wilhelm was doubtless taken with the speed that these cruisers would possess. On the other hand, the size of the cruiser fleet and the fact that it would be stationed all around the globe doubtless appealed to him as well. Not only could cruisers be used to great effect diplomatically (sparing Wilhelm and his subjects the humiliation of not having the ships to represent Germany's interests abroad), but they would insure that Kaiser and Reich would be tangibly represented in every corner of the world.[50]

As a result it was only with difficulty that Tirpitz persuaded the Kaiser to abandon the idea of a navy composed of cruisers in favor of a battlefleet. Following the theories of the American naval captain Alfred Mahan, Tirpitz argued that the outcome of one decisive engagement on the high seas between rival battlefleets would determine not only naval supremacy but the survival of the nation as a great power. The Kaiser's conversion to this view in June 1897 would have fateful consequences. Whereas a cruiser fleet was suited to serve as an instrument of *Weltpolitik* and to symbolze the omnipresence of Kaiser and Reich, the battlefleet—although a symbol of national and imperial omnipotence—posed a direct naval challenge to Britain.[51]

As historians like Volker Berghahn have argued forcefully and for the most part convincingly, Tirpitz and his supporters in the navy saw the battlefleet from the outset as an offensive weapon designed, either through the threat of its use or in combat, to wrest naval and ultimately, perhaps, world hegemony away from the English.[52] In fact, it was precisely because of their ineffectiveness against Britain that Tirpitz opposed the development of high-speed cruisers. As a result of Germany's geographical position and lack of naval bases abroad, a cruiser war with Britain would have been, in his words, "completely out of the question." Therefore he concluded that if the German navy was to pose an effective challenge to Britain "it comes down, also viewed politically, to the battleship war between Helgoland and the Thames."[53] Tirpitz acknowledged that in foreign service in time of peace cruisers had significant benefits. Echoing the Kaiser, he saw these including: "a. demonstrating to the world Germany's interest in shaping local conditions abroad; b. securing the right to have a say and to make our claims valid [*sichert Recht mitreden zu können und Ansprüche geltend zu machen*]; c. creating respect for the Germans among the Chinese and smaller South American states; d. elevating the German element."[54] Still, what was critical for Tirpitz was the navy's function in time of war, especially in a war against Britain. Thus the development of the slow, heavily armored, short-range battleships had to take precedence over the faster, lightly armored, long-range cruisers and over coastal defenses.[55] It seems clear that for Tirpitz the German navy was first and foremost to be composed of battleships whose primary purpose was to challenge English naval supremacy and then, should it come to war, to enable the Reich to supplant Britain as the premier naval and world power.

And yet, despite his logical mind and meticulous plan for naval development, Tirpitz could be inconsistent in defining the purpose of the navy. Believing that the battlefleet would "make possible a policy of world power,"[56] Tirpitz, in defining the navy's role in that policy, appeared occasionally to enter the emotional universe in which Wilhelm II tended to operate. For him, as for the Kaiser, the fleet's ability to uphold national honor was by no means an insignificant part of its value to the nation. Like Wilhelm, he was convinced that the battlefleet would enable the Reich to avoid international humiliation, particularly at the hands of the British.[57] As early as the fall of 1898, Tirpitz argued before the Kaiser that the rapid development of the battlefleet was critical in order to secure "Germany's position of world power," "to preserve world peace," and "to ward off the danger of serious political humiliation." Its importance in wartime he mentioned almost as an afterthought.[58] A year later he told the Kaiser that once an effective force of forty-five ships of the line had been created not only would the fleet have a real chance against the Royal Navy but it would cause the British to treat Reich and Kaiser with respect:

> Apart from the for us by no means prospectless conditions of battle, England, for general political reasons and from the purely sober perspective of the businessman, will have lost every inclination to attack us and as a result will concede such a measure of maritime prestige [*Seegeltung*] to Your Majesty and will enable Your Majesty to practice a grand overseas' policy.[59]

Nevertheless, it seems likely that in making these arguments Tirpitz sought to accommodate himself to the Kaiser—just as there appear to be times when Wilhelm sought to accommodate himself to the state secretary. For when all is said and done England as "the great naval danger"[60] outweighed England as the ceder of "*Seegeltung*" in Tirpitz's thinking and power outweighed prestige in his vocabulary. Conversely, although Wilhelm could on occasion identify England as one of Germany's adversaries,[61] winning the respect of the British dominated his thinking about German naval development in relation to their country. Although he could speak the language of power politics, the primary purpose of the navy for Wilhelm was to secure recognition, "*Geltung*," for Kaiser and Reich.[62]

Before 1896 Wilhelm had little reason to waver in his support for the cruiser fleet. But then came the shock and humiliation of the British reaction to the Krüger telegram. Wilhelm's sense of vulnerability and fear of the British after January 1896 when coupled with the force of Tirpitz's convictions and personality caused him to accept the construction of a battlefleet and the transformation of what had been a global naval policy to one that focused primarily on Britain. Although he made the strategic arguments to the Kaiser, the evidence of Tirpitz's notes suggests that it was his ability to sell the battlefleet to Wilhelm in the familiar terms of honor and prestige—set now primarily in the context of the Anglo-German relationship—that made the difference. From its role in representing Kaiser and Reich around the world and in raising the image of both in the eyes of Chinese and South Americans, the navy's purpose, as Tirpitz presented it to Wilhelm, now became to insure that Kaiser and Reich be spared another humiliation at the hands of the British and that in the future they would treat Wilhelm and the Germans with respect. Indeed, the Kaiser believed that the battlefleet would actually make possible an Anglo-German alliance compatible with Germany's independence and honor.[63] For Tirpitz, the battlefleet would perhaps enable the Reich to supplant Britain; for Wilhelm, it would enable the Reich to become more nearly her equal.

Even after the Tirpitz plan had been instituted, the state secretary constantly needed to bolster the Kaiser's commitment to it by reminding him of the prestige value of the battlefleet and its ability to uphold imperial and national honor.[64] In fact, at least through the summer of 1906, Wilhelm displayed a—to Tirpitz disconcerting—tendency to return to his dream of a vast fleet of high-speed vessels that could be used in foreign service. Tirpitz constantly needed to reassert the priority of the battlefleet over the *Auslandsflotte* and over Germany's coastal defenses and force of torpedo boats, which the Kaiser was also anxious to develop.[65] In late 1903/early 1904 Wilhelm's enthusiasm for fast, long-range vessels was rekindled when he learned that the British had been constructing high-speed, lightly armored ships that had the firepower to join the battleships in the line. To Wilhelm these vessels doubtless represented an ideal compromise between him and his state secretary. They would have all the diplomatic and symbolic advantages of the cruiser fleet in peacetime. Unlike the battlefleet, they were not directed more or less exclusively against the Royal Navy. And yet these ships would be compatible with Tirpitz's battlefleet in a war with England. For the next several years the construction of these "fast ships of the line" became the Kaiser's naval preoccupation. Not only did he bombard his long-suffering state secretary with letters, charts, and memoranda in which he detailed the myriad benefits of these vessels, but, to Tirpitz's dismay, in 1904 he actually published an article in the *Marine Rundschau* under a pseudonym defending his pet naval project.[66] Although Tirpitz always managed to overcome the Kaiser's insistence that the navy construct fast ships of the line and to reaffirm to Wilhelm the priority of the battlefleet, this conflict reflects the fact that despite their shared commitment to naval development—indeed to the development of a battlefleet—Kaiser and state secretary understood the mission of the navy in different terms and defined its purpose in different ways.

Two studies of Bernhard von Bülow's foreign policy suggest that, like Tirpitz, Bülow had a consistent and clearly articulated strategy of using the navy to achieve world power for the Reich at the expense of England.[67] According to Peter Winzen and Barbara Vogel, Bülow's "policy of the free hand" was actually designed to steer the Reich through the hazardous period, the so-called "danger zone," that would exist until the battlefleet was ready and Germany, in alliance with Russia, was in a position to challange British naval and world hegemony.[68] After 1897, Bülow sought to keep England isolated and promote Anglo-Russian antagonism while working toward a rapprochement with Russia that would protect Germany from military assault on the continent. The main reason Bülow did not pursue an alliance with Russia more aggressively, according to this view, was because he did not want to provoke a British naval assault during the period of the fleet's vulnerability. For these two historians, Björkö, rather than the product of Wilhelm's theatrical personal diplomacy, was the culmination of Bülow's carefully orchestrated rapprochement with Russia and would serve, in Vogel's words, as the "cornerstone" of his foreign policy.[69] The chancellor's emphatic rejection of the accord is explained by Winzen as resulting from Bülow's recognition that the restriction of the treaty to Europe made it ineffective against England and by Vogel as resulting from his recognition that since Russia would not be split off from France the treaty would merely antagonize England and expose the fleet to a British preemptive strike.[70] For Winzen and Vogel, the collapse of the Björkö treaty signaled the failure of Bülow's strategy to secure world power for the Reich.

There are problems with this view of Bülow's conception of German foreign policy. In contrast to the more rigid Tirpitz who would not be deflected from the systematic realization of his naval plans, Bülow was an eminently adaptable character, known to contemporaries as "the eely smooth Bülow," and it is difficult to imagine him assiduously realizing a fixed concept of world power. He seems genuinely to have believed in the period after 1897 that, given the apparently irreconcilable differences between England and France and especially between England and Russia, Germany, by keeping nonaligned, could exploit its position at the fulcrum of power in Europe.[71] In Bülow's view, the navy, rather than being the end of German foreign policy, would make "the policy of the free hand" possible: the fleet would enable the Reich to secure its freedom of action in the world just as the army guaranteed Germany's independence on the continent.[72] Indeed, there is evidence that the chancellor never understood Tirpitz's battleship doctrine or North Sea strategy against England.[73]

Although Vogel, in marked contrast to Winzen, portrays the Kaiser as agreeing with Bülow's blueprint for world power, she ignores all the evidence making it impossible to portray Wilhelm II as England's implacable foe, secretly and consistently plotting the destruction of the maritime and imperial power of Britain.[74] Furthermore, this view of Bülow's foreign policy is difficult to reconcile with the policies pursued at various times by the German Foreign Office.[75] Thus Vogel is forced to concede that the Björkö treaty, the culmination and the cornerstone of Bülow's foreign policy, was undertaken behind the back of the secretary of state in the Foreign Office, Oswald Freiherr von Richthofen.[76] Indeed, their view of Bülow's foreign policy causes Vogel and, to a lesser extent, Winzen to adopt a view of Björkö that stands in sharp contrast to the generally accepted version of this episode.[77] Finally, it seems just as logical to argue that an alliance with Russia would deter an English assault upon the German battlefleet as provoke one. And yet, even if Bülow is seen as less dogmatic in his adherence to the objective of replacing Britain as a world power than Winzen and Vogel suggest, it still seems credible that high on Bülow's foreign political agenda was providing "diplomatic cover" while battlefleet and Reich passed through the "danger zone."[78]

As Tirpitz and Bülow recognized themselves, however, the navy for Wilhelm was designed to fulfill an emotional mission: to display and enhance the power and prestige of the German Reich and of the German Kaiser.[79] The navy was a symbol of Germany's status as a great world power and of Wilhelm's status as a great world leader. It was also a weapon to insure that Germany would be treated by the other powers with appropriate deference and respect and that, as Wilhelm told the king of Italy in 1908, "one harkens more to the voice of the German Kaiser."[80] Finally, in the common experience of pride in the Reich's naval and world power, domestic divisions would be overcome.

III

Wilhelm II's vision of naval and world policy was greeted with widespread and intense popular enthusiasm.[81] Those who stood to profit from naval construction and colonial expansion were, of course, zealous proponents of *Weltpolitik*. Its supporters were hardly restricted to those Germans, however. And if the middle classes and their representatives in the Reichstag formed the social and political basis for naval imperialism, within a short time it had acquired the support of the majority of the German people and of the Reichstag deputies.[82] Indeed, some political parties backed naval construction against the economic interests of their constituents.[83] By 1907 support for an expansionistic imperial policy had become so broad and so passionate that it was politically dangerous to oppose *Weltpolitik* for fear of being labeled unpatriotic.[84] Even the Social Democrats, the staunchest adversaries of world politics, were unable to resist the aggressive nationalism that lay behind it; and in 1914, once they had convinced themselves of the defensive character of the war, they joined the patriotic chorus with relief.[85] Although Wilhelm's popularity declined when he was perceived to abandon his message of international prestige and national unity or to fail to fulfill its promise with concrete achievements, the message itself remained broadly and deeply popular in Germany up to the outbreak of the war and beyond.

The immediacy and the intensity of the popular response suggests that the Kaiser's subjects had anticipated his message and needed him only to articulate it for them. Already in 1890 the head of the Colonial Division in the Foreign Office, Paul Kayser, declared that "no government, no Reichstag, would be in the position of giving up colonies without humiliating itself before Germany and Europe. Nowadays a colonial policy has supporters in all parts of the nation and no political party, apart from the Socialists [could ignore this feeling]."[86] Four years later the British ambassador, Sir Edward Malet, reported that enthusiasm for colonial acquisition had become so intense that the Kaiser seemed to be "following, almost of necessity, an unmistakable ebullition of feeling."[87] Thus Wilhelm's speech in the Berlin *Schloss* on 18 January 1896, on the twenty-fifth anniversary of the unification of Germany, was instantly understood by his subjects as the imperial proclamation of *Weltpolitik*.[88] The Kaiser's statements that "the German Empire has become a World Empire" and that it was the task of the German people to stand together in "complete unity" to help their emperor "bind this greater empire firmly to our German homeland" were greeted with excitement.[89] The historian Hans Delbrück professed to see signaled in Wilhelm's speech a "great revolution in German foreign policy" which would "also have profound repercussions for domestic conditions."[90] The leaders of the Pan German movement claimed that in

Wilhelm's words "we find the program of the League."[91] And when the rumor spread during January that the Kaiser planned a major increase in the size of the navy, liberal public opinion was enthusiastic.[92]

The ease with which Kaiser and country fell into step over naval and world policy was remarkable. Despite his initial lack of enthusiasm for the Kaiser's naval dreams, Chancellor Hohenlohe could write on 7 November 1897 that, in wanting to create a fleet, Wilhelm was doing "nothing other than what the German people have been striving for over the past one hundred and fifty years."[93] What had seemed impossible only a few months before, when in March the naval bill had been defeated in the Reichstag, now appeared to Hohenlohe the inevitable culmination of a century and a half of historical development. By 1900 the value of naval and world policy had become accepted as a matter of course. "It is astonishing," Michael Salewski wrote in his study of New Year's 1900 in Germany, "how naturally already at the turn of the century the term '*Weltmacht*' found its way into the mass media, how naturally and naively even the non-political, humorous papers merged *Weltpolitik*, naval construction, and German 'honor' together."[94]

But if Germans were predisposed to receive Wilhelm's message on the purpose of the navy and on the significance of *Weltpolitik*, they were convinced that he deserved the credit for defining and developing naval and world policy and for mobilizing the general populace behind both. Admiral Tirpitz, despite his criticisms of the Kaiser and eagerness to take credit for the navy, wrote in his memoirs that "without the Emperor, Germany's estrangement from the sea, and the interests and tasks bound up with the latter, would never have been overcome. That is his historic merit."[95] Philipp Eulenburg, after his disgrace and as the negative consequences of naval development were becoming increasingly evident, described the Kaiser as having bewitched the "entire" nation through the "power of suggestion" onto this disastrous course.[96] Germans less intimately connected to the Kaiser shared these views—though, until the end of the war, more would have agreed with Tirpitz than with Eulenburg on the value of naval expansion.

On 15 June 1913 Wilhelm's subjects, despite their mounting dissatisfaction with his performance, could still honor the Kaiser on the twenty-fifth anniversary of his accession to the throne as the leader who had transformed Germany into a *Weltmacht* and a *Weltreich* and who had transformed the Germans into a people who thought in global terms. Despite the Eulenburg scandal and the *Daily Telegraph* affair, despite the Moroccan crises and the "encirclement" of the Reich, Friedrich Meinecke could still celebrate Wilhelm at Freiburg University as the *Flottenkaiser*.[97] Meinecke saw Wilhelm's expansion of the navy and even more his having brought his initially skeptical subjects to share his enthusiasm for naval power as the greatest achievement of the reign. "Practically from the beginning," Meinecke told his listeners, "he had ceaselessly converted the nation and enticed it out onto the water—with romantic fantasy, with a sailor's delight, with sober calculation and shining images of glory. Today," Meinecke concluded, "he has the satisfaction of knowing that his conviction has become the conviction of the nation."[98] On the same day and on the same occasion the historian Hermann Oncken, despite his criticism of the Kaiser, could celebrate Wilhelm at Heidelberg University as the moving force behind *Weltpolitik*, the leader who had widened the physical and spiritual horizons of the Germans. "Consciously and with perseverance," Oncken declared, "he directed the politics of the Reich, which under Bismarck had had an essentially continental orientation, out into the world. In this effort he was able to use his personality to its greatest effect; in this effort will lie, as far as we are now able to judge, his unique significance for world history. Here too, the world experiences a new era of German aspirations."[99]

In a speech that captures as well as any single document the spirit of Wilhelmian imperialism, a third historian, Otto Hintze, celebrated the twenty-fifth anniversary of Wilhelm's accession to the throne.[100] Hintze reminded his listeners in the Aula of the Friedrich-Wilhelm University in Berlin that at one point the need for colonies had been questioned since they required that along with its army Germany possess a formidable fleet. "Had this faint-hearted and land-locked policy prevailed," Hintze asserted, Germany "would have sunk slowly but surely to the level of a second-rate power." Either the Reich had to develop a powerful navy "or it had to abandon the attempt to stand in the same row with the great world powers."[101] For Hintze, as for Meinecke and Oncken, Wilhelm II's significance lay in his having recognized before his contemporaries the great and essential world-political tasks confronting the Reich and in his having "thrust the entire weight of his position and personality" behind their fulfillment.[102] It was the Kaiser who was able "to overcome the ingrained habits and prejudices of a purely land-locked conception of state and politics which then dominated our thinking." Thanks to his promotion of world policy and naval development, Hintze declared, "the scales fell from our eyes."[103]

In a sense Hintze was responding to Max Weber's inaugural address at Freiburg University delivered in 1895, before the construction of the fleet and the political thrust out into the world. One year before the outbreak of the war, Hintze was saying in effect that Weber's warning had been heeded. Wilhelm II's reign had not been an "epigonic completion" but "the beginning of a new world era," characterized by a great and soaring imperialistic spirit that had produced a series of advances in culture, technology, commerce, economic life, and world view, culminating in the creation of the battlefleet.[104] It was the Reich's naval might, Hintze proclaimed, which alone guaranteed that measure "of respect in the world" necessary to insure that Germany would "have a say [*mitsprechen*] in the great questions on which the fate of the peoples [of the world] depends."[105] Now the Reich was in a position to realize the goal of world politics: "the securing of our prestige [*Geltung*] alongside the other powers."[106] "Kaiser Wilhelm II," Hintze concluded, "is an epochal figure, who marks a turning point in history."[107]

Although Oncken's speech contained criticism of the Kaiser, these three speeches by these three historians are remarkably similar in tone and content. These speeches, like Weber's before them, echoed Wilhelm II's central message to the Germans—indeed, they used his very words. The immediacy and the intensity of the response of his subjects to the Kaiser's vision of naval development and *Weltpolitik* and their readiness to ascribe those policies to him confirm that Wilhelm and the Germans understood naval and world policy in essentially the same way. Less economic or political self-interest and more feelings of power and glory, purpose and pride inspired the enthusiasm for world and naval policy. Both the Kaiser and his subjects felt personally enhanced by the possession of a battlefleet that increased the power and prestige of the Reich to which they belonged and with which they identified. In their emotional response to naval and world policy and in their understanding of its emotional purpose, Wilhelm II and the Germans had become indistinguishable from one another.

The congruence between the Kaiser and his subjects over naval imperialism extended to their faith in the domestic benefit of naval construction and *Weltpolitik*. Wilhelm's conviction that, by engendering a common feeling of pride and purpose, naval construction and world policy would overcome "national malaise" and strengthen the "feeling of belonging together" was matched by Bülow's expectation that naval and world policy would have an integrative effect.[108] Tirpitz and his supporters believed that the Navy Law would become "the beacon for the rallying together [*Sammlung*] of the national parties" and that the navy possessed the "strength to reinvigorate the national feeling of the classes and to fill them again with patriotic loyalty and love for Kaiser and Reich."[109] Similar sentiments were expressed within the general population. Thus many middle-class intellectuals believed that without increased social and political unity Germany's goal of world power and world empire would have to be renounced. According to Friedrich Meinecke, the greatest task facing the Reich in 1910 was "a rallying together of the nation to defend against the dangers which threaten it," dangers arising "from the nation's position in the world and at the same time from its own unique and powerful impulses." He concluded: "should we fail to unite the whole impulsive force of the nation and all its classes and to overcome the inner divisions which threaten it, then we will stand there internally weak on the day of reckoning."[110]

In 1913, with that day only one year away, it seemed to Hermann Oncken that the external pressure on the Reich had increased German unity: "We are indeed experiencing that the growing demands of *Weltpolitik* also serve domestically to speed up the achievement of social equality and to bring gradually all of the parties to active and joyful work in the service of the nation."[111] In August 1914, in the patriotic fervor that swept the Reich, Germany's internal divisions appeared to have been overcome at last. For Moritz Heimann, a publisher of liberal and social democratic leanings, the war brought the moral unification of Germany to complement its physical unification in 1871.[112] As he had in espousing naval and world policy, the Kaiser spoke for the nation when he declared on 1 August 1914 at the royal palace in Berlin: "In the struggles that stand before us, I know no parties anymore. There are only Germans here now."[113]

IV

The conscious effort of the leaders of Germany to use the campaign on behalf of naval development and the practice of world politics to increase national integration and loyalty to the crown when coupled with the popular enthusiasm for *Weltpolitik* lies at the heart of recent historical debate over the ultimate purpose of naval and world policy. Until the 1960s, historians, with the notable exception of Eckart Kehr and a few others, took it for granted that, as Germany's leaders had evidently assumed themselves, the primary purpose of the navy was to serve the foreign political interests of the Reich. Following the publication of Fritz Fischer's studies of Germany's interests and aims immediately preceding and during the First World War in the 1960s and of Hans-Ulrich Wehler's analyses first of Bismarck's imperialism and then of the *Kaiserreich* as a whole in the 1970s and with the rediscovery of Kehr's *Schlachtflottenbau und Parteipolitik* (Berlin, 1930), a new consensus emerged to assert the primacy of domestic over foreign policy.[114] Naval and world policy was now seen as an attempt of the ruling elites in Imperial Germany to preserve their political authority and social position through two strategies: first, by rallying together the dominant social and political elite, the Prussian aristocracy, and the dominant economic elite, the owners of heavy industry, in an alliance to protect their power and status; and, second, by reconciling the mass of the population to the existing order through naval construction and imperialist policy.[115]

The first strategy has been called "*Sammlungspolitik*," after the statement of the Prussian finance minister, Johannes von Miquel, to General von Waldersee in 1890 that "the great task of the present is . . . to bring together [*sich . . . sammeln*] all the elements that support the State and thus prepare for the perhaps unavoidable battle against the Social Democratic movement."[116] Out of agricultural distress and fear of socialism and recognizing the mutual economic benefits to be derived from an alliance, Junkers and industrialists came together in a compromise. The landowners would tolerate naval construction and colonial acquisition, which would benefit industry, in exchange for grain tariffs, which would protect East Elbian agriculture from foreign competition. This *Sammlung* of the propertied classes, the proponents of this interpretation contend, not only produced the Navy Laws of 1898 and 1900 and the grain tariffs of 1902, but also determined the essential character of the Reich. The second strategy has been called "social imperialism" following Hans-Ulrich Wehler's application of this term to Bismarck's colonial policy of the mid-1880s.[117] It is argued that just as Bismarck sought to deal with the Reich's domestic problems through colonial acquisition, so the leaders of Wilhelmian Germany attempted to distract the German people from their political and social frustration through an expansionist foreign policy. Naval and world policy, then, by appealing to nationalist sentiment, was designed to bring the Germans together behind the crown and generally reconcile them to the status quo.

Despite the popularity of "*Sammlungspolitik*" and "social imperialism" with historians, the application of these models to the *Kaiserreich* has become increasingly controversial. The first tenet of this interpretative constellation to be challenged—generally by historians sympathetic to its point of view—was the notion of the absolute primacy of domestic policy. Was social imperialism the primary purpose of naval construction and the practice of *Weltpolitik*, these critics have asked, or merely a desirable, indeed perhaps essential, domestic side effect of what in the end remained a foreign policy? Peter Winzen, for example, acknowledges that Bülow had "his social imperialist moments," but, Winzen contends, his primary purpose was still the achievement of world power status for the Reich.[118] Like Meinecke, Bülow saw national unity and social harmony not as the goal of naval and world policy but as a precondition for its successful practice.[119] Similarly, Wilhelm Deist has implicitly challenged Berghahn's assertion that the navy was a weapon directed not only against England but also against the Reichstag.[120] Deist argues that the propaganda campaign on behalf of naval development was designed less to defeat the Reichstag than to win its support for the building of the battlefleet.[121] The primary reason the naval bills fixed the course of ship construction was to enable Wilhelm and his admirals to obtain the fleet they wanted without civilian and parliamentary interference. It is also possible to question Berghahn's assertion that German foreign policy was manipulated to insure the passage of the Navy Laws by arguing that international crises, rather than being manufactured, were merely exploited once they had occurred to mobilize the population behind the navy.[122]

Although scholars have found it easy to resolve the debate over the primacy of foreign or domestic policy by adopting the position that a confluence of foreign and domestic factors produced naval imperialism,[123] historians have recently questioned whether *Sammlungspolitik* and social imperialism can even be applied to the *Kaiserreich*.[124] Thus, after two decades' immersion in the correspondence, diaries, and memoirs of the men at the top in Wilhelmian Germany, John Röhl finds little evidence that they regarded the navy as an instrument to achieve a *Sammlung* between agrarians and industrialists.[125] And Geoff Eley, focusing less on the motives of the participants and more on the domestic effects of naval and world policy, has concluded that, instead of bringing together "all the elements that support the State" as Miquel had hoped, naval and world policy fractured the German right and divided it from the government.[126]

Although critics of *Sammlungspolitik* can argue that the model is not sustained by much historical evidence, the same charge cannot be leveled at social imperialism, since the Kaiser, Bülow, and Tirpitz all hoped that naval construction and *Weltpolitik* would have an integrative effect. Here the criticism is based upon evidence of the existence of imperialist sentiment in Germany independent of government manipulation, upon evidence of popular Anglophobia that cannot be attributed to the propaganda campaign conducted by the Reich Naval Office. Here critics are drawn less to the attitudes of the government leaders and more to attitudes expressed in the general population, to the statements of Meinecke, Oncken, and Hintze, Kayser and Malet, to the popular demands for a colonial policy before Wilhelm's "proclamation" of

Weltpolitik in 1896 or the naval campaign in 1897, to the research of Michael Salewski who was so struck by the popular enthusiasm for naval and world policy in 1900 that he wrote: "Wilhelm II and Bülow . . . and numerous representatives of the ruling classes appeared less as leaders into as yet unfamiliar territory and more as promulgators of a widespread 'public opinion.'"[127]

Thus Eley, in considering the motives of the leaders of the Reich, concedes that some hoped naval and world policy would have a domestic effect compatible with social imperialism.[128] But he contends that in espousing *Weltpolitik* those leaders were not so much manipulating society as responding to its demands for an imperialist policy.[129] In considering the domestic effects of the government's imperialist policies, Eley contends that far from creating social and political harmony and rallying the populace behind the existing order they produced division and dissatisfaction. Included among the most vigorous proponents of *Weltpolitik* were social reformers (the most conspicuous being Friedrich Naumann and Max Weber) who asserted that the effective practice of world politics demanded not preservation of the status quo but a fundamental restructuring of state and society. Furthermore, although Germans could agree that the Reich should pursue aggressively nationalistic and imperialist policies, they disagreed over how those policies were to be conducted and over what specific objectives were to be attained. Finally, rather than producing popular satisfaction with the political leadership of the Reich, *Weltpolitik* produced mounting condemnation of the government, which was seen to be overly conciliatory and unable to deliver the promised international successes.[130]

Between the position that the government sought to use naval and world policy as a domestic strategy to stabilize the existing order and the position that naval and world policy was a response to popular pressure, a third position can be discerned. According to this view, the leaders of Germany sought to use naval and world policy as an instrument of national and social integration. Indeed that strategy was initially successful. Within short order, however, the government found itself attacked for being too moderate, too modest, too Anglophile. At that point, rather than attempting to stir up nationalist and imperialist sentiment, the government found itself trying to damp that sentiment down. The attempt to manipulate the public had failed. Like the sorcerer's apprentice, the leaders of the Reich found themselves overwhelmed by forces they had called forth but could not control.[131]

There are two contributions the present study can make to the debate over the application of "*Sammlungspolitik*" and "social imperialism" to Wilhelmian Germany. As we have seen, the Kaiser, Bülow, and Tirpitz all anticipated that the creation of a mighty navy and the practice of *Weltpolitik* would engender feelings of pride and purpose in the German people. In the shared experience of those emotions, Germany's divisions would be surmounted, national identity would be strengthened, and the appeal of social democracy, an internationalist ideology, would be weakened. Naval and world policy were designed to overcome what Wilhelm, in his interview with Ludwig Ganghofer, called "*Reichsverdrossenheit*" and to increase what he called "*Zusammenge-*

hörigkeit." Enthusiasm for Germany's international mission would bring Germans together behind nation and crown.

In translating the domestic purpose of naval and world policy into the language of *Sammlungspolitik* and social imperialism, however, historians frequently use the words "cynical," "strategy," "self-interested," and "manipulation." The attitude suggested by these words does not reflect—indeed it distorts—the self-experience of the historical participants. Certainly Wilhelm II, almost certainly Bülow, and probably Tirpitz did not understand the domestic purpose of naval and world policy in these terms. Their support of *Weltpolitik*, as far as its domestic consequences were concerned, was based not on a cold-blooded assessment of the economic and political advantages they would derive from these policies or on a concern for their political, economic, or physical survival. Their support for naval and world policy was based not on greed and fear but on the belief that naval and world policy was in the best interest of the German nation and of the German people. For the leaders of the Reich, the mobilization of nationalist sentiment was not merely a means to an end, whether that end be defined narrowly as naval development or more broadly as the preservation of the existing order. For the leaders of the Reich, the mobilization of nationalist sentiment was an end greatly to be desired for its own sake. The idea of using world and naval policy to increase national cohesion and social integration and to rally the Germans behind the monarchy was not a cynical strategy or a self-interested manipulation on the part of the leaders of Germany but derived from their most basic beliefs and values, from their understanding of history and of what made life worthwhile.[132]

This study can also contribute to the debate over whether naval and world policy was an attempt to manipulate popular emotion from above or whether that policy was a response to popular pressure from below. Clearly the answer to this question must be that it was both an attempt at manipulation or, perhaps better, at education and a response. And yet the "sorcerer's apprentice" variant of this compromise position, although accurate to a degree, probably muddies over as much as it clarifies. For it would seem unlikely, if not impossible, that propagandists, no matter how skilled, could create feelings and beliefs that were previously unknown to the population. As we have seen, Germans anticipated *Weltpolitik* in their colonialist enthusiasms before its proclamation by the Kaiser in 1896. Certainly the alacrity and excitement with which they responded to that proclamation suggests that Germans were predisposed to accept its message. The propaganda campaign on behalf of the navy was effective—perhaps too effective from the government's point of view—because it was in tune with popular aspirations.

Presumably it has been demonstrated that Wilhelm II was sensitive to the feelings of the Germans and that he sought to say and do and be what he sensed they expected of him. And presumably it has also been demonstrated that the Kaiser sought to "lead" public opinion. There is overwhelming evidence that a sophisticated and successful propaganda campaign was carried out by the government, not the least of which is the testimony of Wilhelm's contemporaries who were convinced that it was he who had brought them "out onto the water" and "out into the world." Hence, the conclusion sustained by this study is that Wilhelm II and his advisers neither created feelings of intense nationalism and imperialism in the Germans nor simply adapted passively to such pre-existing popular sentiments. Rather what they did was to grasp the largely inarticulate popular yearning for national unity and international greatness and translate it into words like "*Mitspracherecht*," "*Gleichberechtigung*," and "*Weltgeltung*" and into deeds like the occupation of Kiaochow, the visit to the Holy Land, and the building of the battlefleet. Perhaps the notion of pure governmental manipulation (or even education) from above posits too great a distinction between state and society and the notion of pure governmental response to popular pressure from below fails to posit enough of one.

Certainly there were divisions in the *Kaiserreich* during the reign of Wilhelm II, divisions between and within government and society. Nevertheless, even if there was disagreement over the specific objectives of *Weltpolitik*, there was agreement that world politics ought to be practiced. Although on the level of self-interest Germans were bitterly and increasingly divided, most could come together in the desire for national unity and international greatness, in the demand for "*Geltung, Anerkennung, Gleichberechtigung*" for the Reich. The essence of Bismarck's political leadership had been to rule Germany by playing one self-interested group off against the other; the essence of Wilhelm II's symbolic leadership was to rule by covering over conflicts of interest through the creation of an emotional consensus.[133]

CHAPTER **10**

Between the British
and the Germans

Before concluding this study of Wilhelm II, it is necessary to consider one last area of his political activity that is as significant as it is puzzling: the Kaiser's attitude and policy toward England. From the moment of his birth, England played an important role in Wilhelm's life. Through his mother and other English relatives, English values and attitudes were deeply rooted in his psyche. It is not too much to say that he possessed a partial English identity. At the same time Wilhelm's affiliation with England created personal and political difficulties for him. Because of its association with figures in his life who were psychologically important and problematic, Victoria par excellence, England was a country about which Wilhelm had powerful and decidedly mixed feelings. Not only was England personally important to the Kaiser, but the Kaiser can be said to have been politically important to England. Although other aspects of Wilhelmian Germany can be understood without reference to the Kaiser, no account of Anglo-German relations during his reign can afford to neglect his contribution. The authority of chancellors and advisers, the pressure of economic, social, and popular political forces notwithstanding, German policy toward England bears the unmistakable stamp of Wilhelm II's personality.[1]

Given its apparently contradictory character, Wilhelm's attitude toward England and the English eludes precise historical definition, however. On the one hand, Wilhelm harbored incredible suspicions of the British. As we have seen, in 1896 he feared an English attack on Germany or at least the seizure of Germany's colonial empire, and in 1906 and 1908 he believed that Edward VII was plotting against him throughout Europe. These were not isolated incidents. In late 1903 he believed the aim of English foreign policy to be the "dissolution of the Triple Alliance, to draw our allies into England's sphere of influence in order to isolate Germany completely, so that it can be destroyed—by England."[2] In 1904/1905 he suspected that the British, as they had done to the Danes in 1807, would now, without warning or declaration of war, attack and destroy the German fleet at anchor.[3] And during the 1905 revolution in Russia

Wilhelm was convinced that "since England has perceived that with the Tsar nothing is to be arranged against us, they want secretly to use and to support the revolution so as to be rid of him, because it serves English interests. Just as they had Paul murdered, so too they will allow Nicholas II to go to ruin! Just as Albion needs Japan to break the Tsar's power on the land and sea, so it will use revolution to cause him to fall and to create a 'liberal' Russia which then with 'liberal' England and France can be unleashed on 'reactionary' Germany!"[4] On the other hand, as we have also seen, the Kaiser admired England greatly and involved himself in English affairs—often against the interests of Germany—as if he were an Englishman. Thus, despite the Krüger telegram, his fears of the British in its aftermath, and the rampant Anglophobia in Germany during the Boer War, Wilhelm carried on a correspondence with his uncle, the Prince of Wales, offering detailed advice on how the Boers might be defeated.[5] Proudly signing himself "Admiral of the Fleet," Wilhelm suggested improvements in the Royal Navy and throughout the first ten years of his reign and beyond complained frequently about England's slow pace of naval modernization and expansion. "As long as your fleet is first and looked upon and feared as invincible," he wrote the Prince of Wales in English in 1900 after the Second German Navy Law had been introduced to the Reichstag, "I do not care a fiddlestick for a few lost fights in Africa! But your fleet must be up to date and on the 'qui vive.'"[6]

Just as historians have been reluctant to ascribe naval and world policy to psychological factors and have thought, in the domestic dimension of those policies, to discover a conscious logic behind the emotion, so they have sought to discover a consistent and conscious rationality in German policy toward England during the reign of Wilhelm II. Given the evident importance of Wilhelm's contribution to Anglo-German relations, it is difficult simply to ignore him. Given his apparent inconsistency, irrationality, and impulsiveness, it is difficult to reconcile him with any German policy toward England that could be described as consistently and consciously rational. With his reactive nature, the Kaiser's attitude seems to have been determined by the responses to him: he hated the English when he felt rejected by them; he loved the English when he felt accepted by them. With his adaptability, he meant every word he said when, in England or talking to the British ambassador in Berlin, he expressed his fervent wish for better and closer relations between the two countries. But he also meant every word he said in the presence of his admirals and generals at the *Kriegsrat*, on 8 December 1912, when the possibility of a preventive war against the enemies of the Reich, including England, was discussed.

Therefore, in dealing with Wilhelm's attitude and policy toward England, historians have tended to adopt one of the following strategies. The first is to ignore the evidence of Wilhelm's contribution to German policy toward England and to dismiss him as capricious and inconsequential.[7] The second is to ignore the evidence of Wilhelm's Anglophobia and to present him as a more or less consistent friend of England.[8] The third is to ignore the evidence of Wilhelm's admiration and affection for Britain and to present him as a more or less consistent foe of England.[9] The final strategy is to admit Wilhelm's importance and inconsistency and to suggest that he simply was ambivalent, vacillating between Anglophilia and Anglophobia depending on his circumstances.[10] But even this approach is not entirely satisfactory, for it remains difficult to define precisely either his attitude toward England or his influence over German policy toward that country.

Not only does the Kaiser's attitude toward England seem important and puzzling, it also appears to have been a larger and a sharper reflection of popular attitudes prevalent in Germany during Wilhelm's reign. On the one hand, Anglophilia and increasingly strident Anglophobia could be found across the social and political spectrum.[11] Wilhelm's ambivalence thus reflected the range of German reactions to Great Britain. On the other hand, Wilhelm's ambivalence also reflected the mixed feelings toward England and the English that many of his subjects experienced individually. Thus Tirpitz was personally Anglophile, yet it was he who designed and executed the plan to challenge Britain's naval hegemony.[12] In the words of Rudolf Stadelmann: "One gets the impression that he sought to educate the Germans after the model of the English, whose self-assured cosmopolitan demeanor, whose national self-confidence and sense of empire, whose worldwide interests and tradition of rule ... had made a deep impression."[13] And, Stadelmann believed, what held true for Tirpitz held true for many of his compatriots: "From the maritime way of life to high politics, from the schools to the ideology of empire, spread the enchantment with the English model with which the entire epoch of Wilhelm II was more or less smitten."[14] The same curious combination of respect and contempt, admiration and hostility that characterized Wilhelm's feelings toward England, then, could also be found in the general population, particularly in the middle classes.[15] As with the Kaiser, it is difficult to be certain whether the wish to emulate England brought Germany into conflict with her or whether the wish to compete with England brought Germany to emulate her.

Although some reasons for the existence of these parallels have been suggested, this congruence should not be pushed too far. For it was over Britain that Wilhelm and his subjects came into their most bitter conflicts. If in relation to England Wilhelm can be described, in the words of Friedrich Naumann, as a "mirror image" of the Germans, it was an image that became increasingly distorted during the course of the reign. As the mixture of popular admiration and hostility toward Britain shifted markedly toward the latter, the mixture of Wilhelm's feelings remained relatively more constant. As the hatred of the English grew within the German population, the Kaiser found himself condemned for being too admiring, too respectful, too conciliatory, indeed for being too English. It was the Kaiser's enduring Anglophilia that perhaps contributed most to his unpopularity with his increasingly Anglophobic subjects.[16] Nevertheless, although the enmity of the Germans burned deeper perhaps than Wilhelm's flare-ups of rage at the British, the source of hostility was the same: both hated Britain when she was seen to frustrate Germany's rightful ambition to comparable world power status and to treat the German Kaiser and the German people as anything less than the leader and the citizens of an equally important imperial power.

Therefore, because the Kaiser's attitude toward England is as important to any study of German foreign policy as it is perplexing and because his attitude both reflected popular attitudes toward England and brought him into conflict with his subjects, it remains to define that attitude more precisely and to discover beneath his ambivalence a consistency of outlook that, if not consciously rational perhaps, can at least be seen to have made personal and political sense.

I

Throughout his life, Wilhelm II was profoundly attached to England. He was deeply involved with his English relatives, and he developed intense and turbulent relationships to two sovereigns among them, his grandmother, Queen Victoria, and his uncle, King Edward VII. Despite his occasional anger at Queen Victoria when he felt slighted or rejected by her, Wilhelm maintained his love and admiration for what he described in his memoirs as "the perfect Queen and perfect woman, mother and grandmother."[17] "How I love my Grandmother, I cannot describe for you," he told Eulenburg. "She is the sum total of all that is noble, good, and intelligent. With her and my feelings for her, England is inextricably connected."[18] It was from his grandmother that Wilhelm received his first watch, and, after 1901, he carried a watch commemorating the queen that he had purchased in London while attending her funeral.[19] Wilhelm's letter to his grandmother after his fortieth birthday gives a clear sense of what she meant to him:

> I fully understand how extraordinary the fact must seem to you that the tiny, weeny little brat you often had in your arms and dear Grandpapa swung about in a napkin has reached his forties! Just half of your prosperous and successful life! . . . It is often full of moments when I fancy that the strain is too strong and the burden too heavy to bear. But then I trust in Him who has thus ordered it to be . . . as well as the happy knowledge that you observe and follow my career with the love of a very, very kind Grandmother. And I venture to believe that, where the Sovereign will sometimes shake her wise head often over the tricks of her queer and impetuous colleague, the good and genial heart of my Grandmother will step in and show that, if he sometimes fails, it is never from want of goodwill, honesty, or truthfulness, and thus mitigate the shake of the head by a genial smile of warm sympathy and interest![20]

Similarly, as manifested in his suspicions of Edward VII and his frequent rages at him, Wilhelm was emotionally invested in his uncle. Bülow was convinced that the Kaiser idealized Edward and wanted nothing more than to win his affection and recognition.[21] It was precisely because his uncle mattered so much that Wilhelm could be so deeply wounded by him.[22] "Unfortunately," Eulenburg wrote of Wilhelm after the *Daily Telegraph* affair and his own disgrace, "his love for England was so great that *nothing* could injure the pride of the Kaiser *sufficiently*, and the undignified courtship reeled on from one disappointment to the next . . . 'Wilhelm the German' is in the air. Wilhelm 'the Englishman' flutters around the fat King Edward like a leaf in the wind around the tower."[23]

If for the Anglophobic Eulenburg it was unfortunate that Wilhelm's attachment to England and to his uncle was so strong as to survive every rejection, for Anglo-German relations it was unfortunate that at those times when the Kaiser felt slighted by his English relatives his anger was directed not only at them but at their country as well.[24] Thus Eulenburg described how in 1899, when Wilhelm felt wounded by his relatives during the Boer War, he "trembled with rage—and hope" that the English, in the Kaiser's words, "would for their rapaciousness be humiliated into the dust." At that moment the Boers were a "heroic people" and the English a "pack of wretches." But then a letter from Queen Victoria arrived, and suddenly the Boers were "a sorry lot" and it was necessary to aid the "poor" English by sending them the battle plan against the Boers he had prepared, with no sense that to do so might very well injure British pride.[25] In fact, Wilhelm's relatives were frequently insulted by what they experienced as his arrogant meddling in British affairs.[26] And, when he sensed their negative reaction, Wilhelm was wounded in turn by the rejection of what he had hoped would win him gratitude, affection, and respect.

The Kaiser felt the right to intervene in the affairs of the British not out of overweening arrogance, but because he felt himself in many ways an Englishman. Wilhelm II was a German Kaiser whose only daily paper was the English *Daily Graphic*;[27] whose yacht, the *Meteor*, was built in England and had, until 1908, an English captain, crew, and cook;[28] who proudly confirmed in 1911 that English had been the language of his own and of his children's early life;[29] whose first words when he crossed the border into Holland in November 1918 were reported to have been "now," eagerly rubbing his hands together, "now, you must give me a cup of hot, good, real English tea";[30] who, in exile, was insistent that the forward to his memoirs be so written that English publishers and booksellers "will clearly recognize that, for example, the description of the '*English*' childhood was unquestionably written by me";[31] and whose principal occupation in Holland, chopping wood, followed the example of the British statesman Gladstone, for whom he had long professed disdain.[32] "I feel absolutely at home in England," he declared to Eulenburg, "it is *home* to me. That, the provincial Germans cannot of course understand!—They have no inkling of what I feel in my heart."[33] It was what Eulenburg caustically called "Wilhelm the Englishman" who, echoing his mother, frequently and indiscreetly compared Germany unfavorably with England.[34] To the bitter end, Wilhelm maintained his attachment to England. Although regarded as a war criminal in England, Wilhelm in exile could still assert proudly to an interviewer:

To understand my character and nature you must understand that I am half English. I have never been able to think purely like a Continental and that is why I have so often been misunderstood or misjudged. Undoubtedly, my

The Kaiser in British uniform (1901). The photograph bears Wilhelm's signature and his inscription, "They say what they say, let 'em say!" Reprinted with the permission of the Bundesarchiv Koblenz.

mother had a great influence on my nature; it was due to her education that I could get along so easily with the English.[35]

As the admiration for Britain, the British Empire, and the British way of life was overwhelmed by popular Anglophobia during the course of Wilhelm's reign, Germans both inside of government and out came to view "Wilhelm the Englishman" with alarm. During the period he was secretary of state in the Foreign Office (1897–1900) and chancellor (1900–1909), Bernhard von Bülow had to exercise as much diplomatic skill in keeping the Kaiser's English sympathies in check as he did in dealing with any foreign government. He struggled constantly to moderate Wilhelm's demands for rapprochement with Britain, and he lived in fear that the Kaiser would impulsively commit Germany to an alliance with England before he, Bülow, could intervene.[36] In the spring of 1898, it took all of Bülow's insight into Wilhelm's psychology and how to manipulate it to dampen the Kaiser's enthusiasm for the alliance feelers of the British colonial minister, Joseph Chamberlain.[37] On a number of occasions the Kaiserin importuned Bülow to use his influence to effect "a somewhat slower rotation of the machinery" in her husband's "full-steam ahead toward England."[38]

Given his adaptability, it was when the Kaiser was in England that his English proclivities became most pronounced, and it was then that his advisers and subjects became most distressed at "Wilhelm the Englishman." With typical flamboyance, Philipp Eulenburg wrote in 1908:

Only one who has seen the Kaiser in England, who has experienced him in the company of the English, will be able to appreciate what I mean. It sounds ghastly to a German ear when I say: the German Emperor is not a German at all, but actually an Englishman. . . . I have frequently had to look away, to avoid seeing him: in his style, movement, gestures, posture—an Englishman. *Only* an Englishman. An Englishman, who had disguised himself as German Kaiser in Prussia, and who now in his English homeland, laughingly, shaking with boyish pleasure, tosses away his Prussian character.[39]

Already during the Kaiser's visit to England in 1895 the undersecretary of state in the Foreign Office, Freiherr Wolfram von Rotenhahn, wrote to Chancellor Hohenlohe: "I very much hope that His Majesty will soon return so that Your Excellency can report to him, for I very much fear the English influence [on the Kaiser], particularly in its anti-Russian direction, since in England there sometimes is no counterweight that can make itself felt."[40] The same concern on the part of Holstein, Richthofen, and Bülow prompted the secretary of state to accompany the Kaiser to Windsor in November 1899. Not only did Bülow and his colleagues in the Foreign Office fear that Wilhelm, if left unattended in Britain, could harm the foreign policy interests of the Reich, particularly as these concerned Russia, they were also deeply worried about the trip's domestic consequences. Given the Anglophobia in Germany resulting from the Boer War and the recent Anglo-German conflict over Samoa, it was bad enough that

Wilhelm had to travel to England at all. What the Kaiser might do and say while among the English to damage his prestige with his subjects was all too easy for Wilhelm's advisers to imagine. The Kaiserin, recognizing how unpopular the visit would be and fearing that her husband would be exploited by the British, urged Bülow to prevent him from going.[41] When the visit was officially announced, the public reaction was as she had anticipated. The *Badische Landeszeitung* editorialized: "Who can deny that the forthcoming journey of the royal family to visit the Queen of England is highly unpopular in all of the German Reich?" Although popular sentiment in Germany "had been transformed into open hatred of England," the Kaiser's "sympathies for the English character and for English sport will never cease," the paper concluded with resignation.[42]

To restrain Wilhelm's enthusiasm for England and prevent him from precipitously concluding an Anglo-German alliance, Holstein drew up a memorandum officially signed by the chancellor to prepare the Kaiser for the trip. The document opened by assuring Wilhelm that "Your Majesty is without doubt more talented than all your [English] relatives, male and female. Nevertheless, your relatives have not shown you the respect that, quite apart from your position of authority as German Kaiser, is in keeping with your outstanding personality." The upcoming visit, the memo continued, presented Wilhelm with the opportunity to correct this situation and "with one blow to secure for yourself the authority to which Your Majesty has claim as a result of your spiritual and intellectual qualities and your position of power." According to the memo, this transformation was easily achieved: Wilhelm simply had to "shun all political conversation" while in England.[43]

The entreaties of the Kaiserin, the negative public reaction, the attempt at psychological manipulation by Holstein, and the presence of Bülow notwithstanding, Wilhelm was overwhelmed on his arrival at Windsor Castle. It was, he declared to Bülow, "the most lovely entrance and the most uplifting experience of my life," and he ordered the secretary of state to write to Kaiserin Friedrich expressing Wilhelm's satisfaction at being able to demonstrate his "devotion and unshakable friendship" for Britain at this moment when she was subject to so much unjust criticism and hostility.[44] Every morning to the annoyance of his military entourage Wilhelm gestured to the Round Tower at Windsor Castle and proudly announced: "From this tower the world is being governed."[45] The British press responded to the Kaiser's visit with great friendliness for Wilhelm, emphasizing his English heritage and inclinations as well as his having proved himself more farsighted than his subjects;[46] the German press was less enthusiastic. On his return, the *Münchener Allgemeine Zeitung* noted with relief that Wilhelm's visit had passed without Germany having become an ally of British imperialism. This fact alone, the paper concluded, in making the best of a bad situation, had brought the English down a peg and was therefore "*a great moral victory for Germany.*"[47] Predictably, Wilhelm was displeased by the negative reaction of his subjects to what he deemed a great personal success.[48]

When in January 1901 Wilhelm rushed across the channel to be at the bedside of his dying grandmother, this scenario was replayed. For the Kaiser the trip was certainly one of the best experiences of his life. Conducting himself with an appropriate mixture of dignity and warmth, he was received with enthusiasm by his English relatives, the English press, and the English people. Adapting himself to his surroundings, he shed his many uniforms in favor of civilian attire and wore a tie clasp bearing Queen Victoria's insignia. For the Kaiser's military entourage, the unaccustomed sight of their commander-in-chief out of uniform was distressing, as were his loudly voiced endorsements of England, the English people, and English customs, which he compared favorably to their German counterparts.[49] Exhilarated and touched by his reception, Wilhelm, to the dismay of his advisers, remained in England a full two weeks with the crown prince. "If only we were safely home with the two of them," General-Adjutant Hans von Plessen lamented to Bülow. "I find it terrible that during these busy and momentous weeks, His Majesty is not in Berlin."[50] For his part, Bülow worked to limit the trip's diplomatic and domestic damage. His worst fear, that Wilhelm would impulsively conclude an alliance with Britain, was not realized, but he did need to suppress the original text of the Kaiser's speech at his departure for Germany in which he called for one.[51] And even when Wilhelm was "safely home" in Berlin, Bülow could not rest easy, for it had been arranged between Wilhelm and his uncle that Edward VII would visit the Kaiser in August in Wilhelmshöhe where the opportunity for a precipitously concluded alliance would once again present itself.

The visit was roundly condemned in the German press.[52] Even the socialist *Vorwärts* denounced the trip: "*There is no point in closing one's eyes* in order to avoid recognizing the *unwelcome fact* that our policy swims out and out in the English wake." There was no reason to be concerned lest the forthcoming visit of the English sovereign to Germany unnecessarily ruin our relations with other powers, the newspaper continued, "THERE IS NOTHING MORE TO RUIN IN OUR POLITICAL POSITION."[53] The editorial in the *Badische Landespost* on 31 January 1901 was plaintive:

> The conduct of the Kaiser in England is becoming more and more incomprehensible and even painful for us Germans as a result of his growing tendency toward English ways and English policies. . . . Oh! If only the Kaiser realized what a wealth of love and trust he loses with his *own* people by so openly manifesting his affection for a *foreign* people and trying to win their favor.

II

Wilhelm's enduring attachment to England posed serious personal and political problems for him. On the one hand, he doubtless experienced psychological tension between the German and the English sides of his personality. Unable to integrate these two important aspects of himself, he could only shift back and forth between his English and his German identity: in England, he became an Englishman; in Germany, he became a German once again. As the two countries grew further apart politically, his inner disharmony can only have increased.[54] On the other hand, he also found himself in a difficult political position. When, as in sending the Krüger telegram, his attitudes and actions were in tune with the Germans, he antagonized his English relatives and the English people whose affection and appreciation he craved. When, as in attending his grandmother's funeral, his attitudes and actions were in tune with his English relatives and the English people, he antagonized the Germans whose support he required for his political and psychological survival. Indeed, his unpopularity in Germany resulting from his attachment to England can only have reminded him of the fate of his parents, whose Anglophilia had cost them personal standing and political influence. Unable to deny either aspect of himself for long, requiring positive responses from both the English and the Germans, and yet experiencing severe personal and political tension as a result, the Kaiser was confronted with a dilemma: how to harmonize these two parts of himself and achieve the reconciliation of these two countries and peoples to whom he was so attached and on whom he was so dependent.

That dilemma helps to account for the excitement with which Wilhelm greeted the racial interpretation of history and culture of the Germanophile British political philosopher, Houston Stewart Chamberlain. Chamberlain's *The Foundations of the Nineteenth Century* was, according to the Kaiser in 1903, "the greatest and most significant work that has ever been written and of such value that every word should be printed in gold,"[55] and he entered into an enthusiastic correspondence, exuding mutual admiration, with the book's author.[56] It is obvious perhaps why Chamberlain's theories would have appealed to the Kaiser. They denied the existence of any significant differences between Germany and England or within the Kaiser's psyche, for both peoples belonged, as Wilhelm wrote to the wife of Rudyard Kipling in 1899 (undoubtedly before he had encountered Chamberlain's writings), to the same "great race."[57] Indeed, the passage that Bülow had censored in the Kaiser's toast of 5 February 1901 on his departure for Germany following his grandmother's funeral expressed the notion that racial kinship formed the basis for an eventual Anglo-German alliance:

> I believe there is a Providence which has decreed that two nations which have produced such men as Shakespeare, Schiller, Luther, and Goethe must have a great future before them; I believe that the two Teutonic nations will, bit by bit, learn to know each other better, and that they will stand together to help in keeping the peace of the world. We ought to form an Anglo-German alliance, you to keep the seas while we would be responsible for the land; with such an alliance not a mouse could stir in Europe without our permission.[58]

Nearly a year later he wrote to Edward VII in English:

> I gladly reciprocate all you say about the relations of our two Countries and our personal ones; they are of the same blood, and they have the same creed, and

they belong to the great Teutonic Race, which Heaven has intrusted with the culture of the world . . . that is I think grounds enough to keep the Peace and to foster *mutual* recognition and *reciprocity* in all what draws us together and to sink everything which could part us![59]

Despite the obvious alienation and antagonism, no matter how tense relations between the two countries became, an Anglo-German alliance was, according to this view, a historical and racial inevitability. Russian ambitions in the Balkans in 1909 were therefore interpreted by the Kaiser as a manifestation of the clash between the Slavic race with "the European cultural and Germanic world. Therefore a uniting of the Germans and the Anglo-Saxons with eventually the Gauls!"[60] To be sure, Wilhelm had his moments of doubt and despair when political realities in Europe did not conform to his racially based expectations. Thus in 1906, during the Moroccan crisis, Wilhelm wrote that the rapprochement between England and Spain and Italy's increasingly doubtful commitment to the Triple Alliance revealed that the "whole, wretched, degenerate Latin people have become nothing but instruments in the hands of England. . . . Not only have we no friends anymore, but the eunuch-species of the ancient Roman chaos of peoples hates us with all its heart. . . . A battle between the Germans and the Latins all down the line! And unfortunately the former are divided!"[61] In his statement at the *Kriegsrat* in December 1912, Wilhelm analyzed the coming world war in racial terms: "the eventual battle for survival, in which the Germans in Europe (Austria, Germany) will have to fight against the Slavs (Russia) supported by the Romans (Gauls), finds the Anglo-Saxons on the side of the Slavs. Reason: envy and fear of our becoming too great!"[62] And yet by May 1913, the Kaiser's faith in the racial impossibility of an Anglo-German conflict had been restored. "In the long-run," he wrote, "it will be absolutely impossible for the Anglo-Saxons to ally with Slavs and Gauls against Germany (the Germanic people)."[63]

III

Like his attraction to the view of history propounded by Houston Stewart Chamberlain, Wilhelm II's support for the construction of the German navy can be understood in part as a response to the personal and political dilemma created by his enduring attachment to England. Whereas Chamberlain's theories promised the reconciliation of the German and the English sides of his personality along with the reconciliation of the two nations, the German navy would be the instrument to effect that personal and political integration.

Given Wilhelm's maritime passion and its connection with Britain, it should come as no surprise that early in his reign the Kaiser manifested a keen interest in all things British relating to the sea and ships. Not only were the royal yacht and its crew English, but, to the annoyance of German seamen, Wilhelm loved to travel on English warships, which he justified by virtue of his rank as British admiral.[64] Possessing an expert's knowledge of the Royal Navy,[65] he corresponded with Lord Salisbury, the Admiralty, and various active and retired British naval officers on its condition,[66] and in marginalia to the dispatches of his diplomats he expressed displeasure at the slow pace of the Royal Navy's modernization and expansion.[67] This was not an interest Wilhelm could maintain as Kaiser. Clearly, he had to translate his English naval passion into German.

In so doing, the Kaiser arrived at a solution reminiscent of that adopted by his mother in dealing with her homesickness by attempting to recreate England in Prussia. Beginning in the gymnasium in Kassel and the barracks of the guard regiment in Potsdam and culminating in the propaganda campaign on behalf of naval development some twenty years later, Wilhelm sought to Anglicize the Germans by awakening in them a naval passion.[68] Just as he imitated the annual regatta at Cowes by creating the *"Kieler Woche,"*[69] Wilhelm sought to recreate the Royal Navy in the German fleet. Thus, following practices in the British navy, he instituted Sunday sermons delivered by the captain on board all German naval vessels and he insisted that each German warship produce a daily paper.[70] His design of the German navy's battle flag looked so much like the British battle flag that Eulenburg had to intervene in order to make the two flags distinguishable from one another.[71] Undoubtedly one of the attractions of Tirpitz's battlefleet over the vast fleet of fast cruisers for the Kaiser was that its construction would make the German navy more like the British. Still, when he learned that the English had begun constructing vessels designed not only for speed but able also to fight in the line, Wilhelm's passion for fast cruisers was rekindled in late 1903, and when it became British practice to outfit their naval vessels with turbine engines, the Kaiser urged the German navy to follow suit.[72] Psychologically, Eulenburg was right when he wrote that it was "'Wilhelm the Englishman' who created the German Navy,"[73] a verdict confirmed by the Kaiser's speech during the *"Kieler Woche"* at the Imperial Yacht Club on 27 June 1904. In the presence of Edward VII and with tears in his eyes, Wilhelm declared (in a passage suppressed before the speech was released to the press):

> Holding on to the hands of kind aunts and friendly admirals, I was allowed to visit Portsmouth and Plymouth and in those two glorious harbors to admire the proud English ships. There the wish was born in me also to build such ships, also to possess a fleet one day as beautiful as the English.[74]

It is difficult to know for certain whether Wilhelm ever appreciated that his attempt to imitate Britain's navy had helped transform her into Germany's enemy. Certainly it is unlikely he recognized the parallel that can be drawn between his relationship with England as Kaiser and his relationship with his mother as a young adult. As he had come into conflict with Victoria by seeking to adopt those features of her personality—her self-assurance, forcefulness, and combativeness—he most admired, he and his country came into conflict with Britain by adopting Britain's admired naval weapon for the Reich. And yet there was a significant difference between what had transpired in Wilhelm's personal history and what occurred in the history of Anglo-German relations during his reign. Whereas Victoria's dream of Anglo-German friendship had been dashed in part because she failed in her campaign to Anglicize Germany, Wilhelm's dream of Anglo-German friendship was dashed in part because his campaign to Anglicize Germany succeeded only too well.

As discussed in the preceding chapter, following the Krüger telegram Wilhelm believed that without a powerful navy Germany was in a weak and vulnerable position. Until such a navy was constructed, the British would treat Kaiser and Reich like "poor relations."[75] In the words of Daisy Pless:

> The Kaiser often criticized England; he always did so impatiently or petulantly as one does when criticizing relatives whom one sincerely likes but who, one feels, are at times lacking in understanding or appreciation. That was the real grievance! The Kaiser felt that he was never understood or appreciated by Queen Victoria, King Edward, King George or the British people.[76]

Wilhelm's frequent use of the phrase that Germany had received an "*Ohrfeige*," a box on the ears, from the British reflects his sense that England contemptuously dismissed him and his country;[77] or England dealt with the Germans as if they were citizens of a third-rate power, like Venezuela, Patagonia, Chile, or Portugal.[78] The degree to which Wilhelm could feel degraded by the British is revealed by his reaction to the suggestion of the English *Daily News* in August 1905 following the Björkö debacle and in the midst of the Moroccan crisis that relations between Germany and England might be improved were the Kaiser to pay a visit to a British naval flagship. Despite the fact that he had already visited two such vessels earlier in the year, Wilhelm now scrawled angrily in the margin of the paper: "It would not occur to me! To kiss the rod [*Rüthe*, meaning also penis and tail] that John Bull holds out menacingly!!!"[79]

German naval development would transform the English attitude, however. A formidable fleet would impress the seafaring British and cause them to treat Reich and Kaiser with respect.[80] Furthermore, Wilhelm was convinced that, like his mother who esteemed those who stood up to her, the English appreciated forceful conduct. Concerned exclusively with their own self-interest,[81] the English, according to the Kaiser, understood "only the cold-blooded brutality of the facts."[82] In one of their first official conversations, Wilhelm informed Bülow how to deal with the British:

> the Englishman . . . was inconsiderate to the point of brutality, for which reason he thoroughly understood anybody who acted similarly toward him; that there must be no playing the diplomatic game, or "finessing" with an Englishman, because it made him distrust those with whom he was dealing.[83]

Therefore the way to deal with the British was with brutal directness. In his famous "Cronberg interview" with Sir Charles Hardinge, permanent undersecretary in the British Foreign Office, in August 1908, it came as no surprise to the Kaiser that Hardinge, after hectoring him about Germany's navy, suddenly became friendly, deferential, and conciliatory when Wilhelm looked Hardinge straight in the eye and threatened him with war should the British continue to insist that Germany stop or reduce its naval building program. "The open discussion with me in which I sharply showed him my teeth did not fail to have the desired effect," Wilhelm telegraphed Bülow describing the interchange. "That is how one always must deal with the English."[84] In fact, the Kaiser believed that one of the reasons the British viewed the German navy with alarm was because the German ambassador in London, Paul Metternich, had not been sufficiently forceful in repudiating the British charges that Germany sought to challenge England's naval supremacy.[85] Wilhelm was convinced that the English were only impressed with countries that frightened them.[86] In the fall of 1897, Baron Axel von Varnbüler, the representative of Württemberg in Berlin, reported the Kaiser to say:

> In the face of such egotism [of the British] finally nothing avails but the actual might that stands behind one's claims. All the skill of diplomacy is of no avail if it cannot threaten and induce fright through this threatening. . . . Only if the armored fist is thus held before his face will the British Lion hide his tail as he recently did in the face of American threats.[87]

Therefore it became the Kaiser's "one overriding idea," in Holstein's words, to intimidate "England to make her more docile."[88]

Given his understanding of the English character and the fact that the German army was in no position to intimidate England, Wilhelm was convinced that only by confronting her with a formidable navy would Germany impress the British and force them to treat Reich and Kaiser honorably and as equals. "We will nonetheless build and increase the size of our fleet," he asserted in the spring of 1904; "with each additional ship of the line England's respect will increase."[89] A few months later Wilhelm noted in the margin of a report concerning derogatory comments by the British ambassador in St. Petersburg to members of the diplomatic corps about Russia's deteriorating position in the Russo-Japanese War: "Typically English. That is how they will treat us as well as long as we do not possess a fleet that fills them with respect."[90]

Because the fleet was designed to impress the British, Wilhelm could not understand his advisers' insistence that the fleet not be displayed to avoid alarming them. To the appeal in the spring of 1905 of Count Johann Bernstorff, chancellor of the German Embassy in London, that given the tension in Anglo-German relations the German navy be exhibited to the English as little as possible, the Kaiser responded sarcastically:

> If the estimable Count would be so good as to indicate to us in what manner this miracle is to be achieved I would be very grateful; because in order for our fleet *not to be seen* (1) it must for a start either burn smokeless coal or consist only of torpedo boats, (2) no Englishman must come to the Kiel Week or travel at all on the sea as he will be able and will in fact encounter our fleet everywhere, (3) the German Navy must be ordered to proceed to the North Sea only secretly

at night and at daybreak to return to secure anchor in the harbor[,] there to evaporate. Because no way has yet been discovered to hide a fleet on the ocean, especially one that burns Westphalian coal.[91]

Again and again the Kaiser's desire to show off the fleet clashed with the desire of his advisers to avoid antagonizing the English until the battlefleet was ready. In spring of 1904, for example, Wilhelm "surprised" Bülow with the news that Edward VII would be coming to Kiel that summer. The chancellor, suspecting that the initiative for the site of the visit had come from the Kaiser, pressed him to choose a location other than Kiel where the German navy was anchored. Tirpitz shared Bülow's concern and feared that "with his childish vanity, the Kaiser would not be able to resist making use of the opportunity to strut before the English with the rapid development of his Navy." Although unable to convince Wilhelm to change the site of the meeting, Bülow and Tirpitz were able to win his assurance that as few ships as possible would be shown to the king. "The next day, however, it was determined," Bülow continued, "that during the night the Kaiser had nonetheless issued a direct order through the Naval Cabinet that every ship, even the smallest barge, be sent to Kiel. Above all else, he wanted to use even this opportunity 'to impress.'"[92]

In March 1904 Friedrich Rosen, councillor in the Foreign Office, reported the Kaiser's comments on the subject of Anglo-German relations to Berlin:

It is the greatest nonsense to assume that we are in a position to practice *Weltpolitik* without, let alone against, England. His Majesty took the opportunity, as on many previous occasions, to object strongly to the conservative-agrarian press which demands that we engage in battle with the whole world and that we should give England and America a piece of our mind. . . . The unreasonable attitude of the German press has strained our relations with England. His Majesty our most gracious Highness alone forms the chain that connects us to England. He is honored by the English not simply as a relative of the Royal Family, but more on account of his person "as Patron of the entire sailors' caste in the world." To this belongs, however, that he be master of a mighty fleet. Therefore, since he alone is in a position to foster good relations with Great Britain, one should not make his task more difficult but easier by approving a more rapid increase in the size of the fleet.[93]

As revealed in his remarks to Rosen, the Kaiser believed not only that a formidable fleet would impress the British but that it was the key to an Anglo-German alliance. Already in the memorandum accompanying the naval budget for 1889/1890, Wilhelm wrote that the size of the navy must be increased and its condition improved in order "to give it that standing among the other seapowers which reflects the political, military, and overseas' interests of the German Reich and which makes an alliance with Germany also in a maritime connection something to be wished for and sought after."[94] In 1903 Wilhelm enthusiastically supported the concentration of the battlefleet in home waters—the very policy that so alarmed the British—for, as he told Tirpitz, he was certain that "a large fleet would draw the other Germanic states to us."[95]

"Nothing will change in England's attitude," he wrote in 1906, "until we are so strong on the seas that we become valuable allies."[96]

Given this expectation, it is no wonder that until the end of the Anglo-German naval race Wilhelm vehemently denied that Germany was racing with England or challenging her naval supremacy. The idea lying behind the Tirpitz-Plan, as presented by Berghahn, or behind Bülow's *Weltmachtkonzept*, as presented by Winzen, of using the navy to wrest naval and hence world power away from the English was foreign to Wilhelm's thinking. From the establishment of the battlefleet in 1898 through its expansion in 1900, the Kaiser, in public *and* in private, rejected the notion that the developing German navy posed a threat to Britain.[97] "Crazy! hysterical women!" he scrawled angrily in response to the assertion of the official British newspaper in India *Pioneer* that the German Navy Law of 1900 represented a challenge to England that had to be squarely met.[98] In the spring of 1906 just before the Reichstag's passage of the *Novelle* of that year (which responded to the construction of Dreadnoughts by the British by expanding the Northeast Sea Canal and the harbor and dock facilities at Wilhelmshaven and by beginning to construct German Dreadnought-type battleships), Wilhelm once more denied in the margins of the reports of his ambassadors that Germany's fleet was designed to challenge Britain's "'Predominance on the seas' or to fight or to achieve it!" Britain's "naval hegemony," he declared, "we will never assail."[99]

In 1908 when the Anglo-German naval rivalry reached its greatest intensity with the Reichstag's passage of the Navy *Novelle* in March (increasing the tempo of German ship construction and producing something of a panic in England and various British attempts to reduce the pace of German naval development),[100] Wilhelm still refused to concede that the German navy posed a threat to Britain. "Nonsense," he declared in January in a marginal comment to the statement that the Reich sought to be able in several years to challenge the Royal Navy. "It would never occur to us!"[101] Shortly thereafter on 16 February 1908 he wrote his extraordinary letter to the first lord of the British Admiralty, Tweedmouth, denying as "*nonsensical* and *untrue* that the German Naval Bill is to provide a Navy meant as a 'Challenge to British Naval Supremacy.'"[102] Again and again during the course of that year the Kaiser denied that the battlefleet was directed against England,[103] that Germany sought to challenge Britain's naval preeminence,[104] that the German navy could ever be powerful in comparison to the Royal Navy or that a naval competition between the two countries even existed.[105] "There is no competition. It exists only in overheated English brains!" he wrote in July in English in the margin of the *Spectator*. "Who dreams of racing?! Britain is racing against its own self!"[106] Wilhelm dismissed the notion that the aim of German policy was the ultimate defeat of Britain. Although Berghahn, Vogel, and Winzen have concluded that Bülow and Tirpitz had precisely this aim in mind, the Kaiser scrawled angrily in the margin of a report from the German ambassador in London to Bülow of 10 July 1908: "There is not one among us who believes in such nonsense!" Those in England who feared Germany, he concluded, "ought to be sent to a hydropathic institution!"[107] The way to resolve the imaginary arms' race and to assuage the irrational fears of the British was "very easy!" he believed: "just make an entente with us. . . . The simplest solution is an entente or an alliance with us, then all their worries will be taken care of. That we are good allies is revealed by our relationship with Austria."[108]

Given the fact that the purpose of the navy was to impress the British, to earn their admiration and respect, and to achieve an Anglo-German alliance, Wilhelm found it more than merely incomprehensible that the British were alarmed by German naval development. They appeared to be deranged. Thus, the notion that Germany sought to contest English naval hegemony was variously "blanc lunacy!"[109] or "a mad house idea of pathological condition"[110] and those who made such assertions were "suffering from delusions."[111] Even more preposterous and insane was the British fear that Germany was preparing to launch an attack on England. "Ripe for Bedlam! for the Commissioners for lunacy!" Wilhelm wrote also in English at the bottom of an English newspaper article suggesting that it would be logical for the Kaiser to want to remove England as "the chief obstacle in his path" to making Germany "a great world power."[112] And when the *Daily Express* warned of an imminent German attack in August 1908 and asserted that it was up to Germany "to prove to us that this fear is groundless," Wilhelm responded once again in English in the margin: "Certainly not! If England suffers from self-suggested hallucinations, it must call the doctor, but *we* have nothing to do with that! . . . The writer ought to be sent to Bedlam for treatment against Germanophobia." The Kaiser concluded: "he has 'invasion on the brain'!"[113]

According to Bülow, the idea of defeating or even of surpassing England was simply not in keeping with the Kaiser's character. "I can assure anyone on my honor and conscience," Bülow wrote in his memoirs, "that at no time during my service to Kaiser Wilhelm II did he think of a war of aggression." Wilhelm's pacific bent was the product of underlying timidity, Bülow believed. The Kaiser loved martial trappings, "a 'smart' conduct and a 'dashing' manner, but no real danger, no serious test."

It was probably even further from Emperor Wilhelm II's mind to attack *England* with his beloved fleet than to invade our neighbors with the German Army. The image which danced before Wilhelm's eyes as the most wonderful prospect for the future was to see himself at the head of a great, a very great German fleet starting out on a peaceful visit to England. At the heights of Portsmouth the English sovereign at the head of his high seas' fleet would await the German Kaiser. The two fleets would file past one another; each of the sovereigns standing on the bridge of their respective flag ships wearing the naval uniform and decorations of the other. Then following the obligatory embraces and kisses, a gala dinner with splendid speeches would be held at Cowes.[114]

From this perspective, lack of self-confidence was the psychological source of Wilhelm's incredulous reaction to the suspicions of the British. The Kaiser may simply have been unable to conceive of himself as posing a threat to anyone. Indeed, it is revealing that at the time of the Jameson raid, Wilhelm identified with the tiny Boer Republics, heroically able perhaps to assert their independence from Britain's world empire but hardly able to endanger England's national security.[115] That the British could feel threatened by Germany's developing fleet was simply incredible.[116] "To my humble notion," he wrote Lord Tweedmouth, "this perpetual quoting of the 'German danger' is utterly unworthy of the great British nation with its worldwide Empire and its mighty navy which is about five times the size of the German Navy. There is something nearly ludicrous about it."[117] Even more preposterous was the notion that the Reich sought to conquer Britain. To the Kaiser, English fear of a German invasion was "approximately the same as if we were to be afraid that Switzerland sought to invade us."[118]

Nevertheless, neither Bülow's theory about the Kaiser's pacifism and underlying weakness nor the Kaiser's belief that the purpose of the navy was to impress the British and win an alliance with them can account for Wilhelm's outrage at the British disarmament proposals or for his stated willingness—in contradiction to Bülow's hypothesis—to go to war should the British persist in making them. The extent to which Wilhelm was stirred over this issue is revealed by his instruction to his ambassador in London that such proposals were to be given "a rude answer such as kiss my etc."[119] He vowed that continued British demands would be met "with grenades" for it would "absolutely [mean] war."[120] Wilhelm's rage at the British effort to limit the pace of German naval construction reached a climax in his "Cronberg interview" with Hardinge. As Wilhelm reported the contents of the conversation to Bülow:

> He: "Can't you put a stop to your building? Or build less ships?" [In English in the Kaiser's telegram.]
>
> I: "The extent of German naval armament is based upon our own interests and our alliances. The Navy serves a defensive purpose and is not directed against anyone, least of all against England. It poses no threat to you. At present you are all afraid of shadows."
>
> He: "But an arrangement must be made in order to limit construction. You must stop or build slower." [Again, in English.]
>
> I: "Then we shall fight for it is a question of national honour and dignity." [Once more, in English.][121]

The Kaiser's outraged belligerence at the British disarmament proposals can be understood in several ways. In the first place, Wilhelm doubtless experienced the British reaction to the German navy as a form of rejection when he had expected to win admiration and acceptance. Old traumas had been repeated. Just as he had felt unappreciated by his mother as a child, now he experienced the British disarmament proposals as a failure to appreciate and esteem the very feature of himself and his country of which he was most proud. Just as he was hurt and angry when his subjects rejected his words (as after his speech to the Brandenburg Provincial Diet in 1897) or his deeds (as after Björkö in 1905), he was hurt and angry when the English in 1908 rejected the navy that was designed to impress them. He even clashed with his own advisers when they manifested a failure to appreciate the fleet by advocating a naval agreement with Britain. When, during his last official meeting with the Kaiser as chancellor on board the *Hohenzollern* on 26 June 1909, Bülow urged Wilhelm to negotiate a halt to the arms' race, the Kaiser responded with annoyance: "Why must you end by bringing up that matter!? Haven't I told you often enough ... that I will not allow myself to be talked into anything that would interfere with naval construction! Every such suggestion is a humiliation to me and to my Navy!" Gesturing to the German fleet assembled at Kiel, he proclaimed: "Whoever casts his eye directly, as I do at this moment, on the fruit of his honest and arduous labor has a right to manifest a certain self-esteem." "I cannot and will not allow John Bull to prescribe to me the tempo of my ship construction," Wilhelm concluded. "I beg you finally to drop the subject. We want to part on good terms, do we not?"[122]

As revealed by his comments to Bülow, Wilhelm regarded the British disarmament proposals as an unwarranted and degrading intrusion in Germany's private affairs. It was a matter of principle for Wilhelm: no foreign government could prescribe German defense policy to Kaiser or Reich.[123] When the possibility arose that the disarmament issue would be raised at the Second International Peace Conference at the Hague in 1906, Wilhelm instructed his ministers to withdraw: "Because I as well as my people will never allow foreigners to make any sort of stipulations about our military or naval situation."[124] Five years later in November 1911 he denounced the suggestion of the German ambassador in London that an agreement be reached with the British to limit the tempo of ship construction. Such a proposal, Wilhelm telegraphed Chancellor Bethmann Hollweg, "allows a foreign people to meddle in our naval affairs, something that I, as Commander-in-Chief and Kaiser, *never can nor ever will agree to*! It means a *humiliation* for our people!"[125] Here, too, a connection with Wilhelm's past can be established. As it had been necessary for Wilhelm as a young man to preserve his psychological autonomy against his mother's domineering personality, as it had been necessary for Wilhelm in the first year of his reign to protect his political authority by rejecting his uncle's advice on how to resolve the succession in Hannover, now it was necessary to defend the independence of the Reich against impertinent English attempts to interfere in this most sensitive area of his sovereignty.

Finally, Wilhelm experienced the British disarmament proposals as more than merely a denigration of his most prized achievement or an attempt to compromise his independence and that of the Reich. They were also insulting.[126] As he told Hardinge, it was "a question of national honour and dignity." By insisting that Germany curtail its naval development, England was treating Germany not as a valued and respected equal but as an inferior, like Spain or Portugal, China or Italy.[127] In April 1909 he wrote Bülow that recent British demands for German naval reductions had created a "situation which was never a negotiation over proposals between two *equal* partners, but always had the effect of being a rather arrogant *request* of one *more powerful* to a *not equally respected* weaker one. Therefore the rejection, since our honor almost always hung in the balance."[128] Once again, a familiar situation had been created for Wilhelm. Whereas Victoria had only attempted to compromise her son's autonomy she had, in his eyes, succeeded only too well as far as Friedrich was concerned. Thus the Kaiser experienced the British demands that Germany disarm as an attempt to put him and his country in the position his father had occupied in the house of his parents, in the toilet of the Cologne railway station, and in his uncle Edward's assertion in 1888 that had he survived Friedrich would have returned Alsace and Lorainne to France.[129] Were he and his country to accede to the British demands and reduce the strength of the navy as the price for closer relations, then, the Kaiser was convinced, the Reich would automatically assume a subordinate position in relation to the overbearing British. Without a mighty navy, Germany would become another of Britain's "vassals and *Lanzknechten*,"[130] like Japan, England's eastern "*Lanzknecht*,"[131] or like Portugal, which had accepted an English "satrapy."[132] Despite his yearning for an alliance with England, Wilhelm would go to war before accepting that status. He wrote in July 1908 that he

> did *not* wish for good relations with England at the cost of the expansion of the German fleet. If England is only prepared to offer us its hand in goodwill on the condition that we must limit our fleet, then that is a boundless insolence, which comprises a profound insult for the German people and their Kaiser.[133]

From the beginning the only relationship with England that Wilhelm had been able to contemplate was one "of absolute equality" between the two countries.[134] As a young man he had been unwilling to sacrifice his autonomy to his domineering mother in order to win her affection. As Kaiser he would not sacrifice the independence of the Reich to win the affection of the British. Nor would he sacrifice his honor as a German or as a man in relation to England as he believed his father had done in relation to Victoria. The creation of a mighty German navy seemed the answer to Wilhelm's personal dilemma. On the one hand, the fleet would impress the British, for they, like his mother, only respected the formidable and the powerful. On the other hand, the navy would simultaneously uphold his honor and the honor of the Reich, for the increased power of the fleet was also an assertion of German armed might and represented Wilhelm's identification of himself with the military tradition of his father and grandfather. Wilhelm's Germany would not be weak and dependent in relation to England as Friedrich had been in relation to Victoria. In Germany's alliance with England, Germany would be strong and dominant or, at the very least, fully equal. Germany would not have to renounce its nationality and manhood. It could still assert its national and military pride. Wilhelm's goal, however, remained an Anglo-German alliance, his parents' fondest wish. Germany was to adopt England's greatest characteristic in his eyes, a powerful navy, so that friendship and kinship could be realized between the two countries. The fleet would also enable Wilhelm to resolve the political dilemma he faced as a result of his enduring attachment to England and desire for an alliance with that country. Unlike Friedrich and Victoria, whose Anglophilia had cost them their popularity and influence, Wilhelm II could not and would not disregard German public opinion. Given the intensity of German nationalism and the criticism of the Kaiser in Germany when he was seen to be overly friendly or conciliatory toward the English, the only Anglo-German alliance Wilhelm could conclude that would be acceptable to his subjects was one on the basis of "absolute equality." Anything less would be experienced as an intolerable blow to the honor of the nation and would be instantly repudiated along with the leader who had concluded it. The creation of a mighty navy that would uphold Germany's honor and preserve the Kaiser's standing with his subjects would make an alliance with England possible politically.

It remains appropriate therefore to characterize Wilhelm II's attitude toward England as inconstant, for that attitude changed depending on when he expressed himself and with whom, on how he was responded to. Clearly he was neither consistently Anglophile nor consistently Anglophobe. But even if his attitude shifted from affection to anger and back again, that inconstancy does not mean either that his attitude toward England cannot be understood or that his shifts did not occur for perfectly intelligible reasons. Wilhelm's consistency lay less on the level of a foreign policy conducted in accordance with a rational self-interest determined by relatively unchanging historical circumstances (Germany's geographical position in the center of Europe, for example).[135] Instead his consistency lay on the level of a foreign policy conducted in accordance with basic emotional and political needs as these were either satisfied or frustrated by specific events and changing circumstances.[136] Wilhelm's policy toward England was developed to harmonize three such needs: the need for the recognition, respect, and affection of his English relatives and of the English people; the need to be in tune with and supported by his associates and by the German people; and the need to uphold his honor and the honor of his nation. With his policy dependent on the reponses of his environment, on the reactions of the British and of his own subjects, when, instead of the harmony he had anticipated, the navy produced discord between England and Germany and disharmony in himself, he sought first to satisfy the two needs that were most important to his psychological and political functioning and were, in addition, compatible with one another. Thus, despite his attachment to England, he was ready to go to war with that country to maintain the support of the Germans and preserve his own and his nation's honor. In that, the Kaiser was consistent or as consistent as variously consistent human beings ever are able to be.

In the course of this study, three German policies toward England have been identified: Tirpitz's plan to use the navy to wrest maritime and world power away from Britain; Bülow's plan to exploit Germany's position at the fulcrum of power in Europe by maintaining a "policy of the free hand," unencumbered by restrictive alliances, in order at critical moments in the disputes of the powers to place its weight on the side that would bring the greatest advantage to the Reich; and Wilhelm's plan to create a navy that would uphold German honor in the world and before Britain, make possible an Anglo-German alliance, and insure that his voice and that of his nation be listened to and respected in all the decisions taken by the great powers. Given the profound divisions in the Wilhelmian establishment, divisions between and within the various branches of government, a number of other German foreign policies can no doubt be identified as well.[137] Therefore we have to accept a Kaiser who can only be described as consistent in the context of a more complex emotional constellation than Anglophilia, Anglophobia, or ambivalence and a German policy toward England that was actually the product of various different policies interacting with one another.[138]

IV

In the beginning of Wilhelm II's reign, the Germans were blind to the necessity of creating a mighty navy. In 1900 an article entitled "Engländerei" appeared in the *Hamburger Nachrichten*, a paper that had been used as a vehicle by Bismarck to criticize the Kaiser. The article was a veiled attack on Wilhelm for his Anglophilia and for his visit to England in November 1899. At the bottom Wilhelm wrote:

> If for years the Hambg. Nachrichten and with it the entire German Press had expended the energy and "wind" to drum into Germany the logic of my policy and to support it through a strong [program of] naval construction, then we would have the fleet and with it the much wished for respect of the British! Instead, however, the H.N. has for years made itself the mouthpiece of a disobedient and deposed minister, to the great applause of my countrymen and subjects, and has abused and defiled everything that their Kaiser has done! Now the consequences are apparent! Had the visit so criticized by them not taken place, then, with the aid of the H.N. the Dresdr. Nach. [*Dresdener Nachrichten*], Tageszeitg. [*Deutsche Tageszeitung*], etc., we would now have war with England![139]

Despite the *Hamburger Nachrichten* and the other papers, the Kaiser was able to convince his subjects, if not of the logic of his policies, then at least of the necessity of creating the fleet that was the key to their success. But then the English, instead of responding as Wilhelm had expected, instead of finding Germany a more attractive ally, instead of understanding the importance of maintaining German honor and independence, instead of appreciating the difficulty of his domestic position and his need to uphold that honor and independence before his subjects, instead of recognizing that the fleet was designed not to defeat the British but to make possible an alliance with them, instead, the English reacted with fear and anger and with demands that Germany stop building the fleet and either renounce its honor and independence or earn the enmity of the one nation in the world whose friendship Wilhelm wanted most.

From this perspective, the Kaiser's notorious interview with the *Daily Telegraph* published in late October 1908 becomes readily intelligible. Wilhelm's remarks were simply a public echo of what he had written at the bottom of the *Hamburger Nachrichten* in 1900, of what he had said to Friedrich Rosen in 1904, or of what he had scrawled in the margin of the reports from the German ambassador in London during 1908. Perhaps one of the reasons that the Foreign Office approved the interview with only minor alterations was because Wilhelm's comments must have seemed completely unexceptional to the officials who vetted the document. The Kaiser's interview was simply another expression of his mounting exasperation and bewilderment over the failure of the British to understand him or the purpose of the navy.

"You English are mad, mad as March hares!" he chided in the pages of the *Daily Telegraph*. "What has come over you that you are so completely given over to suspicions quite unworthy of a great nation? What more can I do than I have done? . . . My actions ought to speak for themselves, but you listen not to them but to those who misinterpret and distort them. This is a personal insult which I feel and resent. To be forever misjudged, to have my repeated offers of friendship weighed and scrutinized with zealous, mistrustful eyes taxes my patience severely. I have said time after time that I am a friend of England, and your Press, or at least a considerable section of it, bids the people of England to refuse my proffered hand and insinuates that the other holds a dagger. How can I convince a nation against its will?" He told his English readers that they did not appreciate the difficulty of his position in Germany. "The prevailing sentiment amongst my own people is not friendly to England. I am in a minority[140] in my own land. . . . That is another reason why I resent your refusal to accept my pledged word that I am the friend of England. I strive without ceasing to improve relations and you retort that I am your arch-enemy. You make it very hard for me. Why is it?" As proof of his goodwill toward Britain, Wilhelm cited his conduct during the Boer War when "German opinion undoubtedly was hostile, bitterly hostile. The Press was hostile, the private opinion was hostile. But official Germany—what of it?" It was he, alone, the Kaiser insisted, who had blocked the attempt of France and Russia "to humiliate England to the dust" by threatening that "Germany would use her armed might to prevent such concerted action,"[141] and he boasted of the battle plan against the Boers he had sent to England, a plan, he added, that "ran very much on the same lines as that which was actually adopted by Lord Roberts." Finally, the Kaiser turned to the German navy. Again denying that the fleet was directed against England and asserting that, as "a young and growing Empire . . . Germany must have a powerful fleet," Wilhelm concluded: "Only those powers which have vast navies will be listened to with respect when the future of the Pacific comes to be solved, and if for that reason only Germany must have a powerful fleet. It may even be that England herself will be glad that Germany has a fleet, when they speak together on the same side in the great debates of the future."[142]

Although the uproar in Germany over the *Daily Telegraph* interview badly shook his confidence, Wilhelm sought to preserve his dream of naval expansion and Anglo-German alliance. On 14 May 1911 the latest British proposal to limit the naval race was now not a mortal insult but, he telegraphed Tirpitz, "proof of the effectiveness of the Navy Law and of our Navy. The latter continues to work directly as pressure [on the British] to [reach] an understanding with us." The navy's "undisturbed expansion and continued development," he concluded, "is an absolute necessity."[143] Despite these brave words and his willingness to contemplate an agreement to control what he now could acknowledge was an arms' race,[144] the Kaiser's policy toward England was in shambles by the spring of 1911—as were the policies of his state secretary and former chancellor. England had not been impressed or intimidated by the battlefleet into an alliance with Germany as Wilhelm had expected. Nor had she allowed herself to be put in the position where the battlefleet either through force or the threat of its use could compel England to relinquish her position of world preeminence to Germany as Tirpitz had planned. Bülow's policy of the "free hand" had produced, instead of the anticipated diplomatic successes, only the suspicion and enmity of the European powers. As a result of all three policies, the Reich's world political ambitions had been frustrated, and Germany found itself encircled by arming adversaries. Having failed diplomatically and strategically, the German navy was pushed into the background, bringing Wilhelm's dream of continuous naval expansion to an end. With the existence of the Reich in jeopardy, what had once seemed essential now became a luxury. Germany's military leaders occupied center-stage, and the focus of German diplomatic and strategic thinking shifted from *Weltpolitik* to a continental policy.[145] Along with his policy of using the navy to secure an Anglo-German alliance and worldwide prestige for himself and for the Reich, Wilhelm's standing with his subjects collapsed in the aftermath of the *Daily Telegraph* affair.[146] Only at the beginning of August 1914 was the Kaiser, for one brief moment, the symbolic leader he had been before.

V

In 1912 after reading an article in the *Strand Magazine* entitled "The Kaiser as He Is," Wilhelm II wrote in English: "This is the Kaiser as he is *not*! I should like to know what he *really* is!!"[147] Wilhelm's policy toward England can be understood as a futile attempt to resolve that question. His effort to achieve the integration of his fractured self through the creation of a battlefleet served only to increase the personal tension within him and the political tension between the two countries. In playing out the unresolved problems of his innermost being, the Kaiser contributed to the deterioration of Anglo-German relations before the First World War.[148] It is one of history's paradoxes that Germany and England were driven toward armed conflict by a leader who in the deepest layers of his personality wished that they would live together in friendship and peace.

And yet, as this chapter has sought to demonstrate, Wilhelm II's contribution to the Anglo-German antagonism cannot be understood in a vacuum. Presumably it has been made clear that the Kaiser's personal agenda, which he sought to realize in his policy toward England, was itself the product of the politics of his past and his present; and in putting his policy toward England into practice, Wilhelm was constrained and directed by the politics of the day. Looking back, it seems obvious that the goal of achieving an Anglo-German alliance through the creation of a mighty German navy, as absolutely sensible and necessary as it was from Wilhelm's point of view, could never have been realized. Quite apart from the improbability that England would react to the battlefleet with an awestruck eagerness to conclude an alliance, the Kaiser's policy was seriously flawed from the start. In the first place, in order to create a fleet that would impress the English, Wilhelm, as he was well aware,[149] had to play to popular Anglophobia in Germany, which, in turn, would inevitably antagonize the British and increase their suspicion of the Kaiser and the Reich.[150] Then when he sought to assure the British of his friendship, as in his visits to England and in his *Daily Telegraph* interview, he managed only to antagonize his subjects. If nothing else, the uproar in Germany over the Kaiser's *Daily Telegraph* interview revealed the depth of popular animosity toward England in the Reich.[151] Second, there was tension between Wilhelm's desire to practice *Weltpolitik* and his desire for an alliance with England. Both objectives required naval development from the Kaiser's perspective. But whereas the practice of *Weltpolitik* meant, through colonial acquisition and the expansion of German influence around the globe, a fundamental redistribution of world power, an alliance with England meant allying the Reich with the country that more than any other sought, as a result of its position of preeminence, to preserve the international status quo.[152] Indeed, Germany and England appear simply to have had a series of competing commercial, colonial, and diplomatic interests. Moreover it is hard to imagine any alliance that would have been experienced by both the English and the Germans as compatible with the national honor. For as the history of Wilhelm II's futile effort to achieve an Anglo-German alliance clearly reveals, in addition to their conflicting economic and political interests, the English and the Germans had conflicting emotional needs as well.

Conclusion

After the First World War a number of psychiatric studies were published in Germany purporting to demonstrate that Wilhelm II was mentally ill.[1] Adolf Friedländer's *Wilhelm II: Versuch einer psychologischen Analyse* is typical of these attempts to diagnose the Kaiser. The author found that Wilhelm "shows all the indications of overbreeding [*Hochzüchtung*] and degeneration."[2] "Wilhelm II reveals himself to us," Friedländer continued, "as a personality in which the positive and negative hereditary characteristics of his ancestors are present in greatly intensified form."[3] Friedländer's study, like the others published in the aftermath of an unexpected and terrible defeat, attributed Wilhelm's erratic and extreme behavior to breeding. These studies share the implicit assumption that the loss of the war could be traced in part to the unstable conduct of the Kaiser, which in turn was a direct result of hereditary hypomania. In the psychiatrist Paul Tesdorpf's *Die Krankheit Wilhelms II*, the connection between Wilhelm's "illness" and Germany's defeat was made explicitly. "We Germans have lost nothing of our honor and inner greatness," the author proclaimed. "We have emerged internally victorious from this struggle." Tesdorpf sought to absolve the German people of responsibility for the collapse of the *Kaiserreich* by attributing it to the sickness of the Kaiser:

> The government of Wilhelm II was spurious. It had to collapse. What was to blame for this spuriousness? Was it his will? His will was perhaps noble and pure. But he was sick, sick, as were his thoughts and emotions. . . . For the experienced physician and psychiatrist there can be no doubt that Wilhelm II, already as a youth was mentally ill. . . . The blame for the war that can be attributed to him was the result of his illness.[4]

Although acknowledging that aspects of Wilhelm's psychopathology could be ascribed to his birth injury, Tesdorpf ultimately accepted Friedländer's diagnosis. All the evidence, he concluded, "leads to the natural conclusion that Wilhelm II presents a typical picture of hereditary psychic degeneration."[5]

Although the diagnoses of Friedländer, Tesdorpf, and their colleagues doubtless represented honest efforts to come to terms with a puzzling and to them historically decisive personality, it seems clear that a diagnosis of inherited "degeneracy," like the veiled imputation of the German defeat to Wilhelm's psychopathology generally, suited the need of Germans to distance themselves from their Kaiser after 1918. Sigmund Freud, writing in the summer of 1906, noted that such a diagnosis reassures people by enabling them to deny their sense of emotional kinship with those suffering from psychological disorders. In his discussion of the novella *Gradiva: A Pompeiian Fancy* by Wilhelm Jensen, Freud observed that because the hero, a young archaeologist, had developed a delusion about an antique bas-relief of a woman, an old-school psychiatrist

> would at once stamp him as a *dégénéré* and would investigate the heredity which had remorselessly driven him to this fate. But here the author does not follow the psychiatrist, and with good reason. He wishes to bring the hero closer to us so as to make "empathy" easier; the diagnosis of "*dégénéré*," whether it is right or wrong, at once puts the young archaeologist at a distance from us, for we readers are the normal people and the standard of humanity.[6]

Ironically, Freud's own remarks on Wilhelm II's psychopathology testify to the attraction of a popular view of the Kaiser that served to increase the psychological distance between the Germans and their leader in defeat. Freud was moved to comment on the Kaiser by Emil Ludwig's biography, *Wilhelm Hohenzollern: The Last of the Kaisers*, which appeared in Germany in 1926. For Ludwig, as for Hinzpeter before him, Wilhelm's withered left arm provided the key to the character of the Kaiser:

> Only those who can appreciate this lifelong struggle against the congenital weakness will be fair to him when the future Emperor is seen to strain too far, or lose, his nervous energy. The perpetual struggle with a defect which every newcomer must instantly perceive and he, for that very reason, the more ostentatiously ignore—this hourly, lifelong effort to conceal a congenital, in no way repulsive, stigma of Nature, was the decisive factor in the development of his character. The weakling sought to emphasize his strength; but instead of doing so intellectually, as his lively intelligence would have permitted, tradition and vainglory urged him to the exhibition of an heroic, that is to say a soldierly personality.[7]

Wilhelm's blustering bellicosity and inner weakness were directly attributable to his birth defect according to Ludwig. Indeed, he implied, a measure of responsibility for the war and the defeat could be traced to this "stigma of Nature." Although Ludwig's biography focused popular attention on the Kaiser's arm as a way to understand his personality, it seems likely that Ludwig had articulated a widely held belief in Germany that the failings and failures of the Kaiser were to be attributed to his physical defect, a defect perhaps the responsibility of the attending English physician—according to one well-known, if apocryphal, version of Wilhelm's birth, which Wilhelm himself may have had a hand in promoting at the height of his conflict with his mother.[8]

The popularity of Ludwig's biography was such that the book came to Freud's attention. He invoked it in 1932 in his "New Introductory Lectures on Psychoanalysis" as part of his effort to refute the theory of the inferiority complex developed by his erstwhile disciple Alfred Adler. Specifically, Freud criticized Ludwig for having

> ventured on an attempt to erect the whole of the development of his hero's character on the sense of inferiority which must have been called up by his physical defect. In doing so, he has overlooked one small but not insignificant fact. It is usual for mothers whom Fate has presented with a child who is sickly or otherwise at a disadvantage to try to compensate him for his unfair handicap by a superabundance of love. In the instance before us, the proud mother behaved otherwise; she withdrew her love from the child on account of his infirmity. When he had grown up into a man of great power, he proved unambiguously by his actions that he had never forgiven his mother. When you consider the importance of a mother's love for the mental life of a child, you will no doubt make a tacit correction of the biographer's inferiority theory.[9]

Freud's subtle shift in emphasis away from Adler-Ludwig's point of view beautifully expresses the revolution he brought about in our understanding of human beings. The defect of nature was not by itself psychologically significant but rather the responses of the environment to the defect. It was Victoria's rejection of her son because of his withered left arm that "stigmatized" the defect, thereby laying the groundwork for his rebellion against his parents as a young man and for his vengeful anger against England as Kaiser.[10] To be sure, Freud's interpretation has a circumscribed validity and is not unlike that presented in Chapter 2. Nevertheless, Freud's understanding was based upon a popular view of the Kaiser in which Germans had a nationalistic investment, a view which directed responsibility for the Kaiser's psychopathology, for his bellicosity toward Britain, for the lost war, away from Germany, an understanding which attributed Wilhelm II's failings and failures not to his weak and distant German father (or to any other Germans who played a role in Wilhelm's upbringing) but solely to the unempathic responses of the foreign English princess who was his mother.[11]

Like Friedländer and Tesdorpf's diagnoses of the Kaiser, the interpretations of Wilhelm suggested by Ludwig and Freud, although accounting for certain aspects of the Kaiser's psychopathology, offer a picture of his personality and behavior that would have appealed to Germans after the war.[12] By attributing Wilhelm's difficulties to his breeding, his physical deformity, the actions of the doctors at his birth, or his English mother, Germans were able to deny their emotional kinship with the Kaiser, their influence on his actions, their contribution to the catastrophe. In the aftermath of an unexpected and humiliating defeat, Wilhelm was made a scapegoat, the target of the ignominy and helpless anger of his former subjects. Paradoxically, in exile in Holland, Wilhelm II continued to personify the feelings of the Germans about themselves. Now he was not the embodiment of national strength and greatness but of national weakness and disgrace. In a symbolic sense, however, the "personal regime" can be said to have continued.

In contrast to the diagnoses of Friedländer and Tesdorpf and the interpretations of Ludwig and Freud, this study has attempted to establish psychological connections between Wilhelm II and the Germans. The Kaiser has been understood, in other words, less as a great man of history who changed the course of events in accordance with his own psychological agenda and more as a figure who is historically significant primarily because his psychological agenda was shaped by the forces of his time. Of course the Germans were not the cause of Wilhelm's narcissistic pathology. Both of his parents and his other caretakers as well as physical and constitutional factors bear primary responsibility for that. And yet, through his parents and caretakers, historical forces exerted political influence on Wilhelm's psychological development. Furthermore, as a result of the nature of his adult personality and, more specifically, of his tendency to blur psychologically the distinction between himself and his country, the Germans influenced his attitudes and actions. Because of his vulnerability to the responses of his subjects, because they had the capacity to exhilarate or devastate him, Wilhelm sought to moniter popular opinion and adapt himself to the various German publics to which he was exposed—as he monitored and adapted to the other environments on which he was also emotionally dependent.

The psychology of the Kaiser worked not only to connect him to the Germans but to connect them to him. Wilhelm's restless search for admiration, his driven need to exhibit himself and his accomplishments, served to focus national attention on his person. Often literally donning the garb of an heroic leader to cover his insecurity, Wilhelm provided his subjects with an imposing figure with whom they could identify and around whom they could unite. Wilhelm's brittle facade of personal sovereignty, his defensive need always to appear right and in control fulfilled the need of Germans to have a powerful and independent Kaiser, a ruler with perhaps a world-historical mission. In the field of foreign policy, Wilhelm's anxious and belligerent insistence that he be listened to and treated with respect expressed the widespread sense that Germany was entitled to take its rightful place as a great imperial power.

As a result of his eternal youth or, put less generously, of his immaturity, the Kaiser came to embody the young and energetic spirit of his newly unified and recently industrialized nation.[13] That Wilhelm's energy and activity realized a popular wish that youthful and vigorous Germany be personified by a youthful and vigorous Kaiser was reflected in an editorial in *Die Badische Presse* on 4 October 1889 following his visit to the area:

> For the first time one can appreciate completely the significance of the words of the greatest statesman of the last century, Prince Bismarck, that the youthful Reich now has the good fortune to have a Kaiser who wants to be his own

chancellor. The wholesome influence that an active and vigorous monarchy can exert on the German Reich has not yet been fully realized in that the great Kaiser Wilhelm I was already aged, and his noble son Friedrich was already infirm. Kaiser Wilhelm II, however, with his youth and energy is "the right man in the right place" for the new phase in the development of the Reich.

Despite its veneration for Bismarck as "the greatest statesman of the last century," this editorial, published six months before his dismissal, already expressed those sentiments that would lead many Germans to applaud the Kaiser's action.[14] Although Wilhelm's conflict with the chancellor was based upon political and, even more, upon personal antagonism, his dismissal of Bismarck was in tune with the popular desire, expressed in *Die Badische Presse*, that the Kaiser be his own chancellor and that Germany be led and represented by a man not of the past but of the future.[15]

Perhaps it would be most accurate to say in fact that, if Wilhelm II was the "mirror image" of the Germans, he reflected with particular clarity those who dominated the stage in Wilhelmian Germany, who set the tone, determined the pace of daily life, and established the order of the day. Those Germans invariably saw themselves as representatives of a more dynamic, enterprising, and aggressively modern generation than the one they were impatiently thrusting aside. Diederich Hessling of Heinrich Mann's *Der Untertan* certainly thought of himself in those terms, and he had little use for those he perceived as old-fashioned, cautious, liberal, or devoid of the energetic spirit of the new Wilhelmian era.[16] Now was a time for "large views," "large-scale enterprise," and "large-scale publicity," for impulsive action and risk-taking, for doing things "in the modern way" and "in the grand manner."[17] It was an era of "personality," of fervent nationalism and aggressive imperialism.[18] For Heinrich Mann, as for his protagonist Hessling, the Kaiser personified the youthful generation that dominated the Wilhelmian Reich.

> Unlike the democratic balderdash in which the departing generation still believed, the Emperor was the representative of youth, the most outstanding personality, charmingly impulsive and a highly original thinker. "One man must be master, and master in every field!" Diederich confessed that he harboured the firmest and most passionate convictions, and declared that an end must be made . . . of the old liberal nonsense. "Now comes the new age!"[19]

Admiring successful businessmen, concerned with commerce, and denounced by conservative Prussians as a "parvenu," Wilhelm II was an apt symbol of the *nouveau riche* Germans and of what Heinrich Mann and Walther Rathenau described as the *nouveau riche* Germany of his day.[20]

Although Wilhelm's psychology allowed him to personify his subjects and symbolize his nation, his weakness and inconsistency made him a singularly ineffective, if not inconsequential, politician. Here, his impressionability, his labile dependence on others to supply him with direction and purpose, his tendency to understand and respond to everything personally, his vulnerability and emotionally reactive character, his lack of diligence and persistence, all contributed to the incoherence of German policy. In domestic affairs, his capricious meddling interfered with consistent government. In foreign affairs, his precipitous and flamboyant bellicosity alarmed Germany's neighbors and contributed to the diplomatic isolation of the Reich. In general, Wilhelm's inability to define a personal self-interest, to decide who he was and what he wanted, found political expression in his inability to determine the self-interest of the nation and take the steps necessary to realize it.

And yet perhaps even in his political incompetence, the Kaiser personified the Reich. Perhaps Germany was simply so badly divided that no significant community of interest could have been developed that might have formed the basis for effective political leadership.[21] Even a politician of genius, Otto von Bismarck, proved unequal to the task of forging national consensus, and the last years of his chancellorship were characterized by stagnation that covered growing social tension and political disaffection. Certainly it was a task beyond the psychological and intellectual resources of Wilhelm II. As a symbolic leader, the Kaiser was able to create a certain emotional unity among Germans, an identity of feeling, a sense of belonging together. As a political leader, he was utterly unable to ameliorate the underlying economic, social, and political conditions that served to drive the Germans apart. And obviously, therefore, he failed to provide his subjects with what has proved to be the most effective leadership in our contemporary world, leadership that integrates politics and symbolism to create a community of interest and sentiment.

Looking back on the Kaiser after the Second World War, this time not as a participant in the tragic events that made up the history of Germany during the first half of the twentieth century but as a historian, Friedrich Meinecke raised the question in his little book, *Die deutsche Katastrophe*, "whether Wilhelm II could not be described as an unfortunate accident in the course of German history."

Had another ruler stood in his place—perhaps one possessing only average talents but with a character more that of the temperate Hohenzollern type—then everything might have turned out differently and more favorably. This possibility cannot be disputed but must promptly be supplemented through a glance at the general historical forces that also manifested themselves in the accident of Wilhelm II. There were certainly . . . signs of degeneration in the German bourgeoisie and general population and those inherent defects in Prussian militarism . . . that worked themselves out in the individual personality of Wilhelm II. Who can ever differentiate clearly and completely between the accidental historical personality and the general historical tendencies that rise out of the depths of the life of a people?[22]

Although we shall never know whether a more psychologically cohesive leader could have helped to create a more truly cohesive national self-interest, Wilhelm II characterized his nation and historical epoch.[23] There is a striking parallel between this youthful, energetic emperor whose psychic disjointedness prevented him from defining a coherent personal self-interest and this newly formed, dynamic nation whose economic, social, regional, religious, political, and intellectual disjointedness seems to have precluded the definition and realization of a national self-interest. And there is a striking fit between an emperor who covered his profound inner disharmony with flamboyant, provocative, and even bellicose self-aggrandizement and a nation that covered its profound lack of domestic consensus with a foreign policy of *Weltpolitik*, a policy of flamboyant, provocative, and even bellicose national self-aggrandizement.

Looking back on the relationship between Wilhelm II and the Germans it seemed to contemporaries that the Kaiser, as a personality, reflected his subjects and his times. "Wilhelm the Second did in one sense actually fulfill the task of a king completely," Egon Friedell wrote in 1926, "in that he almost always was the expression of the overwhelming majority of his subjects, the champion and executor of their ideas, the representative of their outlook on life. Most Germans were nothing more than pocket editions, smaller versions, miniature copies of Kaiser Wilhelm."[24] That, certainly, was the view Heinrich Mann presented in *Der Untertan*. As one of the characters in the novel noted with more than a little irony, the Kaiser's "person so perfectly expresses and represents the tendencies of Germany at this moment as to be almost awe-inspiring."[25] Diederich Hessling, himself the *Untertan*, the "vassal" or "subject" of the novel's title, was portrayed by Mann as the quintessential Wilhelmian German. Hessling sought to model himself on Wilhelm II by wearing medals, by assuming an imperial demeanor, especially the Kaiser's flashing eyes, and by growing an "imperial" moustache whose points "aimed straight at his eyes, which inspired fear in Diederich himself, as though they flashed from the countenance of the all-powerful Emperor."[26] Adopting Wilhelm's social and political views as his own, Hessling became the mini-Kaiser of his paper factory—its twelve workers, his proletariat; its elderly bookkeeper, Sotbier, his Bismarck.[27] Imitating the famous statement that the Kaiser would be his "own chancellor," Hessling told Sotbier: "Times have changed, and don't you forget it. I am my own manager."[28] Delivering passages from Wilhelm's speeches, he proclaimed to his handful of employees:

> "Now I have taken the rudder into my own hands. My course is set straight and I am guiding you to glorious times. Those who wish to help me are heartily welcome, but whoever opposes me in this work I will smash."
> He tried to make his eyes flash and the ends of his moustache rose still higher.
> "There is only one master here, and I am he. I am responsible only to God and my own conscience."[29]

"As the new master, who had firmly grasped the reins of the business, he felt he must immediately launch into new enterprises; success awaited him and events would have to shape themselves to his personality!"[30] For, as the Kaiser would with the Reich, so Hessling would bring his paper business to "a place in the sun!"[31]

In the end, Diederich Hessling, the quintessential Wilhelmian German, could no longer distinguish between himself and the Kaiser:

Wilhelm II and the Germans. The Kaiser accompanied by spectators at maneuvers in 1910. Reprinted with the permission of the Ullstein Bilderdienst.

He subscribed to every word in every speech of the Emperor's, and always in their first and strongest form, not in the modified version which appeared the next day. All these keywords to the character of Germany and of the times— Diederich lived, moved, and had his being in them, as if they had been manifestations of his own nature; they remained in his memory as if he himself had spoken them. Sometimes he really said such things. He confused some of them, on public occasions, with his own remarks, and neither he nor anybody else could tell what came from him and what from one more exalted.[32]

And yet, for Mann, it was less that the Germans took on the character of the Kaiser and more that Wilhelm and the Germans were the same. Despite Hessling's efforts to become the Kaiser, he, the *Untertan*, was able ultimately to determine the actions and put words into the mouth of his master:

Within the depths of his soul he murmured, so that he himself could hardly hear it: "My telegram." He could hardly contain himself for sheer joy. Was it possible? Had he really anticipated what the Emperor would say? Was his intuition so acute? Did his brain work in unison with . . . ? He was overpowered by a sense of mystic relationship. . . . He [Wilhelm II] had adopted Diederich's own words and had taken action in the sense Diederich had indicated! . . . Diederich spread out the newspaper, and gazed into its mirrored reflection of himself draped in imperial ermine."[33]

According to Walther Rathenau it was a mistake to blame Wilhelm II for a defeat that was the responsibility of the German people and the age in which they lived.[34] "Not a single day," he wrote after the war, "could Germany have been governed as it was governed without the consent of the people."[35] It was not possible, he believed, to separate the fate of country and Kaiser:

This people in this period of history, consciously and unconsciously, wanted him to be as he was, in no way different than he was, wanted themselves to be in him as they were, in no way different than they were. In the indescribable drama of her weaving the web of history, it pleased Clio to bind together in a great human destiny the character of the Germans during this period and their alienation, their idol and their downfall.[36]

In his successes and failures, Wilhelm II represented the successes and failures of his subjects. In their adulation of the Kaiser and in their irritation with him, Germans expressed their feelings about themselves. "Criticism of personal rule was usually in evidence," Elisabeth Fehrenbach has written, "when the fiction of the glorious Kaiser threatened to crumble."[37] On the one hand, as revealed by the uproar in Germany following the publication of Wilhelm's *Daily Telegraph* interview, the Kaiser was criticized when he failed to live up to the idealized expectations of his subjects, when he was unable to realize their glorified image of themselves and of their country. Wilhelm's shortcomings frustrated the wish of Germans to be represented by a monarch who was omnipresent, omniscient, and omnipotent. On the other hand, as revealed by the reaction of Germans to Wilhelm after the war, the Kaiser was most bitterly condemned when he personally manifested those features of his subjects of which they themselves were most ashamed. Wilhelm was adored when he reflected back an image of German national greatness. He was reviled when he reflected back an image of German national disharmony, ineffectuality, and weakness. Although the Germans came to dismiss the Kaiser after the war— in the process persuading generations of historians of his insignificance—Wilhelm II was regarded by his contemporaries as a leader of decisive, historic importance. He *seemed* so important to his subjects because he *was* so important to them. In their reactions to the Kaiser, the Germans were on some level reacting to an image of themselves.[38]

The Kaiser's Travels and Public Appearances, 1897–1902

German Cities and Towns Visited by Wilhelm II by Year

	1897	1898	1899	1900	1901	1902
Aachen						*
Altona		*		*		
Amanweiler			*			
Arolsen			*			
Ars on the Mosel			*			
Bad Oeynhausen		*				
Baden-Baden		*				
Barmen				*		
Bethel (Bielefeld)	*					
Bielefeld	*			*		
Biebelried	*					
Blankenburg						*
Bonn	*				*	*
Borby (on the Eckernförder Bight)						*
Bremen	*			*	*	*
Bredow	*					
Bremerhaven		*		**	*	
Breslau	*			*	*	*
Brühl	*					
Brunsbüttel			*			
Camenz		*				
Charlottenburg			*			*
Cologne	*					
Cronberg	*		*		*	
Cuxhaven	*	*			*	*
Danzig	**	**			*	

German Cities and Towns Visited by Wilhelm II by Year (*continued*)

	1897	1898	1899	1900	1901	1902
Darmstadt	*		*			
Deidenhofen			*			
Dortmund			*			
Dortmund-Ems-Canal			*			
Dresden	*	*				*
Düsseldorf						*
Eckernförde	*		*			
Eisenach					*	
Eisleben				*		
Elberfeld				*		
Emden						*
Erfurt				*		
Essen						*
Fehrbellin						*
Forchheim			*			
Frankfurt a. d. Oder						*
Frascati		*			*	
Frauenburg						*
Friedrichsruh	*	**	*			
Gentringer Höhe			*			
Görlitz						*
Gotha					*	
Graudenz	*					
Gross-Strehlitz	*					
Gürzenich	*					
Hamburg	*		*			
Hanau	*					
Hannover		**	*			**
Heiligengrabe (Ost-Priegnitz)					*	
Helgoland	*	*				
Henrichenburg			*			
Hildesheim				*		
Hochkönigsburg				*		
Holtenau				*		
Homburg v. d. Höhe	**	**	*	**	*	*
Kadinen						*
Karlsruhe	**	*	*	*		*
Kassel			*			
Kiel	*****	*	***	***	*	***
Koblenz	*					
Koburg				*		
Königsberg					*	*
Krefeld						*
Kurzel				*		*
Letzlingen			*			

German Cities and Towns Visited by Wilhelm II by Year (*continued*)

	1897	1898	1899	1900	1901	1902
Linden		*				
Liegnitz	*					
Lübeck			*	*		
Magdeburg	*					
Mainz		*	*	**		
Maria Laach	*				*	
Marienburg	**					*
Metz	*	*	*	*		
Minden		*				
Mittelheim				*		
Moers						*
Müngsten			*			
Munich		*				
Münster						*
Nedlitz			*			
Neuwied	*					
Niedermendig	*					
Nürnberg	*					*
Obereschebach	*					
Odilein mountains			*			
Porta		*				
Posen						*
Prenzlau		*				
Rauxal			*			
Remscheid			*			
Rendsburg	*					
Ruhrort						*
Saalburg		*	*	*		
Sassnitz					*	
Schlettstadt			*	*		
Schlitz	*					
Scloss Burg a. d. Wipper			*			
Schweinau	*					
Schwerin						*
Solingen			*			
Stettin	*	**		*		
St. Privat			**			
Strassburg	*	**	**			*
Strehlen	*					
Stuttgart			*			
Swinemünde						*
Tangermünde				*		
Thorn	*					
Tilsit				*		
Travemünde	*	*	*	*		*
Urville		*	*			*

German Cities and Towns Visited by Wilhelm II by Year (*continued*)

	1897	1898	1899	1900	1901	1902
Wiesbaden	**		*	*		*
Wilhelmshaven	*	*	*	*	*	*
Wilhelmshöhe	*			**	*	
Wartburg				*	*	
Wesel						*
Würzburg	**					
	57	34	45	37	19	41

Over the six-year period the Kaiser made at least 233 visits to at least 123 cities and towns in Germany

From Gustav Roloff, ed., *Schulthess' europäischer Geschichtskalender,* 79 vols. (Munich, 1860–1938), and Karl Wippermann, ed., *Deutscher Geschichtskalenders,* 49 vols. (Leipzig, 1885–1933).

The Kaiser's Travels and Public Appearances in 1897

30.I	In **Kiel**, for the christening of the second son of Prince Heinrich.
26.II	In **Berlin**, delivers a speech to the Brandenburg Provincial Diet.
4.III	In **Wilhelmshaven**, for the induction of naval recruits.
5.III	In **Bremen**, to visit his brother, Prince Heinrich.
22.III	In **Berlin**, unveils a monument to Kaiser Wilhelm I.
23.III	In **Berlin**, participates in a parade of citizens' organizations (including veterans' groups, student associations, etc.) before the monument.
21–23.IV	Wilhelm in Vienna.
23.IV	Enters **Strehlen**, for the birthday of King Albert of Saxony.
	In **Dresden**, he visits the studio of the painter Prell.
24.IV	In **Karlsruhe**, where he delivers a speech in response to the mayor's greeting.
28.IV	The Kaiser in **Cronberg** and in **Schlitz**.
4.V	Attends the launching of the steamer *Kaiser Wilhelm der Grosse* in **Bredow**.
10.V	Travels to Alsace-Lorraine.
11.V	Following maneuvers, ceremonial entrance into **Metz**.
15.V	Ceremonial entrance into **Strassburg**.
	Attends rehearsal of play in **Wiesbaden**.
28.V	In **Danzig**, to inspect the shipyards.
	In **Marienburg**.
16.VI	In **Liegnitz**, for the 100th anniversary of the King's Grenadier Regiment.
17.VI	In **Bethel**, where he delivers a speech.
18.VI	In **Bielefeld**, views the workers' communities of Pastor Bodelschwingh and delivers a speech in response to the mayor's greeting.

	In **Cologne**, for the unveiling of a monument to "Kaiser Wilhelm the Victorious," delivers a speech in response to the mayor's greeting.
	In **Gürzenich**, where, at a banquet in his honor, he makes a toast in response to the mayor's greeting.
19.VI	Passing through **Niedermendig**, travels to the Benedictine abbey of **Maria Laach**.
	Visits **Neuwied**, **Bonn**, and **Brühl**.
20.VI	Enters **Cuxhaven** and boards the royal yacht.
21–26.V	Visits **Helgoland**.
26.VI	Travels through the Northeast-Sea-Canal to **Kiel**, for a regatta of the North-German Regatta Association.
28.VI	Attends the regatta at **Eckernförde**.
2–5.VII	In **Travemünde**.
5–30.VII	On Scandinavian cruise.
30.VII	Returning, lands in **Kiel**.
4–14.VIII	Visits Tsar in Russia.
14.VIII	Returning, lands in **Kiel**.
16.VIII	In **Wilhelmshöhe**, receives Count Leopold zur Lippe-Biesterfeld.
25.VIII	In **Magdeburg**, for the unveiling of a monument to Kaiser Wilhelm I; at the city hall, delivers a toast in response to the mayor's greeting.
	Travels to the **Grusenwerk**, where, accompanied by the industrialist Krupp, he inspects the experimental station for ore preparation, several armored towers, and models for armament.
30.VIII	At the Moselle-Bridge in **Koblenz**, delivers a speech in response to the mayor's greeting.
	After a parade, delivers a toast at a banquet in the royal palace in the city.
31.VIII	At the "Deutschen Eck," where a monument to Kaiser Wilhelm I is unveiled.
1.IX	At **Biebelried**, for the "Kaiser Parade" of the 2nd Bavarian Army Corps.
	In **Würzburg**, delivers a speech in response to the greeting of Prince-Regent Luitpold.
2.IX	From **Würzburg** to **Schweinau**, and from there to the parade grounds where the 1st Bavarian Army Corps is marched past the Kaiser.
	In **Nürnberg**, delivers a speech in response to the mayor's greeting. Entrance into **Würzburg**.
3.IX	Official reception of the Kaiser in **Homburg v. d. Höhe**; receives King Humbert of Italy.
4.IX	In **Obereschebach** accompanied by the king, attends a parade by the 11th Army Corps; with king at the head of the flag company, enters **Homburg v. d. Höhe**.
6.IX	In **Hanau** with king, both return to **Homburg v. d. Höhe**.
7.IX	Kaiser and king enter **Wiesbaden**.
12–22.IX	Visit to Austria-Hungary.
22.IX	Enters **Breslau**.

5.X	Visits **Marienburg** and **Danzig**, to attend the christening of the steamer *Kaiser Friedrich.*
18.X	In **Wiesbaden**, attends the unveiling of a monument to Kaiser Friedrich.
21.X	Visits the Tsar in **Darmstadt.**
	In **Karlsruhe**, where, at a monument to Kaiser Wilhelm I, he delivers a speech in response to the mayor's address.
8.XI	Official reception of the Kaiser in **Gross-Strehlitz** in Silesia.
18.XI	In **Berlin**, delivers a speech at the swearing in of the Gardekorps Regiments.
22.XI	In **Kiel**, swears in naval recruits.
30.XI	In **Berlin**, delivers a speech from the throne to open the Reichstag session.
15.XII	In **Hamburg**, visits the city hall and the stock exchange and delivers a speech in response to the greeting of his brother, Heinrich.
16.XII	In **Friedrichsruh**, visits Prince Bismarck.
	In **Rendsburg**, delivers a speech to troops departing for Asia.
21.XII	In **Thorn**, for the dedication of a new garrison church.
	In **Graudenz**, where he delivers a speech in response to the mayor's welcome.

The Kaiser's Travels and Public Appearances in 1898

3.III	From **Wilhelmshaven**, the Kaiser goes on a cruise aboard the warship *Kurfürst Friedrich Wilhelm.*
25.III	From **Bremerhaven**, the Kaiser goes on a cruise aboard the steamer *Kaiser Wilhelm der Grosse*; on his return he delivers a speech in response to the address of the chair of the board of directors of the North German Lloyd.
6.IV	While staying in **Homburg v. d. Höhe**, visits the **Saalburg.**
14.IV	Arrival of the Kaiser in **Wiesbaden.**
18.IV	Visit of the Kaiser to **Karlsruhe.**
22.IV	In **Homburg v. d. Höhe.**
23.IV	Visit of the Kaiser to **Dresden.**
6.V	Delivers a speech from the throne to close the Reichstag session. Travels to **Urville.**
9.V	Visits **Metz**, where he delivers a speech in response to the mayor's welcome.
12.V	At a troop display at **Frascati.**
15.V	Views area where a harbor will be constructed at **Strassburg**, and thereafter rides at the head of the garrison's flag division into the city.
18.V	In **Berlin**, delivers a speech to close the session of the Prussian Landtag.
3.VI	The Kaiser in **Danzig.**
6.VI	The Kaiser in **Stettin.**
11.VI	The Kaiser delivers a speech in **Berlin** to the Berlin constabulary.

16.VI	In **Berlin**, delivers speeches to the members of the Royal Theater in Berlin and to the Leibregiments.
18.VI	The Kaiser attends the unveiling of a monument to Kaiser Wilhelm I at **Altona**.
	From there, he travels to **Cuxhaven**.
21.VI	The Kaiser arrives in **Helgoland**.
22.VI	The Kaiser arrives in **Kiel** after traveling through the Northeast-Sea-Canal.
4.VII	From **Travemünde**, the Kaiser embarks on a Scandinavian cruise.
2.VIII	The Kaiser at the coffin of Bismarck at **Friedrichsruh**.
20.VIII	The Kaiser arrives in **Mainz** where he delivers a speech in response to the mayor's greeting.
2.IX	Arrives in **Hannover** where he delivers a speech in response to the mayor's greeting.
3.IX	At parade in **Linden** where he delivers a speech in response to the mayor's greeting.
4.IX	Returns to **Hannover** where he holds a religious service at the Waterlooplatz, and delivers further speeches.
5.IX	Enters **Minden**, where he delivers a speech in response to the mayor's greeting.
	Enters **Bad Oeynhausen**, where he delivers several speeches.
7.IX	In **Porta**, where at a banquet he delivers a speech in response to the greeting from the speaker of the Westphalian Provincial Diet.
15.IX	The Kaiser enters **Prenzlau**, where he delivers a speech in response to the mayor's greeting.
23.IX	In **Stettin**, delivers a speech at the dedication of the new harbor.
2.X	In **Danzig**.
11.X	In **Camenz**, to attend the funeral of Princess Albrecht.
13.X–23.XI	The Kaiser's visit to the Holy Land.
24.XI	Reception for the Kaiser in **Munich**.
	Reception for the Kaiser in **Baden-Baden**.
1.XII	Ceremonial entrance into **Berlin** and delivers a speech in response to the mayor's greeting.
6.XII	In **Berlin**, delivers a speech from the throne to open the Reichstag session.

The Kaiser's Travels and Public Appearances in 1899

16.I	Delivers a speech in **Berlin** to open the Prussian Landtag.
24.I	Reviews parade at the Waterlooplatz in **Hannover** and delivers several speeches.
3.II	In **Berlin**, delivers a speech to the Brandenburg Provincial Diet.
1.III	In **Wilhelmshaven**, delivers speech to the naval recruits.
16.III	In **Friedrichsruh** for the burial of Prince Bismarck in a mausoleum.
28.IV	Arrival in **Darmstadt**.
3.V	The Kaiser in **Strassburg** and in the **Odilien Mountains**.

4.V	In **Schlettstadt**, to receive from the city the gift of the ruins of the Hochkönigsburg.
9.V	The Kaiser in **Kurzel**.
	In **Ars on the Moselle**, to lay a cornerstone for Fort Häseler.
11.V	In **Metz, Urville**, and at the graves at **St. Privat**.
15.V	The Kaiser in **Homburg v. d. Höhe** and at the **Saalburg**.
18.V	The Kaiser in **Wiesbaden** and delivers a speech to greet the Tsar.
2.VI	In **Kiel**, delivers a speech at the launching of the battleship *Ersatz König Wilhelm.*
18.VI	In **Brunsbüttel**, delivers a speech to a delegation of former Hannoverian officers, attends a sailing regatta, and delivers a speech in response to the greeting of the mayor of Hamburg.
1.VII	Coming from **Travemünde**, the Kaiser enters **Lübeck** and delivers a speech in response to the welcoming addresses of the mayor and the chairman of the yacht club.
4.VII	From **Eckernförde**, embarks on Scandinavian cruise.
1.VIII	Returns from the cruise and lands at **Kiel**.
11.VIII	Coming from **Kassel**, the Kaiser enters the farm community of **Rauxel**.
	From there he proceeds by car along the Dortmund-Ems-Canal.
	Boarding a steamer, he travels up the Canal to **Dortmund**. School children and clubs from the neighboring communities line the banks along the entire route. In Dortmund he delivers speeches in reponse to the mayor's greetings at the landing in the harbor and at the city hall.
12.VIII	From the Villa Hügel, the Krupp estate, the Kaiser visits **Remscheid, Castle Burg an der Wupper, Solingen, Müngsten**, returning to the Villa Hügel.
13.VIII	In **Arolsen**, for the unveiling of a monument to Kaiser Wilhelm I.
18.VIII	Enters **Amanweiler** and rides from there to **St. Privat**, where he delivers a speech at the unveiling of a monument to the 1st Guard Regiment.
19.VIII	Enters **Deidenhofen** and travels from there to the **Gentringer Höhe**.
20.VIII	Arrives in **Cronberg**.
21.VIII	In **Mainz**, where he observes a parade.
22.VIII	In **Nedlitz**, where he receives school and veterans' groups from **Zerbst**.
5.IX	In **Strassburg**, delivers a speech at a banquet.
7.IX	In **Stuttgart**, delivers a speech at a banquet.
8.IX	After observing a parade in **Forchheim**, the Kaiser rides to **Karlsruhe**, where he delivers a speech in response to the mayor's greeting.
19–25.IX	Hunting in Sweden.
18.X	In **Hamburg**, delivers a speech at the city hall after the launching of the warship *Kaiser Karl der Grosse*.
19.X	Delivers a speech at the 100th anniversary of the Institute of Technology in **Charlottenburg**.
10.XI	In **Letzlingen**.
18.XI	In **Kiel**, embarking on his visit to England.
9.XII	Returns to **Potsdam**.

The Kaiser's Travels and Public Appearances in 1900

1.I	In the armory in **Berlin**, the Kaiser delivers a speech at a military ceremony celebrating the turn of the new century.
13.III	The Kaiser in **Bremerhaven**.
	The Kaiser in **Bremen**.
19.III	The Kaiser delivers a speech in the White Hall of the Palace to celebrate the 200th anniversary of the Academy of Science.
19.IV	In **Altona,** to greet the Prince of Wales.
21.IV	The Kaiser at the **Wartburg**.
26.IV	The Kaiser in **Karlsruhe**.
4–6.V	Festivities in **Berlin** on the occasion of the coming of age of the crown prince.
8.V	Arrival in **Kurzel**.
12.V	The Kaiser in **Metz**.
25.V	From **Wiesbaden,** the Kaiser enters **Mainz**, from there traveling down the Rhine on a torpedo boat to **Mittelheim**, returning then to **Wiesbaden**.
26.V	Visits **Schlettstadt** in Alsace and the **Hochkönigsburg**.
30.VI	In **Berlin**, the Kaiser delivers a speech on the occasion of the beginning of the crown prince's active military service.
12.VI	In **Eisleben,** where, on the 700th anniversary of the opening of the Mansfeld mines, he delivers a speech in the market square to the assembled miners and foundry workers.
13.VI	The Kaiser in **Homburg v. d. Höhe**.
16.VI	In **Lübeck**, to open the Elbe-Trave-Canal, he delivers a speech in response to the mayor's greeting.
20.VI	In **Kiel**, delivers a speech at the unveiling of a statue of Christ in front of the Garrison Church.
25.VI	In **Holtenau**, attends the unveiling of a monument to Kaiser Wilhelm I.
29.VI	In **Kiel**, reviews a parade of former soldiers of the guard and delivers a speech.
30.VI	The Kaiser in **Travemünde**.
2.VII	In **Wilhelmshaven**, delivers speech to 1st Naval Battalion, embarking for China.
3.VII	In **Wilhelmshaven**, for the launching of the warship *Wittelsbach.* Delivers a speech at the banquet to celebrate the event.
27.VII	In **Bremerhaven**, delivers speech to troops embarking for China.
2.VIII	In **Bremerhaven**, delivers speech to troops embarking for China.
3.VIII	In **Bremerhaven**, bestows medals on fifteen workers of the North German Lloyd and delivers a speech.
4.VIII	Arrival of the Kaiser in **Koburg**.
6.VIII	In the **Sparen Mountains near Bielefeld**, delivers speech at the unveiling of a monument to the Great Elector.
	Arrival in **Wilhelmshöhe**.
11.VIII	Official reception of the Kaiser in **Mainz**.
18.VIII	The Kaiser in **Wilhelmshöhe**, delivers a speech to General von Waldersee and his staff on their departure for China.
25.VIII	In **Erfurt**, delivers speech in response to the mayor's greeting

	before the city hall at the unveiling of a monument to Kaiser Wilhelm I.
7.IX	Entrance into **Stettin**, where he delivers a speech in response to the mayor's welcome.
22.IX	In **Tilsit**, where he rides to the square where a monument to Queen Luise is to be unveiled; delivers a speech in response to the mayor's greeting.
11.X	On the **Saalburg in Nassau**, to lay the cornerstone of the Reichs-Limes-Museum, where, at the end of an elaborate ceremony, he delivers a speech.
24.X	In **Barmen**.
	Enters **Elberfeld** and delivers speech at the city hall in response to the mayor's welcome.
1.XI	In **Hildesheim**, delivers a speech in response to the mayor's welcome at the unveiling of a monument to Kaiser Wilhelm I.
14.XI	In **Berlin**, delivers a speech from the throne to open the Reichstag session.
16.XI	In **Breslau**, the Kaiser is attacked by a woman as he was leaving the railway station.
23.XI	In **Kiel**, delivers a speech to the naval recruits.
29.XI	In **Tangermünde**, at the unveiling of a monument to Emperor Karl IV, delivers a speech before the city hall.

The Kaiser's Travels and Public Appearances in 1901

18.I	Celebration in **Berlin** of the 200th Anniversary of the Prussian monarchy.
19.I–6.II	In England for the death and funeral of Queen Victoria.
25.II–2.III	In **Cronberg**, meets with Edward VII of England.
4.III	In **Wilhelmshaven**, to deliver speech to naval recruits.
	Travels to **Helgoland**.
5.III	Returning, visits **Bremerhaven** and **Bremen**, where he is wounded in the face by a mentally unbalanced young man.
28.III	In **Berlin**, delivers a speech about 1848.
11.IV	Attends ceremonial unveiling of a monument to Kaiser Wilhelm I in **Potsdam**.
24.IV	In **Bonn**, for the enrollment of the crown prince at the university where he delivers a speech to the students.
25.IV	From Bonn, he visits the Abbey **Maria Laach**, where he delivers a speech in response to the Abbot's welcome.
	Returning to **Bonn**, he delivers a speech to the student corps at the university.
	Received by Grand-Duke Wilhelm Ernst von Saxe-Weimar in **Eisenach**; delivers speech in response to the grand-duke's toast at a banquet in the city palace.
	Visits the **Wartburg**.
18.V	Attends a parade at **Frascati** near **Metz**.
8.VI	In the county of **Ost-Priegnitz**, visits the convent of **Heiligengrabe**, where he delivers a speech to the nuns.

16.VI	In **Berlin**, attends the unveiling of a monument to Bismarck.
18.VI	In **Cuxhaven** for a regatta on the Lower Elbe, delivers a speech in response to the greeting of the mayor of Hamburg.
20.VI	Delivers a speech at the unveiling of a monument to the Great Elector in the park of the Naval Academy in **Kiel**.
8.VII	Embarks from **Sassnitz** on a Scandinavian cruise.
5.VIII	Death of Kaiserin Friedrich with the Kaiser present in **Homburg v. d. Höhe**.
11.VIII	Meets there with Edward VII.
23.VIII	In **Wilhelmshöhe**, receives King Edward VII.
7.IX	Ceremonial entrance into **Königsberg**, where he delivers speeches in response to the mayor's welcome and on the occasion of his gift of portraits of himself and of King Friedrich I to the province of East Prussia.
9.IX	In **Königsberg**, dedicates the Queen Luise-Memorial-Church and delivers a speech at the county seat.
11.IX–13.IX	Meets with Tsar on the royal yacht off Hela.
14.IX	Enters **Danzig** and delivers speech in response to mayor's welcome.
18.XI	In **Berlin**, delivers a speech to the Society of Ships Architects.
12.XII	In **Breslau**, delivers a speech at the unveiling of a monument to the Great Elector.
18.XII	Attends the unveiling of the Siegesallee in **Berlin** and delivers a speech.
26.XII	In **Gotha**, delivers a speech on the occasion of the 300th anniversary of the birth of Duke Ernst the Pious.

The Kaiser's Travels and Public Appearances in 1902

24.I	In **Hannover**, to attend a banquet for retired Hannoverian officers.
25.I	In **Berlin**, delivers a speech at the Handicraft Museum.
11.III	In **Wilhelmshaven**, to deliver speech to the II. Naval Battalion.
14.III	In **Bremen**, where he was "warmly received by the populace."
18.III	In **Cuxhaven** to welcome his brother Heinrich home from America.
20.IV	In **Hannover**, unveils a monument to General of the Cavalry von Rosenberg and delivers a speech.
26.IV	In **Karlsruhe**, for the 50th anniversary of the government of Grand-Duke Friedrich of Baden.
7.V	Official reception in **Strassburg**.
11–15.V	In **Wiesbaden**.
21.V	In **Kurzel**, receives a delegation from the *Landesausschuss* of Alsace-Lorraine and delivers a speech to them.
22.V	In the castle in **Urville** near **Metz**.
5.VI	In **Marienburg**, attends the festivities of the Order of St. John (Knights of Malta) and delivers a speech at a banquet.
16.VI	In **Nürnberg**, to celebrate the 50th anniversary of the German Musueum.
17.VI	In **Bonn**, to deliver speech to the I. Rhenish Hussar Regiment, Nr.

	7, and to celebrate the 75th anniversary of the Borussia Student Corps.
19.VI	In **Aachen**, delivers a speech.
	In **Münster**, delivers a speech.
	Ceremonial entrance into **Mainz**, where Kaiser delivers speeches before the cathedral and in the city hall.
20.VI	In **Moers**, to celebrate the 200th anniversary of the county's incorporation into Prussia.
20.VI	Entrance and speech in **Krefeld**.
21.VI	After staying in **Ruhrort**, visits **Wesel**, where he delivers speech in response to mayor's greeting.
24.VI	In **Dresden**, to attend the funeral of King Albert of Saxony.
2.VII	In **Borby** on the **Eckernförder Bight**, to attend a banquet of the Kiel Yacht Club.
3.VII	In **Kiel**, to receive Crown Prince Friedrich August of Saxe-Weimar.
5.VII	In **Travemünde**, to attend the *Bierabend* of the North German Regatta Association and the Lübeck Yacht Club.
7.VII–30.VII	On Scandinavian Cruise.
30.VII	Arriving in **Emden**, the Kaiser views the monuments to the Great Elector and Friedrich the Great, delivers a speech before the city hall to the crews of the Torpedo Boat S. 42, which had sunk, and delivers a speech in response to the mayor's greeting.
1.VIII	In **Schwerin**, delivers a speech in response to Grand-Duke Friedrich Franz IV's greeting.
4.VIII	Embarks **Kiel,** to meet with Tsar at Reval.
10.VIII	In **Swinemünde** on return to Germany.
15.VIII	Entrance into **Düsseldorf**, where he delivers speech in response to mayor's greeting.
19.VIII	In **Homburg v. d. Höhe**, unveils a monument to Kaiserin Friedrich and delivers a speech.
2.IX	Ceremonial entrance into **Posen**, where Kaiser delivers speech in response to mayor's greeting.
6.IX	On the way to the fall maneuvers, enters **Frankfurt an der Oder** and delivers speech in response to the mayor's greeting.
7.X	The Kaiser in **Königsberg**.
10.X	In **Frauenburg**, where he responds to the greeting of the Bishop and clergy at the main entrance to the cathedral.
15.X	In **Kadinen**.
18.X	Delivers speech at the unveiling of a monument to the Great Elector in **Fehrbellin**.
2.XI	Delivers speech at the dedication of a new building for the academy of art in **Charlottenburg**.
3.XI	The Kaiser in **Blankenburg**.
4.XI	In **Berlin**, delivers a speech to army recruits.
6.XI	In **Kiel**, delivers speech to navy recruits.
	Embarks for England.
26.XI	In **Essen**, after attending the funeral of the industrialist Krupp meets with the Board of Directors and with representatives of the workers of the Krupp Works at the railway station.

29.XI In **Görlitz**, dedicates a Kaiser Friedrich Museum and memorial hall and delivers speech in response to the mayor's greeting.

5.XII Returning from a hunt in **Slawentzitz**, receives a delegation of workers at the railway station in **Breslau** and delivers a speech to them.

APPENDIX **II**

The Navy and
Wilhelm II's Withered Arm

Frequently in writing about the deficiencies of the navy, the Kaiser used language applicable to his physical disability. As already noted in the text, he described the navy to Hohenlohe in 1896 as "ever more shriveled-up [*zusammengeschrümpfende*]."[1] In 1897 he described the Reich as "paralyzed [*lähmt*]" in the absence of an imposing fleet.[2] In 1899, he described his inability to prevent England from "making a slight movement of the elbow" in Africa that would push Germany and France into the sea.[3] As described in Chapter 10, the Kaiser was a vociferous opponent of "disarmament." In addition, the Kaiser wrote in marginalia to a report from the German representative in Cairo, Heyking, to Hohenlohe of 20 May 1895: "Can I stamp vessels out of the earth! Does a squadron grow out of the . . . open palm of my hand!"[4] See, also, his letter to Hohenlohe of 21 January 1895 denying the Foreign Office request to dispatch a naval vessel to Venezuela: "The above is yet another tangible [*handgreiflicher*] proof of the irresponsible conduct of the Reichstag in naval matters which is having ever more harmful consequences for our foreign policy."[5] There is a consistency in his use of language here: Germany's naval inadequacy was described in words applicable to his withered arm; his inability to correct that naval inadequacy and Britain's naval superiority were described in words applicable to motions that he was unable to make with his hand or arm.

Critics of psychoanalysis tend to be skeptical about attempts of this sort to establish connections via word associations or slips of the tongue between an individual's apparently independent feelings, thoughts, and actions. In fact such connections can only be made on the basis of a thorough familiarity with the individual in question and with the particular personal meanings that his or her communications have. In the case of Wilhelm II the evidence suggests that he associated his sense of psychological weakness and inadequacy with his withered left arm and partially paralyzed left hand, both because of any role his arm played in creating that sense of weakness and inadequacy and because the physical deficiency may have come to symbolize and concretize his sense of psychological deficiency. The evidence is compelling that Wilhelm associated German naval inferiority with his sense of personal weakness. Therefore it should come as no great surprise that the Kaiser associated Germany's naval inadequacy with his physical defect. Still, too much significance probably should not be attached to such associative connections in and of themselves.

What should be stressed here is that in talking and writing about the German navy, and particularly about German naval inadequacy in relation to Britain, Wilhelm II frequently used language relating to the body and to bodily functions. In addition to those words and phrases related to his physical defect, he made statements that can be interpreted as being unconsciously concerned with castration: his fear that, given German naval inadequacy, several German ships might be "cut off" by the mobilization of the Russian Black Sea fleet and his association on two separate occasions of British attempts to make the best of a bad naval situation with the fable by La Fontaine about the fox who lost his tail [*Rüthe*, also meaning "penis" in German] and therefore sought to convince the other foxes of the advantage of this condition.[6] Furthermore, Wilhelm wrote of having to "kiss the *Rüthe*" of John Bull because of Germany's naval insufficiency,[7] and he ordered the German ambassador in London in 1908 to give British proposals to limit German naval construction "a rude answer such as kiss my etc."[8] In his letter to Bülow of 29 October 1899, the Kaiser compared Germany's naval unpreparedness to being caught with one's pants down,[9] and he made frequent references in 1908 to German diplomats, especially his ambassador in London, Paul Metternich, whom he regarded as being insufficiently forceful in defending Germany's naval building program before the English, as being "*Hosenscheisser*" and having "*die Hosenvoll*," of having soiled their pants.[10] Again, it should come as no surprise that Wilhelm may have experienced Germany's lack of a mighty navy as a form of castration (that is, he felt as though he were missing something vital to him), as a humiliation akin to having to kiss the penis or the behind of a more powerful adversary, or as a sign of cowardice and disgrace as when one's britches are soiled.[11] And yet, even if the precise psychological meaning of these phrases is subject to other plausible interpretations, what they do unquestionably indicate is the psychological importance of the navy to the Kaiser and the depth of the humiliation he experienced as a result of Germany's naval inferiority, especially in relation to England. As crude as the words and as vulgar as the phrases are, all relate to the human body and to essential bodily functions. They relate, in other words, to the psychologically most basic. They confirm yet again that Wilhelm II's desire to construct a mighty German navy and the humiliation he experienced in the absence of one emerged out of the depths of his psyche.

Notes

List of Abbreviations

BA Koblenz	Federal Archive, Koblenz
BMA Freiburg	Federal Military Archive, Freiburg
GSA	Secret State Archive, Berlin-Dahlem
PA Bonn	Political Archive of the Foreign Ministry, Bonn
RA	Royal Archives, Windsor Castle
GP	Johannes Lepsius et al., eds., *Die grosse Politik der europäischen Kabinette,* 40 vols. (Berlin, 1922–1927)

Introduction

1. Indeed, it was only in 1989 that the first biography of Wilhelm II based on extensive archival research was published, Lamar Cecil's *Wilhelm II: Prince and Emperor, 1859–1900* (Chapel Hill, 1989). John C. G. Röhl is also preparing a scholarly biography of the Kaiser for publication.

2. The best of these perhaps are Michael Balfour's *The Kaiser and His Times* (New York, 1972) and Wilhelm Schüssler's *Kaiser Wilhelm II, Schicksal und Schuld* (Göttingen, 1962). Others include J. Daniel Chamier, *Fabulous Monster* (London, 1934); Joachim von Kürenberg, *The Kaiser: The Life of Wilhelm II., Last Emperor of Germany* (London, 1954); Virginia Cowles, *The Kaiser* (New York, 1963); Harold Kurtz, *The Second Reich: Kaiser Wilhelm II and his Germany* (London, 1970); Tyler Whittle, *The Last Kaiser. A Biography of Wilhelm II, German Emperor and King of Prussia* (London, 1977); and Alan Palmer, *The Kaiser: Warlord of the Second Reich* (New York, 1978).

3. Letter from Eulenburg to Friedrich von Holstein, privy councillor in the Foreign Office, of 2 December 1894, Johannes Haller, *Aus dem Leben des Fürsten Philipp zu Eulenburg-Hertefeld* (Berlin, 1926), p. 180. See also Norman Rich, *Friedrich von Holstein: Politics and Diplomacy in the Era of Bismarck and Wilhelm II,* 2 vols. (Cambridge, 1965), pp. 487–88.

4. F. J. Scherer, *Die Kaiseridee des deutschen Volkes in Liedern seiner Dichter seit dem Jahre 1806* (Arnsberg, 1896), pp. 5–6. Translation is by Terence Cole, quoted in Elisabeth Fehrenbach, "Images of Kaiserdom: German Attitudes to Kaiser Wilhelm II," John C. G. Röhl and Nicolaus Sombart, eds., *Kaiser Wilhelm II: New Interpretations* (Cambridge, 1982), p. 278. See also Elisabeth Fehrenbach, *Wandlungen des deutschen Kaisergedankens, 1871–1918* (Munich, 1969), p. 109.

5. Of course it is true that the distinction between political and symbolic leadership is

artificial. Symbolic acts have political consequences, and acts of political self-interest exert symbolic power. Nor are these two leadership functions incompatible. In fact, the most effective leadership integrates symbolism and the politics of self-interest.

6. Jonathan Steinberg, *Yesterday's Deterrent: Tirpitz and the Birth of the German Battle Fleet* (London, 1965), p. 26.

7. Fehrenbach, *Wandlungen,* p. 12.

8. For the designation of the truly "Wilhelmian" period of the Kaiser's reign, see Volker R. Berghahn, "Zu den Zielen des deutschen Flottenbaus unter Wilhelm II.," *Historische Zeitschrift* 210 (1970), pp. 34–100; Wilhelm Deist, *Flottenpolitik und Flottenpropaganda: Das Nachrichtenbureau des Reichsmarineamtes, 1897–1914* (Stuttgart, 1976); and John C. G. Röhl, *Germany Without Bismarck: The Crisis of Government in the Second Reich, 1890–1900* (Berkeley, 1967).

9. Bismarck quoted in a letter from Wilhelm II's mother, Victoria, to her mother, Queen Victoria, of 6 November 1888, Frederick Ponsonby, ed., *The Letters of the Empress Frederick* (London, 1929), p. 363.

10. Dr. Eduard Martin, "Bericht über die Entbindung Ihrer Königlichen Hoheit der Frau Prinzessin Friedrich Wilhelm Princess Royal von Grossbritanien" of 9 February 1859. This report is included in the deposition about his father's conduct during Wilhelm's birth of Prof. Dr. med. August Martin on 28 April 1931, GSA, BPH, Rep. 53. Letter from Wilhelm's father, Friedrich, to Queen Victoria of 29 January 1859, RA Z63/115. Copy of a letter from the pediatrician who was present at Wilhelm's birth, Dr. Wegner, to Queen Victoria of 8 September 1859, RA Z63/133. I am indebted to two obstetricians, Gertrud Siebeck and Ole Thienhaus, for their help in evaluating these documents.

11. The Kaiser's most notable mentally ill ancestor was his great-great-grandfather, Tsar Paul I of Russia.

12. John C. G. Röhl has asserted that excessive use of chloroform caused brain damage in the future Kaiser. See his article in the *Frankfurter Allgemeine Zeitung* of 22 July 1987, p. 22; "Kaiser Wilhelm II. Eine Charakterskizze," *Kaiser, Hof und Staat: Wilhelm II. und die deutsche Politik* (Munich, 1988), pp. 33–34; and "Kaiser Wilhelm II. 'Eine Studie über Cäsarenwahnsinn,'" *Schriften des Historischen Kollegs,* Vortrag 19 (Munich, 1989), pp. 31–34. There is no evidence that any of the physicians attending the birth thought that Wilhelm had suffered brain damage, however. Cecil, *Wilhelm II,* p. 345, note 48. During World War I, various American, English, French, Italian, Russian, and Swiss psychiatrists diagnosed the Kaiser as manic-depressive, a diagnosis taken up by a number of their German colleagues after the Reich's defeat. See Röhl, "Kaiser Wilhelm II. Eine Charakterskizze," pp. 32–33. Not only had none of these psychiatrists examined Wilhelm, but, given where and when they wrote, factors having nothing to do with psychiatry doubtless influenced their view of the Kaiser's mental condition. See the Conclusion to this study.

13. Beginning when Wilhelm was one month old and throughout the first two years of his life Victoria's letters contain frequent references to his restlessness. She described him as "exceedingly lively and when awake will not be satisfied unless kept dancing about continually," as "well and in wild spirits. . . . a bit of quicksilver, he is never quiet a minute," as "a great 'fidgeon'—and very wild," as "dreadfully lively," as being "too lively and violent" to have yet attempted to speak or walk, as "very well, very wild and violent and never still a minute," as "very wild and unmanageable," as "terribly violent and passionate," and as "fretful and cross and violent and passionate." Letters from Victoria to her mother, Queen Victoria, of 28 February 1859, Ponsonby, *Letters,* p. 20; of 3 September 1859, Roger Fulford, ed., *Dearest Child: Letters between Queen Victoria and the Princess Royal, 1858–1961* (New York, 1964), p. 209; of 26 December 1859, RA Z9/9; of 26 January 1860, RA Z9/21; of 25 February 1860, RA Z9/35; the letter from Victoria to Mary Teck of 31 March 1860, RA Add. Mss. A8/1326; the letters from Victoria to Queen Victoria of 7 April 1860, RA Z9/50; of 14 April 1860, RA Z9/52; and of 23 January 1861, RA Z10/47.

Although its precise etiology is not fully understood, hyperactivity is thought to be either congenital or hereditary. Indeed, one of the causes of hyperactivity may be reduced blood flow to the brain during delivery. There may also have been a history of hyperactivity on the maternal side of Wilhelm's family. See the letter from Wilhelm's mother to her mother, Queen Victoria, of 18 August 1868, Roger Fulford, ed., *Your Dear Letter: Private Correspondence of Queen Victoria and the Crown Princess of Prussia, 1865–1871* (London, 1971), pp. 205–207, and the letter from Queen Victoria to Wilhelm's mother of 3 November 1874, Roger Fulford, ed., *Darling Child: Private Correspondence of Queen Victoria and the Crown Princess of Prussia, 1871–1878* (London, 1976), p. 160.

14. Heinz Kohut, "Psychoanalysis in a Troubled World," Paul H. Ornstein, ed., *The Search for the Self: Selected Writings of Heinz Kohut, 1950–1978,* 2 vols. (New York, 1978), II, pp. 528–29; Thomas A. Kohut, "Psychohistory as History," *The American Historical Review,* 91 (1986), pp. 336–54.

15. Walther Rathenau, "Der Kaiser," Hans Werner Richter, ed., *Walther Rathenau: Schriften und Reden* (Frankfurt, 1964), pp. 239–41.

16. For a thoughtful consideration of the relevance of the classical Freudian model to the study of history, see Peter Gay, *Freud for Historians* (New York, 1985).

17. See Erik Erikson, *Identity and the Life Cycle* (New York, 1959) and *Identity, Youth and Crisis* (New York, 1968); Helene Deutsch, "Some Forms of Emotional Disturbance and Their Relation to Schizophrenia," *Neurosis and Character Types* (New York, 1965), pp. 262–86; W. Ronald Fairbairn, *Psychoanalytic Studies of the Personality* (London, 1952); D. W. Winnicott, *The Maturational Process and the Facilitating Environment: Studies in the Theory of Emotional Development* (London, 1965) and *Through Pediatrics to Psychoanalysis* (London, 1975); Margaret S. Mahler, Fred Pine, and Anni Bergman, *The Psychological Birth of the Human Infant: Symbiosis and Individuation* (New York, 1975).

18. Heinz Kohut, "Forms and Transformations of Narcissism," *Search for the Self,* I, pp. 445–60.

19. Ibid., p. 430.

20. Ibid. See also D. W. Winnicott, "Transitional Objects and Transitional Phenomena," *International Journal of Psychoanalysis* 34 (1953), pp. 89–97; Margaret S. Mahler, "Mother-Child Interaction during Separation-Individuation," *The Psychoanalytic Quarterly* 34 (1965), pp. 483–98; J. F. Bing, F. McLaughlin, and R. Marburg, "The Metapsychology of Narcissism," *The Psychoanalytic Study of the Child* 14 (1959), pp. 9–28; Sandor Ferenczi, "Stages in the Development of the Sense of Reality," *Contributions to Psychoanalysis* (New York, 1950), pp. 213–39; and Ernest Jones, "The God Complex," *Essays in Applied Analysis* (London, 1951), pp. 244–65.

21. As a matter of convenience, the words "he" and "him" will be used to denote all of humanity in this consideration of self psychology.

22. It should be pointed out that no individual is ever completely autonomous psychologically. All people need affirmation to bolster their self-esteem and external ideals to follow. Narcissistic pathology is thus a matter of the intensity and the immaturity of the narcissistic needs.

23. Bülow's notes of 7 April 1897 of conversations with Eulenburg during which the latter quoted Leuthold's assessment of the Kaiser's mental condition, translated and quoted in John C. G. Röhl, "The Emperor's New Clothes: A Character Sketch of Kaiser Wilhelm II," *Kaiser Wilhelm II,* p. 38.

24. Bernhard Fürst von Bülow, *Denkwürdigkeiten,* 4 vols. (Berlin, 1930), I, pp. 56–61. Bülow had come to know Wilhelm in 1885, when the latter was in his mid-twenties. In 1897 Bülow was appointed secretary of state in the Foreign Office, and in 1900 he became chancellor of the Reich, a position he was to hold until his resignation in 1909 in the aftermath of the *Daily Telegraph* affair.

25. Ibid., I, p. 461.

26. Diary entry of 9 July 1891, John Viscount Morley, *Recollections,* 2 vols. (London, 1917), I, p. 272.

27. Hermann Oncken, "Der Kaiser und die Nation: Rede bei dem Festakt der Universität Heidelberg zur Erinnerung an die Befreiungskriege und zur Feier des 25 jährigen Regierungs-Jubiläums Kaiser Wilhelm II." (15 June 1913), Hermann Oncken, *Historisch-politische Aufsätze und Reden,* 2 vols. (Munich and Berlin, 1914), I, p. 12.

28. Bogdan Graf von Hutten-Czapski, *Sechzig Jahre Politik und Gesellschaft,* 2 vols. (Berlin, 1936), I, p. 241.

29. Ernst Johann, ed., *Reden des Kaisers: Ansprachen, Predigten und Trinksprüche Wilhelms II.* (Munich, 1977), p. 155.

30. Letter from Eulenburg to Bülow of July 1899, Bülow, *Denkwürdigkeiten,* I, pp. 351–52.

31. Eulenburg quoted in ibid., I, p. 237.

32. For the relationship between narcissistic psychopathology and messianic personalities, see Heinz Kohut, "Creativeness, Charisma, Group Psychology," *Search for the Self,* II, pp. 823–32.

33. Speech of 25 August 1910 quoted in Karl Wippermann, ed., *Deutscher Geschichtskalender,* 49 vols. (Leipzig, 1885–1933), 1910 (II), p. 9.

34. Letter from Eulenburg to Bülow of 15 July 1900, Bülow, *Denkwürdigkeiten,* I, pp. 456–57.

35. Copy of a telegram from Holstein to Bülow of 5 March 1897, BA Koblenz, Bülow Papers, vol. 90.

36. The Kaiser and General von Kessel both quoted in Röhl, "The Emperor's New Clothes," p. 31.

37. Bülow, *Denkwürdigkeiten,* I, pp. 363–65; Cecil, *Wilhelm II,* pp. 182–87.

38. Philipp Eulenburg, "Kaiser Wilhelm II.," BA Koblenz, Eulenburg Papers, vol. 80.

39. Paul Güssfeldt was a marine painter and frequent companion on the Kaiser's annual Scandinavian cruise. He was Wilhelm's art teacher and friend from the early 1880s.

40. PA Bonn, Holstein Papers, vol. 56.

41. Eulenburg, "Kaiser Wilhelm II.," BA Koblenz, Eulenburg Papers, vol. 80.

42. Admiral Alfred von Tirpitz's notes of 4 January 1905, BMA Freiburg, Tirpitz Papers, N 253, vol. 21.

43. Quoted in Kürenberg, *The Kaiser,* p. 95.

44. Heinz Kohut, *The Analysis of the Self: A Systematic Approach to the Psychoanalytic Treatment of Narcissistic Personality Disorders* (London, 1971), pp. 210–12.

45. Letter from Eulenburg to Bülow of 28 September 1901, Bülow, *Denkwürdigkeiten,* I, p. 546.

46. Daisy, Princess of Pless, *Daisy Pless by Herself* (London, 1928), p. 256.

47. Quoted in the original French in Ignatius Valentine Chirol, *50 Years in a Changing World* (New York, 1928), p. 276.

48. Bülow, *Denkwürdigkeiten,* I, pp. 83–84.

49. See Appendix I.

50. Rathenau, "Der Kaiser," p. 250.

51. Bülow, *Denkwürdigkeiten,* I, p. 5.

52. For the sycophants around the Kaiser, see Lamar Cecil, *The German Diplomatic Service, 1871–1914* (Princeton, 1976), pp. 212–13 and 255–56. The information about the burying of archeological artifacts in the sand comes from Dr. Wilhelm Huebener, former personal physician to the ex-Kaiser in Holland, in a personal communication to the author.

53. Bülow, *Denkwürdigkeiten,* I, p. 140.

Part I

1. BA Koblenz, Bülow Papers, vol. 170.

Chapter 1

1. Letter of 28 January 1858, Hector Bolitho, ed., *The Letters of Queen Victoria: From the Archives of the House of Brandenburg-Prussia* (New Haven, 1938), p. 97.

2. The marriage had been encouraged by both sets of parents, who looked with favor on a Hohenzollern-Hannover union. In contrast to their children, who regarded the marriage as having political and diplomatic implications, Victoria and Albert and Wilhelm and Augusta were concerned with the dynastic significance of the match.

3. For a summary of the political views of Friedrich and Victoria set against the background of Prussian and German politics, see Norman Rich, *Friedrich von Holstein: Politics and Diplomacy in the Era of Bismarck and Wilhelm II,* 2 vols. (Cambridge, 1965), pp. 130–44.

4. Text of Victoria's letter included in a letter from Queen Victoria to her uncle, the king of the Belgians, of 29 January 1861, Arthur Christopher Benson and Viscount Esher, eds., *The Letters of Queen Victoria: 1837–1861,* 3 vols. (New York, 1907), III, pp. 548–49.

5. Letter of 18 February 1884, BA Koblenz, Bülow Papers, vol. 165.

6. Roger Fulford, ed., *Dearest Child: Letters between Queen Victoria and the Princess Royal, 1858–1861* (New York, 1964), pp. 344–45.

7. See, here, Lamar Cecil, *Wilhelm II: Prince and Emperor, 1859–1900* (Chapel Hill, 1989), p. 9. For Friedrich's political views, see Andreas Dorpalen, "Emperor Friedrich III and the German Liberal Movement," *American Historical Review* 54 (1948), pp. 1–31. For Friedrich's admiration for England, the urgency of his desire for an Anglo-German rapprochement, and Victoria's political influence over her husband as well as her own Anglophilia, see Paul M. Kennedy, *The Rise of the Anglo-German Antagonism, 1860–1914* (London, 1982), pp. 129–31.

8. Quoted in Egon Cesar, Count Corti, *The English Empress, a Study in the Relations Between Queen Victoria and her Eldest Daughter* (London, 1957), p. 126.

9. Quoted in Joachim von Kürenberg, *The Kaiser: The Life of Wilhelm II, Last Emperor of Germany* (London, 1954), p. 26.

10. For Friedrich's dependent character, see Cecil, *Wilhelm II,* p. 11, as well as the diary entry of Heinrich Gelzer, adviser to the grand duke of Baden, of 17 December 1881, Walther Peter Fuchs, ed., *Grossherzog Friedrich I. von Baden und die Reichspolitik, 1871–1907,* 4 vols. (Stuttgart, 1968–1980), II, p. 164.

11. Wilhelm II, *My Early Life* (New York, 1926), p. 19.

12. Cecil, *Wilhelm II,* p. 10. Holstein's diary entry of 6 June 1885, Norman Rich and M. H. Fisher, eds., *The Holstein Papers,* 4 vols. (Cambridge, 1955), II, p. 204.

13. Diary entry of 3 March 1885, ibid., p. 170.

14. See Holstein's diary entries of 29 March 1885, ibid., p. 179, and of 9 September 1885, ibid., p. 245.

15. Holstein's diary entry of 3 March 1885, ibid., p. 171.

16. See, here, Cecil, *Wilhelm II,* p. 11.

17. Friedrich's insecurity and depression can be traced back to his relationship with his parents, who failed to provide him with warmth, affection, and affirmation. Ibid. There is evidence suggesting that Friedrich hoped to find an alternative to his own parents in Queen Victoria and Prince Albert. See Queen Victoria's letters of 22 September 1855 to the king of the Belgians, *Letters of Queen Victoria: 1837–1861,* III, pp. 186–87, and to Friedrich's father of 23 October 1885, *From the Archives,* p. 59.

18. Not only the acerbic Holstein but Friedrich's closest relatives regarded him as a tool of his wife. For Friedrich's father, Wilhelm I, see Herbert von Bismarck's letters to his father, Otto von Bismarck, of 9 September 1886 and to Count Kuno von Rantzau of 18 December 1886, Walter Bussmann, ed., *Staatssekretär Graf Herbert von Bismarck: Aus seiner politischen Privatkorrespondenz* (Göttingen, 1964), pp. 403 and 414; Johannes Haller, ed., *Aus 50 Jahren: Erinnerungen, Tagebücher und Briefe aus dem Nachlass des Fürsten Philipp zu Eulenburg-Hertefeld* (Berlin, 1923), pp. 187–88. For Friedrich's uncle, Friedrich I, grand duke of Baden, see his letters to Heinrich Gelzer of 20, 21, and 31 March 1872, *Grossherzog Friedrich I. von Baden,* I, pp. 54–5 and 64.

It should be mentioned that this attitude toward Friedrich was in keeping with the contempt prevalent in nineteenth-century Germany for men who allowed themselves to be dominated by their wives. See in this context the negative historical reputation of King Friedrich I of Prussia (1688–1713) who was also married to a forceful, outgoing, and talented woman.

19. Wilhelm II, *My Early Life,* p. 19.

20. "Kaiserin Friedrich," BA Koblenz, Bülow Papers, vol. 110. See also the essay "Kaiserin Friedrich" written by the historian Hans Delbrück, *Erinnerungen, Aufsätze und Reden* (Berlin, 1905), pp. 606–25. Delbrück had been the tutor of one of Wilhelm's younger siblings.

21. From Wilhelm II's "Introduction" to the German edition of Ponsonby, *Letters,* p. x, quoted in Michael Balfour, *The Kaiser and His Times* (New York, 1972), p. 66.

22. "Kaiserin Friedrich," BA Koblenz, Bülow Papers, vol. 110.

23. A. F. Whyte, ed., *A Field Marshal's Memoirs from the Diary, Correspondence and Papers of Alfred Count von Waldersee* (London, 1924), p. xvii n. See also Baron Hugo von Reischach, *Unter Drei Kaisern* (Berlin, 1925), p. 156.

24. *Holstein Papers,* II, p. 261.

25. Holstein quoting the chancellor in his diary entry of 5 July 1885, ibid., p. 212.

26. Holstein's diary entry of 29 March 1885, ibid., p. 179.

27. "Kaiserin Friedrich," BA Koblenz, Bülow Papers, vol. 110.

28. Bernhard Fürst von Bülow, *Denkwürdigkeiten,* 4 vols. (Berlin, 1930), I, pp. 534–35. Wilhelm did bury his mother in an English coffin as she had requested, but he put it inside of a coffin of German manufacture. He also had her body shrouded in the British Union Jack but covered it over with a German flag. I am indebted to Lamar Cecil for this information.

29. Letter from Victoria to Queen Victoria of 30 January 1871, RA Z25/49.

30. See, among countless examples, Victoria's letter to her mother of 17 November 1860 in which she wrote: "everything that ties my children to my old Home and makes me feel they belong to it also a little bit, makes me indescribably happy." RA Z10/3.

31. Letter from Victoria to Queen Victoria of 31 March 1859, RA Z7/105.

32. First, Miss Innocent, then Mrs. Hobbs in charge during most of Wilhelm's infancy, then Mrs. Cott, and, finally, Miss Byng. Letters from Victoria to Queen Victoria of 18 March 1859, RA Z7/99, and of 11 April 1863, RA Z15/10.

33. Thomas Dealtry, whose task it was to compliment the efforts of Hinzpeter, the German tutor of Wilhelm and his brother Heinrich, by improving their English and increasing their exposure to English literature and history. Letter from Thomas Dealtry to Victoria of 30 April 1870, Frederick Ponsonby, ed., *Letters of the Empress Frederick* (New York, 1930), p. 68.

34. Taking Wilhelm to England would "do him the most good," she wrote her mother on 2 August 1864, "but it would never do to say that here." RA Z16/69. When she and Wilhelm returned to Berlin, Victoria would be "obliged to restrain many an uncomplimentary comparison with their German Home which are ready to burst forth." Letter from Victoria to Queen Victoria of 22 August 1871, RA Z26/6.

35. Letter from Victoria to Queen Victoria of 11 January 1865, Roger Fulford, ed., *Your Dear Letter: Private Correspondence of Queen Victoria and the Crown Princes of Prussia, 1865–1871* (London, 1971), pp. 15–16.

36. Letter from Victoria to Marie Dönhoff of 8 February 1877, BA Koblenz, Bülow Papers, vol. 166. See also the letter from Victoria to Queen Victoria of 1 September 1874, Ponsonby, *Letters,* pp. 134–36.

37. Letter from Queen Victoria to the king of the Belgians of 9 February 1858, *The Letters of Queen Victoria: 1837–1861,* III, p. 334.

38. See letters from Queen Victoria to Princess Augusta of Prussia of 8 April 1856, of 15 April 1856, of 6 October 1856, of 5 September 1857, and of 3 February 1858, *From the Archives,* pp. 63, 64–65, 74, 87, and 97–98, respectively.

39. See, for example, the letter from Queen Victoria to Victoria of 22 August 1874, Roger Fulford, *Darling Child: Private Correspondence of Queen Victoria and the Crown Princess of Prussia, 1871–1878* (London, 1976), pp. 146–47; the letter from Victoria to Queen Victoria of 23 August 1874, ibid., p. 147; and the letter from Queen Victoria to Victoria of 4 September 1877, ibid., pp. 262–63. Various unpublished letters from Victoria to Queen Victoria housed in the Royal Archives testify to Victoria's conviction that her mother expected her to maintain an emotional investment in her parents.

40. Ponsonby, *Letters,* p. 351.

41. It is also possible that Victoria sought to undo the loss of her father by recreating Albert in herself. By educating her family as Albert had once educated her, by adopting Albert's marked Anglophilia and his contempt for Prussia, Victoria identified with her father. This so-called "identification with the lost object" is a way in which people typically attempt to deal with the absence of a loved or needed person. By taking on the attributes of the missing person, by identifying with him or her, the separation from that person becomes more tolerable.

42. Diary entry of 7 May 1884, *Holstein Papers,* II, p. 139.

43. Letter from Victoria to Queen Victoria of 7 February 1863, RA Z14/37. Queen Victoria's complaint in a letter to Victoria of 30 December 1875, *Darling Child,* p. 201, about the handwriting of Wilhelm and his brother produced over the next months and years a series of apologies from Victoria to her mother about this deficiency in her children. Letters from Victoria to Queen Victoria of 16 May 1863, RA Z15/20; of 30 May 1863, RA Z15/27; and of 7 January 1876, RA Z207/22.

44. RA Z21/4.

45. RA Z25/49.

46. Among many examples, her letters to her mother written on 24 May 1871, RA Z25/79, and 7 August 1872, RA Z26/88.

47. See, here, Cecil, *Wilhelm II,* pp. 71–73.

48. "Kaiserin Friedrich," BA Koblenz, Bülow Papers, vol. 110.

49. Diary entry of 11 March 1885, *Holstein Papers,* II, p. 174.

50. Holstein's diary entry of 24 October 1884, ibid., p. 165.

51. Ibid., p. 202.

52. Diary entry of 6 May 1885, ibid., p. 195.

53. As Bismarck angrily told the Prince of Wales after Friedrich's death, "the Salic law did not exist" in the German Empire. Letter from Ambassador Malet in Berlin to Prime Minister Salisbury of 24 June 1888, RA Z68/131. See also Nicolaus Sombart, "The Kaiser in his Epoch: Some Reflexions on Wilhelmian Society, Sexuality, and Culture," John C. G. Röhl and Nicolaus Sombart, eds., *Kaiser Wilhelm II: New Interpretations* (Cambridge, 1982), pp. 287–311.

54. "Political Reflections of ex-Kaiser Wilhelm II" of 28 March 1827 in Doorn, GSA, BHP, Rep. 53, Nr. 165 (1).

55. "Kaiserin Friedrich," *Die Zukunft* 36 (1901), pp. 257–71. Germans were not alone in believing that had they reigned longer Friedrich and Victoria would have sought dramatic changes in German politics and foreign policy. A decade after Friedrich's death King Oscar of Sweden told the German representative: "Believe me, the present Kaiser—Kaiser Wilhelm—is a much better ruler than his father. Had Kaiser Friedrich lived longer, then Germany would have fallen completely under *English influence.* Kaiser Friedrich hated Berlin. He often told me so. He wanted to move the capital to Frankfurt a. M. [site of the 1848 Parliament]; as did the Kaiserin. I often told her—I was good friends with both of them, Kaiser Friedrich was my age—that that would never work, at least not for the foreseeable future; but she hated Berlin and everything Prussian." Report from Stockholm of 2 August 1898, PA Bonn, Preussen 1, Nr. 1c, vol. 4.

56. "Zum Gedächniss des Kaisers und der Kaiserin Friedrich," 13 August 1901.

Chapter 2

1. Letter of 30 January 1859, Hector Bolitho, ed., *The Letters of Queen Victoria: From the Archives of the House of Brandenburg-Prussia* (New Haven, 1938), pp. 103–104.

2. Extract of letter of 27 January 1861, RA Add. Mss. U/32.

3. Letter of 30 January 1861, RA Z10/50.

4. RA Z16/74.

5. Frederick Ponsonby, ed., *Letters of the Empress Frederick* (New York, 1930), p. 28.

6. Letter to her brother Albert Edward of 7 March 1859, RA T2/46. Also her letter to Queen Victoria of 5 May 1859, RA Z7/124.

7. Letter from Queen Victoria to Victoria of 2 February 1866, Roger Fulford, ed., *Your Dear Letter: Private Correspondence of Queen Victoria and the Crown Princess of Prussia, 1865–1871* (London, 1971), p. 57.

8. RA Z7/130.

9. Letters from Victoria to Queen Victoria of 18 March 1859, RA Z7/99; of 3 September 1859, Roger Fulford, ed., *Dearest Child: Letters between Queen Victoria and the Princess Royal, 1858–1861* (New York, 1964), p. 209; and of 23 January 1861, RA Z10/47.

10. Letters from Victoria to Queen Victoria of 24 March 1859, RA Z7/101, and of 30 April 1859, RA Z7/120.

11. In a psychological investigation, a single piece of evidence cannot by itself prove a particular interpretation. Unfortunately, people are able to have very different, indeed contradictory, feelings at the same time. Therefore, the investigator must demonstrate the existence of tendencies or patterns. Testifying to Victoria's delight in her baby is the fact that at least thirty-five letters from Victoria to her mother, her father, and her brother, Albert Edward, housed in the Royal Archives contain positive statements about Wilhelm during the first year of his life.

12. Letter from Victoria to Queen Victoria of 16 April 1859, RA Z7/113.

13. Letter from Victoria to Queen Victoria of 23 April 1859, RA Z7/117.

14. RA Z8/20.

15. Letter from Victoria to Queen Victoria of 2 July 1859, RA Z8/12; and letters from Victoria to Prince Albert of 23 July 1859, RA Z2/29, and 3 August 1859, RA Z2/32.

16. Letter from Victoria to Queen Victoria of 20 August 1859, RA Z8/33.

17. Letter from Victoria to Queen Victoria of 11 August 1859, RA Z8/29.

18. Letter from Victoria to Prince Albert of 16 July 1859, RA Z2/28.

19. Letters from Victoria to Queen Victoria of 2 April 1859, RA Z7/106, and of 4 April 1859, RA Z7/107, and letter from Victoria to Prince Albert of 30 July 1859, RA Z2/30.

20. RA Z8/65. It should be noted that Victoria's fears proved groundless. Queen Victoria and Prince Albert were delighted with their grandson.

21. Letter from Victoria to Prince Albert of 10 December 1859, RA Z2/44. Also the letter from Victoria to Queen Victoria of 13 June 1859, RA Z8/5.

22. *Dearest Child,* p. 224.

23. Letters from Victoria to Queen Victoria of 14 April 1860, RA Z9/52, and of 27 January 1862, RA Z12/69. In contrast to the thirty-five letters from Victoria to her English relatives containing positive references to her son during the first year of his life, I was only able to discover fifteen letters from Victoria housed in the Royal Archives containing positive references to Wilhelm between his first and third birthdays.

24. Letters to her mother of 31 October 1860, RA Z10/8, and of 26 May 1860, RA Z9/63, and her letter to Prince Albert of 8 November 1861, RA Z4/35.

25. Letter from Victoria to Queen Victoria of 12 December 1859, *Dearest Child,* p. 224.

26. Letter from Friedrich to Prince Albert of 20 June 1860, RA Z7/81.

27. Letters from Victoria to Queen Victoria of 10 April 1860, RA Z9/51, and of 30 May 1860, RA Z9/64.

28. Letter to Queen Victoria of 16 June 1860, RA Z9/69.

29. Letters from Victoria to Queen Victoria of 10 January 1860, RA Z9/15; of 18 July 1860, RA Z9/79; and of 10 September 1862, RA Z13/50. Letter to Prince Albert of 18 August 1860, RA Z3/35.

30. Letters from Victoria to Queen Victoria of 19 January 1860, RA Z9/18; of 4 March 1860, RA Z9/39; of 17 March 1860, RA Z9/43; of 28 March 1860, RA Z9/46; and of 22 February 1861, RA Z10/59.

31. Letter from Victoria to Queen Victoria of 14 March 1860, RA Z9/41.

32. Already on 2 May 1859 she had written her mother that she attributed "all my mis-

fortune" with Wilhelm's birth to a fall in September 1858 when she was six months pregnant. RA Z7/121.

33. RA Z3/35.

34. Letter of 27 January 1860, RA Z3/5.

35. Letter from Victoria to Queen Victoria of 15 February 1861 (Victoria had mistakenly written 1860), RA Z10/56.

36. Letter from Victoria to Queen Victoria of 26 January 1861, RA Z10/48. To get a sense of the shift in Victoria's attitude toward her son, compare the fifteen unambiguously positive letters she wrote about him between 1860 and 1862 with the thirty-five positive letters she wrote about him before his first birthday.

37. Letters from Victoria to Queen Victoria of 18 December 1861, RA Z12/52; of 21 December 1861, RA Z12/53; of 29 December 1861, RA Z12/57; of 11 January 1862, RA Z12/63; and of 18 January 1861, RA Z12/66.

38. Letters from Victoria to Queen Victoria of 20 August 1859, RA Z8/33, and of 1 October 1861, RA Z12/17.

39. Copy of letter from Dr. Wegner to Queen Victoria of 8 September 1859, RA Z63/133.

40. Letter from Victoria to Prince Albert of 3 March 1860, RA Z3/11.

41. For example, Victoria's letters to Queen Victoria of 10 November 1861, RA Z10/12, and of 6 November 1863, RA Z15/61.

42. Letters from Victoria to Prince Albert of 18 February 1860, RA Z3/9; of 2 November 1860, RA Z3/42; of 23 November 1860, RA Z3/46; and of 31 May 1861, RA Z4/20; and from Victoria to Queen Victoria of 2 May 1863, RA Z15/16, and of 19 May 1863, RA Z15/21.

43. Letters from Victoria to Prince Albert of 31 May 1861, RA Z4/20, and to Queen Victoria of 17 May 1865, RA Z17/65.

44. Letters from Victoria to Queen Victoria of 10 January 1863, RA Z14/29; and from Queen Victoria to Victoria of 14 January 1863, RA Add. Mss. U/32. Letter from Victoria to Queen Victoria of 26 December 1863, RA Z16/3. Letter from Sir James Clark to Dr. Wegner of 8 January 1866, RA Add. Mss. J/1600. Victoria was more successful three years later in overcoming the resistance of Wegner and Langenbeck to a daily program of gymnastic exercises for Wilhelm. Letter from Victoria to Queen Victoria of 13 February 1866, RA Z18/25.

45. The brace consisted of a belt with a rod up the back. Straps were attached at the top of the rod to hold Wilhelm's head in place.

46. Letters from Victoria to Queen Victoria of 21 April 1863, RA Z15/14, and of 28 April 1863, RA Z15/15.

47. Letter from Victoria to her brother Albert Edward of 7 March 1859, RA T2/46. Also her letters to Queen Victoria of 5 March 1859, RA Z7/90, and of 6 March 1859, RA Z7/93.

48. Letter of 28 April 1863, Roger Fulford, ed., *Dearest Mama: Letters between Queen Victoria and the Crown Princess of Prussia, 1861–1864* (New York, 1964), pp. 203–204.

49. See, here, Lamar Cecil, *Wilhelm II: Prince and Emperor, 1859–1900* (Chapel Hill, 1989), p. 14.

50. RA Z4/20. Also the letter from Victoria to Prince Albert of 2 November 1860, RA Z3/42.

51. Letters from Victoria to Queen Victoria of 12 July 1864, RA Z16/62; of 27 June 1865, RA Z17/75; and of 4 July 1865, RA Z17/76.

52. Letter from Victoria to Queen Victoria of 5 May 1963, RA Z15/17.

53. Letters from Victoria to the Duchess of Argyll of 9 September 1863, RA Add. Mss. A17/87, and from Victoria to Queen Victoria of 3 February 1864, *Dearest Mama*, pp. 278–79.

54. RA Z16/67.

55. Letter from Victoria to Queen Victoria of 6 November 1864, *Dearest Mama*, pp. 278–79.

56. Letter from Victoria to Queen Victoria of 17 May 1865, *Your Dear Letter*, pp. 25–26. Victoria's preoccupation with Wilhelm's arm marred her pride and pleasure at his ability to

write: her letters to Queen Victoria of 3 February 1864, RA Z16/14, and of 26 February 1865, RA Z17/41.

57. Letter from Victoria to Queen Victoria of 17 May 1865, *Your Dear Letter,* pp. 25–26. Also the unpublished portion of this letter, RA Z17/65.

58. Letter from Victoria to Queen Victoria of 31 May 1865, *Your Dear Letter,* pp. 28–29, and letter from Victoria to Queen Victoria of 21 April 1863, *Dearest Mama,* pp. 199–200. I am indebted to Dr. Fedor Hagenauer for pointing out Victoria's sense of inadequacy as a mother expressed in this letter.

59. Letters from Victoria to Queen Victoria of 24 March 1863, RA Z15/4; of 20 July 1864, RA Z16/64; of 18 December 1864, RA Z17/16; of 17 May 1865, RA Z17/65; and of 21 April 1866, RA Z18/42. Already following her confinement with Wilhelm, she had written her mother: "Quite between ourselves, I would not have had a German nurse come near me for the world, you know I am not prejudiced, but they are not, to one accustomed to English habits, nice." Letter of 6 March 1859, RA Z7/93. Particularly after the death of her son, Sigismund, she became anxious whenever her children contracted the inevitable childhood diseases: "Bungling as is the German fashion of treating these illnesses—after dear Sigie's loss I never feel at peace one minute if anything is the matter with one of the children." Letter to Queen Victoria of 26 February 1868, RA Z21/16.

60. Letters from Victoria to Queen Victoria of 22 October 1864, RA Z16/89, and 23 January 1866, RA Z18/18.

61. Letters from Victoria to Queen Victoria of 22 June 1864, RA Z16/54, and of 2 July 1864, RA Z16/59. Letter from Victoria to Queen Victoria of 14 June 1864, *Dearest Mama,* pp. 346–47.

62. Copy of a letter from King Wilhelm I to Crown Prince Friedrich of 6 July 1864, RA I99/30.

63. Letter from Victoria to Queen Victoria of 8 July 1864, RA Z16/61.

64. Friedrich's diary entry of 24 November 1865, *Kaiser Friedrich III, Tagebücher von 1848–1866* (Leipzig, 1929), p. 403.

65. Friedrich's diary entry of 23 March 1864, ibid., p. 386; letter from William Jenner to Queen Victoria of 28 March 1865, RA I42/37a; and letter from Victoria to Queen Victoria of 7 April 1865, RA Z17/54.

66. For example, Friedrich's letter to Prince Albert and Queen Victoria of 20 February 1861(?), RA Z64/26.

67. Wilhelm II, *My Early Life* (New York, 1926), p. 19.

68. Ibid., p. 30. Wilhelm's image of Sophie Dobeneck would appear to be confirmed by Victoria's letter to Queen Victoria of 20 May 1865 in which she reported that the governess tended to emphasize fire and brimstone in discussing religious matters with the children. RA Z17/66.

69. Comment to an interviewer in exile. Joachim von Kürenberg, *The Kaiser: The Life of Wilhelm II, Last Emperor of Germany* (London, 1954), p. 11.

70. *Dearest Mama,* p. 215.

71. Letter of 26 June 1866, Ponsonby, *Letters,* p. 61. Also Victoria's letters to her mother of 5 August 1866, RA Z18/75, and of 10 December 1866, RA Z19/30, in which she expressed her conviction that Sigismund was her brightest and most beautiful child, the one most likely to resemble her father.

72. Her letter to Queen Victoria of 13 May 1867, RA Z20/7, and Queen Victoria's letter to Victoria of 18 May 1867 disapproving of this practice, *Your Dear Letter,* p. 137. The crown princess' attachment to Vicky would (as discussed in Chapter 4) bring Victoria into bitter conflict with Bismarck over the issue of her daughter's marriage. It seems plausible to trace Victoria's absolute unwillingness to subordinate her daughter's happiness to the interests of state to Vicky's original connection with Sigismund and perhaps to Victoria's guilt over his death. One can speculate, in other words, that with the sense that she had failed her little boy she would not fail her "little Vicky."

73. "Today is a sad day for me!" Victoria wrote her friend Marie Dönhoff on 18 June 1877. "I lost my darling little boy 11 years ago, the remembrance of all I suffered comes up

vividly before me,—and *never* shall I cease to mourn and grieve for the little darling of which I was so proud." BA Koblenz, Bülow Papers, vol. 166.

74. Letter of 26 June 1866, Ponsonby, *Letters,* pp. 61–62. It confirms the hypothesis presented in Chapter 1—that Victoria responded to her feelings of inadequacy as a mother by attempting to recreate the home of her parents in her home in Berlin—that her increased involvement with the children after Sigismund's death took the form of her redoubled efforts to Anglicize them. These efforts proved successful with her youngest children—as evidenced by the fact that Vicky spoke only English during the first years of her life and later even refused to say German words when she had finally learned them. Letter from Victoria to Queen Victoria of 10 June 1868, *Your Dear Letter,* pp. 195–96.

75. Letter from Victoria to Queen Victoria of 22 May 1872, Roger Fulford, ed., *Darling Child: Private Correspondence of Queen Victoria and the Crown Princess of Prussia, 1871–1878* (London, 1976), p. 43.

76. Quoted in Michael Balfour, *The Kaiser and His Times* (New York, 1972), p. 76.

77. Kürenberg, *The Kaiser,* p. 9.

78. Wilhelm II, *My Early Life,* pp. 30, 35, 46, and 111. See also Cecil, *Wilhelm II,* pp. 28 and 30.

79. Letter from Victoria to Queen Victoria of 5 November 1866, RA Z19/18.

80. Letter from Queen Victoria to Victoria of 27 January 1865, Fulford, *Your Dear Letter,* pp. 16–17. See also Queen Victoria's journal entry of 27 January 1866, George Earle Buckle, ed., *The Letters of Queen Victoria: 1862–1885,* 3 vols. (New York, 1926), I, pp. 296–97.

81. Letter from Victoria to Queen Victoria of 30 January 1871, Fulford, *Your Dear Letter,* pp. 316–17.

82. Bogdan Graf von Hutten-Czapski, *Sechzig Jahre Politik und Gesellschaft,* 2 vols. (Berlin, 1936), I, p. 312. See also Karl Friedrich Nowak and Friedrich Thimme, eds., *Erinnerungen und Gedanken des Botschafters Anton Graf Monts* (Berlin, 1932), pp. 137–38, and Cecil, *Wilhelm II,* pp. 19–21 and 24.

83. Hutten-Czapski, *Sechzig Jahre,* I, p. 312. He was particularly contemptuous of Wilhelm's "soft friend" Philipp Eulenburg.

84. Franz Ayme, *Wilhelm II und seine Erziehung. Aus den Erinnerungen seines französischen Lehrers* (Leipzig, 1898). Hinzpeter sacrificed his personal life to his obligation to the two princes. During the period that he was Wilhelm's tutor, Hinzpeter fell in love with Sophie Dobeneck's successor as governess, Mlle. Darcourt. Rather than give up his position, Hinzpeter agreed that their marriage should be in name only, and his bride returned to France. Letter from Hinzpeter to Bartelsmann of 22 April 1875, Bielefeld Stadtsarchiv, Hinzpeter Nachlass.

85. Georg Hinzpeter, "Der Prinzenerzieher," GSA, BHP, Rep. 53, Nr. 101.

86. "Der Prinzenerzieher," GSA, BHP, Rep. 53, Nr. 101.

87. Wilhelm II, *My Early Life,* pp. 31–32.

88. Ibid., p. 37.

89. Ibid.

90. Ibid., p. 33.

91. Kürenberg, *The Kaiser,* p. 11; Wilhelm II, *My Early Life,* p. 37.

92. Bernhard Fürst von Bülow, *Denkwürdigkeiten,* 4 vols. (Berlin, 1930), I, p. 106; Cecil, *Wilhelm II,* pp. 35 and 351, notes 17 and 20; and Kürenberg, *The Kaiser,* p. 11.

93. This interpretation is considered in the Conclusion to this study.

94. Bülow, *Denkwürdigkeiten,* I, p. 107.

95. See Cecil, *Wilhelm II,* pp. 14 and 346–47, notes 56 and 57.

96. Among the contemporaries who testified to the Kaiser's riding ability was his chief of the Naval Cabinet, Admiral Georg Alexander von Müller. Müller noted in his diary-memoir: "But I can say, that despite his inability to use his left arm, he was a most unflappable rider. He galloped with absolute self-assurance—even over terrain where one could not see what was coming, as in the gorse bushes of Döberitz." Walter Görlitz, ed., *Der Kaiser: Aufzeichnungen des Chefs des Marinekabinetts Admiral Georg Alexander von Müller über die Ära Wilhelms II* (Göttingen, 1965), pp. 177–78.

97. Wilhelm II, *My Early Life,* pp. 117–18.

98. The saddle desk chair also reflects the Kaiser's imitation of Friedrich the Great, who had such a chair, as well as Wilhelm's restlessness. Even when seated, he had to feel that he was on the move.

99. Ibid., p. 11.

100. Georg Hinzpeter, *Kaiser Wilhelm II. Eine Skizze nach der Natur gezeichnet* (Bielefeld, 1888), p. 10.

101. Letters from Victoria to Prince Albert of 12 March 1859, RA Z2/11; to Queen Victoria of 19 November 1861, RA Z12/37; and of 28(?) December 1872, RA Z27/25.

102. Letter of 10 December 1866, RA Z19/30. Portions of this letter have been published in *Your Dear Letter,* pp. 111–12.

103. RA Z22/11. Portions of this letter have been published in *Your Dear Letter,* pp. 205–206.

104. The letters from Victoria to Queen Victoria of 31 August 1869, RA Z23/72; of 28 May 1870, Ponsonby, *Letters,* p. 68; of 2 June 1870, RA Z24/61; and of 31 January 1872, RA Z26/46, portions of this letter have been published in *Darling Child,* p. 26.

105. Ponsonby, *Letters,* pp. 119–20.

106. See the Conclusion to this study.

107. Ayme, *Wilhelm II und seine Erziehung.* In numerous letters to her mother housed in the Royal Archives, Victoria indicated her preference for Wilhelm over Charlotte and Heinrich.

108. Letters from Victoria to Queen Victoria of 15 February 1867, RA Z19/58; of 18 April 1874, RA Z28/22; of 28 February 1865, RA Z17/42; of 5 November 1866, RA Z19/18; of 16 October 1875, *Darling Child,* p. 196; and of 11 October 1877, ibid., p. 267. Other letters in which Victoria complained about Charlotte to her mother include: of 4 January 1867, RA Z19/42; of 10 July 1879, RA Z33/22; of 27 July 1880, RA Z34/39; and of 13 October 1880, RA Z34/54. See also Holstein's diary entry of 9 June 1886, Norman Rich and M. H. Fisher, eds., *The Holstein Papers,* 4 vols. (Cambridge, 1955–1963), II, p. 205.

109. Letter from Victoria to Queen Victoria of 16 May 1863, RA Z15/20. These measures testify either to Victoria's exaggerated worry about her daughter or to Charlotte's extreme anxiety as a child—or to both.

110. Letters from Victoria to Queen Victoria of 6 May 1870, RA Z24/53; of 23 May 1874, RA Z28/30; of 30 October 1874, RA Z28/70; of 24 June 1874, RA Z28/36; of 20 June 1876, *Darling Child,* p. 215; of 20 July 1879, RA Z33/22; of 7 August 1872, RA Z26/88; and of 14 August 1880, Roger Fulford, ed., *Beloved Mama: Private Correspondence of Queen Victoria and the German Crown Princess, 1878–1885* (London, 1981), p. 87.

111. RA Z28/30.

112. Letter of 17 November 1866, *Your Dear Letter,* pp. 108–109. Also Victoria's letters to Queen Victoria of 14 August 1880, *Beloved Mama,* p. 87, and of 1 October 1880, RA Z34/52.

113. Ponsonby, *Letters,* p. 215.

114. Letter from Victoria to Queen Victoria of 14 December 1877, *Darling Child,* p. 270.

115. Letter from Victoria to Queen Victoria of 6 January 1873, RA Z27/28.

116. At least nine letters housed in the Royal Archives from Victoria to Queen Victoria written while Wilhelm was at Kassel testify to her pleasure in and affection for her son.

117. Letter of 27 March 1875, *Darling Child,* p. 174.

118. Report from Hermann Sahl to Dalton of 19 May 1876, RA Geo. V AA6/149. For details of Wilhelm's life in Kassel, see Cecil, *Wilhelm II,* pp. 30–37, and James C. Albisetti, *Secondary School Reform in Imperial Germany* (Princeton, 1983), pp. 172–76.

119. Letters from Prince Wilhelm to Queen Victoria of 10 January 1877, RA Z79/50, and of 28 January 1877, RA Z64/104.

120. Letter from Victoria to Queen Victoria of 10 February 1877, RA Z31/8.

121. RA Z207/47.

122. Letter from Victoria to Queen Victoria of 10 March 1877, RA Z31/13. Letter from Wilhelm to Queen Victoria of 23 May 1877, RA Z79/70. Letter from Victoria to Queen Victoria of 2 June 1877, RA Z31/29. See, here, Cecil, *Wilhelm II,* p. 37.

123. Even when living in Potsdam, Wilhelm remained close to the house of his parents and saw them fairly frequently.

124. Lamar Cecil, "History as Family Chronicle: Kaiser Wilhelm II and the Dynastic Roots of the Anglo-German Antagonism," John C. G. Röhl and Nicolaus Sombart, eds., *Kaiser Wilhelm II: New Interpretations* (Cambridge, 1982), p. 96. This paragraph is based upon Cecil's description of Wilhelm's student days in Bonn. See also Cecil, *Wilhelm II*, pp. 37–43.

125. Letter to Heinrich Gelzer of 15 August 1878, Walter Peter Fuchs, ed., *Grossherzog Friedrich I. von Baden und die Reichspolitik, 1871–1907*, 4 vols. (Stuttgart, 1968–81), I, p. 322.

126. Letter to Queen Victoria of 17 April 1879, RA Z32/42.

127. Cecil, "History as Family Chronicle," p. 96. This view is confirmed by the fact that it was while Wilhelm was at Bonn that he and his parents disagreed politically over the war between Russia and Turkey, with the prince supporting the Tsar and his parents, the Turks. Cecil, *Wilhelm II*, pp. 37 and 43.

128. Letter in English from Wilhelm to Victoria of 17 July 1879, RA Add. Mss. U34/8.

129. Letter from Victoria in Italy to Queen Victoria of 12 October 1879, RA Z33/40.

130. Letter from Victoria in Italy to Queen Victoria of 27 October 1879, RA Z33/43. See Victoria's complaints to her mother on 17 July 1880 about Wilhelm's excessive zeal in his performance of his military duties and its potentially deleterious impact on his character. *Beloved Mama*, p. 83. For Wilhelm's second tour of duty in the Potsdam Guards, see Cecil, *Wilhelm II*, pp. 46–47 and 58–61.

131. "Kaiser Wilhelm II," BA Koblenz, Eulenburg Papers, vol. 80.

132. "Hineinragende Persönlichkeiten," BA Koblenz, Eulenburg Papers, vol. 81, p. 165. Quoted in Cecil, "History as Family Chronicle," p. 96.

133. Karl Wippermann, ed., *Deutscher Geschichtskalender*, 49 vols. (Leipzig, 1885–1933), 1887 (II), p. 224.

134. Cecil, "History as Family Chronicle," p. 97.

135. "Hineinragende Persönlichkeiten," BA Koblenz, Eulenburg Papers, vol. 81, p. 165. Quoted in Cecil, "History as Family Chronicle," p. 96.

136. Letter in English from Wilhelm to Victoria of 20 May 1879, RA Vic. Add. Mss. U34/4.

Chapter 3

1. Extract of letter from Queen Victoria to Victoria of 16 March 1859, RA Add. Mss. U34; letter from Victoria to Prince Albert of 30 July 1860, RA Z3/32; letters from Victoria to Queen Victoria of 31 July 1860, RA Z9/81; and of 6 November 1860, RA Z10/11; letter from Queen Victoria to Victoria of 2 February 1866, Roger Fulford, ed., *Your Dear Letter: Private Correspondence of Queen Victoria and the Crown Princess of Prussia, 1865–1871* (London, 1971), p. 57; letter from Victoria to Queen Victoria of 3 November 1866, RA Z19/1; letter from Queen Victoria to Victoria of 31 July 1880, Roger Fulford, ed., *Beloved Mama: Private Correspondence of Queen Victoria and the German Crown Princess, 1878–1885* (London, 1981), p. 85; and letter from Victoria to Queen Victoria of 23 March 1883, RA Z36/90.

2. Letter of 3 December 1870, *Your Dear Letter*, p. 311. As was suggested in Chapter 1, although Queen Victoria's sentiments doubtless reflected her distress at the conduct of her eldest son, Albert Edward, Victoria appears to have taken comments of this sort as a personal criticism, prompting her to redouble the effort to Anglicize her children and adopted country.

3. Letter of 17 July 1886, RA Z38/34.

4. As has been suggested, Victoria's dependence was subtly encouraged by her parents, as were her efforts to keep her own children dependent. Queen Victoria believed that it was particularly important in royal families to extend childhood as long as possible, and she urged the Kaiser and Kaiserin not to push Wilhelm into adulthood too quickly. Letters from Queen Victoria to Kaiserin Augusta of 5 September 1874 and to Kaiser Wilhelm I of 25 November 1874, Hector Bolitho, ed., *The Letters of Queen Victoria: From the Archives of the House of*

Brandenburg-Prussia (New Haven, 1938), pp. 199–201. See also notes 17 and 19 to this chapter.

5. "How interesting it is to watch the progress from childhood to manhood," Victoria wrote her mother on 7 December 1874, "and how strange it seems to me who still feel young at times, to have such a big child." RA Z28/78. Portions of this letter have been published in Roger Fulford, ed., *Darling Child: Private Correspondence of Queen Victoria and the Crown Princess of Prussia, 1871–1878* (London, 1976), pp. 164–65.

6. Letter from Victoria to Queen Victoria of 30 June 1866, Frederick Ponsonby, ed., *Letters of the Empress Frederick* (New York, 1930), p. 62. Technically, she experienced her children as "selfobjects."

7. Ibid., p. 135.

8. Letter from Victoria to Queen Victoria of 5 September 1874, RA Z28/57. A portion of this letter has been published in *Darling Child*, pp. 150–51. Letters from Victoria to Queen Victoria of 15 September 1874, ibid., p. 152; of 7 December 1874, RA Z28/78; and of 15 February (?), the year as written, 1874, is in error, RA Z31/9.

9. Letter from Victoria to Marie Dönhoff of 1 August 1878, BA Koblenz, Bülow Papers, vol. 166.

10. Letters from Victoria to Queen Victoria of 30 January 1877 (quoted in the previous chapter) and of 29 October 1880, RA Z34/57.

11. Letters from Victoria to Queen Victoria of 6 May 1874, RA Z28/25; of 29 December 1875, RA Z29/61; of 28 October 1864, RA Z17/1; of 16 December 1864, RA Z17/15; and of 14 August 1865, *Your Dear Letter,* pp. 38–40.

12. Ibid., pp. 24–25.

13. Letters from Victoria to Queen Victoria of 27 August 1867, RA Z20/37, and of 11 September 1867, Fulford, *Your Dear Letter,* pp. 150–51. Although Sophie Dobeneck was a German, Victoria also sought to emphasize to herself and her mother the governess' tenuous connections with England. Letter from Victoria to Queen Victoria of 26 February 1861, RA Z10/62.

14. Letters from Victoria to Queen Victoria of 6 June 1874, *Darling Child,* pp. 141–42; of 29 August 1874, RA Z28/55; of 1 September 1874, Ponsonby, *Letters,* pp. 134–36; of 6 October 1874, *Darling Child,* pp. 155–56; and of 30 January 1877, RA Z207/47.

15. Letter from Victoria to Queen Victoria of 7 December 1874, *Darling Child,* pp. 164–65.

16. BA Koblenz, Bülow Papers, vol. 166.

17. Letter from Victoria to Marie Dönhoff of 9 April 1877, BA Koblenz, Bülow Papers, vol. 166. Her children's growing independence appears to have aroused Victoria's powerful dependent needs. Thus, her psychosomatic ailments expressed Victoria's own need to be cared for, her yearning to be mothered herself. This letter, like the one quoted in the text, concludes with a wish that Countess Dönhoff come to comfort her. See note 19 below.

18. Letters from Victoria to Queen Victoria of 20 February 1878, Ponsonby, *Letters,* p. 168, and of 21 February 1878, ibid., pp. 168–69.

19. Letter of 21 February 1878, ibid., pp. 169–70. This was at least her third letter to her mother in twenty-four hours. Again the independence of her daughter stirred up Victoria's yearning for her own mother, her wish to be a child again—testifying to Victoria's need for the presence of her children and, more specifically, her need for them to be in need of her, in order to prevent Victoria from regressing to a dependent state herself. Being needed, in other words, maintained Victoria's sense of maturity and psychological autonomy. Hence the conclusion to her letter cited above: "I have thought more of you than ever in my life and more than of anyone else. Mothers do not lose their daughters if all love their mothers as much as I do you."

20. Letter from Queen Victoria to Victoria of 4 September 1877, *Darling Child,* pp. 262–63.

21. Ibid., pp. 261–62. A few weeks later, Victoria's distress was increased when Wilhelm failed to stop and talk when they passed one another on the road. RA Z31/47. In early 1879, when Wilhelm reinjured his knee fencing, the reactions of mother and son were the same as

they had been in August 1877. Letter from Victoria to Queen Victoria of 1 February 1879, RA Z32/14.

22. Letter from Victoria to Queen Victoria of 27 March 1879, *Beloved Mama*, p. 38; also her letter to her mother of 17 April 1879, RA Z32/42. As she was after Sigismund's death, Victoria remained inconsolable after the death of Waldemar. Her letters to Queen Victoria of 20 April 1879, RA Z32/43; of 26 January 1880, RA Z34/6; of 18 February 1880, RA Z34/25; and of 7 July 1883, RA Z36/101.

23. Letter of 3 April 1879, BA Koblenz, Bülow Papers, vol. 166.

24. Letters from Wilhelm to Marie Dönhoff of 27 October 1878 and of 30 October 1878, both BA Koblenz, Bülow Papers, vol. 173, and letter from Victoria to Marie Dönhoff of 2 November 1878, BA Koblenz, Bülow Papers, vol. 166.

25. BA Koblenz, Bülow Papers, vol. 173. This letter, which dates from the middle of Wilhelm's correspondence with Marie Dönhoff, also suggests that, without the presence of a father to help him separate from his possessive mother, Wilhelm may have used soldiers to help him achieve autonomy.

26. In the period from 27 October 1878 to 1 January 1880 Wilhelm wrote at least nine letters to Marie Dönhoff.

27. Wilhelm's letters to Victoria of 30 October 1878 and to Marie Dönhoff of 13 November 1878, BA Koblenz, Bülow Papers, vol. 173.

28. Wilhelm's letters to Victoria of 30 October 1873 and to Marie Dönhoff of 5 November and 4 December 1878, BA Koblenz, Bülow Papers, vol. 173.

29. Letter of 5 November 1878, BA Koblenz, Bülow Papers, vol. 173.

30. Letter of 27 October 1878, BA Koblenz, Bülow Papers, vol. 173.

31. Letter of 13 November 1878, BA Koblenz, Bülow Papers, vol. 173.

32. See note 41 of Chapter 1.

33. Letters of 4 December 1878, of 12 February 1879, and of 20 February 1879, all BA Koblenz, Bülow Papers, vol. 173.

34. Letter of 5 November 1878, BA Koblenz, Bülow Papers, vol. 173.

35. Letters from Wilhelm to Marie Dönhoff of 4 December 1878, of 1 January 1879, and of 12 February 1879, BA Koblenz, Bülow Papers, vol. 173.

36. BA Koblenz, Bülow Papers, vol. 173.

37. Wilhelm wrote letters to his aunt on 1 February 1878, GSA, BPH, Rep. 53, Nr. 37; on 25 April 1878, GSA, BPH, Rep. 53, Nr. 39; on 3 March 1879, GSA, BPH, Rep. 53, Nr. 40; on 2 December 1879 (the date on this letter is obviously incorrect, it probably comes from February 1879 or January 1880), GSA, BPH, Rep. 53, Nr. 41; on 2 December 1879, GSA, BPH, Rep. 53, Nr. 42; on 9 February 1881, GSA, BPH, Rep. 53, Nr. 43; on 5 January 1884, GSA, BPH, Rep. 53, Nr. 44; a telegram on 31 May 1891, GSA, BPH, Rep. 53, Nr. 48; and letters on 33 June 1898, GSA, BPH, Rep. 53, Nr. 44; on 14 February 1900, GSA, BPH, Rep. 53, Nr. 57; on 30 January 1905, GSA, BPH, Rep. 53, Nr. 72; and on 1 February 1906, GSA, BPH, Rep. 53, Nr. 76. Unfortunately many of Wilhelm's letters to his aunt appear to have been destroyed.

38. GSA, BPH, Rep. 53, Nr. 37.

39. Wilhelm II, *My Early Life* (New York, 1926), p. 194.

40. Letter from Victoria to Queen Victoria of 18 February 1880, Ponsonby, *Letters*, pp. 177–78. Also the letter from Victoria to the Marquis of Lorne of 22 February 1880, RA Vic. Add. A17/1719, and the letter from Crown Prince Friedrich to a childhood companion of 2 August 1880, GSA, BPH, Rep. 94, Nr. 830.

41. RA Z34/9. This letter has been published in *Beloved Mama*, pp. 64–65, although the order in which it appears there is incorrect. Victoria's letter to her mother of 16 May 1879, RA Z65/159, expresses similar sentiments.

42. Letters from Victoria to Queen Victoria of 26 March 1880, RA Z34/14; of 24 May 1880, Ponsonby, *Letters*, p. 180; and of 18 June 1880, RA Z34/32. Prince Wilhelm's letter to Queen Victoria of 8 March 1881 also concerns the Kaiser's evident affection for Dona, RA Z80/123.

43. Letter from Victoria to Queen Victoria of 29 January 1880, *Beloved Mama*, p. 63.

44. Ponsonby, *Letters,* pp. 179–80.

45. Letter from Crown Prince Friedrich to Marie Dönhoff of 13 October 1880, BA Koblenz, Bülow Papers, vol. 165.

46. Letter from Victoria to Queen Victoria of 29 October 1880, RA Z34/57. A portion of this letter has been published in *Beloved Mama,* p. 91.

47. Letter of 16 November 1880, BA Koblenz, Bülow Papers, vol. 167.

48. Victoria's letters to Queen Victoria of 29 October 1880, RA Z34/57, and of 10 February 1881, RA Z35/3.

49. Letter from Victoria to Queen Victoria of 16 December 1880, RA Z34/65.

50. Ponsonby, *Letters,* p. 183.

51. Letter from Wilhelm to Queen Victoria of 29 January 1881, RA Z80/118.

52. Letter from Victoria to Queen Victoria of 28 February 1881, RA Z35/6. A portion of this letter has been published in *Beloved Mama,* p. 96. Letter from Victoria to Queen Victoria of 27 February 1881, Ponsonby, *Letters,* p. 184. Letters from Victoria to Queen Victoria of 28 February 1881, *Beloved Mama,* p. 96, and of 5 March 1881, RA Z35/7.

53. Letter from Wilhelm to Queen Victoria of 1 March 1881, RA Z80/120.

54. Letter from Queen Victoria to Victoria of 14 February 1887, RA Add. Mss. U32.

55. Mary Theresa Olivia Fürstin von Pless, *Daisy, Princess of Pless by Herself* (London, 1928), p. 160.

56. Bernhard Fürst von Bülow, *Denkwürdigkeiten,* 4 vols. (Berlin, 1930), I, p. 264.

57. For Wilhelm's marriage, see Lamar Cecil, *Wilhelm II: Prince and Emperor, 1859–1900* (Chapel Hill, 1989), pp. 47–54.

58. Wilhelm II quoted in Joachim von Kürenberg, *The Kaiser: The Life of Wilhelm II., Last Emperor of Germany* (London, 1954), p. 88.

59. Bülow, *Denkwürdigkeiten,* I, p. 262.

60. Letters from Victoria to Queen Victoria of 5 September 1881, RA Z35/41; of 16 November 1883, RA Z37/11 (a portion of this letter has been published in *Beloved Mama,* pp. 149–50, although the published version contains errors); and of 10 August 1885, RA Z37/91. Victoria was also distraught at Heinrich's failure to write her. Letter from Victoria to Queen Victoria of 3 March 1884, RA Z37/21.

61. Letter from Arthur, Duke of Connaught to Queen Victoria of 6 November 1881, RA Add. Mss. A15/3463; letter from Queen Victoria to Arthur, Duke of Connaught, of 12 November 1881, RA Add. Mss. A15/3464; and letter from Victoria to Queen Victoria of 12 November 1881, *Beloved Mama,* p. 110.

62. Letters from Victoria to Queen Victoria of 1 December 1883, ibid., p. 151; of 15 December 1883, RA Z30/16; and of 22 December 1883, RA Z37/16.

63. Letter from Victoria to Queen Victoria of 1 December 1883, *Beloved Mama,* p. 151.

64. Letters from Victoria to Marie Dönhoff of 15 April 1882, BA Koblenz, Bülow Papers, vol. 168; and to Queen Victoria of 12 November 1881, *Beloved Mama,* p. 110, and of 16 November 1883, RA Z37/11.

65. Letter from Victoria to Queen Victoria of 1 December 1883, *Beloved Mama,* p. 151.

66. Letter of 8 December 1881, BA Koblenz, Bülow Papers, vol. 167.

67. Carl von Wedel's diary entry of 8 May 1891, Count Erhard von Wedel, ed., *Zwischen Kaiser und Kanzler: Aufzeichnungen des General-adjutanten Grafen Carl von Wedel aus den Jahren 1890–1914* (Leipzig, 1943), p. 173. Indeed, Charlotte went so far as to accuse her mother of attempting to arrange marriages for her and for Wilhelm with lesser aristocrats in order to limit the influence of her children and to keep them under her thumb.

68. Letter from Victoria to Queen Victoria of 6 October 1877, RA Z231/51. A portion of this letter has been published in *Darling Child,* p. 266.

69. RA Z80/48.

70. *Beloved Mama,* p. 85.

71. Letter in German of 9 February 1881, GSA, BPH, Rep. 53, Nr. 43.

72. For the deterioration of Wilhelm's relationship with his parents, see Cecil, *Wilhelm II,* pp. 71–87.

73. RA Z36/5. Portions of this letter have been published in *Beloved Mama,* pp. 114–15.

74. Holstein's diary entry of 17 March 1882: "Yesterday Lord Ampthill [the British ambassador in Berlin] told a lady that the Crown Prince and Princess were grieved at Prince Wilhelm's behaviour. The Crown Princess had had eye trouble for some time. Prince Wilhelm came and went without ever asking after his mother's health. The father reproved him, but his son replied—according to Ampthill—that he didn't wish to hear such language again. Both parents are said to be deeply hurt, 'the father at the lack of respect, the mother at the lack of love.'" Norman Rich and M. H. Fisher, eds., *The Holstein Papers,* 4 vols. (Cambridge, 1955–1963), II, p. 15.

75. Wilhelm II quoted in Lamar Cecil, "History as Family Chronicle: Kaiser Wilhelm II and the Dynastic Roots of the Anglo-German Antagonism," John C. G. Röhl and Nicolaus Sombart, eds., *Kaiser Wilhelm II: New Interpretations* (Cambridge, 1982), p. 98.

76. Ibid., p. 99.

77. Letter from Victoria to Queen Victoria of 26 March 1887, RA Z39/13.

78. Letters from Victoria to Queen Victoria of 2 July 1885, *Beloved Mama,* p. 193, and of 19 April 1887, RA Z39/18.

79. Letter from Victoria to Queen Victoria of 22 April 1887, RA Z39/19. This letter has been published in Ponsonby, *Letters,* pp. 212–15, although with some minor errors. Also the letters from Victoria to Queen Victoria of 11 August 1886, ibid., pp. 206–207; of 28 December 1887, RA Z38/109; of 28 March 1888, RA Add. Mss. A15; of 19 May 1888, Ponsonby, *Letters,* p. 311; of 8 June 1888, RA Z41/59; of 29 June 1888, Ponsonby, *Letters,* pp. 322–23; of 23 August 1888, ibid., p. 329; of 6 November 1888, ibid., pp. 361–64; and of 19 July 1889, ibid., pp. 381–82.

80. Ibid., p. 369. Also the letters from Victoria to Queen Victoria of 22 September 1887, RA Z38/67, and of 28 September 1888, Ponsonby, *Letters,* pp. 347–48.

81. Letter from Victoria to Queen Victoria of 15 March 1890, ibid., p. 369. See also her letter to Queen Victoria of 25 May 1886: "We met him in the garden and I thought him looking all right. [Wilhelm was recovering from an ear infection.] He did not condescend to remember that he had not seen me for two months, or that I had been to England and to Homburg, or that his sisters had the measles. He never asked after them or you, or any of my relations in England, so that I felt hurt and disappointed as I had been tormenting myself so much about him. He is a curious creature! . . . Still, it is very painful to a soft-hearted Mama to feel so plainly that her own child does not care whether he sees her or no, whether she is well or ill, or away, etc. Dona is most devoted to him and never leaves him for one minute; they seem very happy and contented together." Ibid., p. 200.

82. *Your Dear Letter,* p. 111.

83. Letter from Philipp Eulenburg to Bernhard von Bülow of 23 September 1900, John C. G. Röhl, ed., *Philipp Eulenburgs politische Korrespondenz,* 3 vols. (Boppard-am-Rhein, 1976–1983), III, pp. 1990–92. See also Bülow, *Denkwürdigkeiten,* I, pp. 450–51.

84. GSA, BPH, Rep. 53, Nr. 165 (1).

85. Wilhelm II quoted in a letter from Eulenburg to Bülow of 8 November 1896, BA Koblenz, Bülow Papers, vol. 76. Wilhelm II's marginalia to a report from the German ambassador in Vienna, Prince Heinrich VII Reuss, to Chancellor Caprivi of 15 November 1892, *GP,* VII, pp. 410–12. See also Lamar Cecil, "Wilhelm II and his Russian 'Colleagues'," *German Nationalism and the European Response, 1890–1945,* Carole Fink, Isabel V. Hull, and MacGregor Knox, eds. (Norman, Oklahoma, 1985), pp. 119–21.

86. Wilhelm II's marginalia to a report from the German ambassador in St. Petersberg, Werder, to Chancellor Hohenlohe of 15 February 1895, *GP,* IX, pp. 342–44.

87. Hugo von Reischach, *Unter drei Kaisern* (Berlin, 1925), p. 131.

88. Reflections of ex-Kaiser Wilhelm II of 28 March 1927, GSA, BPH, Rep. 53, Nr. 165 (1).

89. See, here, Cecil, *Wilhelm II,* p. 9.

90. Reischach, *Unter drei Kaisern,* p. 158.

91. *Holstein Papers,* II, pp. 214–16.

Chapter 4

1. Telegram of 28 January 1859, RA Z63/106. In contrast to most of his communications with his in-laws, this telegram was written in English. Letter to Queen Victoria and Prince Albert of 27 December 1859, RA Z71/79. Also Queen Victoria's letter to Victoria of 4 May 1859, RA Add. Mss. U32, in which she contrasted "Fritz's ecstacy [sic]" over Wilhelm with Prince Albert's more blasé attitude toward little babies, and Friedrich's letter to Queen Victoria of 21 May 1859, RA Z71/77.

2. Also the letters from Friedrich to Queen Victoria of 12 March 1859, RA Z71/75, and of 18 May 1859, RA Z71/76.

3. Roger Fulford, ed., *Dearest Child: Letters between Queen Victoria and the Princess Royal, 1858–1861* (New York, 1964), p. 209. See also Victoria's letter to her mother of 18 June 1859 in which she wrote that Wilhelm "is fonder of gentlemen than of ladies. He is particularly fond of Fritz—laughs when he sees him at the other end of the room. I do not think he cares much about me." RA Z8/7.

4. Letter from Victoria to Queen Victoria of 31 March 1861, RA Z7/105.

5. "It is so sad to do and settle *everything* without Fritz," Victoria wrote with her husband away during the waning days of the Franco-Prussian War, "he is so much away that *every*-thing in the House and about the children's education falls upon me. It is more responsibility than is quite fair." Letter to Queen Victoria of 26 November 1870, RA Z25/30.

6. Letters from Victoria to Queen Victoria of 1 April 1865, RA Z17/52, and of 5 April 1865, Roger Fulford, ed., *Your Dear Letter: Private Correspondence of Queen Victoria and the Crown Princess of Prussia, 1865–1871* (London, 1971), p. 22.

7. Wilhelm II, *My Early Life* (New York, 1926), p. 127.

8. Diary entry of 27 January 1871, A. R. Allinson ed., *The War Diary of Emperor Frederick III, 1870–1871* (Westport, 1971), p. 285.

9. Indeed Friedrich's lack of involvement with his family seems to have been typical of Prussian aristocrats. The fact that the experience of paternal neglect was typical for the children of these Prussian fathers does not mean that it was without psychological consequences for them, however.

10. Franz Ayme, *Wilhelm II und seine Erziehung. Aus den Erinnerungen seines französischen Lehrers* (Leipzig, 1898), p. 129.

11. Wilhelm II's marginalia to a report from Eckardstein in London to Bülow of 9 August 1901, PA Bonn, Preussen 1, Nr. 1f, vol. 1.

12. Letter of 25 May 1861, RA Z11/15.

13. Letter of 6 July 1864, RA Z16/60.

14. Letter of 16 January 1869, *Your Dear Letter*, pp. 218–19.

15. RA Z23/11.

16. Letter from Victoria to Queen Victoria of 4 May 1869, RA Z23/43.

17. RA Z23/46.

18. *Your Dear Letter*, p. 236. Victoria's anxiety did not diminish with the passage of years; in 1872 she was still convinced that Wilhelm's participation in a parade had "totally upset his equilibrium . . . it is not very good for him I fear—but we cannot avoid it without having almost a quarrel with the Emperor." Letter from Victoria to Queen Victoria of 11 May 1872, RA Z26/70. Three months later, when Heinrich reached the age of commissioning, Victoria wrote: "To my horror Henry will get a uniform on his Birthday as he is 10 years old, his poor ugly face will look worse than ever and he has grown if possible much plainer still since last year! Willie will have to wear a Russian uniform when the Emperor comes—to my horror. I am of course not asked and all these things are arranged without my having a voice in the matter." Roger Fulford, ed., *Darling Child: Private Correspondence of Queen Victoria and the Crown Princess of Prussia, 1871–1878* (London, 1976), p. 57.

19. Letter to Queen Victoria of 20 May 1869, RA Z78/3.

20. Letter from Victoria to Prince Albert of 5 March 1859, RA Z2/10. Holstein's diary

entry of 27 January 1884, Norman Rich and M. H. Fisher, eds., *The Holstein Papers,* 4 vols. (Cambridge, 1955–1963), II, pp. 67–70.

21. Letter of 28 January 1871, Frederick Ponsonby, ed., *Letters of the Empress Frederick* (New York, 1930), pp. 119–20. Allinson, *Frederick III,* p. 285.

22. Letter from Victoria to Queen Victoria of 17 November 1860, RA Z10/14.

23. Letter from Victoria to Queen Victoria of 27 November 1860, RA Z10/19.

24. Letter from Victoria to Prince Albert of 23 February 1861, RA Z4/8.

25. Letter from Victoria to Queen Victoria of 8 June 1861, RA Z11/20.

26. RA Z12/44.

27. Friedrich reported with pride that already by his first birthday Wilhelm had developed the capacity to observe and imitate. Letter from Friedrich to Queen Victoria and Prince Albert of 6 February 1860, RA Z71/80.

28. Letter from Victoria to Queen Victoria of 1 January 1869, RA Z23/3.

29. Letter of 28 January 1871, RA Z78/25.

30. Letter in English of 2 September 1874, RA Z64/58.

31. *Darling Child,* pp. 164–65.

32. Letter from Prince Wilhelm to Queen Victoria of 29 January 1876, RA Z79/3.

33. Letters from Prince Wilhelm to Queen Victoria of 22 May 1876, RA Z79/18; of 30 December 1877, RA Z79/100; and of 13 November 1878, RA Z79/152.

34. Letters from Wilhelm to Queen Victoria of 30 December 1877, RA Z79/100, and of 13 September 1878, RA Z79/152.

35. Letter from Victoria to Queen Victoria of 12 January 1878, RA J40/150.

36. Letter of 25 May 1878, RA Z79/137.

37. Lamar Cecil, *Wilhelm II: Prince and Emperor, 1859–1900* (Chapel Hill, 1989), pp. 55–66. For Alfred von Waldersee's relationship with Wilhelm, see Heinrich O. Meisner, ed., *Denkwürdigkeiten des General Feldmarschalls Alfred Grafen von Waldersee,* 3 vols. (Stuttgart and Berlin, 1923–25), passim. For Adolf von Bülow's relationship with Wilhelm, see also the memoirs of his brother, Bernhard von Bülow, *Denkwürdigkeiten,* 4 vols. (Berlin, 1930), I, p. 182.

38. Cecil, *Wilhelm II,* p. 60.

39. Count Hugo Lerchenfeld-Koefering, *Erinnerungen und Denkwürdigkeiten* (Berlin, 1935), p. 345.

40. Lamar Cecil, "History as Family Chronicle: Kaiser Wilhelm II and the Dynastic Roots of the Anglo-German Antagonism," John C. G. Röhl and Nicolaus Sombart, eds., *Kaiser Wilhelm II: New Interpretations* (Cambridge, 1982), p. 97.

41. Eulenburg, "Hineinragende Persönlichkeiten," BA Koblenz, Eulenburg Papers, vol. 81, p. 166. Letter from Victoria to Queen Victoria of 17 November 1882, Roger Fulford, ed., *Beloved Mama: Private Correspondence of Queen Victoria and the German Crown Princess, 1878–1885* (London, 1981), p. 121.

42. Wilhelm I quoted in Cecil, "History as Family Chronicle," p. 97. Gelzer's diary entry of 21 June 1884, Walther Peter Fuchs, ed., *Grossherzog Friedrich I. von Baden und die Reichspolitik, 1871–1907,* 4 vols. (Stuttgart, 1968–1980), II, p. 347.

43. Wilhelm II, *My Early Life,* p. 193.

44. Letter from Victoria to Queen Victoria of 1 December 1883, *Beloved Mama,* p. 151.

45. Letter of 2 May 1886, GSA, BPH, Rep. 53, Nr. 45.

46. See, here, Lamar Cecil, *The German Diplomatic Service, 1871–1914* (Princeton, 1976), pp. 206–209, and Cecil, *Wilhelm II,* pp. 80–82 and 85–87.

47. Holstein's diary entry of 22 March 1883, *Holstein Papers,* II, p. 37. Friedrich's fear that Bismarck sought to use Wilhelm against him was not unjustified. See Holstein's diary entry of 3 October 1886 in which he wrote that "Bismarck's plan is to repress the next Kaiser [Friedrich] with Prince Wilhelm." Ibid., pp. 305–307.

48. Report from St. Petersburg of 22 May 1884, *GP,* III, pp. 340–41. See also the report of the German ambassador in St. Petersburg, Schweinitz, to Bismarck of 21 May 1884, ibid., pp. 339–40.

49. Copy of the letter from Wilhelm to Tsar Alexander III of 19 June 1884, GSA, BPH, Rep. 53a, Nr. 5.

50. Holstein's diary entry of 6 June 1884, *Holstein Papers*, II, pp. 153–55. Also the copy of Wilhelm's letter to the Tsar of 19 June 1884, GSA, BPH, Rep. 53a, Nr. 5.

51. Letter from Victoria to Queen Victoria of 11 August 1886, Ponsonby, *Letters*, pp. 206–207.

52. Letter of 12 August 1886, *GP*, V, pp. 55–56.

53. Holstein's diary entry of 19 August 1886, *Holstein Papers*, II, p. 298.

54. Letter of 17 August 1886 (also the editors' footnote to this letter), *GP*, V, p. 57.

55. BA Koblenz, Moritz Busch Papers, vol. 66.

56. Letter from Kaiser Wilhelm I to Bismarck of 13 December 1886, GSA, BPH, Rep. 94. This letter came in response to a letter from Friedrich to Bismarck of 2 December 1886, in which he again expressed his opposition to the decision to send Wilhelm to the Foreign Office, GSA, BPH, Rep. 94.

57. Letter from Wilhelm to Philipp Eulenburg of 11 August 1886, John C. G. Röhl, ed., *Philipp Eulenburgs politische Korrespondenz*, 3 vols. (Boppard-am-Rhein, 1976–1983), I, pp. 191–93. Letter from Victoria to Queen Victoria of 2 June 1887, Ponsonby, *Letters*, p. 238.

58. Diary entry of 17 August 1886, *Holstein Papers*, II, pp. 296–97.

59. Holstein's diary entry of 27 December 1886, ibid., p. 327.

60. Political reflections of the ex-Kaiser Wilhelm II on 14 and 15 January 1927, GSA, BPH, Rep. 53.

61. Political reflections of the ex-Kaiser Wilhelm II on 14 and 15 January 1927, GSA, BPH, Rep. 53.

62. Prince Wilhelm quoted in a letter from Herbert von Bismarck to Otto von Bismarck of 8 October 1886, Walter Bussmann, ed., *Staatssekretär Graf Herbert von Bismarck: Aus seiner politischen Privatkorrespondenz* (Göttingen, 1964), p. 391. In 1884, during Wilhelm's visit to St. Petersburg, he had become friendly with Herbert von Bismarck, at the time a secretary in the German Embassy there and the eldest son of the chancellor. In the course of the next several years, the two became quite close, cementing Wilhelm's alliance with the chancellor. For Wilhelm's friendship with Herbert von Bismarck, see Cecil, *Wilhelm II*, p. 64.

63. Adolf von Wilke, *Alt-Berliner Erinnerungen* (Berlin, 1930), p. 107. See also Waldersee's diary entry of 10 June 1884, *Denkwürdigkeiten Waldersee*, I, pp. 239–40.

64. The reader may have noted the parallel between Wilhelm's attitude toward his father and Victoria's attitude toward her son. Each saw the other as unalterably dependent, did not blame the other directly, and believed all would be well if only they could gain influence over the other. For more on this parallel, see the following chapter.

65. Prince Wilhelm quoted in a letter from Herbert von Bismarck to Otto von Bismarck of 4 October 1886, Bussman, *Herbert von Bismarck*, p. 388.

66. *Holstein Papers*, II, pp. 153–55.

67. Prince Wilhelm quoted in a letter from Herbert von Bismarck to Otto von Bismarck of 4 October 1886, Bussmann, *Herbert von Bismarck*, p. 388.

68. Bülow, *Denkwürdigkeiten*, I, pp. 248–49.

69. Cyril Spencer Fox, ed., *This was Germany; An Observer at the Court of Berlin; Letters of Princess Marie Radziwill to General di Robilant . . . One Time Italian Military Attaché at Berlin* (London, 1937), p. 16.

70. Michael Balfour, *The Kaiser and His Times* (New York, 1972), p. 88.

71. *Denkwürdigkeiten*, I, pp. 248 and 261–65.

72. In raising their children, Wilhelm and Dona also set a public example markedly different from the English orientation of Wilhelm's early life. Although making certain that his children were exposed to the English language and to English values, Wilhelm did so without fanfare. Instead he played up the Germanness of his children's upbringing. In contrast to his mother, who sought to adopt a modest, understated, "English" tone in celebrating family occasions, Wilhelm celebrated events like the christening of his eldest son with a flamboyance in keeping with the ostentatious spirit of the newly unified German Empire. Letter from Victoria to Queen Victoria of 4 June 1882, RA Z36/27. The nurseries were not set up in the

English manner, and the English nurse who had initially been hired to take care of the children was soon replaced by a German woman. Letter from Queen Victoria to Victoria of 22 August 1883, *Beloved Mama*, p. 146.

73. Report of the secretary of state in the Foreign Office, Herbert von Bismarck, of 25 July 1888, *GP*, VI, pp. 326–33.

74. Letter from Victoria to Queen Victoria of 7 March 1887, RA Z39/5.

75. For a typical rendition of this version of the relationship between Wilhelm and his parents and of its inevitable political consequences, see Lerchenfeld-Koefering, *Erinnerungen*, p. 344.

76. Holstein's diary entry of 16 January 1883, *Holstein Papers*, II, pp. 29–30.

77. Lucius von Ballhausen's diary entry of 16 December 1882, Freiherr Lucius von Ballhausen, *Bismarck-Erinnerungen* (Stuttgart, 1920), pp. 243–44.

78. Letter from Prince Wilhelm to Queen Victoria of 28 January 1883, RA Z81/62.

79. Letter of 10 April 1884, RA Z66/31.

80. RA Z81/116.

81. Cecil, *Wilhelm II*, pp. 104–107.

82. General von Waldersee, for example. Holstein's diary entry of 18 February 1883, *Holstein Papers*, II, pp. 34–35.

83. Ballhausen, *Bismarck-Erinnerungen*, pp. 243–44.

84. Sidney Lee, *King Edward VII: A Biography*, 2 vols. (New York, 1925), I, p. 478.

85. Letter of 13 December 1882, RA L1/109.

86. See in this context Wilhelm's proud description of his participation in the English quadrille at the upcoming costume ball in a letter to Queen Victoria of 26 December 1882. RA Z81/56.

87. Holstein's diary entry of 18 February 1883, *Holstein Papers*, II, pp. 34–35.

88. Holstein's diary entry of 6 January 1884, ibid., pp. 46–47.

89. Ibid.

90. Holstein's diary entry of 17 November 1884, ibid., pp. 167–69.

91. Holstein's diary entry of 18 February 1883, ibid., pp. 34–35. The accuracy of these observations on the relations between Prince Wilhelm and his parents is less important in the present context than in the fact that these observations accurately reflected the image of those relations held by the Prussian elite.

92. Diary entry of 12 April 1885, ibid., p. 190. Already by mid-1883 Wilhelm's popularity had grown at the expense of his father to such an extent that Friedrich became depressed and apathetic. He apparently even contemplated renouncing his claim to the throne in favor of his eldest son. Gelzer's diary entry of 5 June 1883, *Grossherzog Friedrich I. von Baden*, II, pp. 206–207. Gelzer's diary entries of 17 June 1883 and 21 June 1885 testify to Wilhelm's popularity not only in elite circles but with the general public. Ibid., pp. 207–208 and 347.

93. For a consideration of the diplomatic dimension of the Battenberg affair, see Norman Rich, *Friedrich von Holstein: Politics and Diplomacy in the Era of Bismarck and Wilhelm II*, 2 vols. (Cambridge, 1965), pp. 150–61, 180–82, 186–92, 204–207, 222–25, and 239–42; for the political and personal dimensions of the affair, see Cecil, *Wilhelm II*, pp. 82–87.

94. Letter from Queen Victoria to Empress Augusta of 27 July 1883, Hector Bolitho, ed., *The Letters of queen Victoria: From the Archives of the House of Brandenburg-Prussia* (New Haven, 1938), pp. 248–50.

95. Diary entry of 14 April 1884, *Holstein Papers*, II, pp. 111–15. Since both Bernhard von Meiningen and Alexander von Battenberg were lower-born than Victoria's children, it was thought that they were likely to be especially dependent on Victoria—even by her daughter Charlotte (see note 67 of Chapter 3).

96. See Chapter 2, especially note 72.

97. Letter from Queen Victoria to Empress Augusta of 27 July 1883, *From the Archives*, pp. 248–50; as well as Holstein's diary entries of 14 April 1884 and 4 May 1884, *Holstein Papers*, II, pp. 111–15 and 134–37 respectively.

98. *Beloved Mama*, pp. 165–66. Also the letter from Queen Victoria to Victoria of 21 May

1884, ibid., pp. 166–67; Victoria's reply of 23 May 1884, RA Z30/22; and her letter to Marie Dönhoff of 27 December 1885, BA Koblenz, Bülow Papers, vol. 169.

99. Letters from Herbert to Otto von Bismarck of 9 and 10 September 1885, Bussmann, *Herbert von Bismarck*, pp. 310–12 and 314; Holstein's diary entry of 4 May 1884, *Holstein Papers*, pp. 134–37, and also of 12 May 1885, ibid., pp. 197–98, in which Friedrich is reported to have poured out his heart "with disparaging" comments about the Battenbergs. He was said to be particularly distressed that a Battenberg would become the son-in-law of Queen Victoria. (A view confirmed by the letter from Queen Victoria to Victoria of 10 January 1885 in *Beloved Mama*, pp. 178–79.) It seems most likely that Friedrich feared that Battenberg's low birth would diminish his own stature.

100. Holstein's diary entries of 12 May 1884, *Holstein Papers*, pp. 143–44; of 26 May 1884, ibid., pp. 152–53; of 6 June 1884, ibid., pp. 153–55; and of 11 August 1885, ibid., pp. 217–21.

101. Holstein's diary entry of 12 May 1884, ibid., pp. 143–44. Distress over Victoria's promotion of English interests in the Reich and specifically of the Battenberg marriage prompted Duke Ernest II of Sachsen-Coburg-Gotha to publish an anonymous brochure in Zurich in 1886 entitled "Co-Regents and Foreign Hands in Germany," in which he denounced "female politics" and "ladies' campaigns." Editor's note to the letter from Grand Duke Friedrich II of Baden to Duke Ernest II of Sachsen-Coburg-Gotha of 6 February 1886, *Grossherzog Friedrich II. von Baden,* II, p. 376.

102. Holstein's diary entry of 5 July 1885, *Holstein Papers,* pp. 211–14.

103. Holstein's diary entry of 16 March 1885, ibid., pp. 176–77.

104. BA Koblenz, Bülow Papers, vol. 169.

105. RA Add. Mss. A15/4374.

106. RA Z37/56.

107. Letter from Wilhelm to Philipp Eulenburg of 8 January 1887, *Eulenburgs Korrespondenz,* I, pp. 207–208. Lamar Cecil, "History as Family Chronicle," p. 100.

108. Ibid., p. 101. For other expressions of Wilhelm's hatred toward England, his English relatives, and his mother, see his letters to Eulenburg of 8 January 1887 and 10 April 1887, *Eulenburgs Korrespondenz,* I, pp. 207–208 and 221–22 respectively.

109. Letter from Wilhelm to Eulenburg of 11 August 1886, ibid., pp. 191–93.

110. During this period when he was publicly Anglophobic, Wilhelm was drawing pictures of British warships and sending them to his grandmother. Letter from Wilhelm to Queen Victoria of 22 May 1885, RA Z82/23.

111. Letter to Victoria of 13 February 1885, *Beloved Mama,* p. 183. See also Queen Victoria's letter to her daughter of 14 January 1884, ibid., p. 179.

112. Lamar Cecil, "History as Family Chronicle," p. 101; Holstein's diary entry of 16 October 1885, *Holstein Papers,* II, pp. 254–55.

113. Letter from Victoria to her mother of 30 October 1885, RA Z30/26.

114. Report from Herbert von Bismarck to his father of 22 May 1884, *GP,* III, pp. 340–341; and report from Schweinitz to Bismarck of 21 May 1884, ibid., pp. 339–40. Report from Herbert von Bismarck to Kaiser Wilhelm I of 2 September 1886, ibid., V, pp. 57–61; and report from Bülow to Bismarck of 22 September 1886, ibid., pp. 63–65.

115. Copy of letter of 25 May 1884, GSA, BPH, Rep. 53a, Nr. 5.

116. Copy of letter of 19 June 1884, GSA, BPH, Rep. 53a, Nr. 5. Here again the parallel between Wilhelm and Victoria should be noted: both had the tendency to see those to whom they were attached but who had disappointed them as dependent on the wrong people. For Victoria, her eldest children were "in the pocket" of Bismarck et al.; for Wilhelm, his father was dependent on his mother who, in turn, was "in the pocket" of Alexander of Battenberg. See, here, note 64 of this chapter and the following chapter.

117. Copy of the letter of 13 March 1885, GSA, BPH, Rep. 53a, Nr. 5.

118. Copies of letters of 6 and 20 May 1885, GSA, BPH, Rep. 53a, Nr. 5.

119. Diary entry of Carl von Wedel of 20 March 1890, Count Erhard von Wedel, ed., *Zwischen Kaiser und Kanzler: Aufzeichnungen des General-adjutanten Grafen Carl von Wedel aus den Jahren 1890–1914* (Leipzig, 1943), p. 42.

120. Report from Schweinitz to Herbert von Bismarck of 9 December 1886, *GP,* V, p. 93.
121. Report from Wedel to the German ambassador in Vienna, Prince Heinrich VII Reuss, of 15 January 1887, ibid., pp. 15!–53.
122. Report of the German ambassador in London, Count Paul von Hatzfeldt-Wildenburg, to Bismarck of 12 November 1887, with marginalia of Herbert and Otto von Bismarck, ibid., IV, pp. 368–73. Abstract of the report of the British ambassador in Berlin of 19 November 1887, RA I55/78. Letter from Otto von Bismarck to Lord Salisbury of 22 November 1887, Bernhard Schwertfeger, ed., *Die diplomatischen Akten des Auswärtigen Amtes, 1871–1914,* 5 vols. with two additional vols. (Berlin, 1923–1925), IV, pp. 288–91 (see also Chapter 6). Letter from Bismarck to Salisbury of 22 November 1887, *GP,* IV, p. 380.
123. Letter from Eulenburg to Holstein of 5 August 1886, *Eulenburgs Korrespondenz,* I, pp. 190–91. See also the letter from Eulenburg to Holstein of 28 February 1887, ibid., pp. 219–21. For Holstein's concern about Wilhelm's "foolish hatred of England," see his diary entry of 25 April 1888, *Holstein Papers,* II, pp. 273–74.
124. Wilhelm's toast to the Diet of 8 February 1888, Karl Wippermann, ed., *Deutscher Geschichtskalender,* 49 vols. (Leipzig, 1885–1933), 1888 (I), p. 3.
125. Rather than making individual references to the principal secondary works relevant to the next two sections of this chapter, readers interested in a detailed history of Friedrich's illness and the medical and political controversy surrounding it are advised to consult Hans-Joachim Wolf, *Die Krankheit Friedrichs III. und ihre Wirkung auf die deutsche und englische Öffentlichkeit* (Berlin-Lichterfelde, 1958) and Michael Freund, *Das Drama der 99 Tage: Krankheit und Tod Friedrichs III.* (Cologne and Berlin, 1966). For a good synthesis of these events, see Cecil, *Wilhelm II,* pp. 88–109. For a detailed and useful consideration of German political history from early 1887 to Wilhelm II's accession, one that integrates the medical controversies and the divisions in the royal family into the political conflicts of the period, see J. Alden Nichols, *The Year of the Three Kaisers: Bismarck and the German Succession, 1887–1888* (Urbana and Chicago, 1987).
126. Letter from Victoria to Queen Victoria of 7 March 1887, RA Z39/5.
127. Holstein's diary entry of 17 May 1887 reveals that he was already fully informed about Bergmann's diagnosis and recommendation. *Holstein Papers,* II, p. 343. Victoria's letter to Queen Victoria of 17 May 1887, RA Z39/23.
128. As she had been unable to tolerate neck surgery on her four-year-old son, Victoria now was unable to contemplate the prospect of surgery to remove a substantial portion of her husband's larynx, an operation that would leave him mute. Years later when it was discovered that she had cancer herself, Victoria was adamant in opposing surgery, and she again sought to prevent anyone from learning about her condition. Baron Hugo von Reischach, *Unter drei Kaisern* (Berlin, 1925), pp. 203–206.
129. Letter of 17 May 1887, RA Z39/23.
130. Letter from Victoria to Queen Victoria of 20 May 1887, RA Z39/25.
131. According to Jain I. Lin, Virchow's rigid adherence to a traditional view of cancer prevented him from being able to recognize the presence of a malignancy. Lin assigns Virchow's misdiagnosis ultimate responsibility for the controversy over Friedrich's medical treatment, a point overlooked at the time by all the participants in their eagerness to turn the medical controversy into a national dispute. "Virchow's Pathological Reports on Friedrich III's Cancer," *New England Journal of Medicine* 311 (1984), pp. 1261–64.
132. Letter from Victoria to Queen Victoria of 9 June 1887, RA Z39/36.
133. Holstein's diary entry of 17 May 1887, *Holstein Papers,* II, p. 343.
134. Holstein's diary entry of 20 May 1887, ibid., pp. 343–44.
135. Letter from Victoria to Queen Victoria of 24 May 1887, RA Z39/27.
136. RA Z39/34.
137. Letter from Friedrich to Queen Victoria of 30 May 1887, RA Z71/103.
138. Letter from Victoria to Queen Victoria of 30 May 1887, RA Z39/30.
139. Letter from Victoria to Queen Victoria of 3 June 1887, RA Z39/34; postscript to letter from Victoria to Queen Victoria of 4 June 1887, RA Z39/36; and letter from Victoria to Queen Victoria of 11 June 1887, RA Z39/38.

140. Letters from Victoria to Queen Victoria of 30 May 1887, RA Z39/30; of 31 May 1887, RA Z39/31; of 2 June 1887, RA Z39/33; and letter from Friedrich to Queen Victoria of 30 May 1887, RA Z71/103.

141. Extracts of letters from Queen Victoria to Victoria of 4 June 1887, RA Add. Mss. U32, and of 7 June 1887, RA Add. Mss. U32. Also, letters from Queen Victoria to Victoria of 31 May 1887, RA Add. Mss. U32, and to Friedrich of 2 June 1887, RA Z66/69. Letter from Victoria to Queen Victoria of 5 June 1887, RA Z39/35.

142. Letter from Victoria to Queen Victoria of 15 June 1887, RA Z39/40.

143. Letter from Hedwig von Bruehl, lady-in-waiting to Victoria, to Holstein of 26 July 1887, *Holstein Papers,* III, pp. 218–19.

144. Ibid. and letter from Hugo von Radolinski to Holstein of 4 July 1887, ibid., III, p. 214.

145. Letter from Bruehl to Holstein of 26 July 1887, ibid., pp. 218–19. Letter from Queen Victoria to Lord Salisbury of 25 August 1887, RA Z66/75. Lord Salisbury urged the queen to wait before bestowing a knighthood on Mackenzie until it was clear that Friedrich had recovered completely (letter of 26 August 1887, RA Z66/76), but the queen insisted that the knighthood be bestowed right away (letter to Salisbury of 26 August 1887, RA Z66/77). Friedrich responded to Queen Victoria's gesture with effusive expressions of gratitude (letter of 27 August 1887, RA Z66/79).

146. Letter probably from Lyncker to Radolinski of 24 September 1887, *Holstein Papers,* II, pp. 349–52. Even Mackenzie apparently became concerned that Victoria's refusal to acknowledge Friedrich's illness was having a harmful effect upon his health. Letter probably from Lyncker to Radolinski of 28 September 1887, ibid., pp. 352–53.

147. Ibid., pp. 348–49.

148. Letter from Victoria to Queen Victoria of 17 October 1887, Ponsonby, *Letters,* p. 249.

149. Letter of 6 October 1887, *Eulenburgs Korrespondenz,* I, pp. 244–45.

150. Letter from Wilhelm to King Albert of Saxony on 22 October 1887, GSA, BPH, Rep. 53, Nr. 376.

151. Article of 14 October 1887.

152. Letters from Victoria to Queen Victoria of 17 October 1887, RA Z38/74, and of 27 October 1887, RA Z38/80.

153. Letter from Victoria to Queen Victoria of 6 November 1887, RA Z38/83.

154. Letter from Victoria to Queen Victoria of 9 November 1887, Ponsonby, *Letters,* pp. 252–53, and letter from Victoria to Marie Dönhoff of 3 December 1887, BA Koblenz, Bülow Papers, vol. 170.

155. Letter of 15 November 1887, RA Z38/87. Portions of this letter are published in Ponsonby, *Letters,* pp. 256–57.

156. Wilhelm II, *My Early Life,* p. 288.

157. Letter from Victoria to Queen Victoria of 18 November 1887, RA Z38/91. See also her comments to her mother on 11 November 1887, "To say the truth, I do *not* think Fritz *realized* the whole meaning of what he [Virchow, the pathologist] said." RA Z38/85.

158. RA Z66/109.

159. Wilhelm II, *My Early Life,* p. 335.

160. Letter from Victoria to Queen Victoria of 21 November 1887, RA Z38/92, portions of which have been published in Ponsonby, *Letters,* pp. 262–63; letter from Hugo von Radolinski to Holstein of 21 November 1887, *Holstein Papers,* II, pp. 228–30; and Wilhelm II, *My Early Life,* p. 292.

161. Diary entry of 11 November 1887, *Holstein Papers,* II, pp. 356–57.

162. Holstein's diary entry of 14 November 1887, ibid., pp. 357–58. See also Holstein's diary entries of 9 and 18 November, ibid., pp. 355–56 and 358–59, and the letter from Victoria to Queen Victoria of 18 November 1887, RA Z38/91.

163. Letter from Victoria to Queen Victoria of 14 December 1887, RA Z38/103.

164. Letter from Victoria to Queen Victoria of 29 November 1887, RA Z38/97.

165. Letters from Victoria to Queen Victoria of 12 February 1888, RA Z40/16; of 15 February 1888, RA Z40/17; and of 28 February 1888, RA Z40/24.

166. Already on the 28 November Victoria felt the need to defend herself to her mother for having resisted the idea of surgery in May. RA Z38/96.

167. Letters from Victoria to Queen Victoria of 2 December 1887, RA Z38/98, and of 8 December 1887, RA Z38/101. Memo from Queen Victoria to Sir Henry Ponsonby of 13 December 1887, RA Add. Mss. A12/1509.

168. Letters from Victoria to Queen Victoria of 18 December 1887, RA Z38/106, and of 18 February 1888, RA Z40/19. See also the letter from Radolinski to Holstein of 28 February 1888, *Holstein Papers,* III, pp. 265–66.

169. Letter from Radolinski to Holstein of 12 February 1888, ibid., pp. 257–61.

170. Letter from Wilhelm to Queen Victoria of 22 December 1887, RA Z82/120.

171. Letter from Wilhelm to Eulenburg of 19 February 1888, *Eulenburgs Korrespondenz,* I, pp. 269–70. Letter from Wilhelm to Prince Albrecht von Preussen of 29 February 1888, GSA, BPH, Rep. 53, Nr. 266.

172. Radolinski wrote to Holstein on 23 November 1887: "I am terribly sorry for the poor woman. She keeps up his morale, but when she is alone she gives way to tears. Only she should not smile so much in public. It does her harm and one cannot help thinking that she does not feel deeply. Which is not so." *Holstein Papers,* III, pp. 230–31. But as Eulenburg wrote to Georg Count von Werthern on 29 November 1887: "The hatred for the Crown Princess grows from day to day." *Eulenburgs Korrespondenz,* I, pp. 251–53.

173. Letter from Victoria to Queen Victoria of 16 November 1887, RA Z38/89. Various German newspaper reports between 14 and 28 February, *Deutscher Geschichtskalender,* 1888 (I), pp. 8–11.

174. RA Z40/23.

175. Letter from Victoria to Queen Victoria of 1 March 1888, RA Z40/25. Letter from Radolinski to Holstein of 2 March 1888, *Holstein Papers,* III, pp. 266–68.

176. Letter from Mlle. de Perpigna to Lady Emily Ampthill of 3 March 1888, RA Z66/161.

177. Letter from Radolinski to Holstein of 6 March 1888, *Holstein Papers,* III, pp. 269–71. Letter from Victoria to Queen Victoria of 6 March 1888, Ponsonby, *Letters,* pp. 278–79.

178. Letter from Victoria to Queen Victoria of 2 March 1888, RA Z40/26.

179. Newspaper editorials of 2, 5, and 10 March 1888, *Deutscher Geschichtskalender,* 1888 (I), p. 12.

180. For a summary of Friedrich's illness and reign, see Rich, *Holstein,* pp. 226–28 and 235–42; Cecil, *Wilhelm II,* pp. 110–23; and Otto Pflanze, *Bismarck and the Development of Germany,* 3 vols. (Princeton, 1990), III, Chapter 13. For the fullest treatment, see Nicholls, *Year.*

181. Letter of 16 March 1888, RA Z41/27.

182. "Political Reflections of Kaiser Wilhelm II" in exile, GSA, BPH, Rep. 53, Nr. 165 (1). In his memoirs, Wilhelm described the reaction to Puttkamer's dismissal as being one of "a terrible rage against my mother." At the time, Wilhelm blamed his mother for Puttkamer's fall. Letter from Wilhelm to the grand duke of Baden of 10 June 1888, *Grossherzog Friedrich II. von Baden,* II, p. 554.

183. Letter from Victoria to Queen Victoria of 12 May 1888, RA Z41/47. Holstein's diary entry of 11 April 1888, *Holstein Papers,* II, pp. 368–70.

184. Holstein's diary entry of 15 May 1888, ibid., pp. 376–77. Friedrich was unable to prohibit the issuance of passbooks for Alsace or suppress a pamphlet put out by the group around Stoecker denouncing Friedrich and extolling Wilhelm as the hope of the future. Letter from Victoria to Queen Victoria of 4 June 1888, RA Z41/57.

185. PA Bonn, Preussen 1, Nr. 1c *secr.,* vol. 1.

186. That threat was confirmed three days earlier by Wilhelm himself in a letter to his great-uncle, Duke Ernest II of Sachsen-Coburg-Gotha. In his letter, Wilhelm praised the article that the duke had published anonymously two years before, denouncing Victoria's efforts on behalf of Battenberg and English interests generally, entitled "Co-Regents and Foreign Hands in Germany." "The devil take them," Wilhelm concluded. *Grossherzog Friedrich II. von Baden,* II, pp. 525–26.

187. Holstein's diary entry of 27 March 1888, *Holstein Papers,* II, pp. 365–66. Adolf Her-

mann Marschall von Bieberstein, then Badenese envoy to Berlin, to Ludwig Turban of 9 April 1888, *Grossherzog Friedrich II. von Baden,* II, pp. 528–32.

188. Diary entry of 15 May 1888, *Holstein Papers,* II, pp. 376–77.

189. For a consideration of the press controversy surrounding Friedrich's illness and its treatment, see Kurt Koszyk, *Deutsche Presse im 19. Jahrhundert: Geschichte der deutschen Presse,* 4 vols. (Berlin, 1966), II, pp. 246–47.

190. Including *Worth, The Daily Telegraph, The British Medical Journal, The Weekly Dispatch, The Times, The Sunday-Times,* and *The Pall Mall Gazette* and *Die neue Stettiner Zeitung, Germania, Die Berliner Volkszeitung,* and *Die Schlesische Zeitung.*

191. Including *Das deutsche Tageblatt, Die Kölnische Zeitung, Die Kreuzzeitung, Die allgemeine medizinische Zentral Zeitung, Die Hamburger Nachrichten, Die deutsche medizinische Wochenschrift,* and *Die Berliner klinische Wochenschrift.*

192. *Deutscher Geschichtskalender,* 1888 (I), pp. 191–208. This source contains lengthy quotations and synopses of the newspaper debate, including the newspapers listed above and many others as well.

193. On 9 April 1888, Friedrich bestowed a medal on Mackenzie. On 12 April 1888, Queen Victoria gave a present to Mackenzie. And on 15 April 1888, Friedrich and Victoria gave Mackenzie a golden bowl. Ibid., p. 194.

194. Holstein's diary entry of 27 March 1888, *Holstein Papers,* II, pp. 365–66. Bogdan Graf von Hutten-Czapski, *Sechzig Jahre Politik und Gesellschaft,* 2 vols. (Berlin, 1936), I, p. 142.

195. *My Early Life,* p. 300. Wilhelm's account in his memoirs is confirmed by his letter to his uncle, Friedrich II, grand duke of Baden, of 29 May 1888, *Grossherzog Friedrich II. von Baden,* II, pp. 546–47.

196. *Eulenburgs Korrespondenz,* I, p. 284.

197. Diary entry of 29 April 1888, *Zwischen Kaiser und Kanzler,* pp. 29–30.

198. Memo, Queen Victoria of 9 April 1888, RA Add. Mss. A25/757; letters from Queen Victoria to Victoria of 10 March 1888, RA Add. Mss. U32; and of 10 April 1888, RA Add. Mss. U32.

199. RA Add. Mss. U32.

200. Memo from Queen Victoria to Sir Henry Ponsonby of 9 April 1888, RA Add. A12/1565. The queen's sentiments were shared by Wilhelm's other English relatives. Letters from Arthur, Duke of Connaught, to Queen Victoria of 25 and 26 April 1888, RA Z184/28 and 29.

201. Memo from Lord Salisbury to Queen Victoria of 21 April 1888, George Earle Buckle, ed., *The Letters of Queen Victoria: 1886–1901,* 3 vols. (New York, 1930), I, pp. 397–99. Holstein's diary entry of 25 April 1888, *Holstein Papers,* II, pp. 373–74.

202. Carl von Wedel's diary entry of 29 April 1888, *Zwischen Kaiser und Kanzler,* pp. 29–30. Letter from Bismarck to the German ambassador in Vienna, Prince Heinrich VII Reuss, of 28 April 1888, *GP,* IV, pp. 177–78.

203. Letter from the British ambassador in Berlin, Sir Edward Malet, to Lord Salisbury of 28 April 1888, Ponsonby, *Letters,* p. 304. Carl von Wedel's diary entry of 29 April 1888, *Zwischen Kaiser und Kanzler,* pp. 29–30. Diary entry of 25 April 1888, *Holstein Papers,* II, pp. 373–74.

204. Letter from Queen Victoria to Victoria of 27 April 1888, RA Add. Mss. U32.

205. See, here, Cecil, *Wilhelm II,* pp. 115–18, and Rich, *Holstein,* pp. 216–20.

206. Wilhelm's marginalia to report from Prince Heinrich VII Reuss to Bismarck of 28 April 1888, *GP,* VI, pp. 301–302. Wilhelm's marginalia with Bismarck's marginal responses to report from Bismarck to Reuss of 3 May 1888, ibid., pp. 302–303.

207. Holstein's diary entry of 13 May 1888, *Holstein Papers,* II, pp. 374–76.

208. Letter of 9 May 1888, *GP,* VI, pp. 304–307.

209. Reprinted from Bismarck's *Gedanken und Erinnerungen,* ibid., pp. 307–309.

210. *Denkwürdigkeiten Waldersee,* I, pp. 349, 387, 391, and 395–99.

211. During his reign Wilhelm would often shift from Anglophobia to Anglophilia following positive interaction with England or his English relatives.

212. In fact, in explaining his dismissal of Bismarck to the British ambassador, Sir Edward Malet, Wilhelm contended that it was not so much differences over foreign or domestic policy that had led to the break between the two men but the fact that the chancellor had treated him "like a schoolboy." Quoted in Cecil, *Wilhelm II*, p. 169. The Kaiser expressed similar sentiments to the Austrian emperor, Franz Joseph, claiming that he had determined to get rid of Bismarck "when he took his master for a nobody and tried to degrade him to a retainer." Quoted in ibid., p. 170. Wilhelm's comparable reactions when he felt himself dominated and degraded diplomatically are considered in Chapters 9 and 10.

213. Letter from Wilhelm probably to Prince Albrecht of Prussia on 12 June 1888, GSA, BPH, Rep. 53, Nr. 349.

214. Official bulletin of 14 June 1888, *Deutscher Geschichtskalender,* 1888 (I), p. 204.

215. Ponsonby, *Letters,* pp. 315–16.

216. Telegram of 15 June 1888, *The Letters of Queen Victoria: 1886–1901,* I, p. 417.

217. Letter from Edward Malet to Bismarck of 18 June 1888, PA Bonn, Preussen 1, Nr. 1c, vol. 1.

218. Telegram from Malet to Queen Victoria of 14 June 1888 at 11:45 P.M., RA Z68/97.

219. Holstein's diary entry of 17 April 1888, *Holstein Papers,* II, pp. 370–72.

220. Kürenberg, *The Kaiser,* pp. 65–66.

221. Political reflections of ex-Kaiser Wilhelm II on 14 and 15 January 1927 with Wilhelm's marginalia, GSA, BPH, Rep. 53, Nr. 165.

222. Letters from Victoria to Queen Victoria of 3 June 1887, RA Z39/34; of 11 June 1887, RA Z39/38; and of 20 June 1888, RA Z41/66.

223. Letter from Edward Malet, the British ambassador in Berlin, to Queen Victoria on 14 May 1888, RA Z68/71. Even before Wilhelm's threat, Victoria in a letter of 2 May 1888 told her mother she was planning to take this action. RA Z41/42.

224. Letter from Malet to Queen Victoria of 14 May 1888, RA Z68/71.

225. Letter from Victoria to Queen Victoria of 20 June 1888, RA Z41/66.

226. Letter from Victoria to Queen Victoria of 20 June 1888, RA Z41/66, and memo from Victoria of 20 June 1888, RA Z41/67.

227. Letter from Malet to Queen Victoria of 16 June 1888, RA Z68/106. Letter from the minister of the royal house, Carl von Wedel, to Bismarck of 29 August 1888, PA Bonn, Preussen 1, Nr. 1c, *secr.,* vol. 1.

228. But see the letter from Wedel to Bismarck cited in the previous note. Telegram from Lord Salisbury to Queen Victoria of 20 July 1888, RA Z68/162. For the history of Friedrich and Victoria's personal papers, see Cecil, *Wilhelm II,* pp. 121–23.

229. Letter from Malet to Queen Victoria of 16 June 1888, RA Z68/106.

230. Draft of a letter from Queen Victoria to Wilhelm II of 3 July 1888 and the letter from Wilhelm II to Queen Victoria of 6 July 1888, *The Letters of Queen Victoria: 1886–1901,* I, pp. 423–25. Letter from Victoria to Queen Victoria of 28 September 1888, Ponsonby, *Letters,* pp. 347–48.

231. Letter to Queen Victoria of 9 July 1888, RA Z68/146.

232. Letter from Victoria to Queen Victoria of 28 September 1888, Ponsonby, *Letters,* pp. 347–48. In the letter, Victoria appeared more distressed by her son's neglect of her than by his apparent lack of respect for his father. See also Queen Victoria's letter to the Prince of Wales of 24 July 1888 in which she described Wilhelm's failure to mourn Friedrich publicly as "sickening. . . . indecent and very unfeeling!" *Letters of Queen Victoria: 1886–1901,* I, pp. 433–34.

233. Draft of a letter from Queen Victoria to Wilhelm II of 3 July 1888, ibid., pp. 423–24.

234. Letter from Wilhelm II to Queen Victoria of 6 July 1888, ibid., p. 424.

235. Ibid., p. 425.

236. Georg Hinzpeter, *Kaiser Wilhelm II. Eine Skizze nach der Natur gezeichnet* (Bielefeld, 1888), p. 10.

237. Ibid., p. 12.

238. Bülow, *Denkwürdigkeiten,* I, p. 173.

239. PA Bonn, Deutschland 125, Nr. 2, vol. 1.

240. Extracts from Queen Victoria's journal of 27 June 1888, *Letters of Queen Victoria: 1886–1901,* I, p. 421.

241. See in this context Wilhelm's plan dating from April 1888 to replace the older generation of generals with the younger generals that he believed would be more effective in a two-front war. Diary entry of Carl von Wedel of 29 April 1888, *Zwischen Kaiser und Kanzler,* pp. 29–30. See also Cecil, *Wilhelm II,* pp. 124–25 and 200–201. In this plan can already be seen the tendency that would result some two years later in Wilhelm's dismissal of Bismarck. For the events leading up to and including the dismissal of Bismarck, see ibid., pp. 124–70, and especially Pflanze, *Bismarck,* III, Book Four.

242. Report of the secretary of state in the Foreign Office, Herbert von Bismarck, of 25 July 1888, *GP,* VI, pp. 326–33.

243. Copy of a report from Count Rantzau to the Foreign Office of 28 August 1888, PA Bonn, England 81, Nr. 1a, vol. 1. Draft of a letter from Berchem, undersecretary of state in the Foreign Office, to Prince Heinrich VII Reuss, German ambassador to Vienna, of 6 September 1888, PA Bonn, England 81, Nr. 1a, vol. 1.

244. *Deutscher Geschichtskalender,* 1888 (II), p. 2.

245. Report from Count Rantzau to the Foreign Office of 4 September 1888, PA Bonn, England 81, Nr. 1a, vol. 1.

246. Reports from Prince Heinrich VII Reuss in Vienna to Bismarck of 9 September 1888 and of 13 September 1888, PA Bonn, England 81, Nr. 1a, vol. 1.

247. Copy of a letter from Arthur Ellis to Colonel Swaine of 12 September 1888, PA Bonn, England 81, Nr. 1a *secr.,* vol. 1. The letter was given to Wilhelm by the British military attaché in Berlin, and it contains his marginal comments.

248. Paul M. Kennedy, *The Rise of the Anglo-German Antagonism, 1860–1914* (London, 1982), p. 195. For more on this episode, see Cecil, *Wilhelm II,* pp. 267–69.

249. Memo of 13 October 1888, *The Letters of Queen Victoria: 1886–1901,* I, p. 439.

250. Copy of a letter from Queen Victoria to Salisbury of 15 October 1888, ibid., pp. 140–41.

Chapter 5

1. Norman Rich and M. H. Fisher, eds., *The Holstein Papers,* 4 vols. (Cambridge, 1955–1963), II, p. 178; Wilhelm II, *My Early Life* (New York, 1926), p. 70.

2. "Kaiser Wilhelm II," BA Koblenz, Eulenburg Papers, vol. 80.

3. Bernhard Fürst von Bülow, *Denkwürdigkeiten,* 4 vols. (Berlin, 1930), I, pp. 56–61, 518–19, and 634; "Kaiser Wilhelm II," BA Koblenz, Eulenburg Papers, vol. 80.

4. Wilhelm II, *My Early Life,* pp. 19, 57, and 59.

5. Bülow, *Denkwürdigkeiten,* I, p. 243; Otto von Bismarck, *Gedanken und Erinnerungen* (Stuttgart and Berlin, 1928), p. 121; and Wilhelm's marginalia to Bismarck's *Gedanken und Erinnerungen,* GSA, BPH, Rep. 57, Nr. 170.

6. Victoria's letters to Queen Victoria of 8 June 1861, RA Z11/20, and of 31 May 1865, Roger Fulford, ed., *Your Dear Letter: Private Correspondence of Queen Victoria and the Crown Princess of Prussia, 1865–1871* (London, 1971), pp. 28–29.

7. Wilhelm's letters to Eulenburg of 28 August and 4 September 1888 in John C. G. Röhl, ed., *Philipp Eulenburgs politische Korrespondenz,* 3 vols. (Boppard-am-Rhein, 1976–1983), I, pp. 310–11.

8. See Isabel V. Hull's *The Entourage of Kaiser Wilhelm II, 1888–1918* (Cambridge, 1982); Wilhelm Deist's articles, "Die Armee in Staat und Gesellschaft, 1890–1914," Michael Stürmer, ed., *Das kaiserliche Deutschland* (Düsseldorf, 1970), and "Kaiser Wilhelm II in the Context of his Military Entourage," John C. G. Röhl and Nicolaus Sombart, eds., *Kaiser Wilhelm II: New Interpretations* (Cambridge, 1982), pp. 169–92; Manfred Messerschmidt, *Militär und Politik in der Bismarckzeit und im Wilhelminischen Deutschland,* Erträge der

Forschung, vol. 43 (Darmstadt, 1975); and John C. G. Röhl, *Germany Without Bismarck: The Crisis of Government in the Second Reich, 1890–1900* (Berkeley, 1967).

9. See Hull, *Entourage;* Röhl, "Einleitung" to *Eulenburgs Korrespondenz, I,* pp. 35–53; Röhl, "The Emperor's New Clothes: A Character Sketch of Kaiser Wilhelm II," and Sombart, "The Kaiser in his Epoch: Some Reflexions on Wilhelmine Society, Sexuality and Culture," *Kaiser Wilhelm II,* pp. 23–61 and 287–312, respectively.

10. In addition to Eulenburg and Bülow cited above, see Mary Theresa Olivia Princess of Pless, *Daisy, Princess of Pless by Herself* (London, 1928), pp. 225, 265, and 269.

11. Graf Robert Zedlitz-Trützschler, *Zwölf Jahre am deutschen Kaiserhof* (Berlin and Leipzig, 1924), p. 236; Cyril Spencer Fox, ed., *This was Germany; An Observer at the Court of Berlin; Letters of Princess Marie Radziwill to General di Robilant . . . One Time Military Attaché at Berlin* (London, 1937), pp. 30–31; and "Die Nordlandreise, 1903: in Briefen an Fürstin Augusta zu Eulenburg-Hertefeld," BA Koblenz, Eulenburg Papers, vol. 74.

12. For more on the homosexuality of the men around the Kaiser and the Eulenburg scandal, see Hull, *Entourage,* pp. 57–63 and 130–45; Hull, "Kaiser Wilhelm II and the 'Liebenberg Circle'," *Kaiser Wilhelm II,* pp. 193–220; and Röhl's "Einleitung" to *Eulenburgs Korrespondenz, I,* pp. 35–53.

13. There is evidence to suggest that already as a little boy Wilhelm viewed his father as an object of romantic affection, and his campaign to win his father away from the influence of his mother had the character of a courtship. See Victoria's letter to Queen Victoria of 8 December 1861, RA Z12/44, quoted in Chapter 4. Wilhelm's campaign to win Friedrich away from Victoria would be described in psychoanalytic terms as manifesting a "negative Oedipus complex."

14. For Wilhelm's efforts to exclude women from his environment, see Eulenburg's letter to Holstein of 1 August 1890, *Holstein Papers,* III, pp. 352–54. See also Wilhelm's letter to Eulenburg of 28 August 1888 in which the Kaiser expressed his pleasure over his visit to Copenhagen. After describing the "beautiful women telephone operators" who had strewn flowers in his path and "a pretty red-haired woman with a dazzling tint! Which I admire especially! What more could one want? Answer: Darkness and a military encampment!" *Eulenburgs Korrespondenz,* I, p. 310. Wilhelm apparently was a devotee of mother-in-law jokes. In 1906, Zedlitz reported one such joke in which the Kaiser asked his listeners to identify the difference between a mother-in-law and a good Havana cigar. "With a good Havana one generally most enjoys the first inhalations, and with a mother-in-law one generally most enjoys the last." *Zwölf Jahre,* pp. 137–41. Revealing the sadistic quality of Wilhelm's wit is another mother-in-law joke that he told in the presence of his mother-in-law. Karl Alexander von Müller, ed., *Fürst Chlodwig zu Hohenlohe-Schillingsfürst: Denkwürdigkeiten der Reichskanzlerzeit* (Stuttgart and Berlin, 1931), p. 10. For Wilhelm's contempt for "ladies' men," see his disparaging comments about the king of Spain (Holstein's diary entry of 1 September 1885, *Holstein Papers,* II, p. 242) and his hostility toward the Marquis de Soveral of Portugal who had been first secretary in the Portuguese Embassy in Berlin in the 1880s (Bülow, *Denkwürdigkeiten,* II, pp. 38–39). For Wilhelm's misogyny, see Lamar Cecil, *Wilhelm II: Prince and Emperor, 1859–1900* (Chapel Hill, 1989), pp. 56–59 and 357–58, note 13.

15. "*Männerbund*" is an untranslatable word meaning a group of men bound together by powerful emotional and intellectual ties. Glorifying masculine virtues and disparaging the feminine, the "*Männerbund*" is defined by its total exclusion not only of women but of anything connected with them. Given the intensity of the bond connecting its members, the "*Männerbund*" has a definite homosexual dimension. See Nicolaus Sombart, "Männerbund und politische Kultur in Deutschland," *TAZ,* 23 January 1988, pp. 17–19, and Sombart, "The Kaiser in His Epoch," pp. 287–312.

16. Wilhelm II, *My Early Life,* p. 117.

17. Hull, *Entourage,* pp. 184–85.

18. See all three volumes of *Eulenburgs Korrespondenz* and Johannes Haller, ed., *Aus 50 Jahren: Erinnerungen, Tagebücher und Briefe aus dem Nachlass des Fürsten Philipp zu Eulenburg-Hertefeld* (Berlin, 1923).

19. See letters of 23, 24, 25, and 27 September, and from 1 October 1900, *Eulenburgs*

Korrespondenz, III, pp. 1990–2005. For an earlier instance in which Eulenburg described strained marital relations between Wilhelm and Dona, see his letter to Bülow of 20 July 1898, ibid., pp. 1908–10. A later instance can be found in "Die Nordlandreise, 1903: in Briefen an Fürstin Augusta zu Eulenburg-Hertefeld," BA Koblenz, Eulenburg Papers, vol. 74.

20. Bülow, *Denkwürdigkeiten*, I, pp. 450–51.

21. Letter from Eulenburg to Bülow of 21 March 1902, BA Koblenz, Bülow Papers, vol. 77.

22. Former and present graduate students may be able to recognize something of their own exaggerated responses to their thesis advisers in the extreme responses of the entourage to the Kaiser. For a perceptive discussion of the transferences established in graduate school, see Peter Loewenberg, "The Graduate Years: What Kind of Passage?" and "Love and Hate in the Academy," *Decoding the Past: The Psychohistorical Approach* (New York, 1983), pp. 59–80.

23. For insightful considerations of the relationship between Wilhelm II and Eulenburg, see Röhl's "Einleitung" to *Eulenburgs Korrespondenz* and Hull, *Entourage*.

24. Johannes Haller, *Aus dem Leben des Fürsten Philipp zu Eulenburg-Hertefeld* (Berlin, 1926), p. 48.

25. N1 to "Aufzeichnung" by Eulenburg of 11 July 1892, *Eulenburgs Korrespondenz*, II, p. 912, and Haller, *Aus dem Leben*, p. 128. Eulenburg continued to address Wilhelm as "Your Majesty."

26. Actually in the fall of 1906 Harden had already dropped veiled hints about Eulenburg's homosexuality in *Die Zukunft* in the hope that the threat of public exposure would force Eulenburg to vacate his position as the Kaiser's confidant. When these hints failed to have the desired effect, Harden made more explicit accusations during the first months of 1907.

27. For more on the Eulenburg scandal in addition to Röhl, "Einleitung" and Hull, *Entourage*, see Norman Rich, *Friedrich von Holstein: Politics and Diplomacy in the Era of Bismarck and Wilhelm II*, 2 vols. (Cambridge, 1965), pp. 765–97; Helmuth Rogge, *Holstein und Harden. Politisch-publizistisches Zusammenspiel zweier Aussenseiter des Wilhelminischen Reiches* (Munich, 1959), containing the correspondence between Holstein and Harden that relates to the Eulenburg scandal; and Harry F. Young, *Maximilian Harden: Censor Germaniae* (The Hague, 1959), pp. 82–125.

28. For more on the psychological strain on Wilhelm during the Eulenburg scandal, see the letter from the Kaiserin to Bülow of December 1906, Bülow, *Denkwürdigkeiten*, II, p. 270.

29. Wilhelm's marginalia to a telegram from Count Paul von Wolff-Metternich zur Bracht, German ambassador in London, to the Foreign Office of 1 November 1907, PA Bonn, Preussen 1, Nr. 1, Nr. 40, vol. 15. Actually, Wilhelm asked his uncle whether the visit could be postponed until the next spring or summer or whether his eldest son could travel to England in his place. Sidney Lee, *King Edward VII: A Biography*, 2 vols. (New York, 1925), II, p. 554.

30. Two telegrams from Metternich to the Foreign Office both of 1 November 1907, PA Bonn, Preussen 1, Nr. 1, Nr. 40, vol. 15; Bülow, *Denkwürdigkeiten*, II, pp. 305–306.

31. Wilhelm's marginalia to a memorandum to Wilhelm's marginalia to the telegram from Metternich to the Foreign Office of 1 November 1907, PA Bonn, Preussen 1, Nr. 1, Nr. 40, vol. 15.

32. See also August Eulenburg's suspicion that the fainting spell was the product of Wilhelm's imagination. Bülow, *Denkwürdigkeiten*, II, p. 305.

33. Documents relating to Wilhelm's animosity toward England and Edward VII and his reluctance to travel to England can be found in *GP*, XXI (2), pp. 507–18; XXIV, pp. 10–12; XXV (1), pp. 42–48 and 74–75; PA Bonn, Preussen 1, Nr. 40 *secr.*, vols. 11 and 12; PA Bonn, England 78, vol. 59; BMA Freiburg, RM 2, vol. 181; Lee, *Edward VII*, II, pp. 546–48 and 554; Bülow, *Denkwürdigkeiten*, II, pp. 296–97.

34. Witness Wilhelm's description of his collapse which he used to justify canceling the trip: "Yesterday I was so miserable, had a sudden spell of unconsciousness which would have left me prostrate on the ground had I not in falling grabbed the back of a chair which threw me onto the sofa; I was brought to my senses again by the Kaiserin who had rushed into the

room by chance." Wilhelm's marginalia to the telegram from Metternich to the Foreign Office of 1 November 1907, PA Bonn, Preussen 1, Nr. 1, Nr. 40, vol. 15.

35. August Eulenburg found the Kaiser surrounded by a swarm of adjutants and looking pleased with himself in the Berlin Tiergarten shortly after his "complete collapse." Bülow, *Denkwürdigkeiten,* II, p. 305.

36. That is, had Wilhelm been overwhelmed psychologically by Harden's acquittal, and not simply weakened by it, he would not have been able to use his reaction to the verdict in such a calculated way.

37. Whereas Eulenburg wrote Wilhelm frequently and at length, the Kaiser rarely responded and then usually by telegram. It should be pointed out, however, that Wilhelm was not a good correspondent with anyone. Lacking the time and the patience to write letters, his favorite forms of communication were telegrams and comments scribbled in the margins of the reports he received.

38. At Friedrich's death, for example, Eulenburg displayed a sensitivity to Wilhelm's feelings not shared by Wilhelm's relatives or, apparently, by most of his other friends. In contrast to Victoria, who was preoccupied with her own anguish and that of her younger daughters, and to Queen Victoria, who was preoccupied with the suffering of Victoria, Eulenburg expressed sadness to Wilhelm at the loss of his father. Most of Wilhelm's friends, in their elation at Wilhelm's accession to the throne, also appear to have forgotten that the new Kaiser had just lost his father. See the letter from Victoria to Queen Victoria of 15 June 1888, Frederick Ponsonby, ed., *Letters of the Empress Frederick* (New York, 1930), pp. 315–16; the letter from Victoria to Marie Dönhoff of 4 July 1888, BA Koblenz, Bülow Papers, vol. 170; the extract from Queen Victoria's journal of 15 June 1888 and the telegram from Queen Victoria to Wilhelm II of 15 June 1888, George Earle Buckle, ed., *The Letters of Queen Victoria: 1886–1901,* 3 vols. (New York, 1930), I, 416–17; and the letter from Eulenburg to Wilhelm II of 15 June 1888, Haller, *Aus dem Leben,* p. 48.

39. Letter from Eulenburg to Bülow of 10 December 1896, *Eulenburgs Korrespondenz,* III, pp. 1765–68.

40. Letter from Eulenburg to Bülow of 27 September 1900, BA Koblenz, Eulenburg Papers, vol. 77.

41. For an example of the two friends' romantic effusions, see Wilhelm's letter to Eulenburg of 28 August 1888, *Eulenburgs Korrespondenz,* I, p. 310. For their shared interest in spiritism, see the letter from Eulenburg to his sister of 23 February 1889, ibid., I, p. 329; the letters from Eulenburg to Bülow of 27 September 1900, ibid., III, pp. 1997–98; and of 24 July 1901, ibid., p. 2024. For a consideration of the relationship of Wilhelm and Eulenburg to spiritism, see Röhl, "Einleitung," ibid., I, pp. 35–53. Spiritism was fashionable in aristocratic circles. Bülow, *Denkwürdigkeiten,* II, p. 43.

42. To get a sense of Eulenburg's enthusiasm for Wilhelm, see his letter to the Kaiser of 1 March 1889: "It makes me indescribably happy to experience [*herausfühlen*] how Your Majesty has grasped the spirit of my friendship. To my last breath, I will be the same!" *Eulenburgs Korrespondenz,* I, pp. 330–31. And when Eulenburg learned that Wilhelm had appointed his friend Kuno von Moltke to the position of aide-de-camp, Eulenburg wrote Wilhelm that he was "filled with a gratifying, comfortable feeling to know that precisely *he* is with my hotly beloved Kaiser." Ibid., II, p. 1062.

For Wilhelm's ability to boast unashamedly about his activities, see his letters to Eulenburg of 8 September 1886, in which he described leading his regiment past his grandfather "cum laude!" ibid., I, pp. 198–99; of 6 October 1887, in which he described his long hours on horseback and his defeat of Prince Friedrich von Hohenzollern-Sigmaringen in military maneuvers, ibid., pp. 244–45; of 28 August 1888, in which he described his pride at entering the harbor in Stockholm as German Kaiser, ibid., p. 310. And, finally, see his letter to Eulenburg of 4 September 1888, in which he described his pride in commanding his 30,000 strong Gardekorps and his pleasure at the parade which made the king of Sweden "absolutely 'beside himself [in English]' at the powerful impression [created by the German soldiers]." "What a feeling," he concluded, "to be able to call these troops *mine!*" Ibid., p. 311.

43. Letter from Wilhelm to Eulenburg of 11 August 1886, ibid., pp. 191–93. See also the letter from Wilhelm to Eulenburg of 27 February 1889, ibid., p. 330.

44. Eulenburg and the Kaiser liked to think themselves superior to what they regarded as the prosaic Prussian aristocracy.

45. Telegram of 16 June 1898, ten years and one day after Friedrich's death. Bülow, *Denkwürdigkeiten,* I, pp. 223–24.

46. For example, "Die Nordlandreise, 1903: in Briefen an Fürstin Augusta zu Eulenburg-Hertefeld," BA Koblenz, Eulenburg Papers, vol. 74.

47. Letters from Eulenburg to Wilhelm of 30 August 1892, *Eulenburgs Korrespondenz,* I, pp. 924–25, of 10 September 1892, ibid., p. 939.

48. "Aufzeichnung Eulenburgs" of his visit to Wilhelm II on 8 November 1896, ibid., III, pp. 1749–51.

49. "Kaiser Wilhelm II," BA Koblenz, Eulenburg Papers, vol. 80.

50. See, here, Lamar Cecil, "Wilhelm II and his Russian 'Colleagues'," *German Nationalism and the European Response, 1890–1945,* Carole Fink, Isabel V. Hull, and MacGregor Knox, eds. (Norman, Oklahoma, 1985), pp. 98–99.

51. *Eulenburgs Korrespondenz,* I, pp. 198–99. Bülow, *Denkwürdigkeiten,* II, p. 472.

52. Apart from the jokes about mothers-in-law recounted in note 14, Wilhelm's humor appears almost always to have been directed at men.

53. Letter from Alfred von Kiderlen-Wächter to Holstein of 15 July 1890, PA Bonn, Holstein Papers, vol. 55. The incident recounted by the Kaiser probably occurred during Wilhelm's visit to Bremen in April 1890.

54. Ernst Jäckh, ed., *Kiderlen-Wächter, der Staatsmann und der Mensch,* 2 vols. (Berlin, 1924), I, p. 124. Letter from Eulenburg to Bülow of 26 July 1903, *Eulenburgs Korrespondenz,* III, pp. 2092–93. Translation in the *Kölnische Volkszeitung* of 6 August 1893 of an article from the *Westminster Gazette,* portions of which are reprinted in ibid., II, p. 1095, n. 2. "Die Nordlandreise, 1903: in Briefen an Fürstin Augusta zu Eulenburg-Hertefeld," BA Koblenz, Eulenburg Papers, vol. 74. Haller, *Aus dem Leben,* p. 116. Walther Görlitz, ed., *Der Kaiser: Aufzeichnungen des Chefs des Marinekabinetts Admiral Georg Alexander von Müller über die Ära Wilhelms II.* (Göttingen, 1965), p. 172.

55. "Die Nordlandreise, 1903: in Briefen an Fürstin Augusta zu Eulenburg-Hertefeld," BA Koblenz, Eulenburg Papers, vol. 74.

56. Letter from Georg von Hülsen to Görtz of 17 October 1892. Translated and printed in Röhl, "The Emperor's New Clothes," p. 35. Hülsen was the Prussian military attaché in Munich and theater intendant first in Wiesbaden and then at the Berlin Court Theater. He was the brother of Dietrich von Hülsen, chief of the Military Cabinet from 1901 until his untimely death in 1908. Görtz was a mediatized ruling prince and a boyhood friend of Wilhelm. See Hull, "'Liebenberg Circle'," pp. 194 and 203.

57. Wilhelm's pleasure in relating obscene anecdotes and in telling dirty jokes should be understood in this context. "We always take our meals at H.M.'s table," Kiderlen-Wächter wrote to Holstein on 16 July 1888; "up to now the chief subjects of conversation have been shitting, vomitting, pissing, and fucking; pardon me for hurting your ears with these harsh words, but I cannot choose any others if I am to give you a true picture." *Holstein Papers,* III, pp. 279–81. See also Görlitz, *Der Kaiser,* p. 35 and footnote 30.

58. Bülow, *Denkwürdigkeiten,* II, pp. 260–61.

59. It was also not an uncommon practice in the Prussian military. Translation in the *Kölnische Volkszeitung* of 6 August 1893 of an article in the *Westminster Gazette,* portions of which are reprinted in *Eulenburgs Korrespondenz,* II, p. 1095, n. 2. Hull, *Entourage,* p. 69.

60. Eulenburg suffered from a variety of ailments, including gout and rheumatism. Most of these appear to have been either psychosomatic or at least exacerbated by Eulenburg's delicate psychological constitution.

61. For the importance of Eulenburg's mother to him, see Haller, *Aus dem Leben,* pp. 3 and 6; Hull, *Entourage,* pp. 49–50; and Röhl, "Einleitung," *Eulenburgs Korrespondenz,* I, p. 15.

62. See, for example, Wilhelm's letter to Eulenburg of 5 January 1897, ibid., III, pp. 1772–

73, and his telegram to Eulenburg quoted in the latter's letter to Bülow of 24 April 1897, ibid., pp. 1818–22.

63. "Kaiserliche Privatverkehr," BA Koblenz, Eulenburg Papers, vol. 74.

64. "Ein Zwiegespräch," 29 August 1903, BA Koblenz, Eulenburg Papers, vol. 74.

65. Zedlitz, *Zwölf Jahre,* p. 49. In November a biopsy was performed on a polyp in Wilhelm's throat. Bülow, *Denkwürdigkeiten,* I, p. 634.

66. Both of Wilhelm's parents had died of cancer, his mother only two years before this conversation, and, ever since the death of his father, Wilhelm had worried that he too might develop the disease. "Kaiser Wilhelm II," BA Koblenz, Eulenburg Papers, vol. 80.

67. "Ein Zwiegespräch," BA Koblenz, Eulenburg Papers, vol. 74. Portions are quoted in Chapter 8. According to his biographer, Eulenburg transcribed this conversation immediately after it occurred on 29 August 1903. Haller, *Aus dem Leben,* pp. 320–21. Röhl suspects, however, that Eulenburg prepared the document after November 1908. *Eulenburgs Korrespondenz,* III, p. 2099, note 7. For present purposes it does not appear to matter greatly when Eulenburg recorded this conversation. It is difficult to imagine any motive that might have caused Eulenburg to distort his or the Kaiser's remarks quoted either here or in Chapter 8. By contrast, the dialogue in which Eulenburg presented himself as heroically accusing Wilhelm of absolutist tendencies could well have been added after the uproar in Germany over the Kaiser's "personal rule" during the *Daily Telegraph* affair.

68. Ibid., pp. 2022–25.

69. Already as a child, Wilhelm had adopted a nurturing, maternal role vis-à-vis his younger siblings and had sought to comfort and care for his mother when she was ill. Letters from Friedrich to Queen Victoria of 18 August 1862, RA Z7/94, and of 20 August 1862, RA Z7/95. Letters from Victoria to Queen Victoria of 17 February 1863, RA Z14/40; of 8 August 1865, RA Z17/84; of 26 June 1866, RA Z18/62; and of 7 March 1868, RA Z21/19.

70. Holstein's diary entry of 24 October 1884, *Holstein Papers,* II, pp. 164–65.

71. Bülow, *Denkwürdigkeiten,* I, pp. 151–52.

72. "Kaiser Wilhelm II," BA Koblenz, Eulenburg Papers, vol. 80. Wilhelm had little use for the way Eulenburg raised his sons: "There everything was too soft, too feminine, too pampered." "Kaiser Wilhelm II und Gräfin Mathilde Stubenberg," 16 January 1903, BA Koblenz, Eulenburg Papers, vol. 84.

73. Letter from Victoria to Queen Victoria of 27 December 1890, Ponsonby, *Letters,* p. 422. Some four years before, Wilhelm had told his mother after the birth of his son that he was "delighted that it is a boy and does not wish for girls who he considers 'no use.'" Letter from Victoria to Queen Victoria of 29 January 1887, RA Z66/53.

74. In Wilhelm's letter to Tsar Nicholas II of 20 February 1896 he boasted about his three-and-a-half-year-old daughter, using the phrase "she is a real piece of living quicksilver and tyrannizes her papa tremendously"—the same words that his mother had used in describing him as a child (quoted in note 13 of the Introduction). Issac Don Levine, ed., *Letters from the Kaiser to the Czar* (New York, 1920), pp. 30–32.

75. Letter from Eulenburg to Bülow of 26 September 1901, *Eulenburgs Korrespondenz,* III, pp. 2030–34. The Kaiser's efforts to Anglicize his son appear to have been successful. Court Marshal Count Robert von Zedlitz-Trützschler lamented in 1909 that the crown prince had become "half an Englishman and half a sportsman." *Zwölf Jahre,* pp. 228–29.

76. Bülow, *Denkwürdigkeiten,* I, pp. 56–61, 80, 148–49, 151–52, and 190 and II, pp. 85–86.

77. Diary entry of 6 June 1890, Erhard von Wedel, *Carl von Wedel. Zwischen Kaiser und Kanzler* (Leipzig, 1943), pp. 103–104.

78. Diary entry of 5 March 1884, *Holstein Papers,* II, pp. 96–97; "Kaiser Wilhelm II," BA Koblenz, Eulenburg Papers, vol. 80.

79. Letter from Eulenburg to Holstein of 25 January 1890, *Eulenburgs Korrespondenz,* I, p. 421. Among the attributes that Wilhelm shared with his mother was a tendency toward pedantry. Another shared attribute was their need to have their days planned out in detail in advance. For Victoria's need for scheduling, see Hugo von Reischach, *Unter drei Kaisern* (Berlin, 1925), pp. 163–64. Wilhelm's need for scheduling became particularly pronounced

when he was in exile. Author's conversation with Dr. Wilhelm Huebener, personal physician to the ex-Kaiser in exile.

80. Bülow, *Denkwürdigkeiten,* I, pp. 190, also 56–57.

81. For Victoria's enjoyment of tennis, see Holstein's diary entry of 26 March 1885, *Holstein Papers,* II, pp. 178–79. Her passion for riding is described in various places by Reischach in *Unter Drei Kaisern* and by Bogdan Graf von Hutten-Czapski in *Sechzig Jahre Politik und Gesellschaft,* 2 vols. (Berlin, 1936), I, p. 187.

82. Despite the years of personal recrimination and political opposition, Wilhelm became indignant when the German press ignored the unveiling of a statue of Victoria in Bad Homburg one year after her death. "He had thought," the Kaiser's aide Heinrich von Tschirschky-Bögendorff telegraphed Bülow on 22 August 1902, "that an account of the life of this woman and Kaiserin would have provided the Germans with a noble subject for consideration." It was the wish of the Kaiser, Tschirschky informed the chancellor, that these sentiments be expressed in the press. PA Bonn, Preussen 1, Nr. 1f, vol. 2. See also Bülow, *Denkwürdigkeiten,* I, pp. 148 and 262.

83. Article in the June 1899 issue of *Munsey's Magazine.*

84. Wilhelm II, *My Early Life,* p. 28.

85. He loved reading to his family and, on occasion, to his entourage.

86. Letter from Victoria to Queen Victoria of 16 May 1871, RA Z25/76–75 (there is an error in the archival numbering of this document). Also the letters from Victoria to Queen Victoria of 6 July 1864, RA Z16/60; of 16 August 1864, RA Z16/74; and of 14 August 1869, Fulford, *Your Dear Letter,* pp. 242–43.

87. "Kaiser Wilhelm II," BA Koblenz, Eulenburg Papers, vol. 80. Bülow also confirmed the fact that both Wilhelm and Victoria, despite their love for the sea, suffered from seasickness. *Denkwürdigkeiten,* I, p. 83. See also the letter from Alfred von Kiderlen-Wächter to Holstein of 16 July 1888, *Holstein Papers,* III, pp. 279–81.

88. Wilhelm II, *My Early Life,* p. 229.

89. Diary entry of 11 November 1888, *Holstein Papers,* II, pp. 382–83.

90. "Kaiser Wilhelm II," BA Koblenz, Eulenburg Papers, vol. 80.

91. Bülow, *Denkwürdigkeiten,* I, p. 152. See also the report from Count Hugo Lerchenfeld-Koefering, Bavarian representative in Berlin, to Bavarian Foreign Minister Crailsheim of 29 March 1890, Graf Hugo Lerchenfeld-Koefering, *Erinnerungen und Denkwürdigkeiten* (Berlin, 1935), p. 365.

92. Letter from Edward Malet to the Marquis of Salisbury of 30 March 1889, *Letters of Queen Victoria: 1886–1901,* I, p. 485.

93. See, for example, Wilhelm's marginalia to a report from Metternich in London to Bülow of 9 April 1904, *GP,* XX (1), pp. 13–14.

94. See the epigraphs at the beginning of Part II.

95. See, to cite three examples, Paul M. Kennedy, *The Rise of the Anglo-German Antagonism, 1860–1914* (London, 1982); Charles E. McClelland, *The German Historians and England: A Study in Nineteenth Century Views* (Cambridge, 1971); and Raymond James Sontag, *Germany and England: Background to the Conflict, 1848–1894* (New York, 1969).

96. Kennedy, *Antagonism,* pp. 69–71. Even the emerging S.P.D. tended to be sympathetic toward Britain. Ibid., p. 83. See also McClelland, *German Historians,* pp. 61–158.

97. The notion, criticized by David Blackbourn and Geoff Eley, of an inevitable economic, social, and political development based upon what was supposedly the English model had its roots in the nineteenth century. Not only subsequent generations of historians but the historical participants themselves assumed that industrialization and modernization would lead to the introduction of democratic political institutions accompanying the economic and social ascendance of the bourgeoisie. Blackbourn and Eley, *The Peculiarities of German History* (Oxford, 1984).

98. Kennedy, *Antagonism,* p. 74. For a general consideration of the attitude of the various German political parties toward Britain in the 1870s and 1880s, see ibid., pp. 69–75.

99. See, here, McClelland, *German Historians,* pp. 161–89.

100. For the congruence between Wilhelm II's mixed feelings and those of his subjects,

see, Roger Fletcher, *Revisionism and Empire: Socialist Imperialism in Germany, 1897–1914* (London, 1984), pp. 56–57, 89–91, 129–30, 154, 157, and 165–66; Walther Hubatsch, *Die Ära Tirpitz: Studien zur deutschen Marinepolitik, 1890–1918* (Göttingen, 1955), pp. 14–15; Charles E. McClelland, "Berlin Historians and German Politics," *Journal of Contemporary History* 8 (1973), pp. 3–33; McClelland, *German Historians,* pp. 161–224; Woodruff D. Smith, *The Ideological Origins of Nazi Imperialism* (New York, 1986), pp. 73–75; Sontag, *Germany and England,* p. x; Rudolf Stadelmann, "Die Epoche der deutsch-englischen Flottenrivalität," *Deutschland und Westeuropa* (Schloss Laupheim, 1948), p. 98; Jonathan Steinberg, *Yesterday's Deterrent: Tirpitz and the Birth of the German Battle Fleet* (London, 1965), pp. 202–203; and Ferdinand Tönnies, *Kritik der öffentlichen Meinung* (Bad Honnef, 1981 reprint of the 1922 edition), pp. 507–10. In Chapter 10 this congruence and its limitations are considered in more detail.

101. Friedrich's father was no admirer of England. Cecil, *Wilhelm II,* p. 6.

102. The political differences between Friedrich and Victoria, on the one hand, and Wilhelm I and Augusta, on the other, increased the personal tension between the two couples. Ibid.

103. Indeed, Prussian reactionaries viewed the marriage with suspicion and alarm from the first. Ibid., p. 4.

Part II

1. Friedrich Naumann, *Hilfe,* January 1909, Gerhard Ritter, ed., *Das deutsche Kaiserreich* (Göttingen, 1975), p. 318.

2. Walther Rathenau, "Der Kaiser," Hans Werner Richter, ed., *Walther Rathenau: Schriften und Reden* (Frankfurt, 1964), p. 247.

Chapter 6

1. Hermann von Petersdorff et al., eds., *Bismarck: Die gesammelten Werke,* 15 vols. (Berlin, 1922–1933), II, p. 231; XIV, p. 473.

2. Otto P. Pflanze, *Bismarck and the Development of Germany: The Period of Unification, 1815–1871* (Princeton, 1963), pp. 84–85.

3. In part as a result of this attitude, Bismarck was particularly hostile toward the Center and Social Democratic parties, which presented themselves as transcending self-interest in the service of religious and ideological values.

4. *Bismarck: Die gesammelten Werke,* XIV, pp. 160–61.

5. Bismarck's marginalia to the report from Hatzfeldt to Bismarck of 12 November 1887, *GP,* XIV, pp. 368–73.

6. Letter from Bismarck to Salisbury of 22 November 1887, Bernhard Schwertfeger, ed., *Die diplomatischen Akten des auswärtigen Amtes, 1871–1914,* 5 vols. with two additional vols. (Berlin, 1923–1925), I, pp. 288–91.

7. Woodruff D. Smith, *The Ideological Origins of Nazi Imperialism* (New York, 1986), pp. 56–58; and Raymond J. Sontag, *Germany and England: Background of the Conflict, 1848–1894* (New York, 1969), p. 263.

8. Letter from Holstein to Prince Hugo von Radolin of 28 November 1889, Norman Rich and M. H. Fisher, eds., *The Holstein Papers,* 4 vols. (Cambridge, 1955–1963), II, p. 323. For Holstein's political philosophy, see Norman Rich, *Friedrich von Holstein: Politics and Diplomacy in the Era of Bismarck and Wilhelm II,* 2 vols. (Cambridge, 1965).

9. "Kaiser Wilhelm II.," BA Koblenz, Eulenburg Papers, vol. 80. See also Kurt Koszyk, *Deutsche Presse im 19. Jahrhundert: Geschichte der deutschen Presse,* 4 vols. (Berlin, 1966), II, pp. 258–60.

10. Wilhelm II's letter to Secretary of State in the Foreign Office Marschall of 25 October 1895, *GP,* XI, pp. 8–11.

11. Letter in English of 1 February 1906, ibid., XXI (1), pp. 110–11.

12. Here again one can see evidence of Wilhelm II's adaptability. Because Edward spoke in French, the Kaiser's marginal comment was also written in French. In fact Wilhelm frequently adopted the language he was reading in his marginal comments.

13. Wilhelm II's marginalia to a report from the German representative in Portugal to Bülow of 7 April 1903, PA Bonn, England Nr. 81, Nr. 1, vol. 11a.

14. Wilhelm II's marginalia to a report from Metternich to Hohenlohe of 7 April 1900, PA Bonn, Afrika Generalia 13, Nr. 2b, vol. 3.

15. Wilhelm II's marginalia to a report from Metternich in London to Bülow of 9 June 1905, *GP,* XX (2), pp. 625–26. Also Wilhelm's marginalia to a report from Metternich to Bülow of 27 January 1905, PA Bonn, England 78, vol. 24.

16. Wilhelm II's marginalia to report from Count Anton von Monts in Rome to Bülow of 3 March 1906, *GP,* XXI (1), pp. 246–48.

17. Telegram from Wilhelm II to Hohenlohe of 25 October 1896, ibid., XIII, pp. 3–4. Nine years later Wilhelm still regarded the British press as a portent and a producer of war. Count Robert von Zedlitz-Trützschler's diary entry of 21 November 1904, *Zwölf Jahre am deutschen Kaiserhof* (Berlin and Leipzig, 1924), pp. 97–98.

18. For the role of public opinion in modern political life, see Wilhelm Bauer, *Die öffentliche Meinung in der Weltgeschichte* (Potsdam, 1930); E. Frankel, *öffentliche Meinung und Internationale Politik* (Tübingen, 1962); Jürgen Habermas, *Strukturwandel der Öffentlichkeit: Untersuchungen zu einer Kategorie der bürgerlichen Gesellschaft* (Neuwied, 1968); Friedrich Lanz, *Werden und Wesen der öffentlichen Meinung: Ein Beitrag zur politischen Soziologie* (Munich, 1956); Martin Löffler, ed., *Die öffentliche Meinung: Publizistik als Medium und Faktor der öffentlichen Meinung* (Munich, 1962); Eberhard Naujoks, "Pressepolitik und Geschichtswissenschaft," *Geschichte in Wissenschaft und Unterricht* 22 (1971), pp. 7–22; and Elisabeth Noelle, *Öffentliche Meinung und soziale Kontrolle* (Tübingen, 1966).

19. See Wilhelm II's letter in English to Edward VII of 30 December 1901: "The Press is awful on both sides, but here it has nothing to say, for I am the sole arbiter and Master of German Foreign Policy and the Government and Country *must* follow me, even if I have to face the musik [sic]!" *GP,* XVII, pp. 110–11. See, here, Peter Winzen, *Bülows Weltmachtkonzept: Untersuchungen zur Frühphase seiner Aussenpolitik, 1897–1901* (Boppard-am-Rhein, 1977), pp. 364–65.

20. Telegram from Wilhelm II to Hohenlohe of 2 December 1896, *GP,* XII, pp. 9–10. For more on this incident, see Oron Hale, *Publicity and Diplomacy with Special Reference to England and Germany, 1890–1914* (Gloucester, Mass., 1964 reprint), pp. 141–43. Ten years later the Kaiser still denied that he was able to influence Anglo-German relations. "I am completely powerless," he wrote at the height of the naval race between the two countries. "The English press is to blame for everything." Wilhelm II's marginalia to a report from Metternich in London to Bülow of 2 January 1905, PA Bonn, England 78, vol. 74.

21. Wilhelm probably needed to blurt out his opinions because they were formed as reactions and because he required immediate external recognition and validation of his views before he could feel secure about them himself. The tendency to deliver snap and sweeping judgments had actually been promoted by Wilhelm's tutor. Hinzpeter told Hans von Plessen that "he had educated the Kaiser in such a way that when people told or presented something to the Kaiser, the Kaiser should only appear and present himself as if he already knew and had considered everything." Tirpitz's notes of 28 November 1903, BMA Freiburg, Tirpitz Papers, N253, vol. 20.

22. Diary entry of 6 February 1906, Zedlitz, *Zwölf Jahre,* p. 223. The value of Wilhelm's marginalia to the historian is illustrated in this study where they are cited many times over. See also Lydia Franke's unjustly neglected portrait of the Kaiser and of his political views, *Die Randbemerkungen Wilhelms II. in den Akten der auswärtigen Politik als historische und psychologische Quelle* (Strassburg, 1934); as well as Friedrich Freska, *Menschliche Rechtfertigung Wilhelms II. nach seiner Randbemerkungen in den Akten des Auswärtigen Amtes*

(Munich, 1920). Peter G. Thielen has pointed out in his article "Die Marginalien Kaiser Wilhelms II." that Wilhelm's marginalia imitated Friedrich the Great's communication with his aides through marginal comments. *Die Welt als Geschichte* 20 (1960), pp. 249–59.

23. Bernhard Fürst von Bülow, *Denkwürdigkeiten,* 4 vols. (Berlin, 1930), I, pp. 164–65.

24. Barbara Vogel, *Deutsche Russlandpolitik: Das Scheitern der deutschen Weltpolitik unter Bülow, 1900–1906* (Düsseldorf, 1973), p. 169.

25. Bülow, *Denkwürdigkeiten,* II, p. 19.

26. The clearest example of this phenomenon occurred in the months following the death of Queen Victoria in January 1901. During a period when German public opinion was strongly hostile to England as a result of the Boer War, Wilhelm, because of the favorable reaction in Britain to his conduct during and immediately after his grandmother's final illness, nevertheless sought to pursue a pro-English foreign policy. Wilhelm's attitude toward England also underwent a dramatic transformation after positive interaction with his English relatives and the British public in late-summer 1889. See, here, Lamar Cecil, *Wilhelm II: Prince and Emperor, 1859–1900* (Chapel Hill, 1989), pp. 269–70.

27. According to Wilhelm's French tutor in Kassel, the glow of popular approval was the Kaiser's *raison d'être.* Franz Ayme, *Wilhelm und seine Erziehung* (Leipzig, 1878), p. 67.

28. In the course of this study considerable attention has been devoted to the basic selfobject functions that public opinion (like Wilhelm's other selfobjects) served for the Kaiser, and the reader may well have experienced discomfort at the emphasis placed on these selfobject needs of Wilhelm II. After all, everyone needs the responses of others throughout life to help in establishing goals and setting priorities as well as in assessing the appropriateness of behavior. Finally, everyone needs the affirming responses of others throughout life in order to feel truly alive and worthwhile. No one is ever wholly psychologically autonomous. What made Wilhelm unusual was not that he needed selfobjects to sustain him, but that he needed them so much. Wilhelm's dilemma, in other words, was less his dependence on public opinion than it was the extent of his dependence.

29. Chancellor Hohenlohe's journal entry of 7 March 1897, Karl Alexander von Müller, ed., *Fürst Chlodwig zu Hohenlohe-Schillingsfürst: Denkwürdigkeiten der Reichskanzlerzeit* (Berlin, 1931), p. 311; letter from Holstein to Bülow of 24 March 1897, BA Koblenz, Bülow Papers, vol. 90.

30. Letter from Auguste Victoria to Bülow of 18 August 1899, Bülow, *Denkwürdigkeiten,* I, p. 295.

31. Wilhelm's marginalia to a report from Theodor von Holleben in Washington to Bülow of 31 January 1901, PA Bonn, England Nr. 81, Nr. 1, vol. 7.

32. Diary entry of 21 November 1904, Zedlitz, *Zwölf Jahre,* p. 97.

33. Wilhelm clearly also experienced the efforts of his aides to suppress politically sensitive portions of his speeches as an implied criticism of his words, and he was deeply hurt when phrases of which he was particularly proud were deleted as inappropriate and ill advised.

34. This was the phrase used by the Kaiser's aides and by the Kaiser himself to characterize these episodes.

35. Gustav Roloff, ed., *Schulthess' europäischer Geschichtskalender,* 79 vols. (Munich, 1860–1938), 1908, pp. 167–68.

36. Telegram from Jenisch to Bülow of 14 November 1908, BA Koblenz, Bülow Papers, vol. 33.

37. Bülow, *Denkwürdigkeiten,* II, pp. 377 and 386.

38. Letter from August Eulenburg to Bülow of 25 November 1908, BA Koblenz, Bülow Papers, vol. 33; Zedlitz's diary entry of 26 November 1908, *Zwölf Jahre,* pp. 194–95.

39. Letters from August Eulenburg to Bülow of 26 November 1908 and of 3 December 1908, BA Koblenz, Bülow Papers, vol. 33; Zedlitz's diary entry of 22 December 1908, *Zwölf Jahre,* pp. 198–201. Zedlitz noted in his diary on 30 December 1908 that Wilhelm, despite his low spirits, had suddenly become ecstatic over the news that diamond fields had been discovered in South Africa. He was unable to stop talking about the subject, each time increasing the magnitude of the discovery. His reaction here appears to parallel his uncontrolled excitement over Count Zeppelin at the beginning of the November Crisis. And just as he had

derived relief from watching Hülsen perform as a ballerina immediately following the Reichstag debates, so now Wilhelm treated Major von Neumann like a court jester and unmercifully pinched and tickled a Lieutenant-Commander von H. as well as several of the adjutants. Zedlitz feared a new scandal should news of the Kaiser's conduct leak out. Ibid., pp. 202–205.

40. Ernst Johann, ed., *Reden des Kaisers* (Munich, 1966), pp. 68–70.

41. Bülow, *Denkwürdigkeiten*, I, p. 50.

42. Letter in English of 9 May 1909, Isaac Don Levine, ed., *Letters from the Kaiser to the Czar* (New York, 1920), pp. 230–34.

43. For the role of press and public opinion in Germany during the reign of Wilhelm II, see Pauline R. Anderson, *The Background of Anti-English Feeling in Germany, 1890–1902* (New York, 1969) passim; Wilhelm Deist, *Flottenpolitik und Flottenpropaganda: Das Nachrichtenbüro des Reichsmarineamts, 1897–1914* (Stuttgart, 1976), pp. 14–17; Johannes Dreyer, *Deutschland und England und ihrer Politik und Presse im Jahre 1901* (Berlin, 1934) passim; Hale, *Publicity and Diplomacy*, pp. 3–13 and 42–80; Paul M. Kennedy, *The Rise of the Anglo-German Antagonism, 1860–1914* (London, 1980), pp. 87–102; Isolde Rieger, *Die wilhelminische Presse im Überblick* (Munich, 1957) passim; and Ferdinand Tönnies, *Kritik der öffentlichen Meinung* (Bad Honnef, 1981, reprint of the 1922 edition), pp. 434–36.

44. For the Kaiser's manipulation of public opinion as well as that of his leading ministers, see Kennedy, *Antagonism*, pp. 361–69; Koszyk, *Deutsche Presse*, pp. 255–56 and 260–62; Tönnies, *Kritik*, pp. 434–36; and Winzen, *Bülows Weltmachtkonzept*, pp. 228–30.

45. In the spring of 1898, for example, he suspected that Russian agents were planting anti-German stories in the British press in order to produce Anglophobic press reaction in Germany, thereby poisoning relations between the two countries. Wilhelm II's marginalia to a report from Hatzfeldt in London to Hohenlohe of 26 April 1898, *GP*, XIV (1), pp. 221–27. In December 1902 he attributed a Germanophobic letter to the editor of *The Times* to "the rabble-rousing and insolence of our press that has gone on for years as well as the press campaign conducted by the Ultramontane Irish in alliance with Russian and French money." Wilhelm II's marginalia to the report from Metternich in London to Bülow of 18 December 1902, PA Bonn, England 78, vol. 18. Six years later he attributed the growing chauvinism and hostility toward Germany in Russia to newspaper articles published, the Kaiser apparently believed, with English and French money. Wilhelm II's marginalia to a report from Pourtalès in St. Petersburg to Bülow of 29 February 1908, *GP*, XXV (2), pp. 338–40.

46. Wilhelm's marginalia to a telegram from Tschirschky to the Foreign Office of 27 October 1899, PA Bonn, England 78, vol. 12.

47. Wilhelm II's marginalia to a report concerning an article published on 1 March 1900 from the Prussian representative in Dresden, Count Carl Dönhoff, to Hohenlohe of 4 March 1900, *GP*, XV, footnote on p. 487. Also Wilhelm's order to end all critical press comment in Germany about the forthcoming visit to Berlin of the "Institution of Naval Architects" in 1896. Wilhelm II's marginalia to a report from Hatzfeldt in London to Hohenlohe of 25 May 1896, PA Bonn, England 81, vol. 9. His order in October 1904 to supress the *Weser Zeitung* during the Russo-Japanese War when it sought to report on provision of coal to the Russian fleet by the HAPAG in violation of Germany's declared neutrality in the conflict. Vogel, *Deutsche Russlandpolitik*, pp. 196–97, and Lamar Cecil, "Coal for the Fleet That Had to Die," *American Historical Review* 69 (1964), pp. 990–1005. His insistence that the German press keep calm in order to reassure English public opinion in 1903. Wilhelm II's marginalia to a report from Count Johann Heinrich von Bernstorff in London to Bülow of 7 October 1903, PA Bonn, England 78, vol. 20. In fact Wilhelm was even able on occasion to stop the attacks of foreign papers on Germany, as in the case of the *Englishman* published in India. Report from Waldshausen in Simla to Hohenlohe of 3 May 1900, PA Bonn, England 78, vol. 14.

48. On 28 May 1896 Chancellor Hohenlohe wrote to Holstein that, at his last meeting with the Kaiser, Wilhelm had angrily produced an article critical of him and of his entourage. "Thereupon followed the usual conversation about the means available and not available to the government to prevent the publication of this sort of article or to punish those responsible." PA Bonn, Holstein Papers, vol. 54.

49. See, here, Hale, *Publicity and Diplomacy*, pp. 73–76.

50. See Bülow, *Denkwürdigkeiten,* II, p. 34; Kennedy, *Antagonism,* p. 270; and note 92 to Chapter 10.

51. *"Dieser vorlaute Knabe muss mal gehörig eins auf den Kasten kriegen!"* Wilhelm II's marginalia to the *Münchner neueste Nachrichten* of 18 August 1904, PA Bonn, Deutschland 138, vol. 28.

52. Wilhelm's marginalia to a telegram from Metternich in London to the Foreign Office of 14 January 1902, PA Bonn, England 81, Nr. 1b *secr.,* vol. 1. See also Winzen, *Bülows Weltmachtkonzept,* pp. 395–96.

53. For the attempts to control the German press in relation to England, see Kennedy, *Antagonism,* pp. 239–40, 257–58, and 265–66.

54. Telegram from Tschirschky with Wilhelm in Donaueschingen to the Foreign Office of 28 April 1900, PA Bonn, England 78, vol. 14; Wilhelm II's marginalia to *The Daily News* of 5 June 1900, PA Bonn, England 78, vol. 14; to a report from Metternich in London to Bülow of 26 February 1902, PA Bonn, England 78, vol. 16; to a report from Bernstorff in London to Bülow of 17 May 1904, PA Bonn, Preussen 1, Nr. 1, Nr. 40, vol. 7; to the *Hamburger Nachrichten* of 30 September 1904, PA Bonn, England 78, vol. 22; to a report from Metternich in London to Bülow of 27 December 1904, PA Bonn, England 78, vol. 23a; to a report from Metternich in London to Bülow and to an article in *The Daily Telegraph* both of 19 April 1905, PA Bonn, England 78, vol. 27; to a report from Kühlmann to Bülow of 7 June 1909, PA Bonn, England 78, vol. 73; and to *The Daily News* of 15 May 1913, PA Bonn, England 78, vol. 14c.

55. Wilhelm II's marginalia to the *Weser Zeitung* of 10 April 1900, PA Bonn, England 78, vol. 14.

56. Wilhelm II's marginalia to a report from Hatzfeldt in London to Hohenlohe of 6 July 1899, *GP,* XIV (1), pp. 281–84; to Edward Dicey's article "The British Press and the Law of Nations" in *The Empire Review* of October 1904, PA Bonn, England 78, vol. 22; to a report from Bernstorff in London to Bülow of 30 November 1904, PA Bonn, England 78, vol. 22; and to an article in *The Daily Mail* of 19 April 1905 by Lord Lonsdale, PA Bonn, England 78, vol. 27.

57. Wilhelm II's marginalia to a report from Tschirschky in Hamburg to Bülow of 31 December 1905, PA Bonn, England 78, vol. 45.

58. *Hohenlohe: Denkwürdigkeiten,* pp. 94–95. For more on this episode, see John C. G. Röhl, *Germany Without Bismarck: The Crisis of Government in the Second Reich, 1890–1900* (Berkeley, 1967), pp. 136–38.

59. The most recent treatment of this event is John C. G. Röhl's "Der militärpolitische Entscheidungsprozess in Deutschland am Vorabend des Ersten Weltkriegs," John C. G. Röhl, *Kaiser, Hof und Staat: Wilhelm II und die deutsche Politik* (Munich, 1987), pp. 175–202, which is a revised version of his earlier articles on this topic. Röhl's article contains an extensive bibliography of the *Kriegsrat.*

60. Documents as published in John C. G. Röhl, "An der Schwelle zum Weltkrieg: Eine Dokumentation über den 'Kriegsrat' von 8. Dezember 1912," *Militärgeschichtliche Mitteilungen* 21 (1977), p. 100.

61. Ibid.

62. See, for example, Martin Winckler, "Die Rolle der Presse bei der Vorbereitung des deutsch-französischen Krieges 1870/71," *Presse und Geschichte: Beiträge zur historischen Kommunikationsforschung,* vol. 23 of *Studien für Publizistik* (Munich, 1977), pp. 149–56.

63. It is evident to anyone glancing through the ambassadorial reports submitted to the Foreign Office that during Wilhelm's reign the diplomatic corps devoted considerably more attention to the foreign press than they had before Bismarck's dismissal. For the importance that the Foreign Office placed on the press under Wilhelm II, see Kennedy, *Antagonism,* pp. 364–65. First published in 1940, Oron Hale's *Publicity and Diplomacy* remains an excellent study of the relationship between press, public opinion, and foreign policy under Wilhelm II.

64. For Hammann's role in the manipulation of the press, see Hale, *Publicity and Diplomacy,* pp. 67–73, and Winzen, *Bülows Weltmachtkonzept,* pp. 228–30. For Heeringen's role, see Deist, *Flottenpolitik, passim.*

65. These issues are considered in Chapters 9 and 10.

66. Wilhelm II's marginalia to *The Speaker* of 25 January 1896, PA Bonn, England 81, Nr. 2, vol. 12.

Chapter 7

1. Elisabeth Fehrenbach, *Wandlungen des deutschen Kaisergedankens, 1871–1918* (Munich, 1969), p. 93.

2. Quoted in Henry Wickham Steed, *Through Thirty Years,* 2 vols. (New York, 1924), I, p. 21. Originally printed in *The Times.*

3. Fürst Bernhard von Bülow, *Denkwürdigkeiten,* 4 vols. (Berlin, 1930), I, p. 61.

4. Walther Rathenau, "Der Kaiser," *Walther Rathenau: Schriften und Reden,* Hans Werner Richter, ed. (Frankfurt, 1964), p. 255.

5. Ibid., p. 250. For the enthusiasm with which the Kaiser's speeches were received, see Fehrenbach, *Wandlungen,* p. 99.

6. Karl Lamprecht quoted in ibid., p. 93.

7. For the extent of the Kaiser's personal contact with his subjects, see Appendix I.

8. This point was made by Heinrich Mann in his satire of Wilhelmian Germany and of this new breed of Wilhelmian German, *Der Untertan,* unaccountably translated into English as *Man of Straw* (New York, 1984).

9. Fehrenbach, *Wandlungen,* p. 198.

10. Walther Görlitz, ed., *Der Kaiser: Aufzeichnungen des Chefs des Marinekabinetts Admiral Georg Alexander von Müller über die Ära Wilhelms II.* (Göttingen, 1965), p. 34.

11. Bogdan Graf von Hutten-Czapski, *Sechzig Jahre Politik und Gesellschaft,* 2 vols. (Berlin, 1936), I, p. 183.

12. Diary entry of 27 September 1908, Maurice V. Brett and Oliver, Viscount Esher, eds., *Journals and Letters of Reginald Viscount Esher,* 4 vols. (London, 1934–1938), II, p. 344.

13. Mann, *Man of Straw,* pp. 168, 282, and 287.

14. Ibid., pp. 146–47.

15. Ibid., p. 146.

16. In early 1907 Wilhelm presented the "British nation" with a statue of William III of Orange bearing the inscription "Champion of Europe Against the French Policy of Conquest Directed by Louis XIV" in the hope that English sympathy for Germany would increase and that England could be drawn away from France through the symbolically expressed memory of Anglo-German opposition to France. Letter from Metternich in London to Tschirschky of 29 December 1906, PA Bonn, England 78 *secr.,* vol. 9, and report from Hermann von Lucanus to Metternich of 17 January 1907, PA Bonn, England 78 *secr.,* vol. 9.

17. Telegram from Wilhelm II to Bülow of 20 August 1901, *GP,* XVIII (1), pp. 14–16.

18. Wilhelm's marginalia to a report from Metternich in London to Bülow of 25 June 1908, ibid., XXV (2), pp. 479–81.

19. Bülow, for example, criticized Wilhelm for his tendency "to regard banal civilities and empty phrases as material successes of political consequence." Bülow, *Denkwürdigkeiten,* I, p. 526.

20. Telegram from Wilhelm II to the Foreign Office of 25 January 1901, PA Bonn, Preussen 1, Nr. 1d, vol. 10.

21. Bülow, *Denkwürdigkeiten,* I, pp. 93–95.

22. Throughout his reign the Kaiser sent suggestions to the British Admiralty, Lord Salisbury, and others in England on ways to improve the Royal Navy. He also offered advice to Nicholas II—particularly during the Russo-Japanese War—with similarly unfortunate results.

23. Letter of 16 February 1908, *GP,* XXIV, p. 34.

24. Telegram from Wilhelm Schoen to Metternich in London of 3 March 1903, PA Bonn, England 78 *secr.,* vol. 11. For Tirpitz's outraged reaction, see Bülow, *Denkwürdigkeiten,* II, pp. 324–25.

25. *The Times* of 6 March 1908.

26. Wilhelm II's marginalia to a telegram from Metternich in London to the Foreign Office of 6 March 1908, *GP,* XXIV, pp. 39–40.

27. Ibid., p. 36; Wilhelm's marginalia to the telegram from Metternich to the Foreign Office of 6 March 1908, ibid., pp. 39–40.

28. Bülow, *Denkwürdigkeiten,* I, p. 570.

29. Speech quoted in Michael Balfour, *The Kaiser and His Times* (New York, 1972), pp. 226–27. On the attempts to keep this speech from being reported in the press, see Bernd Sösemann, "Die sogenannte Hunnenrede Wilhelms II. Textkritische und interpretatorische Bermerkungen zur Ansprache des Kaisers vom 27. Juli in Bremerhaven," *Historische Zeitschrift* 222 (1976), pp. 342–58.

30. *GP,* XIX (2), pp. 458–65.

31. Bülow, *Denkwürdigkeiten,* II, p. 149.

32. Ibid.

33. See his dinner speech in Damascus on 8 November 1898 in Ernst Johann, ed., *Reden des Kaisers: Ansprachen, Predigten, und Trinksprüche Wilhelms II.* (Munich, 1977), p. 81. For more on the symbolic value of the Kaiser's visit to the Holy Land, see Fehrenbach, *Wandlungen,* p. 117.

34. *Simplicissimus: Eine satirische Zeitschrift, 1896–1944,* catalogue for the exhibition on *Simplicissimus* at the Haus der Kunst in Munich from 19 November 1977 to 15 January 1978, p. 56. The verses read in German:

So sei uns denn noch einmal hochwillkommen
Und lass dir unsre tiefste Ehrfurcht weihn,
Der du die Schmach vom heilgen Land genommen,
Von dir bisher noch nicht besucht zu sein.
Mit Stolz erfüllst du Millionen Christen;
Wie wird von nun an Golgatha sich brüsten,
Das einst vernahm das letzte Wort vom Kreuz
Und heute nun das erste deinerseits.

Der Menschheit Durst nach Thaten lässt sich stillen,
Doch nach Bewundrung ist ihr Durst enorm.
Der du ihr beide Durste zu erfüllen
Vermagst, seis in der Tropen-Uniform,
Sei es in Seemannstracht, im Purpurkleide,
Im Rokoko-Kostüm aus starrer Seide,
Sei es im Jagdrock oder Sportgewand,
Willkommen, teurer Fürst, im heilgen Land!

35. Ibid.

36. Ibid., pp. 41–42.

37. Letter from Eulenburg to Bülow of 26 July 1903, "Nordlandreise II: Psyche," BA Koblenz, Eulenburg Papers, vol. 74. Lamar Cecil has described Wilhelm II's "habitual inclination to act almost entirely on the basis of his personal feelings" as his "most pronounced—and fatal—characteristic." *Wilhelm II,* p. xii.

38. For more on the psychological meaning of this episode to Wilhelm II as part of a general reflection on the historical, psychohistorical, and psychoanalytic method, see Thomas A. Kohut, "Psychohistory as History," *The American Historical Review* 91 (1986), pp. 350–51.

39. Wilhelm II's marginalia of 24 May 1913 to a report from the representative in Hamburg to Chancellor Bethmann Hollweg, PA Bonn, Preussen 1, Nr. 1d, *secr.* Albert Ballin, director of the Hamburg-Amerika line, reported that, although some passive resistance on the part of the workers had delayed the ship's completion, the resistance was due not to animosity toward the Kaiser but to the fact that workers would be laid off once the ship was completed.

40. Cecil, *Wilhelm II,* pp. 206–11 and 225–27. The Badenese representative in Berlin, Arthur Brauer, had recognized already in late 1891 that Wilhelm was personally offended that

his efforts on behalf of the workers had not produced a complete transformation in their attitude. Brauer feared that in his disappointment and anger the Kaiser might adopt violent measures in dealing with the German proletariat. Letter from Brauer to Turban of 6 December
1891, Walther Peter Fuchs, ed., *Grossherzog Friedrich I. von Baden und die deutsche Politik,
1871–1907,* 4 vols. (Stuttgart, 1968–1980), III, pp. 91–93.

41. Norman Rich and M. H. Fisher, eds., *The Holstein Papers,* 4 vols. (Cambridge, 1955–
1963); John C. G. Röhl, ed., *Philipp Eulenburgs politische Korrespondenz,* 3 vols. (Boppard-
am-Rhein, 1976–1983).

Both Tirpitz's efforts to secure and preserve his control over naval development against
his rivals within the navy and without and the decisive role played by the Kaiser's favor in
determining who succeeded and who failed in this contest are revealed in various volumes of
the Tirpitz Papers, N253 (BMA Freiburg). See, for example, Tirpitz's notes to his audience
with the Kaiser of 28 January 1896 in vol. 3, his notes for October 1903 to January 1904 in
vol. 20, and his notes for 2 to 8 September 1904 in vol. 21. See also the correspondence
between Admiral Baron Gustav von Senden und Bibran, chief of the Naval Cabinet, and
Tirpitz recorded by Admiral Adolf von Trotha in February 1906, BMA Freiburg, RM3, vol.
6, and the copy of the letter from Senden's successor in office, Admiral von Müller, to Tirpitz
of 11 July 1906, BMA Freiburg, RM3, vol. 7. See, here, Volker R. Berghahn, *Der Tirpitz-
Plan: Genesis und Verfall einer innenpolitischen Krisenstrategie unter Wilhelm II.* (Düsseldorf, 1971), pp. 23–45, 108–109, 165–69, and 346–59; Ivo N. Lambi, *The Navy and German
Power Politics, 1862–1914* (Boston, 1984), pp. 115, 139–40, 165, and 167–68.

42. Isabel V. Hull, *The Entourage of Kaiser Wilhelm II, 1888–1918* (Cambridge,
1982); Katharine Anne Lerman, *The Chancellor as Courtier: Bernhard von Bülow and the
Governance of Germany, 1900–1909* (Cambridge, 1990); and John C. G. Röhl, *Germany
Without Bismarck: The Crisis of Government in the Second Reich, 1890–1900* (Berkeley,
1967).

43. Hans-Ulrich Wehler, *Das deutsche Kaiserreich, 1871–1918* (Göttingen, 1980), p. 69.

44. For an excellent analysis of the structure of Wilhelmian government, see the chapter
"Der 'Königsmechanismus' im wilhelminischen Deutschland," in John C. G. Röhl, *Kaiser,
Hof und Staat: Wilhelm II. und die deutsche Politik* (Munich, 1988), pp. 116–40. See also
Röhl, *Germany Without Bismarck,* pp. 271–79, and Nicolaus Sombart, "'Ich sage, unterge-
hen': Zum zweiten Band von Philipp Eulenburgs politische Korrespondenz," *Merkur* 34
(1980), pp. 542–54.

45. See Röhl, *Germany Without Bismarck* and Hull, *The Entourage.*

46. Because those occupying positions of authority generally did so because the Kaiser
found them personally congenial, John Röhl has described the ruling elite within government
as representing an "institutionalization of the imperial personality." Röhl, "'Königsmechanismus','" p. 127. See also Hull, *Entourage,* pp. 4–14.

47. For the Kaiser's tendency to understand politics and particularly foreign policy
in terms of personalities, see Lamar Cecil, *The German Diplomatic Service, 1871–1914*
(Princeton, 1976), pp. 211 and 214–15; Lamar Cecil, "Wilhelm II and his Russian 'Col-
leagues'," *German Nationalism and the European Response, 1890–1945,* Carole Fink, Isabel
V. Hull, and MacGregor Knox, eds. (Norman, Oklahoma, 1985), pp. 95–134; Lamar Cecil,
"History as Family Chronicle: Kaiser Wilhelm II and the Dynastic Roots of the Anglo-Ger-
man Antagonism," John C. G. Röhl and Nicolaus Sombart, eds., *Kaiser Wilhelm II: New
Interpretations* (Cambridge, 1982), pp. 91–119; Fehrenbach, *Wandlungen,* p. 90; and Paul M.
Kennedy, *The Rise of the Anglo-German Antagonism, 1860–1914* (London, 1980), p. 402.

48. Robert Graf von Zedlitz-Trützschler, *Zwölf Jahre am deutschen Kaiserhof* (Berlin,
1924), p. 153.

49. Wilhelm II's marginalia to the *New York Times* of 7 June 1908, PA Bonn, England
78 *secr.,* vol. 14, and to a report from Wilhelm von Stumm in London to Bülow of 8 September 1908, PA Bonn, England 78, vol. 66.

50. While in exile, Wilhelm actually assigned genders to various nations. Not surprisingly,
England was female; Germany, male according to the ex-Kaiser.

51. Letter from Bülow in Windsor with Wilhelm to Holstein of 24 November 1899, BA Koblenz, Bülow Papers, vol. 91.

52. Telegram from Wilhelm II to the Foreign Office of 6 November 1897, *GP,* XIV (1), p. 67.

53. Telegram from Wilhelm II to Bülow of 7 November 1897, ibid., pp. 69–71.

54. Telegram from Bülow to Metternich in London of 21 January 1902, PA Bonn, England 81, Nr. 1b, *secr.,* vol. 1. For more on this incident, see Kennedy, *Antagonism,* p. 255, and Peter Winzen, *Bülows Weltmachtkonzept: Untersuchungen zur Frühphase seiner Aussenpolitik, 1897–1901* (Boppard-am-Rhein, 1977), pp. 395–96.

55. For a brief summary of the European crisis over Samoa, see William L. Langer, *The Diplomacy of Imperialism, 1890–1902* (New York, 1965), pp. 619–22. For a brief consideration of the Samoan crisis in the context of the Anglo-German relationship, see Kennedy, *Antagonism,* pp. 237–51. For a lengthy and detailed consideration of the crisis in the context of that relationship, see Paul M. Kennedy, *The Samoan Tangle: A Study in Anglo-German Relations, 1878–1900* (Dublin, 1974), especially pp. 145–239. See also Rich, *Holstein,* pp. 590–601; Oron J. Hale, *Publicity and Diplomacy: With Special Reference to England and Germany, 1890–1914* (Gloucester, Mass., 1964 rpt.), pp. 192–93; Paul M. Kennedy, "German World Policy and the Alliance Negotiations with England, 1897–1900," *Journal of Modern History* 45 (1973), pp. 616–18; Winzen, *Bülows Weltmachtkonzept,* pp. 94–98 and 186–202; and Cecil, *Wilhelm II,* pp. 324–26.

56. In her letter Queen Victoria had urged Wilhelm officially to deny reports in the German press that she had refused to invite her grandson to the annual regatta at Cowes as was her custom. The contents of Queen Victoria's letter to Wilhelm II were reported by the Kaiser in a telegram to Bülow of 20 May 1899, footnote to the letter from Wilhelm II to Queen Victoria of 22 May 1899, *GP,* XIV (2), pp. 615–16.

57. Peter Winzen interprets Wilhelm's anger at Salisbury as a displacement of his anger at Queen Victoria because he had not been invited to attend her birthday in May. *Bülows Weltmachtkonzept,* pp. 190–93.

58. See, here, Hale, *Publicity and Diplomacy,* pp. 172–73, and especially Winzen, *Bülows Weltmachtkonzept,* pp. 187–88.

59. The use of the titles of two of Paul Kennedy's books is intentional. Kennedy appears to have come to a similar conclusion about the Kaiser's motives in the Samoan affair.

60. Wilhelm II's letter to Queen Victoria of 22 May 1899, *GP,* XIV (2), pp. 615–17.

61. Kennedy, *Antagonism,* pp. 237–39; Kennedy, *Samoan Tangle,* especially pp. 240–41, 263–72, and 297–99; Ferdinand Tönnies, *Kritik der öffentlichen Meinung* (Bad Honnef, 1981 reprint of the 1922 edition), p. 508; and Winzen, *Bülows Weltmachtkonzept,* pp. 198–202.

62. "I doubt whether any Sovereign ever wrote in such terms to another Sovereign, and that Sovereign his own Grand Mother about her Prime Ministre [sic]," Queen Victoria wrote Wilhelm on 12 June 1899. *GP,* XIV (2), pp. 620–23.

63. See, here, Kennedy, *Antagonism,* p. 431.

64. These issues are considered in Chapters 9 and 10.

65. Bülow's telegram to the Foreign Office of 3 August 1900, *GP,* XVI, pp. 78–79.

66. Telegram from Wilhelm II to Bülow of 19 July 1900, ibid., p. 14.

67. Bülow quoting Eulenburg in *Denkwürdigkeiten,* I, p. 456.

68. Memorandum of 2 March 1894, Johannes Haller, *Aus dem Leben des Fürsten Philipp zu Eulenburg-Hertefeld* (Berlin, 1926), pp. 114–15.

69. As was noted earlier, even before his accession to the throne, Wilhelm's sudden shifts of opinion and indiscreet remarks had led him to be suspected of wanting war with Russia in St. Petersburg and of wanting war with England in London. See also the letter from Lord Salisbury to Queen Victoria of 21 April 1888, quoted in Cecil, *Wilhelm II,* p. 280.

70. George P. Gooch and Harold Temperley, eds., *British Documents on the Origins of the War,* 11 vols. (London, 1926–1938), III, p. 420.

71. Dudley Sommers, *Haldane of Cloan: His Life and Times, 1856–1928* (London, 1960), p. 203.

Chapter 8

1. This chapter owes inspiration and a number of its arguments to Elisabeth Fehrenbach's *Wandlungen des deutschen Kaisergedankens, 1871–1918* (Munich, 1969) and to her article "Images of Kaiserdom: German Attitudes to Kaiser Wilhelm II," *Kaiser Wilhelm II: New Interpretations,* John C. G. Röhl and Nicolaus Sombart, eds. (Cambridge, 1982), pp. 269–86.

2. John C. G. Röhl, *Kaiser, Hof und Staat: Wilhelm II. und die deutsche Politik* (Munich, 1988), p. 12.

3. For considerations of Germany's viability as nation-state and of the divisions within Germany see, among others, Robert Berdahl, "New Thoughts on German Nationalism," *American Historical Review* 77 (1972), pp. 65–80; David Calleo, *The German Problem Reconsidered: Germany and the World Order, 1870 to the Present* (Cambridge, 1978); Geoff Eley, *Reshaping the German Right: Radical Nationalism and Political Change after Bismarck* (New Haven and London, 1980); Eley, "State Formation, Nationalism, and Political Culture: Some Thoughts on the Unification of Germany," *From Unification to Nazism: Reinterpreting the German Past* (Boston, 1986), pp. 61–84; Fehrenbach, *Wandlungen*; Friedrich Meinecke, *Weltbürgertum und Nationalstaat* (Munich, 1962); Manfred Messerschmidt, "Reich und Nation im Bewusstsein der wilhelminischen Gesellschaft," *Marine und Marinepolitik im kaiserlichen Deutschland, 1871–1914,* Herbert Schottelius and Wilhelm Deist, eds. (Düsseldorf, 1972), pp. 11–33; Thomas Nipperdey, "Nationalidee und Nationaldenkmal in Deutschland im 19. Jahrhundert," *Historische Zeitschrift* 206 (1968), pp. 529–85; Röhl, "Der 'Königsmechanismus' im Kaiserreich," *Kaiser, Hof und Staat,* pp. 116–40; Theodor Schieder, *Das deutsche Kaiserreich als Nationalstaat* (Cologne, 1961); James J. Sheehan, "What is German History? Reflections on the Role of the *Nation* in German History and Historiography," *Journal of Modern History* 53 (1981), pp. 1–23; and Hans-Ulrich Wehler, *Das deutsche Kaiserreich, 1871–1918* (Göttingen, 1975).

4. Fehrenbach, *Wandlungen,* p. 111. For Wilhelm as the personal symbol of the nation, see pp. 89–184.

5. Marschall quoted in ibid., pp. 117–18. For a consideration of the conflict confronting Wilhelm between Prussian dynastic ritual and national ritual, see Isabel V. Hull, "Prussian Dynastic Ritual and the End of the Monarchy," *German Nationalism and the European Response, 1890–1945,* Carole Fink, Isabel V. Hull, and MacGregor Knox, eds. (Norman, Oklahoma, 1985), pp. 13–41.

6. Karl Alexander von Müller, ed., *Fürst Chlodwig zu Hohenlohe-Schillingsfürst: Denkwürdigkeiten der Reichskanzlerzeit* (Stuttgart and Berlin, 1931), p. 474.

7. Karl Friedrich Nowak and Friedrich Thimme, eds., *Erinnerungen und Gedanken des Botschafters Anton Graf Monts* (Berlin, 1932), pp. 143–44. Wilhelm's first serious crisis with Chancellor Caprivi, for example, came in late 1891/early 1892 over the school reform proposal of the Prussian minister of public worship and education, Zedlitz-Trützschler, which, the Kaiser was convinced, would alienate South German progressives, hence weakening their loyalty to the Reich. See, here, Lamar Cecil, *Wilhelm II: Prince and Emperor, 1859–1900* (Chapel Hill, 1989), pp. 197–200.

8. Fehrenbach *Wandlungen,* pp. 144–57. As Lamar Cecil has pointed out, Wilhelm also alienated the princes with his arrogance toward them, the product, Cecil believes, of the fact that their age and the distinction of their dynasties exacerbated the Kaiser's insecurity.

9. For the use of ceremony and symbol to increase national consciousness in Europe, see Elisabeth Fehrenbach, "Über die Bedeutung der politischen Symbole im Nationalstaat," *Historische Zeitschrift* 213 (1971), pp. 296–357, a comparative study containing excellent references on the use of symbols in French politics; Eric Hobsbawm, "Mass Producing Traditions: Europe, 1870–1914," Eric Hobsbawm and Terence Ranger, eds., *The Invention of Tradition* (Cambridge, 1983), pp. 263–307; George Mosse, "Caesarism, Circuses, and Monuments," *Journal of Contemporary History* 6 (1971), pp. 167–82; Mosse, *The Nationalization of the Masses: Political Symbolism and Mass Movements in Germany from the Napoleonic Wars Through the Third Reich* (New York, 1975); Nipperdey, "Nationaldenkmal," pp. 529–85; and Schieder, *Kaiserreich,* especially Chapter 5 and the book's appendixes.

10. See, here, Nipperdey's consideration of the National Monument to Kaiser Wilhelm I erected in 1897 in Berlin, of the Kyffhäuser Monument erected between 1892 and 1897 on pp. 543–46, and the "Battle of the Peoples' Monument" erected in Leipzig in 1913 on pp. 573–77, all in "Nationaldenkmal"; Fehrenbach, *Wandlungen*, pp. 100–102; and Appendix I of this study. For Wilhelm's efforts at educational reform, including his desire to instill nationalist spirit through school instruction in German history, the school conference of 1890, and his speech on 4 December 1890 at its opening, see James C. Albisetti, *Secondary School Reform in Imperial Germany* (Princeton, 1983), pp. 172–291; Cecil, *Wilhelm II*, pp. 195–200. Wilhelm's speech quoted in ibid., p. 197. For the school conference of 1890 and Wilhelm's attempts to use education as a national-political instrument generally, see Konrad H. Jarausch, *Students, Society, and Politics in Imperial Germany: The Rise of Academic Illiberalism* (Princeton, 1982), pp. 37, 60, 70, 107–109, 218, 219, 222, 226, 234, 335, 360, and 388–89. The report from the Badenese representative in Berlin, Arthur von Brauer, to Ludwig Turban of 7 December 1890 testifies to the popularity of Wilhelm's speech with "the younger generation" and the "broad masses" of the German people and to the enthusiasm greeting the Kaiser's idea that instilling nationalist sentiment was a primary responsibility of German pedagogy. Walther Peter Fuchs, ed., *Grossherzog Friedrich II. von Baden und die Reichspolitik, 1871–1907*, 4 vols. (Stuttgart, 1968–1980), III, pp. 34–36.

11. Fehrenbach, *Wandlungen*, pp. 69–80. Wilhelm regarded the institution of the monarchy as an effective national symbol. Ibid., p. 89. See also Werner K. Blessing, "The Cult of Monarchy, Political Loyalty and the Workers' Movement in Imperial Germany," *Journal of Contemporary History* 13 (1978), pp. 357–75; Hull, "Prussian Dynastic Ritual," p. 20.

12. Wilhelm's marginalia to the *Deutsche Zeitung* of 21 February 1903, PA Bonn, Preussen 1, Nr. 1d, vol. 9. During the course of Wilhelm II's reign three to four hundred "National Monuments" to "Wilhelm the Great" were erected throughout Germany. Nipperdey, "Nationaldenkmal," p. 503. For more on Wilhelm's efforts to make his grandfather into a national hero, see Fehrenbach, *Wandlungen*, pp. 111–15, and Hull, "Dynastic Ritual," pp. 20–23.

13. *Hohenlohe: Denkwürdigkeiten*, pp. 285–86.

14. Quoted in John C. G. Röhl, *Germany Without Bismarck: The Crisis of Government in the Second Reich, 1890–1900* (Berkeley, 1967), p. 206.

15. Bogdan Graf von Hutten-Czapski, *Sechzig Jahre Politik und Gesellschaft*, 2 vols. (Berlin, 1936), I, p. 314.

16. The rulers of Saxony and Bavaria vehemently opposed the imposition of the cockade, the prince regent of Bavaria declaring that no king of Bavaria could ever accept it. Letter from Ferdinand Freiherr von und zu Bodman, Badenese representative in Munich, to Brauer of 14 November 1896, *Grossherzog Friedrich II. von Baden*, III, p. 568. By contrast, the grand duke of Baden, a nationalist, was enthusiastic about the cockade as a way to strengthen German unity. Letter from Brauer to Eugen von Jagemann of 21 January 1897, ibid., p. 586.

17. Hutten-Czapski, *Sechzig Jahre*, p. 315.

18. Ibid., pp. 314–15. See also Fehrenbach, *Wandlungen*, pp. 174–75.

19. Bernhard Fürst von Bülow, *Denkwürdigkeiten*, 4 vols. (Berlin, 1930), I, pp. 229–30.

20. Letter from Hohenlohe to his son, Alexander, of 17 August 1898, *Hohenlohe: Denkwürdigkeiten*, p. 458.

21. Letter from Eulenburg to Bülow, Bülow, *Denkwürdigkeiten*, I, p. 352. See, here, the attempt to promote national unity through monuments to Bismarck. The Bismarck monuments, however, were often used by nationalist opponents of the Kaiser as a symbolic alternative to his flamboyant brand of national integration. Nipperdey, "Nationaldenkmal," pp. 577–82. For more on the use of Bismarck as a symbolic alternative to the Kaiser, see Fehrenbach, *Wandlungen*, pp. 112–16.

22. See, for example, the Kaiser's Throne Speech of 4 July 1893 as well as his famous speech at Döberitz in May 1908 when he openly spoke of the efforts of Germany's enemies to "encircle" her and warned that Germans never fight better together than when they are attacked on all sides. This speech, although attempts were made to suppress it, was made in the presence of, among others, the Russian general, Tatischeff. Rumors of Wilhelm's remarks

produced excitement in Germany and consternation throughout Europe and in the German Foreign Office. Graf Robert von Zedlitz-Trützschler, *Zwölf Jahre am deutschen Kaiserhof* (Berlin and Leipzig, 1924), pp. 193–94.

23. Telegram from Bülow to the Foreign Office of 22 November 1898, PA Bonn, Deutschland 138, vol. 14. Paul M. Kennedy, *The Rise of the Anglo-German Antagonism, 1860–1914* (London, 1982), p. 237.

24. Royal Message of 18 January 1896, PA Bonn, Deutschland 125, Nr. 2.

25. "Ein Zwiegespräch," BA Koblenz, Eulenburg Papers, vol. 74.

26. Letter from Eulenburg to Bülow of 18 February 1902, John C. G. Röhl, ed., *Philipp Eulenburgs politsche Korrespondenz*, 3 vols. (Boppard-am-Rhein, 1976–1983), III, p. 2058.

27. Ibid., pp. 2030–34.

28. Michael Salewski, "'Neujahr 1900': Die Säkularwende in zeitgenössischer Sicht," *Archiv für Kulturgeschichte* 53 (1971), pp. 342–50.

29. Letter from Eulenburg to Bülow of 8 June 1896, *Eulenburgs Korrespondenz*, III, pp. 1693–97.

30. Walther Rathenau, "Der Kaiser," *Walther Rathenau: Schriften und Reden*, Hans Werner Richter, ed. (Frankfurt, 1964), p. 251.

31. Fehrenbach, "Images of Kaiserdom," p. 276. Fehrenbach, *Wandlungen*, pp. 102–104 and 116. Hull, "Prussian Dynastic Ritual," pp. 30–32.

32. Friedrich Wilhelm von Loebell, "Rückblick und Ausblick," *Deutschland unter Kaiser Wilhelm II*, Philipp Zorn and Herbert von Berger, eds., 4 vols. (Berlin, 1914), IV, pp. 1698–99. See, here, Fehrenbach, *Wandlungen*, pp. 90–91.

33. Friedrich Meinecke, "Deutsche Jahrhundertfeier und Kaiserfeier," *Logos* 4 (1913), p. 172. See, here, Fehrenbach, *Wandlungen*, pp. 102–104.

34. Hermann Oncken, "Der Kaiser und die Nation: Rede bei dem Festakt der Universität Heidelberg zur Erinnerung an die Befreiungskriege und zur Feier des 25 jährigen Regierungs-Jubiläums Kaiser Wilhelm II.," *Historisch-politische Aufsätze und Reden*, 2 vols. (Munich, 1914), I, p. 11.

35. Rathenau, "Der Kaiser," p. 243.

36. Ibid., p. 244.

37. Thomas Mann, *Gesammelte Werke*, 12 vols. (Oldenburg, 1960), II, p. 43.

38. Quoted in Friedrich Hartau, *Wilhelm II: In Selbstzeugnissen und Bilddokumenten* (Reinbek, 1978), p. 144. Walther Rathenau also used an operatic metaphor to characterize Wilhelmian Germany. "The course of history," he wrote, "was an opera libretto." "Der Kaiser," p. 257.

39. In the language of self psychology, the Germans were a selfobject for Wilhelm and Wilhelm was a selfobject for the Germans. For more on the selfobject relationship between ruler and subject, leader and follower, see Heinz Kohut, "Creativity, Charisma, Group Psychology: Reflections on the Self-Analysis of Freud," *The Search for the Self: Selected Writings of Heinz Kohut, 1950–1978*, Paul H. Ornstein, ed., 2 vols. (New York, 1978), II, pp. 793–844; Charles B. Strozier, "Heinz Kohut and the Historical Imagination," *Advances in Self Psychology*, Arnold Goldberg, ed. (New York, 1980), pp. 397–406. Although he ignores the psychological dimension of national identity (i.e., the need of human beings to enhance themselves psychologically by identifying with a collective identity larger and more powerful than the self), see Geoff Eley's "State Formation."

40. As Friedrich Naumann put it in 1909: "Humanity wants to have representatives, signal persons, presidents, be they called Bebel or Tolstoy, Ballin or Kirdorff, Mendelsohn or Kanitz, Röntgen or Zeppelin, Roosevelt or Wilhelm II." Quoted in Fehrenbach, *Wandlungen*, p. 211.

41. Ibid., pp. 177–83.

42. The period of Wilhelm II's greatest popularity with the Germans was from approximately 1897 to approximately 1908, with a marked fall-off already discernable in 1905—that is the period corresponding to that defined in the Introduction as the truly Wilhelmian period of German history. For increasing rightwing criticism of the Kaiser especially after 1905, see Roger Chickering, *We Men Who Feel Most German: A Cultural Study of the Pan German League, 1886–1914* (Boston, 1984), pp. 218–23; Wilhelm Deist, *Flottenpolitik und Flotten-*

propaganda: Das Nachrichtenbureau des Reichsmarineamtes, 1897–1914 (Stuttgart, 1976), passim; and Eley, *Reshaping,* passim. For the collapse of Wilhelm II's popularity after the *Daily Telegraph* affair, see ibid., pp. 285–90; Fehrenbach, *Wandlungen,* pp. 135–42; Ferdinand Tönnies, *Kritik der öffentlichen Meinung* (Bad Honnef, 1981, reprint of the 1922 edition), pp. 277–79 and 310–11.

43. Generalizing about popular attitudes, feelings, and opinions is one of the historian's most important tasks, yet one invariably undertaken with misgiving. Needless to say, given present historical methods and the available evidence, it is impossible to determine the Germans' response to Wilhelm II precisely. Lacking quantitative measures of the popular mood, the historian is forced to rely upon the comments of contemporary observers to get a sense of what the Germans thought and felt about the Kaiser. That evidence, drawn from the Kaiser's supporters and detractors, suggests that for much of his reign Wilhelm II enjoyed significant popularity among large sections of the German population.

And yet, this generalization oversimplifies the experience of the Germans not only across time and place but within the same person. Obviously opinions about Wilhelm II varied within individual Germans. When identifying themselves with a particular social class, political party, or region of the country, individuals found it easy to criticize Wilhelm. When identifying themselves as Germans, those same individuals tended to be less critical of the Kaiser. No matter how much he may have been disliked from other perspectives, as the personal symbol of the nation, Wilhelm II could evoke widespread and intense popular enthusiasm. Thus one senses, but cannot of course prove, that there was an underlying feeling, experienced by most Germans at one time or another, often against their better judgment, of proud identification with the heroic image of the German Kaiser.

44. For the extent of Wilhelm's travels and the number of his ceremonial entrances, see Appendix I. Just how unprecedented the Kaiser's travels were is revealed by a comparison with his contemporary, Grover Cleveland. Despite conducting two presidential campaigns (in 1884 and 1892), the U.S. president never once in his life traveled west of Buffalo.

45. Ernst Johann, ed., *Reden des Kaisers: Ansprachen, Predigten und Trinksprüche Wilhelms II* (Munich, 1966), pp. 118–19.

46. Wilhelm's attempt to overcome his vulnerability to narcissistic injury and his ongoing struggle against depression is also revealed by the numerous mottos hung over his desk at his hunting lodge in Rominten and at his home in Berlin. These included: "Be strong in pain; desire not that which is unattainable or worthless; be content with the day as it comes; look for the good in all things; and take pleasure in nature and in men as they are." "For a thousand bitter hours console thyself with a single one that is beautiful; ever give heartily and of thy best, even when repaid with ingratitude. He who is able to learn so to act is a happy, free, and proud man, and his life will always be beautiful." "The man who is distrustful commits an injustice against others and injures himself. It is our duty to consider every man good as long as he does not prove himself to the contrary." "Everything in the world must be as it is; and, be as it may, it is always good in the sight of the Creator." Mottos copied and published by J. L. Bashford in *The Westminster Gazette* of 11 November 1907.

47. Report of 10 September 1889, PA Bonn, Preussen 1, Nr. 1d, vol. 3.

48. Nicolaus Sombart, "Der letzte Kaiser war so, wie die Deutschen waren," *Frankfurter Allgemeine Zeitung,* 27 January 1979. See also Fehrenbach, *Wandlungen,* p. 99.

49. Fehrenbach, "Images of Kaiserdom," p. 278.

50. Ibid., p. 276. See also Fehrenbach, *Wandlungen,* p. 89.

51. Rathenau, "Der Kaiser," p. 242.

52. In satirizing Wilhelm's pilgrimage to the Holy Land in 1898, Frank Wedekind acknowledged the Kaiser's ability to satisfy both mankind's "thirst for deeds" and its even more "immense" thirst to "admire" through his versatile theatricality. Indeed, the frequency of the Kaiser's travels testifies to his popularity. Were the responses of his subjects less than enthusiastic, Wilhelm would not have derived the psychological gratification that caused him to travel so much. I am indebted to Dr. John Hall for this observation.

53. "Ein Zwiegespräch," Eulenburg Papers, BA Koblenz, vol. 74.

54. Rathenau, "Der Kaiser," pp. 235–36.

55. Naumann, *Demokratie und Kaisertum: Ein Handbuch für innere Politik* (Berlin, 1904), pp. 167–68. Translated and quoted in Röhl, *Germany Without Bismarck*, p. 279. It was Naumann's hope that Wilhelm would become a *Volkskaiser*, a people's emperor, and that through a more powerful monarchy and more democracy the working class could be won over to the imperial power state. For more on Naumann and his attitude toward Wilhelm II, see Fehrenbach, *Wandlungen*, pp. 200–20.

56. See Kurt Koszyk, *Deutsche Presse im 19. Jahrhundert: Geschichte der deutschen Presse*, 4 vols. (Berlin, 1966), II, pp. 256–57.

57. Ludwig Quidde, *Caligula—eine Studie über römischen Cäsarenwahnsinn* (Leipzig, 1894), pp. 8, 10, 11, 12, 15, and 16.

58. Ibid., p. 16. Despite the vast political and philosophical distance separating him from the liberal pacifist, Quidde, the racist cultural pessimist, Julius Langbehn reached a similar conclusion about the Kaiser's popularity and influence. Hans Kohn, *The Mind of Germany: The Education of a Nation* (New York, 1965), p. 274.

59. For Wilhelm's personal regime and its critics, see Fehrenbach, *Wandlungen*, pp. 116–58. According to Fehrenbach, despite the fact that Wilhelm's diminished public presence after the *Daily Telegraph* affair reflected the will of the Reichstag, "the increasingly passive role of the Kaiser had by no means favorable consequences, and the criticism of contemporaries as well as the degree of their disappointment demonstrates that in the end they too wanted to preserve the fiction of autocracy and wished it to succeed." Ibid., p. 97. Similarly, Tönnies pointed out that before 1908 criticism of the Kaiser was directed not so much at his personal regime as at the influence of the so-called camarilla. *Kritik*, p. 272.

60. Quoted in Fehrenbach, *Wandlungen*, p. 119.

61. Friedrich Meinecke, "Deutsche Jahrhundertfeier," p. 162.

62. Ibid., p. 172.

63. Ibid., p. 174.

64. Ibid., p. 171. See Fehrenbach, *Wandlungen*, p. 91. See, here, the similar appraisal of the theologian Adolf von Harnack on the occasion of the Kaiser's birthday in 1907 quoted in ibid., p. 104.

65. Eugen Fischer, "Des Kaisers Glaube an seinen göttlichen Beruf," *Die Tat* 5 (1913), p. 574.

66. Fehrenbach, *Wandlungen*, pp. 89–90.

67. Quoted in ibid., p. 129.

68. Quoted in ibid., p. 130.

69. Letter of late March. George Earle Buckle, ed., *The Letters of Queen Victoria, 1886–1901*, 3 vols. (New York, 1930), II, p. 350.

70. Letter from Chancellor Hohenlohe to his son, Alexander, of 31 October 1897, *Hohenlohe: Denkwürdigkeiten*, p. 398.

71. Those interested in recent views on this issue should see Lamar Cecil's assessment in *Wilhelm II*, pp. 259–61 and 416–17, note 92; as well as Röhl, "Introduction," *Kaiser Wilhelm II*, pp. 1–22, which contains a summary of the debate over the Kaiser's significance. Röhl also makes a forceful case for Wilhelm's importance in *Kaiser, Hof und Staat*. See also the contributions to *Kaiser Wilhelm II* of Paul Kennedy, "The Kaiser and German *Weltpolitik*: Reflexions on Wilhelm II's Place in the Making of German Foreign Policy," pp. 143–68; Katharine Anne Lerman, "The Decisive Relationship: Kaiser Wilhelm II and Chancellor Bernhard von Bülow, 1900–1905," pp. 221–47; and Terence Cole, "The *Daily Telegraph* Affair and its Aftermath: The Kaiser, Bülow and the Reichstag, 1908–1909," pp. 249–68. See, here, Geoff Eley, "The View from the Throne: The Personal Rule of Kaiser Wilhelm II," *Historical Journal* 28 (1985), pp. 469–85. Other considerations of this issue include Lamar Cecil, *The German Diplomatic Service, 1871–1914* (Princeton, 1976), pp. 211–25 and 321–22; Fehrenbach, *Wandlungen*, pp. 95–96; Kennedy, *Antagonism*, pp. 403–409; and Barbara Vogel, *Deutsche Russlandpolitik: Das Scheitern der deutschen Weltpolitik unter Bülow, 1900–1906* (Düsseldorf, 1973), pp. 44–48. For earlier controversy over Wilhelm II's personal rule, see Erich Eyck, *Das persönliche Regiment Wilhelms II* (Zürich, 1948); Ernst Rudolf Huber,

"Das persönliche Regiment Wilhelms II," *Zeitschrift für Religion und Geistesgeschichte* 3 (1951), pp. 134–48; and Fritz Hartung, "Das persönliche Regiment Kaiser Wilhelms II," *Sitzungsberichte der deutschen Akademie der Wissenschaften zu Berlin* (Berlin, 1952).

72. "Kaiser Wilhelm II," BA Koblenz, Eulenburg Papers, vol. 80.

73. As his comments on the Kaiser's personality quoted in this study reveal, Bernhard von Bülow had a keen understanding of Wilhelm II's psyche. He used that understanding to great personal and political effect. Indeed, as Katharine Anne Lerman's *The Chancellor as Courtier: Bernhard von Bülow and the Governance of Germany, 1900–1909* (Cambridge, 1990) demonstrates, it was Bülow's ability to maintain a favored personal position with the Kaiser that formed the basis of his political authority and influence. See also Cecil, *Diplomatic Service,* pp. 281–84.

74. For Hohenlohe's skill in managing the Kaiser, see Cecil, *Wilhelm II,* pp. 212–62 and 335–36, and J. David Fraley, "Government by Procrastination: Chancellor Hohenlohe and Kaiser Wilhelm II, 1894–1900," *Central European History* 7 (1974), pp. 159–83. For Tirpitz's skill in managing the Kaiser, see Cecil, *Wilhelm II,* p. 314.

75. See, here, Cecil, *Diplomatic Service,* pp. 275–81; Norman Rich, *Friedrich von Holstein: Politics and Diplomacy in the Era of Bismarck and Wilhelm II,* 2 vols. (Cambridge, 1965), pp. 491–543; and Röhl, *Germany Without Bismarck,* pp. 132–240. Another example of Wilhelm's powerlessness in the face of the determined opposition of his advisers was the Köller crisis, when the threat of the mass resignation of his ministers forced the Kaiser against his will to dismiss Ernst Matthias von Köller as minister of the interior in 1895. For more on this incident, see Cecil, *Wilhelm II,* pp. 228–33; Rich, *Holstein,* pp. 494–96; and Röhl, *Germany Without Bismarck,* pp. 136–46.

76. See Chapter 10.

77. See, for example, the comments of Fitzmaurice and Grey quoted at the conclusion of the previous chapter.

78. Bülow, *Denkwürdigkeiten,* I, pp. 235–37.

79. "Ein Zwiegespräch," BA Koblenz, Eulenburg Papers, vol. 74.

80. Already by the death of Wilhelm I the changing character of the Hohenzollern monarchy was clearly evident. J. Alden Nichols, *The Year of the Three Kaisers: Bismarck and the German Succession, 1887–1888* (Urbana and Chicago, 1987), p. 178.

81. The use of the term "narcissistic" should be understood not in its popular pejorative sense but as a technical term. To say that the Kaiser was the narcissistic object (selfobject) of the Germans simply means that Germans experienced Wilhelm II psychologically as part of themselves.

82. The choice of a psychoanalytic model drawn from self psychology to assist in the investigation of Wilhelm II's leadership of the Germans seems appropriate given the fact that his role was less that of a father to his subjects and more that of a narcissistic extension of his subjects. Presumably an oedipal model would be better suited to aid in understanding a more paternalistic relationship between ruler and subject.

83. Heinrich Mann, *Man of Straw* (New York, 1984), p. 44.

84. Rathenau, "Der Kaiser," p. 236.

85. "Die Feinde des Kaisers," *Die Zukunft* 40 (1902), p. 340. See, here, Fehrenbach, *Wandlungen,* p. 97.

86. Fehrenbach, "Images of Kaiserdom," pp. 269–85. Meinecke, "Deutsche Jahrhundertfeier," pp. 161–75.

87. Friedrich Meinecke, "Drei Generationen deutscher Gelehrtenpolitik: Friedrich Vischer, Gustav Schmoller, Max Weber," *Brandenburg, Preussen, Deutschland: Kleine Schriften zur Geschichte und Politik,* Eberhard Kessel, ed. (Stuttgart, 1979), pp. 495–505.

88. Wolfgang J. Mommsen, *Max Weber und die deutsche Politik, 1890–1920,* 2nd ed. (Tübingen, 1974), pp. 147–76, especially 151–59. See Weber's essays "Zur Lage der bürgerlichen Demokratie in Russland," pp. 30–65, and "Russlands Übergang zum Scheinkonstitutionalismus," pp. 66–108, in Max Weber, *Gesammelte politische Schriften,* 2nd ed., Johannes Winckelmann, ed. (Tübingen, 1958).

89. Mommsen, *Weber,* pp. 40–43.

90. Weber, "Deutschland unter den europäischen Weltmächten," *Schriften,* pp. 152–72, see especially 170–71. See also Mommsen, *Weber,* p. 69.

91. Ibid., pp. 73 and 147–49.

92. Ibid., pp. 150–51. Weber, "Bismarcks Aussenpolitik und die Gegenwart," *Schriften,* pp. 109–26, especially 111–14.

93. Mommsen, *Weber,* pp. 94–95. Weber, "Der Nationalstaat und die Volkswirtschafts-politik," *Schriften,* pp. 1–25.

94. Mommsen, *Weber,* p. 74.

95. Weber, "Die Nationalstaat," p. 23.

96. Mommsen, *Weber,* p. 86.

97. Weber, "Deutschland unter den europäischen Mächten," p. 154.

98. Letter of 24 February 1896, Bülow, *Denkwürdigkeiten,* I, pp. 34–36.

99. For the popular identification with the Boers in Germany, see, for example, the reports in the Berlin papers on 2 January 1900 about the youth of Berlin which had celebrated the new year by pretending to be Boers and making a tremendous racket with "smokeless powder from the Transvaal" and with "*Burenbackpfeifen,*" that is, with the weapons the Boers were using to give the British a slap in the face. Salewski, "'Neujahr 1900'," p. 342.

100. For the popularity of the Krüger telegram in Germany and general German sympathy for the Boers, see Pauline R. Anderson, *The Background of Anti-English Feeling in Germany, 1890–1902* (Washington, 1939), pp. 227–61 and 285–360; Deist, *Flottenpolitik,* p. 15, note 30; Oron J. Hale, *Publicity and Diplomacy: With Special Reference to England and Germany, 1890–1914* (Gloucester, Mass., 1964 reprint), pp. 190–265; Friedrich Thimme, "Die Krüger-Depesche: Genesis und historische Bedeutung," *Europäische Gespräche. Hamburger Monats-hefte für auswärtige Politik* 2 (1924), pp. 201–44. According to the correspondent of *The Times* in Berlin, Chirol, "never perhaps was a royal declaration greeted with such jubilation as the Krüger-Telegram. In that sense it was a 'hit' of the first order." Ibid., p. 232. Hermann Oncken also reported on the sympathy of all social classes and parts of the country for the Boers. Oncken, "Politik, Geschichtsschreibung und öffentliche Meinung," *Aufsätze und Reden,* I, pp. 205–207. See also Cecil, *Diplomatic Service,* pp. 221–23; Cecil, *Wilhelm II,* pp. 326–28; and Rich, *Holstein,* pp. 466–72.

101. Meinecke, "Deutsche Jahrhundertfeier," p. 173.

102. Ibid. Another historian, if one more critical of the Kaiser than Friedrich Meinecke, reached a similar conclusion about Wilhelm II's success on the same occasion. At Heidelberg University on 15 June 1913 Hermann Oncken declared: "Only posterity . . . will be able to speak the last word of historical judgment: as far as one . . . can judge today we are in the course of secure and uninterrupted progress and that too is in large measure to be attributed to the work of the Kaiser." "Der Kaiser und die Nation," p. 18.

103. Rathenau, "Der Kaiser," p. 259.

104. That Wilhelm's response to the Boxer Rebellion and his fear of the "yellow peril" expressed popular anxiety is confirmed in Siegfried A. Kaehler's letter to Friedrich Meinecke of 14 June 1949. Friedrich Meinecke, *Ausgewählter Briefwechsel,* Ludwig Dehio and Peter Classen, eds. (Stuttgart, 1962), p. 541.

105. "Ein Zwiegespräch," BA Koblenz, Eulenburg Papers, vol. 74.

Chapter 9

1. Elisabeth Fehrenbach, *Wandlungen des deutschen Kaisergedankens, 1871–1918* (Munich, 1969), p. 169; Rudolf Stadelmann, "Die Epoche der deutsch-englischen Flottenri-valität," *Deutschland und Westeuropa* (Schloss Laupheim, 1948), pp. 98–99; and Jonathan Steinberg, "The Copenhagen Complex," *Journal of Contemporary History* 1 (1966), p. 43. The effort of historians to detect rational self-interest behind the naval building program will be considered below.

2. See, here, Lamar Cecil, *Wilhelm II: Prince and Emperor, 1859–1900* (Chapel Hill, 1989), pp. 291–318, especially 304–305 and 312–13; Paul M. Kennedy, *The Rise of the Anglo-German Antagonism, 1860–1914* (London, 1982), p. 408; and John C. G. Röhl, "Der 'Königsmechanismus' im Kaiserreich," *Kaiser, Hof und Staat: Wilhelm II und die deutsche Politik* (Munich, 1988), p. 129. Even Volker R. Berghahn, for whom the conclusion poses interpretative problems, and Hans Hallmann, for whom it poses political problems, assign the Kaiser a central role in German naval development. Berghahn regards the navy as a weapon designed to wrest naval and world power away from Britain. As will be considered in the following chapter, this view is difficult to reconcile with the Kaiser's Anglophilia and conviction that a formidable fleet would demonstrate the Reich's value as an ally to the British. For Berghahn's view of the Kaiser's role in naval development, see *Der Tirpitz-Plan: Genesis und Verfall einer innenpolitischen Krisenstrategie unter Wilhelm II.* (Düsseldorf, 1971), pp. 354–80 and 456–58, and "Zu den Zielen des deutschen Flottenbaus unter Wilhelm II.," *Historische Zeitschrift* 210 (1970), pp. 78–82. Hallmann, writing in 1933, sought to establish Tirpitz as a German hero and dedicated his book, *Der Weg zum deutschen Schlachtflottenbau* (Stuttgart, 1933), to him. By crediting Wilhelm with the inspiration for naval expansion, Hallmann not only reduced Tirpitz's responsibility for this achievement but associated him with the unpopular figure of the ex-Kaiser.

3. Wilhelm II, *My Early Life* (New York, 1926), pp. 49 and 230.

4. Joachim von Kürenberg, *The Kaiser: The Life of Wilhelm II., Last Emperor of Germany* (London, 1954), p. 158.

5. For more on Wilhelm II's feelings on board ship, see the complete text of the Ganghofer interview in Ernst Johann, ed., *Reden des Kaisers: Ansprachen, Predigten und Trinksprüche Wilhelms II.* (Munich, 1966), pp. 118–19. See also Wilhelm II, *My Early Life*, p. 52.

6. See, for example, the letters from Alfred von Kiderlen-Wächter to Holstein of 16 July 1888 and of 19 July 1888, Norman Rich and M. H. Fisher, eds., *The Holstein Papers*, 4 vols. (Cambridge, 1955–1963), III, pp. 279–85; the letter from Wilhelm II to Philipp Eulenburg of 28 August 1888, John C. G. Röhl, ed., *Philipp Eulenburgs politische Korrespondenz*, 3 vols. (Boppard-am-Rhein, 1976–1983), I, p. 310; and Wilhelm II's marginalia to the reports from the German representative in the Hague to Bismarck of 10 August 1889 and 11 August 1889, PA Bonn, Preussen 1, Nr. 1, Nr. 4°, vol. 3.

7. For the decisive role played by the Krüger telegram in German naval development, see Cecil, *Wilhelm II*, pp. 282–90. See also Cecil, *The German Diplomatic Service, 1871–1914* (Princeton, 1976), pp. 221–23; Wilhelm Deist, *Flottenpolitik und Flottenpropaganda: Das Nachrichtenbureau des Reichsmarineamtes, 1897–1914* (Stuttgart, 1976), pp. 58–69; Hans Hallmann, *Krügerdepesche und Flottenfrage* (Stuttgart, 1927); Hallmann, *Der Weg*, pp. 171–201; Kennedy, *Antagonism*, pp. 220–21; Norman Rich, *Friedrich von Holstein: Politics and Diplomacy in the Era of Bismarck and Wilhelm II*, 2 vols. (Cambridge, 1965), pp. 466–72, 504–506, and 527; John C. G. Röhl, *Germany Without Bismarck: The Crisis of Government in the Second Reich, 1890–1900* (Berkeley, 1967), pp. 160–68; Jonathan Steinberg, *Yesterday's Deterrent: Tirpitz and the Birth of the German Battle Fleet* (London, 1965), pp. 82–96; and Friedrich Thimme, "Die Krüger-Depesche: Genesis und historische Bedeutung," *Europäische Gespräche. Hamburger Monatshefte für auswärtige Politik* 2 (1924), pp. 201–44.

8. Ivo Nikolai Lambi, *The Navy and German Power Politics, 1862–1914* (Boston, 1984), pp. 25 and 57.

9. Already before the Krüger telegram Tirpitz had been an advocate of battleship construction and had sought to make England the focus of the navy's strategic thinking. Ibid., pp. 83 and 86.

10. Ibid., pp. 118 and 124–25.

11. Wilhelm's word was "*zusammengeschrümpfende.*" See Appendix II.

12. BMA Freiburg, RM 2, vol. 1558. A version of this document dated 8 January 1896 was published in *Fürst Chlodwig zu Hohenlohe-Schillingsfürst: Denkwürdigkeiten der Reichskanzlerzeit*, Karl Alexander von Müller, ed. (Stuttgart and Berlin, 1931), pp. 153–54.

13. Letter from Court Marshal August Eulenburg to Hohenlohe of 15 January 1896, ibid., pp. 158–59.

14. Order of 16 January 1896, ibid., p. 152.

15. See, here, the Kaiser's insistence following Germany's failure to redeem its honor after the Boxer Rebellion that an immediate alliance with Japan be concluded.

16. *GP*, XIII, pp. 3–4. A portion of this telegram has been quoted in Chapter 6.

17. See Appendix II.

18. Ibid., XV, pp. 406–408.

19. Wilhelm II's marginalia to Tirpitz's notes to his audience with the Kaiser of 5 December 1903, BMA Freiburg, Tirpitz Papers, N253, vol. 20, in which Wilhelm characterized the period before naval expansion as a "*Schamm Zeit.*" See note 23 below and Wilhelm II's marginalia to the *Berliner neueste Nachrichten* of 17 September 1897, PA Bonn, Preussen 1, Nr. 1d, vol. 8. See Appendix II.

20. PA Bonn, Deutschland 138, vol. 7. See also Hohenlohe's memorandum of 1 February 1896, *Hohenlohe: Denkwürdigkeiten*, p. 164. For the recall of the *Kaiser*, see Hallmann, *Krügerdepesche*, p. 41; Hallmann, *Der Weg*, p. 179; and Steinberg, *Deterrent*, pp. 87–89.

21. Already before the Krüger telegram, Wilhelm sought to convince his advisers of the need for naval expansion by refusing to dispatch naval vessels to areas where they were needed. Thus he was unwilling to grant the request of the Foreign Office to send ships to Samoa, Venezuela, or the eastern Mediterranean. Wilhelm's letter to Hohenlohe of 21 January 1895, PA Bonn, Deutschland 138, vol. 5; Hohenlohe's memorandum of 31 January 1895, *Hohenlohe: Denkwürdigkeiten*, p. 32; Wilhelm II's marginalia to the telegram from Marschall to Hohenlohe of 16 November 1895, *GP*, X, pp. 179–80; and to the telegram from Saurma to the Foreign Office of 19 November 1895, ibid., p. 187.

22. See Eulenburg's letter to Hohenlohe of 1 November 1897 informing the chancellor of Wilhelm's refusal to dispatch a training vessel to Guatemala because "it is imperative that the German flag be taken 'seriously.'" The Kaiser contended "that unfortunately we have no other ships to send, and Germany must simply get used to the fact that the nation and its overseas interests will be harmed and embarrassed since the necessary vessels are not being approved." PA Bonn, Deutschland 138, vol. 11.

23. "*Marineschmach.*" Wilhelm II's marginalia to a letter from Hohenlohe of 6 February 1897, PA Bonn, Deutschland 122, Nr. 11, Nr. 2, vol. 2. See Appendix II. For the German reaction to the revolt against Turkish rule on Crete and its aftermath, see Cecil, *Wilhelm II*, pp. 321–22; and Rich, *Holstein*, pp. 477–83.

24. Wilhelm's word was "*lähmt.*" See Appendix II.

25. Wilhelm II's marginalia to the report from Plessen in Athens to Hohenlohe of 28 March 1897, *GP*, XII (2), pp. 395–96. Lambi, *Navy*, p. 35.

26. See Chapter 7.

27. Wilhelm II's marginalia to a report from Undersecretary of State in the Foreign Office Oswald Freiherr von Richthofen to Eulenburg with the Kaiser in Skjoldeharn of 20 July 1898, PA Bonn, England 78, Nr. 1, *secr.*, vol. 4. See, here, Paul M. Kennedy, "German World Policy and the Alliance Negotiations with England, 1897–1900," *Journal of Modern History* 45 (1973), p. 614; Kennedy, *The Samoan Tangle: A Study in Anglo-German-American Relations, 1878–1900* (Dublin, 1974), pp. 130–31; Kennedy, *Antagonism*, pp. 235–36; Rich, *Holstein*, pp. 586–89; and Peter Winzen, *Bülows Weltmachtkonzept: Untersuchungen zur Frühphase seiner Aussenpolitik, 1897–1901* (Boppard-am-Rhein, 1977), pp. 93–94.

28. Report from Bülow to the Foreign Office of 4 September 1897, PA Bonn, Deutschland 138, vol. 11. Also Wilhelm II's marginalia to the report of Senden of 9 May 1897, BMA Freiburg, RM2, vol. 143.

29. PA Bonn, England 78, vol. 31. In May 1902 Wilhelm thought to use the British naval revue celebrating the coronation of Edward VII to impress on the Reichstag deputies the need to increase the size of the German navy. Deist, *Flottenpolitik*, p. 99.

30. Ibid., p. 326.

31. Ibid., pp. 28–33. For a general consideration of Wilhelm II's role in the early years of naval propaganda, see pp. 19–69.

32. Wilhelm II's marginalia to the reports from the German ambassador in Tokyo to Chancellor Caprivi of 22 December 1893, PA Bonn, Deutschland 138, vol. 3, and of 6 July 1894, PA Bonn, Deutschland 138, vol. 4. Deist, *Flottenpolitik*, pp. 94–95.

33. Order of 28 May 1896, BMA Freiburg, RM 2, vol. 1730. There is some debate about Admiral Tirpitz's influence on this Order. Jonathan Steinberg in *Deterrent*, pp. 99–100, discerns the influence of the chief of the Naval Cabinet, Admiral Baron Gustav von Senden und Bibran, behind the document. Berghahn in *Tirpitz-Plan*, p. 119, and Deist in *Flottenpolitik*, pp. 61–63, present Tirpitz as the moving spirit behind the Order. Nevertheless, it was the Kaiser's insistence on the central importance to the propaganda campaign of the continuous manipulation of the press that, in Deist's words, "showed" Tirpitz "the way." Ibid., p. 57. See also Wilhelm II's letter to Hollmann of 28 May 1896 stressing the need for the naval authorities and naval officers to increase their involvement in the propaganda campaign on behalf of naval development. BMA Freiburg, RM 2, vol. 1558.

34. See Hohenlohe's memoranda of 22 and 25 January 1896, *Hohenlohe: Denkwürdigkeiten*, pp. 161–62.

35. Bogdan Graf von Hutten-Czapski, *Sechzig Jahre Politik und Gesellschaft*, 2 vols. (Berlin, 1936), I, p. 277.

36. A coup d'état from above, suspending the constitution of the Reich.

37. Wilhelm II's marginalia to a report from Monts in Munich to Hohenlohe of 23 March 1897, PA Bonn. Deutschland 138, vol. 10. See Deist, *Flottenpolitik*, p. 100.

38. Memorandum of late March 1897, *Hohenlohe: Denkwürdigkeiten*, p. 325. For Hollmann's fall and his replacement by Tirpitz as secretary of state in the Reich Naval Office, see Berghahn, *Tirpitz-Plan*, pp. 90–107; Hallmann, *Der Weg*, pp. 202–37; Rich, *Holstein*, pp. 526–43 (passim); Röhl, *Germany Without Bismarck*, pp. 166–71, 210–17, and 246–58; and Steinberg, *Deterrent*, pp. 97–124.

39. Letter from Wilhelm II to Eulenburg of 20 August 1897, Bernhard Fürst von Bülow, *Denkwürdigkeiten*, 4 vols. (Berlin, 1930), I, pp. 137–39. For more on the propaganda campaign in addition to Deist's book, see Volker R. Berghahn, *Rüstung und Machtpolitik: Zur Anatomie des 'Kalten Krieges' vor 1914* (Düsseldorf, 1974), pp. 36–46; Berghahn, *Tirpitz-Plan*, pp. 118–29; Oron J. Hale, *Publicity and Diplomacy: With Special Reference to England and Germany, 1890–1914* (Gloucester, Mass., 1964 reprint), pp. 153–67 and 216–26; Eckart Kehr, *Schlachtflottenbau und Parteipolitik: Versuch eines Querschnitts durch die innenpolitischen, sozialen und ideologischen Voraussetzungen des deutschen Imperialismus* (Berlin, 1930), pp. 93–120; Gustav Oldenhage, *Die deutsche Flottenfrage von 1897 und die öffentliche Meinung* (Gütersloh im Westfalen, 1935); Röhl, *Germany Without Bismarck*, pp. 251–58; and Steinberg, *Deterrent*, pp. 131–48 and 158–63. For later propaganda on behalf of the navy, see Klaus Wernecke, *Die Wille zur Weltgeltung: Aussenpolitik und Öffentlichkeit am Vorabend des Ersten Weltkrieges* (Düsseldorf, 1970).

40. See Wilhelm II's telegram to Chancellor Hohenlohe of 31 August 1895 in which he declared that if Russia occupied Korean territory Germany must seize Wei-hai-wei. Not only would such decisive action win the respect of the other powers, but "it would make a splendid impression on our joyfully enthusiastic people and would substantially raise the self-esteem of the nation." *Hohenlohe: Dendwürdigkeiten*, pp. 94–95. The Kaiser expressed similar sentiments in marginalia to a report from the German vice-consul in Buschär of 6 April 1899, PA Bonn, Deutschland 138, vol. 15.

41. Bülow, *Denkwürdigkeiten*, I, p. 60.

42. Wilhelm II's telegram to Prince Ludwig of Bavaria of 1 May 1904, PA Bonn, Deutschland 138, vol. 26. Wilhelm II's message to the Hauptverband deutscher Flottenvereine im Ausland of 9 June 1898, PA Bonn, Deutschland 138, Nr. 5, vol. 1.

43. On the navy as a symbol, see Roger Chickering, *We Men Who Feel Most German: A Cultural Study of the Pan German League, 1896–1914* (Boston, 1984), p. 56; Deist, *Flottenpolitik*, p. 15; Fehrenbach, *Wandlungen*, pp. 170–73; and Steinberg, *Deterrent*, pp. 31–60.

44. Telegram from Metternich with Wilhelm II in Sandringham, England to the Foreign Office of 9 November 1902, PA Bonn, Deutschland 138, *secr.*, vol. 5. Similar sentiments are expressed in Wilhelm II's marginalia to the report from Monts in Munich to Chancellor

Hohenlohe of 15 November 1899, PA Bonn, Deutschland 138, *secr.,* vol. 2, and in his marginalia to the *Manchester Guardian* of 17 June 1908, PA Bonn, Preussen 1, Nr. 1d, vol. 19. See also the Kaiser's statement to the American minister in Copenhagen, Root, of 7 April 1906 that the navy was an instrument to integrate the particularistic Germans. Quoted in Pauline R. Anderson, *The Background of Anti-English Feeling in Germany, 1890–1902* (Washington, 1939), p. 28. Jonathan Steinberg has written that the navy was "the one truly national institution in the unstable and unfinished German Empire." Indeed, according to Steinberg, "unless the Navy is placed in the perspective of the struggle for national unification we cannot understand why it could grow so rapidly after 1898." *Deterrent,* p. 287.

45. Letter from Hohenlohe to Wilhelm II of 23 March 1898, *Hohenlohe: Denkwürdigkeiten,* pp. 435–36. Letter from Wilhelm II to Hohenlohe of 27 March 1898, ibid., pp. 436–37. Letter from Jagemann, Badenese representative in Berlin, to Brauer of 31 March 1898, Walther Peter Fuchs, ed., *Grossherzog Friedrich II. von Baden und die Reichspolitik, 1871–1907,* 4 vols. (Stuttgart, 1968–1980), IV, pp. 34–35. For other implications of Tirpitz's appointment, see Berghahn, *Tirpitz-Plan,* pp. 158–59; Cecil, *Wilhelm II,* pp. 317–18; and Steinberg, *Deterrent,* pp. 197–98.

46. Wilhelm II's letters in English to Tsar Nicholas II of 22 August 1901, 17 December 1901, 3 January 1902, and 1 February 1907, Issac Don Levine, ed., *Letters from the Kaiser to the Czar* (New York, 1920), pp. 71–81 and 216–17.

47. Report from the chief of the Naval Cabinet, Senden, to the Foreign Office of 22 January 1907, BMA Freiburg, RM 2, vol. 118.

48. Report from Senden to the Foreign Office of 4 November 1902, PA Bonn, Deutschland 138, vol. 23.

49. Deist, *Flottenpolitik,* p. 51; Lambi, *Navy,* pp. 33 and 37.

50. Berghahn, *Tirpitz-Plan,* p. 360; Cecil, *Wilhelm II,* pp. 302–306.

51. For more on the cruiser/battleship controversy and for the political and strategic consequences of the decision to build a battlefleet, see Berghahn, *Tirpitz-Plan,* passim, but especially pp. 55–89, 108–10, and 184–201; Berghahn, "Zielen," pp. 61–66; Deist, *Flottenpolitik,* pp. 43–47; Hallmann, *Der Weg,* pp. 238–49; and Lambi, *Navy,* pp. 62–68, 83, 114, 118, 138, and 164–66.

52. Berghahn, *Tirpitz-Plan;* Berghahn, "Zielen;" Berghahn, *Rüstung;* Berghahn, *Germany and the Approach of War in 1914* (London, 1973); Ludwig Dehio, "Thoughts on Germany's Mission, 1900–1918," *Germany and World Politics in the Twentieth Century* (New York, 1967), pp. 72–108; Kennedy, *Antagonism,* pp. 417–19; Kennedy, "Tirpitz, England and the German Navy Law of 1900: A Strategical Critique," *Militärgeschichtliche Mitteilungen* 2 (1970), pp. 33–57; Kennedy, "German World Policy," pp. 605–25; Lambi, *The Navy;* various contributions to *Marine und Marinepolitik im kaiserlichen Deutschland, 1871–1914,* Herbert Schottelius and Wilhelm Deist, eds. (Düsseldorf, 1972); and Wernecke, *Weltgeltung.*

53. Tirpitz's notes to his audience with Wilhelm II of 15 June 1897, BMA Freiburg, Tirpitz Papers, N 253, vol. 4; also Tirpitz's reports to Wilhelm II, with Wilhelm's marginalia, of 29 January 1904, BMA Freiburg, RM 2, vol. 1601. Berghahn, *Tirpitz-Plan,* pp. 108–10; Cecil, *Wilhelm II,* pp. 315–16; Hallmann, *Der Weg,* pp. 248–49; Lambi, *Navy,* pp. 139–40; and Steinberg, *Deterrent,* pp. 126–29 and 208–23.

54. Tirpitz's notes to his audience with Wilhelm II of 20 February 1899, BMA Freiburg, Tirpitz Papers, N 253, vol. 4.

55. Tirpitz's notes to his audience with Wilhelm II of 28 November 1899, BMA Freiburg, Tirpitz Papers, N 253, vol. 4; copy of Tirpitz's notes to his audience with Wilhelm II of 31 January 1900, BMA Freiburg, RM 3, vol. 1; and Tirpitz's notes of 21 December 1905, BMA Freiburg, Tirpitz Papers, N 253, vol. 21. Berghahn, *Tirpitz-Plan,* pp. 161–62, 362, and 371–72.

56. Tirpitz's notes to his audience with Wilhelm II of 19 August 1897, BMA Freiburg, Tirpitz Papers, N 253, vol. 4; Tirpitz's letter to Finance Minister Johannes von Miquel of 5 August 1897, BMA Freiburg, Tirpitz Papers, N 253, vol. 4. Lambi, *Navy,* pp. 142 and 145; Hallmann, *Der Weg,* p. 266.

57. "Without a battlefleet," Tirpitz wrote on 4 January 1909, "we would be exposed to every insolence on the part of England." Translated and quoted in Lambi, *Navy,* p. 297.

58. Tirpitz's notes to his audience with Wilhelm II of 28 November 1898, BMA Freiburg, Tirpitz Papers, N 253, vol. 4. Berghahn, *Tirpitz-Plan,* pp. 161–62.

59. Copy of Tirpitz's notes to his audience with Wilhelm II of 28 September 1899, BMA Freiburg, RM 3, vol. 1. Lambi, *Navy,* p. 146.

60. Tirpitz's notes, with Wilhelm II's marginalia, of 29 January 1904, BMA Freiburg, RM 2, vol. 1601.

61. Letter to Tirpitz of 20 July 1905, BMA Freiburg, RM 3, vol. 5.

62. The differences between Tirpitz and Wilhelm in their understanding of the purpose of naval development can be attributed in part to their differing personalities and attitudes toward England, in part to the positions the two men occupied. For Tirpitz, as a naval captain and later admiral and state secretary in the Reich Naval Office, the role of the navy in wartime took precedence over its functions in time of peace. Already in the spring of 1894 Tirpitz had concluded that, in the words of Ivo Lambi, "the peacetime development of the navy must be toward its preparation for battle." *Navy,* p. 76. Just as it made sense for Germany's military leaders to regard France and Russia as posing the gravest danger to the Reich, so it made sense from the perspective of a leader of the navy to regard England as Germany's principal adversary. With the role of the navy in a war with Britain his primary concern, it was logical for Tirpitz to advocate the construction not of cruisers, which would not be effective in such a conflict, but of battleships, which would. Although commander-in-chief of both army and navy, Wilhelm, as Kaiser, was more concerned with the navy's impact during peacetime. The fleet's diplomatic and symbolic value took precedence over strategic considerations for him. A fleet of high-speed, long-range cruisers was better suited to realize that value than was a fleet of squat, slow-moving, short-range battleships.

63. See Chapter 10.

64. That Tirpitz still needed to sell the battlefleet to the Kaiser long after he had approved the Tirpitz plan (see Tirpitz's notes to numerous audiences with Wilhelm after 1898) suggests clearly that the Kaiser's commitment to the battlefleet was insecure. Wilhelm's commitment to the general notion of naval expansion was, of course, unmatched, even by Tirpitz himself. In the words of Ivo Lambi, "Wilhelm . . . wanted ships for their own sake and as an essential prerequisite for the successful conduct of an imperialist policy. He appears never to have become fully converted to Tirpitz's battleship doctrine and continued to promote schemes such as that of the fast ship of the line." *Navy,* pp. 155 and 164.

65. For the ongoing debate between Wilhelm and Tirpitz over foreign service ships versus the battlefleet, see the copy of Tirpitz's notes to his audience with Wilhelm II of 31 January 1900, BMA Freiburg, RM 3, vol. 1; Tirpitz's notes of his stay with Wilhelm II in Rominten and Hubertusstock between 25 September and 18 October 1903, BMA Freiburg, Tirpitz Papers, N 253, vol. 20; Wilhelm II's letter and questionnaire with the Kaiser's answers to it in October 1903, BMA Freiburg, RM 3, vol. 1; and Tirpitz's notes to his audience with Wilhelm II of 14 November 1903, BMA Freiburg, RM 3, vol. 3. In a letter of 14 November 1903, Wilhelm assured Tirpitz of his readiness to sacrifice the development of the foreign service fleet for the development of the battlefleet, BMA Freiburg, RM 3, vol. 3. And yet on 11 February 1905 Tirpitz reported to Bülow that Wilhelm had ordered that a naval bill be drawn up calling for the construction of six large cruisers to be used in foreign service. For the debate between Wilhelm and Tirpitz over coastal defenses versus the battlefleet, see Tirpitz's notes to his audience with Wilhelm II of 28 November 1898, BMA Freiburg, Tirpitz Papers, N 253, vol. 4, and Tirpitz's notes of 21 December 1904, BMA Freiburg, Tirpitz Papers, N 253, vol. 21. For the debate between Wilhelm and Tirpitz over torpedo boats versus the battlefleet, see the report from Tirpitz to Bülow of 11 February 1905, BMA Freiburg, RM 3, vol. 4, and especially the letter from Tirpitz to Wilhelm II of 30 July 1905, BMA Freiburg, RM 2, vol. 1601. Lambi, *Navy,* pp. 271–72.

66. The number of communications in which Wilhelm II made his case for the "fast ship of the line" are too numerous to cite individually. They occurred regularly between winter

1903 and the end of 1906. As late as the fall of 1909 the Kaiser was still lamenting that the Reich Naval Office had not followed his advice to create fast ships of the line. These communications are to be found in BMA Freiburg, RM 2, vols. 168, 173, 177, 188, 1601, and 1604; in BMA Freiburg, RM 3, vols. 3, 4, 5, 6, 7, 31, 1034, 1035, 2782, 2785, and 2786; in BMA Freiburg, Tirpitz Papers, N 253, vols. 20, 22, 23, and 40; and in BMA Freiburg, Senden Papers, N 160, vol. 1. For the conflict between Wilhelm and Tirpitz over the "fast ship of the line" and over Wilhelm's article, see Berghahn, *Tirpitz-Plan,* pp. 206, 360–70, 451–56, and 512, and Lambi, *Navy,* pp. 77 and 273–74.

67. Winzen, *Weltmachtkonzept,* p. 427. There are significant differences between Winzen's book and Vogel's *Deutsche Russlandpolitik: Das Scheitern der deutschen Weltpolitik unter Bülow, 1900–1906* (Düsseldorf, 1973). In contrast to Vogel, Winzen, who considers Bülow's foreign policy from 1897 to 1901, tends to adopt a more moderate tone and does not see Bülow's foreign policy as determined ultimately by domestic politics.

68. Winzen, *Weltmachtkonzept,* p. 81.

69. Vogel, *Russlandpolitik,* p. 233.

70. Winzen, *Weltmachtkonzept,* pp. 417–19; Vogel, *Russlandpolitik,* pp. 201–31.

71. Cecil, *Wilhelm II,* pp. 323–24 and 331; Kennedy, *Antagonism,* pp. 227 and 235; and Rich, *Holstein,* pp. 843–45. Bülow's foreign policy so defined is in harmony with his conduct in domestic politics as presented in Katharine Anne Lerman's *The Chancellor as Courtier: Bernhard von Bülow and the Governance of Germany, 1900–1909* (Cambridge, 1990). In domestic affairs, Bülow had no fixed goal or agenda but rather sought to exploit each situation as it presented itself to maximize his authority and prestige. Likewise in foreign affairs, he maintained his flexibility and sought to exploit each situation as it presented itself to maximize the power and prestige of the Reich.

72. Bernhard Fürst von Bülow, *Deutsche Politik* (Berlin, 1916), p. 29; Lambi, *Navy,* pp. 157–58.

73. Ibid., pp. 159 and 164.

74. Vogel, *Russlandpolitik,* pp. 44, 106–18, 155–59, 161–69, 172–73, 176, 178–79, 183, and 210–31.

75. A. Harding Ganz, "Colonial Policy and the Imperial German Navy," *Militärgeschichtliche Mitteilungen* (1977), Nr. 1, pp. 35–52; Kennedy, *Antagonism,* p. 245.

76. Vogel, *Russlandpolitik,* pp. 216–27.

77. See, for example, Lamar Cecil, "Wilhelm II and his Russian 'Colleagues'," *German Nationalism and the European Response, 1890–1945,* Carole Fink, Isabel V. Hull, and MacGregor Knox, eds. (Norman, Oklahoma, 1985), pp. 129–30; Kennedy, *Antagonism,* p. 281; and Rich, *Holstein,* pp. 417–19.

78. Kennedy, *Antagonism,* p. 225.

79. See, here, Cecil, *Wilhelm II,* pp. 299–300.

80. Bülow, *Denkwürdigkeiten,* II, p. 319.

81. For the popularity of the navy, see Deist, *Flottenpolitik,* pp. 14–15, especially note 28 which contains bibliographic references. For the popularity of Wilhelm's version of *Weltpolitik* with Germans of widely different backgrounds and social agendas, see Berghahn, *Tirpitz-Plan,* p. 19; Fehrenbach, *Wandlungen,* pp. 158–83; Charles E. McClelland, *The German Historians and England: A Study in Nineteenth Century Views* (Cambridge, 1971), pp. 191–224; McClelland, "Berlin Historians and German Politics," *Journal of Contemporary History* 8 (1973), pp. 12–21; Michael Salewski, "'Neujahr 1900': Die Säkularwende in zeitgenössischer Sicht," *Archiv für Kulturgeschichte* 53 (1972), pp. 352 and 366–67; and Manfred Sell, *Der deutsch-englische Abkommen von 1890: Über Helgoland und die afrikanische Kolonien im Lichte der deutschen Presse* (Berlin and Bonn, 1926).

82. Kennedy, *Antagonism,* pp. 382 and 321–60.

83. Ibid., pp. 350–51.

84. Ibid., pp. 383–84.

85. Ibid., pp. 379 and 382. Roger Fletcher, *Revisionism and Empire: Socialist Imperialism in Germany, 1897–1914* (London, 1984); Peter Gay, *The Dilemma of Democratic Socialism: Eduard Bernstein's Challenge to Marx* (New York, 1962 reprint), pp. 271–80; and Carl E.

Schorske, *German Social Democracy, 1905–1917: The Development of the Great Schism* (New York, 1972 reprint), pp. 59–87, 243–48, 263–67, and 285–94.

86. Quoted in Kennedy, *Antagonism,* p. 209.

87. Malet quoted in ibid., p. 215.

88. Winzen, *Weltmachtkonzept,* pp. 69–70.

89. Gustav Roloff, ed., *Schulthess' europäischer Geschichtskalender,* 79 vols. (Munich, 1860–1938), 1896, pp. 12–13. Deist, *Flottenpolitik,* p. 59.

90. Delbrück quoted in ibid.

91. Quoted in Chickering, *We Men,* p. 56.

92. See the articles in *Die Post,* the *Hamburgische Korrespondenz,* the *National Zeitung,* the *Schwäbische Merkur,* and the *Täglichen Rundschau,* as well as the statements of the Pan German League, Karl Peters, and Hans Delbrück, all quoted in Hallmann, *Der Weg,* pp. 189–92.

93. Letter to Freiherr von Völderndorff, Friedrich Curtius, ed., *Denkwürdigkeiten des Fürsten Chlodwig zu Hohenlohe-Schillingsfürst,* 2 vols. (Stuttgart and Leipzig, 1907), II, pp. 531–32.

94. "'Neujahr'," p. 352.

95. Alfred Peter Friedrich von Tirpitz, *My Memoirs,* 2 vols. (New York, 1919), I, p. 204.

96. Philipp Eulenburg, "Kaiserliche Indiskretion," 1 and 2 November 1908, BA Koblenz, Eulenburg Papers, vol. 74.

97. Fehrenbach, *Wandlungen,* p. 173.

98. "Deutsche Jahrhundertfeier und Kaiserfeier," *Logos* 4 (1913), p. 173.

99. Hermann Oncken, "Der Kaiser und die Nation: Rede bei dem Festakt der Universität Heidelberg zur Erinnerung an die Befreiungskriege und zur Feier des 25 jährigen Regierungs-Jubiläums Kaiser Wilhelm II." (15 June 1913), *Historisch-politische Aufsätze und Reden,* 2 vols. (Munich and Berlin, 1914), I, p. 15. For Oncken's view that Wilhelm bore primary responsibility for bringing the Germans behind *Weltpolitik,* see pp. 15–16. For Oncken's support of the navy, see McClelland, *Historians,* pp. 207–10.

100. Fehrenbach, *Wandlungen,* p. 158. Otto Hintze, "Rede, Gehalten zur Feier der fünfundzwanzigjährigen Regierung Seiner Majestät des Kaisers und Königs Wilhelm II.," *Hohenzollern Jahrbuch: Forschungen und Abbildungen zur Geschichte der Hohenzollern in Brandenburg-Preussen,* Paul Seidel, ed. (Berlin and Leipzig, 1913), pp. 78–95. For Hintze's support of the navy, see McClelland, *Historians,* pp. 207–10.

101. Hintze, "Rede," p. 82.

102. Ibid., p. 82. See also p. 84.

103. Ibid., p. 87.

104. Ibid., p. 79.

105. Ibid., p. 82.

106. Ibid., p. 84. As a result of naval development, "it is already a significant accomplishment," Hintze concluded, "that we are capable . . . of asserting our claim to a place in the sun with honor." Ibid., p. 85.

107. Ibid., p. 94.

108. For the similarity between Bülow and the Kaiser on the domestic benefits of navy and *Weltpolitik,* see Winzen, *Weltmachtkonzept,* pp. 25–59, especially 36–42.

109. Tirpitz's notes to his audience with Wilhelm II on 23 October 1899, BMA Freiburg, Tirpitz Papers, N253, vol. 5; excerpt from an article published in 1900 in the organ of the Reich Naval Office, *Nauticus,* quoted in Berghahn, *Tirpitz-Plan,* p. 150. Tirpitz and his colleagues in the Reich Naval Office sought to give the campaign on behalf of the navy as broad a base as possible, not only to insure the passage of the naval bills, but also because they were convinced that the mobilization of nationalistic fervor would be domestically beneficial. Ibid., pp. 229–31.

110. "Sammlungspolitik und Liberalismus," Friedrich Meinecke, *Schriften und Reden,* Georg Kotowski, ed. (Darmstadt, 1966), pp. 40–41. See also Hintze, "Rede," p. 92.

111. Hermann Oncken, "Der Kaiser und die Nation," p. 19.

112. Klaus Schrötter, "Chauvinism and its Tradition: German Writers at the Outbreak of

the First World War," *The Germanic Review* 43 (1968), p. 128. Schrötter shows that the enthusiasm of the literati for the war derived significantly from their assessment of its integrative domestic effect. Ibid., pp. 120–35.

113. *Schulthess' Geschichtskalender,* 1914 (I), p. 371.

114. Fischer's *Griff nach der Weltmacht* (Düsseldorf, 1961) and *Krieg der Illusionen* (Düsseldorf, 1969); Wehler's *Bismarck und der Imperialismus* (Cologne, 1969), *Krisenherde des Kaiserreichs, 1871–1918* (Göttingen, 1979), and *Das deutsche Kaiserreich, 1871–1918* (Göttingen, 1980).

115. In addition to those works cited above, see Berghahn, "Zu den Zielen," especially pp. 56–57; Berghahn, *Tirpitz-Plan,* especially pp. 129–57 and 205–48; as well as Berghahn's *Rüstung und Machtpolitik* and *Germany and the Approach of War in 1914*; Dieter Groh, *Negative Integration und revolutionärer Attentismus: Die deutsche Sozial-Demokratie am Vorabend des Ersten Weltkrieges* (Frankfurt, 1973); the collection of Eckart Kehr's essays edited by Wehler and published under the title *Primat der Innenpolitik* (Berlin, 1965); Röhl, *Germany Without Bismarck,* pp. 246–57; Dirk Stegmann, *Die Erben Bismarcks: Parteien und Verbände in der Spätphase des wilhelminischen Deutschlands: Sammlungspolitik, 1897–1918* (Cologne, 1970); and Vogel, *Russlandpolitik.*

116. Hans Herzfeld, *Johannes von Miquel,* 2 vols. (Detmold, 1938), II, p. 183.

117. Wehler, *Bismarck und der Imperialismus.*

118. Winzen, *Weltmachtkonzept,* p. 21.

119. Ibid., pp. 148–56 and 428–33.

120. Berghahn, "Zu den Zielen," pp. 48–77, and *Tirpitz-Plan,* pp. 23–201.

121. Deist, *Flottenpolitik,* pp. 330–31.

122. Compare Berghahn, "Zu den Zielen," pp. 56–57, with Jonathan Steinberg, "The Tirpitz Plan," *The Historical Journal* 16 (1973), p. 202.

123. For example, Paul Kennedy in *Antagonism,* pp. 223–50; "German World Policy," pp. 605–25; and *Samoan Tangle,* pp. 122–33 and 298–305. The distinction between foreign and domestic policy would seem artificial. In the end foreign policy is always a response to present or anticipated domestic circumstances and is inevitably designed to preserve or to improve domestic conditions. A purely "foreign" policy is unimaginable.

124. For the critique of the application of these models to Bismarckian Germany, see Lothar Gall, "Bismarck und der Bonapartismus," *Historische Zeitschrift* 223 (1976), pp. 618–32; Paul M. Kennedy, "German Colonial Expansion: Has the 'Manipulated Social Imperialism' Been Ante-Dated?" *Past and Present* 54 (1972), pp. 134–41; Otto Pflanze, "Bismarcks Herrschaftstechnik als Problem der gegenwärtigen Historiographie," *Historische Zeitschrift* 234 (1982), pp. 561–99; Pflanze, "'*Sammlungspolitik*', 1875–1886: Kritische Bemerkungen zu einem Modell," *Innenpolitischen Probleme des Bismarck-Reiches, Schriften des Historischen Kollegs,* Kolloquium 2, pp. 155–93. There is controversy not just over the application of these models but over the approach to the *Kaiserreich* of Wehler and the so-called "Bielefeld school." See Werner Conze, "Zur Sozialgeschichte des Kaiserreichs und der Weimarer Republik," *Neue politische Literatur* 21 (1976), pp. 511–13; Klaus Hildebrand, "Geschichte oder 'Gesellschaftsgeschichte'?" *Historische Zeitschrift* 223 (1976), pp. 328–57; Wolfgang J. Mommsen, "Domestic Factors in German Foreign Policy before 1914," *Central European History* 6 (1973), pp. 3–43; Thomas Nipperdey, "Wehlers Kaiserreich," *Geschichte und Gesellschaft* 1 (1975), pp. 539–60; and H. G. Zmarzlik, "Das Kaiserreich in neuer Sicht?" *Historische Zeitschrift* 222 (1976), pp. 105–26. For Wehler's response to his critics, see his "Kritik und kritische Antikritik," *Historische Zeitschrift* 225 (1977), pp. 347–84. The debate over Germany's "*Sonderweg*" is also relevant here.

125. Röhl, "'Königsmechanismus'," pp. 121–22.

126. Geoff Eley, "*Sammlungspolitik,* Social Imperialism and the Navy Law of 1898," *From Unification to Nazism: Reinterpreting the German Past* (Boston, 1986), pp. 110–53, and Eley, *Reshaping the German Right: Radical Nationalism and Political Change after Bismarck* (New Haven and London, 1980), pp. 41–98.

127. Salewski, "'Neujahr 1900'," p. 353. See also Kennedy, *Antagonism,* pp. 209, 246–47, and 249.

128. Eley, *Reshaping,* p. 162.

129. It was the increasingly assertive middle classes that voiced those demands most loudly and insistently. Kennedy, *Antagonism,* pp. 214–15.

130. Eley, "Defining Social Imperialism: Use and Abuse of an Idea," *Social History* 1 (1976), pp. 265–90; Eley, "*Sammlungspolitik,*" pp. 110–53; Eley, "The German Right, 1860–1945: How It Changed?" *From Unification,* pp. 231–53; and Eley, *Reshaping,* pp. 19–98.

131. Chickering, *We Men,* pp. 301–304; Deist, *Flottenpolitik,* pp. 147–247; Kennedy, *Samoan Tangle,* pp. 265 and 271–72; Kennedy, *Antagonism,* pp. 223–50, 265–66, and 384; and Röhl, *Germany Without Bismarck,* p. 255.

132. Compare here Eley, *Reshaping,* p. 162.

133. Compare here Raymond James Sontag, *Germany and England: Background of the Conflict, 1848–1894* (New York, 1969), p. 263, and J. Alden Nichols, *The Year of the Three Kaisers: Bismarck and the German Succession, 1887–88* (Urbana and Chicago, 1987), pp. 342–43.

Chapter 10

1. Paul M. Kennedy, *The Rise of the Anglo-German Antagonism, 1860–1914* (London, 1982), pp. 407–408.

2. Wilhelm II's marginalia to the *Standard* of 26 December 1903, PA Bonn, England 78, vol. 20.

3. Jonathan Steinberg, "The Copenhagen Complex," *Journal of Contemporary History* 1 (1966), pp. 23–46; Kennedy, *Antagonism,* p. 275.

4. See also Wilhelm II's marginalia to a report from Metternich to Bülow of 1 November 1905, PA Bonn, England 78 *secr.,* vol. 8, and to Friedrich Paulson's article "Die politische Lage Europas" in the *Neue Freie Presse* of 18 March 1906, PA Bonn, England 78, vol. 49. In February and March 1908 Wilhelm expected the British to seize the entire Portuguese empire. His marginalia to reports from Count Christian Tattenbach in Portugal to Bülow of 14 February 1908, PA Bonn, England 78, Nr. 1 *secr.,* vol. 20, and of 17 March 1908, PA Bonn, England 78, Nr. 1 *secr.,* vol. 21.

5. *GP,* XV, pp. 553–61.

6. Letter of 23 February 1900, ibid., p. 560.

7. This would probably be the conventional view.

8. Peter Winzen's *Bülows Weltmachtkonzept: Untersuchungen zur Frühphase seiner Aussenpolitik, 1897–1901* (Boppard-am-Rhein, 1977) tends in this direction.

9. Volker Berghahn's "Zu den Zielen des deutschen Flottenbaus unter Wilhelm II.," *Historische Zeitschrift* 210 (1970), pp. 34–100, his *Der Tirpitz-Plan: Genesis und Verfall einer innenpolitischen Krisenstrategie unter Wilhelm II.* (Düsseldorf, 1971), and Barbara Vogel's *Deutsche Russlandpolitik: Das Scheitern der deutschen Weltpolitik unter Bülow, 1900–1906* (Düsseldorf, 1973) tend in this direction. To be precise, what Vogel appears to do is cite Wilhelm when he was being Anglophobic to support the argument that the Reich pursued a consistently anti-English policy and to dismiss Wilhelm when he was being Anglophile as inconsequential.

10. Paul Kennedy's *Antagonism* tends in this direction (pp. 224, 226, and 236), although Kennedy concludes that on balance Wilhelm tended more to exacerbate than to ameliorate the Anglo-German antagonism (p. 407). This would probably also characterize Lamar Cecil's view in *Wilhelm II: Prince and Emperor, 1859–1900* (Chapel Hill, 1989), pp. 263–90.

11. Pauline R. Anderson, *The Background of Anti-English Feeling in Germany, 1890–1902* (Washington, 1939), pp. 31–130; Kennedy, *Antagonism,* pp. 69–75, 83, 246–47, 249, 321–60, 366, 371–72, 379, 382, 383–84, and 444. On the revisionist wing of the Social Democratic movement there was tension between Anglophilia and Anglophobia. See Roger

Fletcher, *Revisionism and Empire: Socialist Imperialism in Germany, 1897–1914* (London, 1984), pp. 56–57, 89–91, 129–30, 154, 157, and 165–66.

12. Tirpitz spoke fluent English, was interested in British history and economic policy, and sent his daughters to an English finishing school.

13. Rudolf Stadelmann, "Die Epoche der deutsch-englischen Flottenrivalität," *Deutschland und Westeuropa* (Schloss Laupheim, 1948), p. 98. See also Walther Hubatsch, *Die Ära Tirpitz: Studien zur deutschen Marinepolitik, 1890–1918* (Göttingen, 1955), pp. 14–15.

14. Stadelmann, "Epoche," p. 98. Like Tirpitz, whose wife was the daughter of Karl Twesten, many German navalists were heir to the German liberal tradition. Admiral Müller's brother fought in Dresden in 1848, for example. I am indebted to Jonathan Steinberg for this information.

15. See note 11 above and note 100 of Chapter 5.

16. Heinrich von Treitschke became disillusioned with Wilhelm precisely because of the Kaiser's attachment to Britain. Kennedy, *Antagonism*, p. 209. For Wilhelm's unpopularity with the Germans over this issue, see Isolde Rieger, *Die wilhelminische Presse im Überblick* (Munich, 1957), pp. 9–18. For the hostility of the Wilhelmian establishment toward England, see Cecil, *Wilhelm II*, pp. 277–78.

17. Wilhelm II, *My Early Life* (New York, 1926), p. 75. See also Kennedy, *Antagonism*, pp. 400–401.

18. "Kaiserliche Indiskretion," BA Koblenz, Eulenburg Papers, vol. 74. See also Bernhard Fürst von Bülow, *Denkwürdigkeiten*, 4 vols. (Berlin, 1930), I, p. 503.

19. Letter from Victoria to Queen Victoria of 21 January 1871, RA Z25/46. Wilhelm II's marginalia to the *Chemnitzer Tageblatt* of 24 March 1913, PA Bonn, Preussen 1, Nr. 1d, *secr.*, vol. 4.

20. Letter from Wilhelm II to Queen Victoria of 2 February 1899, George Earle Buckle, ed., *The Letters of Queen Victoria: 1886–1901*, 3 vols. (New York, 1930), III, pp. 336–37.

21. Bülow, *Denkwürdigkeiten*, I, pp. 341–42.

22. See, for example, Wilhelm's jealous anger in 1908 when he believed that Edward had canceled a visit to Berlin in order to visit the Tsar at Reval. Wilhelm II's marginalia to a report from Metternich to Bülow of 30 June 1908, *GP*, XXIV, pp. 81–88.

23. "Kaiserliche Indiskretion," BA Koblenz, Eulenburg Papers, vol. 74.

24. Bülow, *Denkwürdigkeiten*, I, p. 509; Kennedy, *Antagonism*, p. 126.

25. "Kaiserliche Indiskretion," BA Koblenz, Eulenburg Papers, vol. 74.

26. Edward VII's memorandum of 22 March 1906 quoted in Sidney Lee, *King Edward VII: A Biography*, 2 vols. (New York, 1925), II, p. 565. See also ibid., I, pp. 787–88.

27. Letter from Freiherr Martin von Jenisch to Bülow of 20 July 1907, PA Bonn, Preussen 1, Nr. 1d, vol. 18.

28. Walter Görlitz, ed., *Der Kaiser: Aufzeichnungen des Chefs des Marinekabinetts Admiral Georg Alexander von Müller über die Ära Wilhelms II.* (Göttingen, 1965), p. 179. Eulenburg liked to complain about "the English" food he was served on board the royal yacht, the *Hohenzollern*. "Nordlandreise, 1903: In Briefen an Fürstin Augusta zu Eulenburg-Hertefeld," BA Koblenz, Eulenburg Papers, vol. 74.

29. Wilhelm II's marginalia to the *Tägliche Rundscnau* of 2 July 1911, PA Bonn, Preussen 1, Nr. 1d, vol. 21.

30. Bülow, *Denkwürdigkeiten*, vol. III, p. 298.

31. Letter from ex-Kaiser Wilhelm II to Dr. Kurt Jagow of 30 July 1926, GSA, BPH, Rep. 53, Nr. 423.

32. Interestingly, Gladstone was one of the statesmen Victoria most admired and Bismarck most disparaged, in part because of his wood chopping. Holstein's diary entries of 18 January 1884 and 6 April 1885, Norman Rich and M. H. Fisher, eds., *The Holstein Papers*, 4 vols. (Cambridge, 1955–1963), II, pp. 60 and 186.

33. "Kaiserliche Indiskretion," BA Koblenz, Eulenburg Papers, vol. 74; Wilhelm II, *My Early Life*, pp. 78–79.

34. Wilhelm's speech in 1906 to German naval recruits which praised English soldiers to such an extent that it had to be edited before being publicly released. Zedlitz's diary entry of

13 March 1906, Graf Robert Zedlitz-Trützschler, *Zwölf Jahre am deutschen Kaiserhof* (Berlin and Leipzig, 1924), p. 141; "Die Nordlandreise, 1903," Part II, "Zur Psyche und Politik Kaiser Wilhelms II.," BA Koblenz, Eulenburg Papers, vol. 74; Wilhelm II's marginalia to a report from Baron Hermann von Eckartstein in London to Bülow of 27 March 1902, PA Bonn, England 81, Nr. 2, vol. 20; and to the article "Zur Fahrt der 'Lusitania'" in the *Neue preussische Zeitung* of 17 September 1907, BMA Freiburg, RM 2, vol. 181.

35. Joachim von Kürenberg, *The Kaiser: The Life of Wilhelm II., Last Emperor of Germany* (London, 1954), p. 331. For Wilhelm's adopton of English styles and customs, see Cecil, *Wilhelm II,* pp. 271–75.

36. Winzen, *Weltmachtkonzept,* pp. 187–230. For Wilhelm's desire for an Anglo-German alliance, see Cecil, *Wilhelm II,* pp. 275–78.

37. Ibid., pp. 328–34, and Winzen, *Weltmachtkonzept,* pp. 166–81. For the general unpopularity of an alliance with England in Germany, see Oron J. Hale, *Publicity and Diplomacy: With Special Reference to England and Germany, 1890–1914* (Gloucester, Mass., 1964 reprint), pp. 181–89.

38. Dona's letter to Bülow of March 1899 quoted in Bülow, *Denkwürdigkeiten,* I, pp. 290–91.

39. "Kaiserliche Indiskretion," BA Koblenz, Eulenburg Papers, vol. 74.

40. Letter of 5 August 1895, BA Koblenz, Hohenlohe Papers, vol. 1634. Already during this visit the German press responded negatively to the favorable coverage the Kaiser received in the British press. Hale, *Publicity,* pp. 105–108.

41. Letter of 6 November 1899, Bülow, *Denkwürdigkeiten,* I, p. 303.

42. Article of 15 November 1899.

43. Promemoria from Hohenlohe to Wilhelm II of 20 November 1899, printed in Bülow, *Denkwürdigkeiten,* I, pp. 311–13.

44. Ibid., pp. 307 and 344.

45. Ibid., p. 307.

46. See the editorials in *The Times* and *Daily Mail* of 29 November 1899.

47. Editorial of 2 December 1899.

48. Wilhelm II's marginalia to a report from Karl von Eisendecher in Karlsruhe to Hohenlohe of 12 November 1899, PA Bonn, England 78, vol. 12, and the telegram from Hatzfeldt in London to Holstein of 25 November 1899, *Holstein Papers,* IV, p. 167. For the domestic and foreign political background and consequences of Wilhelm's 1899 visit, including its unpopularity in Germany, see Hale, *Publicity,* pp. 198 and 210–11; Paul M. Kennedy, *The Samoan Tangle: A Study in Anglo-German-American Relations, 1878–1900* (Dublin, 1974), pp. 180–243; Norman Rich, *Friedrich von Holstein: Politics and Diplomacy in the Era of Bismarck and Wilhelm II,* 2 vols. (Cambridge, 1965), pp. 611–15; and Winzen, *Weltmachtkonzept,* pp. 103, 107, and 188–243.

For an earlier instance of Wilhelm's anger at his subjects for experiencing his predilection for England as an affront to the honor of the nation, see his outraged reaction to the furor produced in Germany by an editorial in *The Times* of 5 June 1896 claiming that, as a result of the Kaiser's English heritage, German policy would be friendlier toward Britain were he to have his way completely. Holstein's letter to Bülow of 10 June 1896, BA Koblenz, Bülow Papers, vol. 90.

49. Bülow, *Denkwürdigkeiten,* I, pp. 508–509. Letter from Eulenburg to Bülow of 26 January 1901, ibid., p. 506.

50. Ibid., pp. 507–508.

51. Quoted later in this chapter.

52. For Wilhelm's visit to England in 1901 and its unpopularity in Germany, see Hale, *Publicity,* pp. 234–36; Kennedy, *Antagonism,* pp. 243–44; Rich, *Holstein,* pp. 629–33; and Winzen, *Weltmachtkonzept,* pp. 293–307 and 344.

53. Editorial of 22 February 1901.

54. It should be pointed out that what are characterized as the "German" and the "English" sides of Wilhelm's personality refer not simply to two national identities but to the

values, attitudes, character traits, and personalities that over the course of his development had come to be associated with those national identities.

55. "Kaiser Wilhelm II und Gräfin Mathilde Stubenberg," 16 January 1903, BA Koblenz, Eulenburg Papers, vol. 84.

56. See Houston Stewart Chamberlain, *Briefe 1882–1924 und Briefwechsel mit Kaiser Wilhelm II,* 2 vols. (Munich, 1928).

57. Telegram of 5 March 1899, PA Bonn, Preussen 1, Nr. 1d, vol. 9.

58. Lee, *Edward VII,* II, pp. 11–12.

59. Letter of 30 December 1901, *GP,* XVII, pp. 110–11. Despite the fact that in both of these statements the Kaiser called for closer relations between Germany and England as a result of their racial identity, two points should be noted: (1) Wilhelm's toast, in which he conceded the seas to Britain, was made approximately six months after the Reichstag had passed the Second German Navy Law and (2) Wilhelm's letter to his uncle placed special emphasis on "*mutual* recognition and *reciprocity.*"

60. Wilhelm II's marginalia to a report from Naval Captain Paul von Hintze in St. Petersburg to the Kaiser of 24 February 1909, ibid., XXVI (2), pp. 567–68.

61. Wilhelm II's marginalia to a report from Stumm in Madrid to Bülow of 9 March 1906, ibid., XXI (1), pp. 267–68.

62. Telegram from Wilhelm II to the secretary of state in the Foreign Office, Kiderlen-Wächter, of 8 December 1912, ibid., XXXIX, pp. 123–25.

63. Wilhelm II's marginalia to the *Daily News* of 15 May 1913, PA Bonn, England 78, vol. 14c.

64. Bülow, *Denkwürdigkeiten,* IV, p. 659.

65. See, here, BMA Freiburg, RM 2, vol. 163.

66. Görlitz, *Der Kaiser,* p. 33; Wilhelm II's marginalia to a copy of a letter from George Hamilton to Lord Salisbury of 21 February 1891, BMA Freiburg, RM 2, vol. 137; the letter from Wilhelm II to Lord Salisbury of 20 December 1893, BMA Freiburg, RM 2, vol. 120.

67. Wilhelm II's marginalia to the two reports from Wilhelm Schröder in London to the Foreign Office both of 14 December 1888, PA Bonn, England 71 b, vol. 6; his marginalia to a telegram from Hatzfeldt in London to the Foreign Office of 17 November 1893, PA Bonn, England 92, Nr. 3, vol 3; to the reports from Hatzfeldt to Caprivi of 18 November 1893, PA Bonn, England 71 b, vol. 21; of 20 November 1893, PA Bonn, England 92, Nr. 3, vol. 3; of 6 December 1893, *GP,* IX, pp. 102–104; of 15 December 1893, PA Bonn, England 71 b, vol. 22; to the telegram from Saurma in Washington to Caprivi of 22 December 1893, PA Bonn, England 71 b, vol. 22; to *The Times* of 28 December 1893, PA Bonn, England 71 b, vol. 22; to the telegram from Hatzfeldt to the Foreign Office of 29 December 1893, PA Bonn, England 92, Nr. 3, vol. 4; to the reports from Hatzfeldt to Caprivi of 29 December 1893, 10 January 1894, and of 12 January 1894, all PA Bonn, England 71 b, vol. 22; and to the report from Hatzfeldt to Hohenlohe of 23 January 1895, PA Bonn, England 69, vol. 35. See also Cecil, *Wilhelm II,* pp. 276–77 and 294, and Steinberg, *Deterrent,* pp. 61–62.

68. Wilhelm II, *My Early Life,* p. 123; Georg Hinzpeter, *Kaiser Wilhelm II. Eine Skizze nach der Natur gezeichnet* (Bielefeld, 1888), p. 7. Letter from Wilhelm to Queen Victoria of 3 July 1887, RA Z82/103. See also Wilhelm's speech at the launching of the cruiser-corvette *Alexandria* in Kiel on 7 February 1885, Karl Wippermann, ed., *Deutscher Geschichtskalender,* 49 vols. (Leipzig, 1885–1933), 1885, pp. 318–19.

69. Bülow, *Denkwürdigkeiten,* II, p. 32.

70. Ibid., I, p. 582, and Wilhelm II's marginalia to an article in the *Berliner neueste Nachrichten* of 29 August 1905, BMA Freiburg, RM 2, vol. 173.

71. "Nordlandreise," BA Koblenz, Eulenburg Papers, vol. 74.

72. Letter from Müller to Tirpitz of 4 June 1905, BMA Freiburg, RM 3, vol. 5; Wilhelm II's marginalia to a report from Naval Attaché Carl Coerper to Tirpitz of 4 January 1906, BMA Freiburg, RM 3, vol. 2785; and Wilhelm II's marginalia to an article in *The Shipping World* of 31 July 1907, BMA Freiburg, RM 2, vol. 181.

73. "Kaiserliche Indiskretion," BA Koblenz, Eulenburg Papers, vol. 74.

74. Bülow, *Denkwürdigkeiten,* II, pp. 30–31.

75. Wilhelm II's marginalia to the *Pall Mall Gazette* of 16 March 1900, PA Bonn, England 78, vol. 13.

76. Daisy Princess of Pless, *Daisy Pless By Herself* (London, 1928), p. 263. See also Kennedy, *Samoan Tangle,* pp. 179–80.

77. Telegram from Wilhelm II to Hohenlohe of 25 October 1896, *GP,* XIII, pp. 3–4; Wilhelm II's marginalia to a report from Hatzfeldt to Hohenlohe of 14 January 1900, PA Bonn, Afrika Generalia 13, Nr. 2b, vol. 1; to a report from Metternich to Bülow of 10 August 1905, PA Bonn, Preussen 1, Nr. 1, Nr. 4°, vol. 9; and to a report from Metternich to Bethmann Hollweg of 28 July 1909, *GP,* XXVIII, pp. 194–97.

78. Wilhelm II's comments to the British ambassador in Berlin, Sir Edward Malet, in 1895, quoted in Kennedy, *Antagonism,* p. 219; Wilhelm's letter to Queen Victoria of 22 May 1899, quoted in Chapter 7; and his marginalia to a report from Metternich to Bethmann Hollweg of 28 July 1909, *GP,* XXVIII, pp. 194–97.

79. Wilhelm II's marginalia to a report from Metternich to Bülow of 9 August 1905, PA Bonn, Preussen 1, Nr. 1, Nr. 4°, vol. 9. See also Appendix II.

80. See, here, Cecil, *Wilhelm II,* pp. 296 and 333.

81. Wilhelm II's marginalia to a telegram from Metternich to Bülow of 1 November 1905, PA Bonn, England 78 *secr.,* vol. 8, and to a report from Tattenbach in Lisbon to Bülow of 17 March 1908, PA Bonn, England 78, Nr. 1 *secr.,* vol. 21.

82. [*kaltschnauzige Brutalität der Fakten*]. Wilhelm II's marginalia to the article "England, Deutschland und die Entente" in the *Kölnische Zeitung* of 7 November 1911, PA Bonn, England 78, vol. 84.

83. Wilhelm II, *The Kaiser's Memoirs* (New York, 1922), pp. 97–98.

84. Telegram from Wilhelm II to Bülow of 13 August 1908, *GP,* XXIV, pp. 126–29. For an earlier example of Wilhelm's sense that the English responded to intimidation, see Cecil, *Wilhelm II,* p. 285.

85. Bülow, *Denkwürdigkeiten,* II, p. 429. Believing that former British Prime Minister Arthur Balfour had been backed into a corner when Metternich spoke bluntly to him, Wilhelm wrote: "If only Metternich had spoken this way last winter [during negotiations to reach an Anglo-German naval understanding], then many things would have turned out differently." Wilhelm II's marginalia to a report from Metternich to Bethmann Hollweg of 10 February 1910, *GP,* XXVIII, pp. 291–97.

86. Wilhelm II's marginalia to a report from the German ambassador in Washington, Holleben, to Hohenlohe of 27 February 1899, PA Bonn, England 81, Nr. 2, vol. 18, and to a report from the German representative in The Hague to Hohenlohe of 11 May 1900, PA Bonn, Afrika Generalia 13, Nr. 2c, vol. 3.

87. Report from Varnbüler to the prime minister of Württemberg, Freiherr Hermann von Mittnacht, of 2 November 1899 of a conversation of 31 October 1899, quoted in Ivo Nikolai Lambi, *The Navy and German Power Politics, 1862–1914* (Boston, 1984), pp. 35–36.

88. *Holstein Papers,* I, p. 187. See also Holstein's letter to Bülow of 29 August 1907 ibid., IV, pp. 487–90.

89. Wilhelm II's marginalia to a report from Bernstorff in London to Bülow of 1 May 1904, PA Bonn, England 78, vol. 184.

90. Wilhelm II's marginalia to a report from the German ambassador in St. Petersburg, Count Friedrich von Alvensleben, to Bülow of 25 August 1904, *GP,* XIX (1), pp. 212–15. See also Wilhelm II's marginalia to a report from Richthofen to Eulenburg of 20 July 1898, quoted in Chapter 9; his speech to the crew of the cruiser *Falke* in the fall of 1899, quoted in Kennedy, *Samoan Tangle,* p. 226; his marginalia to the report from Hatzfeldt in London to Holstein of 22 April 1899, *GP,* XIV (2), pp. 611–13; and the report from the British ambassador in Berlin, Sir Frank Lascelles, to Lord Salisbury of 26 May 1899, Lee, *Edward VII,* I, p. 743.

91. Wilhelm II's marginalia to a report from Bernstorff to the Foreign Office of 8 May 1905, PA Bonn, Deutschland 138, vol. 30.

92. Bülow, *Denkwürdigkeiten,* II, pp. 23–24; Berghahn, *Tirpitz-Plan,* pp. 328–83. See also Lambi, *Navy,* p. 175. During Edward VII's visit to Kiel, Wilhelm apparently was able to convince the king to invite the German navy to visit Plymouth later in the year.

93. Report from Rosen in Rome to the secretary of state in the Foreign Office, Richthofen, of 31 March 1904, PA Bonn, England 78 *secr.,* vol. 7.

94. Quoted in Hans Hallmann, *Der Weg zum deutschen Schlachtflottenbau* (Stuttgart, 1933), pp. 56–57. For more on Wilhelm's sense that the navy would make the Reich an attractive ally, see ibid., pp. 99–101.

95. Tirpitz's notes of 17 October 1903, BMA Freiburg, Tirpitz Papers, N253, vol. 20.

96. Wilhelm II's marginalia to a report from Metternich to Bülow of 17 October 1906, *GP,* XXI (2), p. 464. Lydia Franke in her study of Wilhelm's marginalia, *Die Randbemerkungen Wilhelms II. in den Akten der auswärtigen Politik als historische und psychologische Quelle* (Strassburg, 1934), reached the same conclusion, that the purpose of the navy for the Kaiser was not only to win the respect of the British (p. 159) but also an alliance with them (pp. 161–62).

97. Wilhelm II's marginalia to a report from Hatzfeldt to Hohenlohe of 4 December 1897, PA Bonn, Deutschland 138, vol. 12, and his speech from the throne of 6 May 1898 closing the session of the Reichstag that had passed the 1898 Navy Law, PA Bonn, Deutschland 125, Nr. 2, vol. 4.

98. Wilhelm II's marginalia to a report from the German consul in Calcutta to Hohenlohe of 23 February 1900, PA Bonn, Deutschland 138 *secr.,* vol. 4.

99. Wilhelm II's marginalia to a report from Metternich to Bülow of 23 April 1906, PA Bonn, England 78, vol. 50. See also his marginalia to a report from Stumm in London to Bülow of 10 May 1906, *GP,* XXIII (1), pp. 76–77.

100. These events culminated in Hardinge's "Cronberg interview" with the Kaiser. See also Jonathan Steinberg, "The *Novelle* of 1908: Necessities and Choices in the Anglo-German Naval Arms Race," *Transactions of the Royal Historical Society* 21 (1971), pp. 25–43.

101. Wilhelm II's marginalia to a report from Metternich to Bülow of 25 January 1908, PA Bonn, England 78 *secr.,* vol. 11.

102. *GP,* XXIV, pp. 32–35. For the background of the letter, see Hale, *Publicity,* pp. 303–307, and Kennedy, *Antagonism,* p. 443.

103. Wilhelm II's marginalia to a report from Metternich to Bülow of 8 March 1908, *GP,* XXIV, pp. 44–46; his marginalia to a report from Metternich to Bülow of 16 July 1908, ibid., pp. 99–104.

104. Wilhelm II's marginalia to a report from Metternich to Bülow of 30 June 1908, ibid., pp. 81–88.

105. Wilhelm II's marginalia to a report from Metternich to Bülow of 16 July 1908, ibid., pp. 99–104; to a report from Metternich to Bülow of 1 August 1908, ibid., pp. 107–16; telegram from Wilhelm II to Bülow of 13 August 1908, ibid., pp. 126–29; and telegram from Bülow to the Foreign Office of 20 August 1908, ibid., p. 136.

106. Wilhelm's marginalia to the *Spectator* of 18 July 1908, BMA Freiburg, RM 2, vol. 184.

107. *GP,* XXIV, pp. 92–96.

108. Wilhelm II's marginalia to a report from Metternich to Bülow of 30 June 1908, ibid., pp. 81–88. Wilhelm expressed similar sentiments in marginalia to reports from Metternich to Bülow of 8 March 1908, ibid., pp. 44–46; of 10 July 1908, ibid., pp. 92–96; and of 1 August 1908, ibid., pp. 107–16; and in Bülow's memorandum of 17 April 1909, ibid., XXVIII, p. 150, in which the chancellor presented the Kaiser as convinced that Britain was not Germany's principal naval adversary, that a conflict with England would be a disaster, and as asserting that he wanted no arms race with the British.

At least until February 1910, Wilhelm continued to insist that the British were "simply 'crazy'!" (Wilhelm II's marginalia to a report from Metternich to Bülow of 9 January 1909, PA Bonn, Preussen 1, Nr. 1, Nr. 4°, vol. 19), that the naval race existed "only in English fantasy!" (Wilhelm II's marginalia to a report from Metternich to Bülow of 2 February 1909, PA Bonn, England 78 *secr.,* vol. 18), and to deny that the German navy posed a threat to the

Royal Navy or to England (Wilhelm II's marginalia to a report from Metternich to Bethmann Hollweg of 10 February 1910, *GP,* XXVIII, pp. 291–97).

109. Wilhelm II's marginalia to the *Spectator* of 18 July 1908, BMA Freiburg, RM 2, vol. 184.

110. Wilhelm II's marginalia of 7 March 1909 to a report from Metternich in London to Bülow of 3 March 1909, *GP,* XXVIII, pp. 93–100.

111. In this instance Lord Charles Beresford, former commander of the English Channel Squadron and first sea lord. Wilhelm II's marginalia to a report from Metternich in London to Bülow of 16 December 1909, PA Bonn, England 78, vol. 76.

112. Wilhelm II's marginalia to the *Navy League Journal* of October 1908, BMA Freiburg, RM 2, vol. 184.

113. Wilhelm II's marginalia to an article of 12 August 1908, PA Bonn, England 78, vol. 65. The Kaiser's adaptability is again reflected in these marginal comments. To these English newspaper articles, Wilhelm responded in English.

114. Bülow, *Denkwürdigkeiten,* I, pp. 444–45. See also ibid., I, p. 354, and IV, p. 677.

115. See also his identification with another victim of the mighty British, the Ashanti people, discussed in Chapter 6.

116. See Wilhelm II's marginalia to a report from Stumm in London to Bülow of 10 May 1906, *GP,* XXIII, pp. 76–77; to a report from Metternich to Bülow of 16 July 1908, ibid., pp. 99–104; and to a report from Metternich to Bethmann Hollweg of 10 February 1910, ibid., XXVIII, pp. 291–97; and his letter to Queen Victoria of 22 May 1899, quoted in Chapter 7; and his telegram to Bülow of 29 October 1899, quoted in Chapter 9.

117. Letter from Wilhelm II to Lord Tweedmouth of 16 February 1908, ibid., XXIV, pp. 32–35.

118. Wilhelm II's marginalia to a report from the German naval attaché in London, Coerper, to Tirpitz of 17 March 1903, BMA Freiburg, RM 3, vol. 2973.

119. Wilhelm II's marginalia to a report from Metternich to Bülow of 1 August 1908, *GP,* XXIV, pp. 107–16. See also Appendix II.

120. Wilhelm II's marginalia to a report from Metternich to Bülow of 16 July 1908, ibid., pp. 99–104.

121. Telegram of 13 August 1908, ibid., XXIV, pp. 126–29. It should be pointed out that, although the English accounts of this discussion reveal that Hardinge and Edward VII understood the Kaiser to reject emphatically all efforts to restrain German naval development, they contain no mention of Wilhelm's threat that Germany was prepared to go to war over the arms' limitation issue. It is possible that since Hardinge regarded his interview with the Kaiser as a private conversation he simply did not report Wilhelm's threat out of discretion or embarrassment. But it is also not unlikely that Wilhelm's account reflects more what he wished he had said to Hardinge than the actual contents of their conversation. As we have seen, given his adaptability, Wilhelm was often Anglophile with the English and Anglophobic with the Germans. From a psychological standpoint, it would not seem to matter greatly, however, whether Wilhelm actually uttered these words or merely wished he had.

122. Bülow, *Denkwürdigkeiten,* II, pp. 511–14.

123. See, for example, Wilhelm II's marginalia to a report from Metternich to Bülow of 16 July 1908, *GP,* XXIV, pp. 99–104, and to a report from Metternich to Bülow of 1 August 1908, ibid., pp. 107–16.

124. Memorandum by Wilhelm II of 15 August 1906, ibid., XXIII (1), pp. 84–86. See also Wilhelm II's marginalia to the *Tägliche Rundschau* of 10 August 1906, ibid., footnote to Nr. 7813, p. 81. For more on Wilhelm's opposition to disarmament proposals and to the Hague Peace Conference, see Kennedy, *Antagonism,* pp. 442–43.

125. Telegram of 27 November 1911, *GP,* XXXI, pp. 34–35. See also Wilhelm II's marginalia to a report from Count Friedrich von Pourtalès, deputy secretary of state in the Foreign Office, to Wilhelm II of 13 October 1906, ibid., XXIII (1), p. 90.

126. On 30 March 1909, Müller informed Tirpitz that Wilhelm regarded as an "insult" the British suggestion that naval vessels under construction in the two countries be inspected by the respective naval attachés. The Kaiser compared the British suggestion to the one made

316   *Notes*

in 1870 by the French ambassador, Benedetti, to Wilhelm I that had precipitated the Franco-Prussian War. Tirpitz's notes to his audience with the Kaiser of 3 April 1909, BMA Freiburg, RM 2, vol. 1762.

127. Wilhelm II's marginalia to a report from Metternich to Bülow of 16 July 1908, *GP,* XXIV, pp. 99–104; to a report from Metternich to Bülow of 1 August 1908, ibid., pp. 107–16; and the letter from Wilhelm II to Bülow of 3 April 1909, ibid., XVIII, pp. 145–47.

128. Ibid. See also Bülow's memorandum of 17 April 1909, ibid., p. 150.

129. It is not unlikely that there also was a psychological connection for Wilhelm between these disarmament proposals and his physical disability. As a child Wilhelm had felt "unfit to be a king" as a result of his handicap. Now the British appeared to insist that as the price of good relations he would have to accept a return to a disadvantaged, even handicapped, status for his country: Germany would have to renounce something crucial to the self-esteem and self-confidence of the Kaiser and his subjects in order to appease the British. That was a higher price than Wilhelm was willing to pay. See Appendix II.

130. Wilhelm II's marginalia to a report from Metternich to Bülow of 25 January 1908, PA Bonn, England 78 *secr.,* vol. 21. Wilhelm expressed similar sentiments in his marginalia to a report from Stumm in London to Bülow of 20 April 1907, PA Bonn, England 78, vol. 57, and to a report from Richard von Kühlmann in The Hague to Bethmann Hollweg of 21 October 1915, PA Bonn, England 81, Nr. 2, vol. 31.

131. Wilhelm II's marginalia to a report from Bernstorff in London to Bülow of 22 April 1905, PA Bonn, England 78 *secr.,* vol. 7.

132. Wilhelm II's marginalia to a report from Tattenbach in Portugal to Bülow of 14 February 1908, PA Bonn, England 78, Nr. 1 *secr.,* vol. 20.

133. Wilhelm II's marginalia to a report from Metternich to Bülow of 16 July 1908, *GP,* XXIV, pp. 99–104.

134. Wilhelm II's marginalia to a report from Hatzfeldt to Hohenlohe of 14 January 1898, PA Bonn, England 78, vol. 11. See also his letter to Queen Victoria of 22 May 1899, quoted in Chapter 7.

135. See Bismarck's letter to Lord Salisbury of 22 November 1887 quoted in Chapter 6.

136. Indeed, German foreign policy during the reign of the Kaiser seems better understood historically as a series of uncoordinated reactions to specific events and changing circumstances than as a coordinated attempt to realize a clearly articulated and coherent political objective that the leaders of the Reich all understood in the same way and to which they were all equally committed.

137. See in this context Kennedy, *Antagonism,* p. 433; Lambi, *Navy,* pp. 160, 164–65, 196, 208–209, 249, 253, and 424; Smith, *Ideological Origins.*

138. Jonathan Steinberg, "The Tirpitz Plan," *The Historical Journal* 16 (1973), pp. 200–202.

139. Wilhelm II's marginalia to the *Hamburger Nachrichten* of 21 March 1900, PA Bonn, England 78 *secr.,* vol. 4.

140. This was the phrase originally submitted to the German Foreign Office for approval. At the suggestion of the Foreign Office, the phrase was changed to read: "The prevailing sentiment amongst large parts of the middle and lower classes of my own people is not friendly to England. So I am, as to say, in a minority."

141. This last phrase was considerably toned down by the Foreign Office.

142. *Holstein Papers,* I, pp. 203–207.

143. BMA Freiburg, RM 2, vol. 1762.

144. In late July 1910 Wilhelm acknowledged the necessity of maintaining a "certain numerical relation to the British fleet as it is now" and of introducing a *Novelle* should that relation be upset by the English. Copy of Wilhelm II's marginalia to an article in the *Westminster Gazette* of 16 July 1910, PA Bonn, England 78, Nr. 3 *secr.,* vol. 6. And in marginalia to an article in the same paper of 31 October 1911, he acknowledged that there had been a naval race between the two countries and that, by implication, it had not simply been a product of "overheated English brains." "Envy and arrogance drive the British toward enmity to Germany," he wrote, "and as long as those [feelings] do not dissipate than nothing will change

between us. They must get used to regarding us as their equal." PA Bonn, England 78 *secr.*, vol. 26.

145. Kennedy, *Antagonism*, p. 445, and Lambi, *Navy*, p. xi. See also Wilhelm Deist, *Flottenpolitik und Flottenpropaganda: Das Nachrichtenbureau des Reichsmarineamtes, 1897–1914* (Stuttgart, 1976), pp. 249–324, and, although he dates the collapse of the Tirpitz Plan earlier, Berghahn, *Tirpitz-Plan*, pp. 419–591.

146. For the impact of the *Daily Telegraph* affair on Wilhelm's popularity and influence, see Lamar Cecil, *The German Diplomatic Service, 1871–1914* (Princeton, 1976), pp. 303–307; Terrence L. Cole, "The *Daily Telegraph* Affair and its Aftermath: The Kaiser, Bülow and the Reichstag, 1908–1909," John C. G. Röhl and Nicolaus Sombart, eds., *Kaiser Wilhelm II: New Interpretations* (Cambridge, 1982), pp. 249–68; Hale, *Publicity*, pp. 302–303 and 313–324; Kurt Koszyk, *Deutsche Presse im 19. Jahrhundert. Geschichte der deutschen Presse*, 4 vols. (Berlin, 1966), II, pp. 262–64; Norman Rich, *Holstein*, pp. 818–27; and Wilhelm Schüssler, *Die Daily-Telegraph-Affaire: Fürst Bülow, Kaiser Wilhelm und die Krise des zweiten Reiches* (Göttingen, 1952).

147. Wilhelm II's marginalia to the *Strand Magazine* of March 1912, PA Bonn, Preussen 1, Nr. 1d, vol. 22.

148. See, here, Kennedy, *Antagonism*, pp. 408–409.

149. See Bülow's description of his meeting with the Kaiser in Kiel on 3 August 1897, *Denkwürdigkeiten*, I, pp. 56–61.

150. See, here, Kennedy, *Antagonism*, pp. 240 and 366. The extent of Wilhelm's dilemma was revealed by the British seizure of the German post steamer *Bundesrath* off Delagoa Bay in December 1899. Wilhelm sought simultaneously to play the incident up so as to get the 1900 Navy Law through the Reichstag and to play the incident down so as not to antagonize the British. See, here, the report from Bülow to Hammann and Esternaux of 31 December 1899, quoted in Winzen, *Weltmachtkonzept*, pp. 104–105.

151. Kennedy, *Antagonism*, p. 444; Hale, *Publicity*, pp. 256–66.

152. Kennedy, *Antagonism*, pp. 437 and 466–70.

Conclusion

1. These include Franz Kleinschrod, *Die Geisteskrankheit Wilhelms II.* (Wörrishofen, 1919); Herman Lutz, *Wilhelm II. periodisch Geisteskrank! Ein Charakterbild des wahren Kaisers* (Leipzig, 1919); Dr. Julius Michelsohn's article in the *Neue Hamburger Zeitung* of 30 November 1918, Abendausgabe; and H. Wilm, *Wilhelm II. als Krüppel und Psychopath* (Berlin, 1919).

2. Adolf Friedländer, *Wilhelm II: Versuch einer psychologischen Analyse* (Halle, 1919), p. 44.

3. Ibid., p. 48.

4. Paul Tesdorpf, *Die Krankheit Wilhelms II.* (Munich, 1919), p. 4.

5. Ibid., p. 11.

6. Sigmund Freud, "Delusions and Dreams in Jensen's *Gradiva*," *The Standard Edition of the Complete Psychological Works of Sigmund Freud*, James Strachey, ed., 24 vols. (London, 1964), IX, p. 45.

7. Emil Ludwig, *Wilhelm Hohenzollern: The Last of the Kaisers* (New York, 1927), p. 30.

8. See, here, Lamar Cecil, *Wilhelm II: Prince and Emperor, 1859–1900* (Chapel Hill, 1989), p. 346, note 56. The fictitious version of the events surrounding the future Kaiser's birth has proved exceptionally hardy. It appears in Michael Balfour's otherwise admirable biography of Wilhelm II, *The Kaiser and His Times* (New York, 1972), p. 74.

9. Sigmund Freud, "Lecture XXXI. Dissection of the Psychical Personality," *The Standard Edition*, XXII, p. 66.

10. Significantly, although the Kaiser's withered arm was the focus of his analysis, Ludwig also blamed Victoria for rejecting Wilhelm because of his disability and saw that rejection as

laying the psychological foundation both for Wilhelm's rebellion against his parents and for his hostility toward England as Kaiser: "She cherished in her heart a secret grudge against her misshapen son. . . . Never through all his life does a child forget a slight of this nature. . . . Sooner or later it will be avenged." *Wilhelm Hohenzollern,* p. 6.

11. This is not to suggest that Freud was a German nationalist. To the contrary, Freud was rather anti-German and pleased at the collapse of the German Empire. What I am suggesting is that Freud, in his comments on Wilhelm II, simply picked up on the view of the Kaiser that was "in the air."

12. Not only did these interpretations exert a psychological and a political attraction for Germans after 1918, they exerted, and continue to exert, the intellectual attraction common to all reductionistic explanations. A complex and confusing problem has been explained on the basis of a single causal factor. The Kaiser's psychopathology, indeed his entire personality, can be accounted for with one not further reducible explanation: namely, Wilhelm is understood psychologically on the basis of his breeding, his handicap, or the rejection of his English mother.

13. Throughout his reign Wilhelm II was popularly regarded as a young man. John C. G. Röhl, "The Emperor's New Clothes: A Character Sketch of Kaiser Wilhelm II," Röhl and Sombart, eds., *Kaiser Wilhelm II: New Interpretations* (Cambridge, 1982), p. 28. See also Röhl, *Kaiser, Hof und Staat: Wilhelm II und die deutsche Politik* (Munich, 1987), pp. 17–34. "I know two people who will always remain young (he meant immature), no matter how old they become," the historian Heinrich von Sybel once told Friedrich Meinecke, "the one is Hans Delbrück, the other is the Kaiser." Eberhard Kessel, ed., Friedrich Meinecke, *Autobiographische Schriften* (Stuttgart, 1979), p. 111. Similarly, Queen Victoria, in 1895, referred to her nearly thirty-six-year-old grandson as an "impetuous and conceited youth." Sidney Lee, *King Edward VII: A Biography,* 2 vols. (New York, 1925), I, p. 670. Her daughter, Victoria, once apparently remarked that "her son had never been a young man and would never be a mature man." Tirpitz's notes of 4 January 1905, BMA Freiburg, Tirpitz Papers, N253, vol. 21.

14. For the popularity of Wilhelm's dismissal of Bismarck, see Ferdinand Tönnies, *Kritik der öffentlichen Meinung* (Bad Honnef, 1981 reprint of the 1922 edition), pp. 434–35.

15. For the symbolic value of Bismarck's dismissal, see Elisabeth Fehrenbach, *Wandlungen des deutschen Kaisergedankens, 1870–1918* (Munich, 1969), pp. 89–90.

16. For Mann, that generation was venally bourgeois, crassly racist, and crudely sexist, even if it included members of various social classes (from the aristocrat von Wulchow to the proletarian Napoleon Fischer), of different ethnic groups (including the converted Jew Jadassohn), and of both sexes.

17. Heinrich Mann, *Man of Straw* (New York, 1984), pp. 114, 123, 285, 286, 226, and 113.

18. Ibid., pp. 91 and 102.

19. Ibid., p. 88.

20. Wilhelm was drawn to self-made men, particularly the American millionaires who appeared with increasing frequency in Europe during this period. The Kaiser thought to recognize a kindred spirit in Theodore Roosevelt, whom he saw as enterprising and daring. "That's my man!" he often used to cry out according to Bülow. Bernhard Fürst von Bülow, *Denkwürdigkeiten,* 4 vols. (Berlin, 1930), I, pp. 572–75. For aristocratic disdain for Wilhelm as a parvenu, see Lamar Cecil, *Albert Ballin: Business and Politics in Imperial Germany, 1888–1918* (Princeton, 1967), p. 101.

21. John C. G. Röhl, *Germany Without Bismarck: The Crisis of Government in the Second Reich, 1890–1900* (Berkeley, 1976), p. 10.

22. Friedrich Meinecke, *Autobiographische Schriften,* p. 382.

23. A number of historians have come to this conclusion. According to Elisabeth Fehrenbach, "the contradictions found in the character of the Kaiser, which the biographers have sought in vain to resolve, fundamentally mirrored the contradictions of the age." *Wandlungen,* p. 95. Similarly, Paul Kennedy has written: "The inner contradictions of German politics and society at the end of the nineteenth century are well known to historians; but in

some curiously appropriate way, Wilhelm's personality symbolized many of those paradoxes." *The Rise of the Anglo-German Antagonism, 1860–1914* (London, 1982), p. 405.
Again Kennedy: "It would not be fair to say that post-Bismarckian Germany got the leader it
deserved; but simply to focus on his personal eccentricities is to ignore the way in which the
Kaiser both reflected and intermeshed with the country's broader problems." Ibid., p. 406.
Most recently J. Alden Nichols has written: "The future Wilhelm II would always dramatize,
even caricature, in his own personality the contradictions, uncertainties, strengths, and weaknesses of his own 'fin-de-siècle' generation, its loss of the simple certainties of previous generations, its curiosity and taste for new experiences, its compulsive activity, its rather callow
posturing, and its yearning after new certainties, as yet unfound or untried." *The Year of the
Three Kaisers: Bismarck and the German Succession, 1887–88* (Urbana and Chicago, 1987),
p. 59. In his textbook written in the aftermath of the Second World War, Hans Herzfeld
reached a similar conclusion about the Kaiser and the Germans: "Precisely the weaknesses of
Wilhelm II were, for the most part, not only personal qualities but qualities of his age and
weaknesses also of the German people." Hans Herzfeld, *Die moderne Welt, 1789–1945* , 2
vols. (Braunschweig, 1952), *Band II: Weltmächte und Weltkriege. Die Geschichte unsere
Epoche, 1890–1945*, p. 14. See also Nicolaus Sombart, "Der letzte Kaiser war so, wie die
Deutschen waren," *Frankfurter Allgemeine Zeitung*, 27 January 1979, and Hermann Glaser,
"Ansichten wilhelminischer Kultur," *Neue Züricher Zeitung*, 20 October 1984, pp. 37–41.

24. Egon Friedell, *Kulturgeschichte der Neuzeit*, 3 vols. (Munich, 1931), III, p. 421.

25. Mann, *Man of Straw*, p. 168.

26. Ibid., pp. 228, 75, and 71.

27. Ibid., pp. 56, 163, 272, 274, 276–77, and 289.

28. Ibid., p. 178.

29. Ibid., p. 75.

30. Ibid., p. 131.

31. Ibid., p. 75.

32. Ibid., p. 277.

33. Ibid., p. 121.

34. Walther Rathenau, "Der Kaiser," *Walther Rathenau: Schriften und Reden*, Hans Werner Richter, ed. (Frankfurt, 1964), p. 260.

35. Ibid., p. 247.

36. Ibid.

37. Elisabeth Fehrenbach, "Images of Kaiserdom: German Attitudes to Kaiser Wilhelm
II," *Kaiser Wilhelm II*, p. 282. See also *Wandlungen*, pp. 133 as well as 97, 177–83, and 227.

38. It is tempting to speculate at this point about the narcissistic psychopathology of the
Kaiser defining the narcissistic psychopathology of a nation, a people, an era. Not only are
there a host of psychological and historical problems with such generalizations, but there is
no need for the psychologist or the historian to make them. Perhaps it makes more sense
simply to say that Wilhelm and the Germans belonged to the same historical period and were
the product of many of the same or similar historical experiences. Their common past was
considered in Part I of this study. Part II has considered their common present. Specifically,
Wilhelm II and the Germans lived in an era of intense nationalism. To the extent that Wilhelm experienced the Germans as "his subjects," he experienced them as a part of himself.
To the extent that the Germans experienced Wilhelm as "their Kaiser," they experienced him
as part of themselves. And to the extent that Wilhelm and his subjects experienced Germany
as "their nation," they experienced the Reich as a part of themselves. Of course, their national
identity was neither the only nor necessarily the primary identity of either the Kaiser or his
subjects. They had a host of other identities and loyalties—political, social, sexual, familial,
occupational, regional, religious—that were by no means compatible with their national identity and loyalty to the Reich. But to the extent that they experienced themselves as Germans
and Germany as an extension of themselves, the Reich's domestic fragmentation was their
fragmentation, the Reich's lack of international respect was their humiliation. In a period of
intense German nationalism, sovereign and people and nation were psychologically interfused. Partially as a result, Wilhelmian Germany had a fitting Kaiser in Wilhelm II. Through

a childhood, adolescence, and young adulthood in which personal issues were politicized and through a reign in which political issues were personalized, Wilhelm II came to symbolize the epoch of German history that bears his name.

Appendix II

1. Passage quoted in Chapter 9.
2. Passage quoted in Chapter 9.
3. Quoted in Chapter 9.
4. PA Bonn, Deutschland 138, vol. 6.
5. PA Bonn, Deutschland 138, vol. 5.
6. Wilhelm's marginalia to a report from the German ambassador in St. Petersburg, Prince Hugo Radolin, of 16 October 1895, *GP,* X, p. 185; Wilhelm's marginalia to *The Times* of 13 May 1902, BMA Freiburg, RM 2, vol. 165; and his marginalia to *The Daily Graphic* of 1 November 1906, BMA Freiburg, RM 2, vol. 178.
7. Quoted in Chapter 10.
8. Quoted in Chapter 10.
9. Quoted in Chapter 9.
10. See, for example, his marginalia to the report from Metternich to Bülow of 10 March 1908, *GP,* XXIV, p. 48. In the published version of this document, Wilhelm's phrase "Er hat maritim immer noch die Hosen voll" is not printed in full.
11. See Wilhelm's marginalia to a report from Metternich to Bülow of 1 August 1908, quoted in Chapter 10.

Index